DATE DUE

This book offers the first detailed examination for many years of the transatlantic trade and shipping of Bristol during the eighteenth century. It compares the performance of Bristol as a port during this period with the growth of other outports, especially Liverpool and Glasgow. Dr Morgan's analysis shows that the absolute growth of Bristol's Atlantic trade between 1700 and 1800 was concomitant with the relative decline of Bristol as a port. The main reasons for this decline were the lack of improvement to port facilities, increasing specialisation among the Bristol merchant community, the impact of war on trade, and more skilful business acumen in the tobacco and slave trades manifested by Glasgow and Liverpool merchants respectively. *Bristol and the Atlantic Trade* is based on a great variety of primary sources in the British Isles, the USA, the West Indies, Australia and continental Europe.

Bristol and the Atlantic trade
in the eighteenth century

Bristol and the Atlantic trade in the eighteenth century

Kenneth Morgan

Principal Lecturer in History,
West London Institute of Higher Education

CAMBRIDGE
UNIVERSITY PRESS

Published by the Press Syndicate of the University of Cambridge
The Pitt Building, Trumpington Street, Cambridge CB2 1RP
40 West 20th Street, New York, NY 10011–4211, USA
10 Stamford Road, Oakleigh, Victoria 3166, Australia

First published 1993

Printed in Great Britain by Redwood Books, Trowbridge, Wiltshire

A catalogue record for this book is available from the British Library

Library of Congress cataloguing in publication data

Morgan, Kenneth.
Bristol and the Atlantic trade in the eighteenth century – Kenneth Morgan.
    p.   cm.
Includes bibliographical references.
ISBN 0 521 33017 3
1. Shipping – England – Bristol – History – 18th century.   2. Merchant marine
– Great Britain – History – 18th century.   3. Bristol (England) – Commerce –
History – 18th century.   4. Great Britain – Colonies – Commerce – History –
18th century.   5. Great Britain – Commerce – America.   6. America –
Commerce – Great Britain.   I. Title.
HE823.M67   1993   92–27535
382′.0942393′009034 – dc20   CIP

ISBN 0 521 33017 3 hardback

BP

To my parents and my brother –
Kenneth Albert Morgan, Clare Frances Morgan,
Philip Richard Morgan

Contents

List of maps	*page* x	
List of tables	xi	
Preface	xiv	
Note on textual conventions	xviii	
List of abbreviations	xx	
Introduction	1	
1 Atlantic trade and the port of Bristol	7	
2 Shipping	33	
3 Shipping patterns	55	
4 The export trade	89	
5 The slave trade	128	
6 The tobacco trade	152	
7 The sugar trade	184	
Conclusion	219	
Appendix	225	
Bibliography	232	
Index	268	

Maps

1   Port area installations, trades and industries for Bristol   *page* 8
2   Bristol's major Atlantic markets in the eighteenth century   12
3   Vessels entering Bristol from the West Indies, 1773–1775   24
4   The situation of Bristol as an eighteenth-century port   30
5   The West African slave coast in the eighteenth century   130
6   Trading regions in the Chesapeake around 1760   171

Tables

1.1 Ships entering Bristol from transatlantic destinations,
1700–1797   *page* 14
1.2 Number and tonnage of ships entering selected British
ports from the American mainland colonies, 1721–1730   17
1.3 Number and tonnage of ships entering selected British
ports from the British Caribbean, 1721–1730   17
1.4 Tobacco imports at selected English ports from the British
West Indies, 1777–1780   27
2.1 Ships entering Bristol from North America and the West
Indies, 1729–1797, arranged by place of ownership   35
2.2 Percentages of ships and tonnage clearing Bristol for North
America and the West Indies, 1730–1799, according to place
of build   39
2.3 Average tonnage of ships entering Bristol from transatlantic
regions, 1729–1797   43
2.4 Average tonnage of ships clearing from Bristol to Africa,
North America and the West Indies, 1730–1799, according to
place of build   44
2.5 Characteristics of ships trading on direct routes between
Bristol and Virginia, 1725–1776   48
2.6 Characteristics of ships trading on direct routes between
Bristol and Jamaica, 1712–1798   48
2.7 Characteristics of ships engaged in slaving voyages between
Bristol and Virginia, 1725–1776   49
2.8 Characteristics of ships engaged in slaving voyages between
Bristol and Jamaica, 1712–1788   49
2.9 Tobacco hogsheads per ton on ships clearing from Virginia to
Bristol, 1725–1776   50
2.10 Sugar hogsheads per ton on ships clearing from Jamaica to
Bristol, 1712–1788   51
2.11 Voyage and turn-around times on direct voyages in the
Bristol–Virginia trade, 1749–1770   52

2.12 Voyage and turn-around times on direct voyages in the Bristol–
      Jamaica trade, 1749–1770   52
3.1   Distribution of Bristol ships completing round–trip
      transatlantic voyages, 1749–1770   60–1
3.2   Shipping routes followed by ships trading between Bristol
      and Newfoundland, 1749–1770   64
3.3   Shipping routes followed by ships trading between Bristol
      and Boston, 1749–1770   65
3.4   Shipping routes followed by ships trading between Bristol
      and Philadelphia, 1749–1770   68
3.5   Shipping routes followed by ships trading between Bristol
      and Virginia, 1749–1770   69
3.6   Shipping routes followed by ships trading between Bristol
      and South Carolina, 1749–1770   72
3.7   Shipping routes followed by ships trading between Bristol
      and Jamaica, 1749–1770   73
3.8   Shipping routes followed by ships trading between Bristol
      and St Kitts, 1749–1770   76
3.9   Shipping routes followed by ships trading between Bristol
      and Barbados, 1749–1770   77
3.10 Distribution of regular and occasional ships sailing on direct
      routes between Bristol and Virginia, 1749–1770   86
3.11 Distribution of regular and occasional ships sailing on direct
      routes between Bristol and Jamaica, 1749–1770   87
4.1   Exports and re-exports sent to North America and the West
      Indies from the outports of England and Wales, 1700–1780   92
4.2   Percentage distribution of exports from the outports of England
      and Wales to regions of North America and the British West
      Indies, 1700–1780   94
5.1   Distribution of the slave trade from London, Bristol and
      Liverpool, 1699–1807   133
5.2   Leading agents of Bristol slaving voyages, 1698–1807   144
6.1   British tobacco imports at the five principal centres,
      1722–1800   155
6.2   Tobacco imports and re-exports at selected English ports,
      1722–1731   156
6.3   Activity of Bristol tobacco importers, 1702–1799   158
6.4   Size of Bristol tobacco importers, 1728–1788   159
6.5   Leading tobacco importers at Bristol, 1728–1800   161
6.6   Virginia tobacco exports to Bristol by district, 1737–1762   172
6.7   Tobacco re-exports from Bristol, 1773–1776   181

6.8   Tobacco re-exports from Bristol to Northern Europe, 1773–1776   182

7.1   Sugar exports from the British West Indies to London, Bristol, Liverpool and Glasgow, 1773   190

7.2   British sugar imports at the five principal centres, 1790–1800   190

7.3   Activity of Bristol sugar importers, 1728–1800   191

7.4   Size of Bristol sugar importers, 1728–1788   192

7.5   Leading sugar importers at Bristol, 1728–1800   194–5

7.6   Distribution of Bristol sugar imports by island of origin, 1702–1742   196

7.7   Sources of sugar imported by leading Bristol West India merchants, 1770–1780   197

7.8   Sugar sale prices offered by Devonsheir & Reeve of Bristol, 22 August 1764   206

7.9   Sale prices of Jamaican sugar at Bristol, 1763–1783   208

7.10 Sugar sale prices at Bristol, 1776–1800   210

Preface

The impulse to research and write this book came partly from my curiosity about the commercial links between my native city and the New World in the early modern era, and partly from an interest in Colonial American History acquired when I was an undergraduate at the University of Leicester. A study of Bristol's Atlantic Trade in the eighteenth century brought these dual interests together very well. In carrying out the project, I have been fortunate in gaining financial support from various quarters. My initial research for an Oxford doctorate was funded by a Major State Studentship from the Department of Education and Science. Archive work in the United States and Australia was made possible by the award of various fellowships. The United States–United Kingdom Educational Commission offered me a Fulbright-Hays Scholarship for the 1978/9 academic year, which enabled me to study at the University of Pennsylvania. This was topped up by an Andrew W. Mellon Fellowship at the Philadelphia Center for Early American Studies plus a shorter summer fellowship at the same Center in 1981. An Archie K. Davis Fellowship from the North Caroliniana Society enabled me to research relevant manuscript sources in the tarheel state. A Samuel Foster Haven Fellowship at the American Antiquarian Society gave me time and resources to gather much of the material for chapter 3. A visiting Fellowship in the Economic History Department at the University of Melbourne was invaluable for incorporation of essential material from the Bright Family Papers. The Warden and Fellows of New College, Oxford and the Staff Research Fund at the West London Institute of Higher Education also provided some financial aid. I am grateful for all this help: my book would not have been possible without it.

Historians in scattered places have helped to mould whatever analytical skills I possess. J. B. Harris set a fine example of academic history teaching when I was a pupil at Kingswood Grammar School, Bristol. He helped to lay the foundations for my university career. While I was an undergraduate, John Runcie introduced me to the study of early American History in a humane and interesting way. At Oxford I benefited from the lively teaching of Duncan MacLeod and from the supervision of Barry Supple. David Richardson exchanged information, read all the chapters of my doctoral thesis, and provided helpful written critiques of my drafts. I hope he will recognise my debt to his own work on the Bristol slave trade. Patrick McGrath and Patrick O'Brien were kindly examiners who told me that I had passed before the viva for my doctoral thesis – a welcome relief to my nerves – and who suggested that I should publish my findings as a monograph. The late Professor McGrath also gave me opportunities for early publication of my historical research. Frank Strahan greatly facilitated my work by helping to secure funding towards my research in the University of Melbourne Archives, and by providing me with two research assistants, Karen Twigg and Dolly MacKinnon. I would not have been able to complete my work in Australia, during an intensive research trip, without their capable help.

My largest academic debts are to four gentlemen who have assisted me throughout the genesis of this project. John J. McCusker furnished plenty of bibliographical and critical suggestions and paid me the compliment of assuming that I had his own knowledge of available source materials. Jacob M. Price has encouraged my work, helped with discussions of technical pitfalls, and spared time to read the draft manuscript of this book with a fine toothcomb. To have Messrs. McCusker and Price supporting one's work on the eighteenth-century Atlantic economy is a considerable boon. Richard S. Dunn has acted as an informal mentor to me ever since I was a young postgraduate student in Philadelphia. He, too, has read my work closely and has encouraged its broad Atlantic perspective. Together with his wife, Mary Maples Dunn, he has also extended hospitality to me on several research trips to the United States. Peter Mathias, my doctoral supervisor at Oxford, has always had a ready supply of shrewd scholarly advice and practical help. From an early stage, he realised that research in American archives would greatly benefit my work. He has been a staunch supporter of my efforts to establish an academic career. The various perspectives of these gentlemen on my project has enhanced my historical development, and I am happy to acknowledge my obligations to them.

Many others have helped in the course of writing this book; too many, in fact, to mention by name. I have learned much from informal discussions with my contemporaries, especially Jonathan Barry, James Horn, Thomas L. Purvis and Marcus Rediker. Chapter 3 received the critical scrutiny of Stuart Bruchey, John J. McCusker, Michael McGiffert and Gary M. Walton. It was awarded the Beit Prize at Oxford in 1984 – an annual award for the best essay on British Imperial History submitted by a member of the university. It is reprinted here by permission, with some amendments, from the July 1989 issue of *The William and Mary Quarterly*. Alan F. Williams kindly agreed to my inclusion of two maps which he originally designed for an article in the *Transactions of the Bristol and Gloucestershire Archaeological Society* (1962). Paul G. E. Clemens allowed me to copy his design for the map of the Chesapeake in chapter 6, and furnished me with data for table 7.6. J. R. Ward sent me references to sources on the Bristol sugar trade. H. E. S. Fisher supplied some material from Portuguese archives. In addition, two families extended hospitality to me while I investigated their records. Lt Colonel and Mrs Hector MacNeal of Losset, by Campeltown, allowed me to read through the papers of their ancestor, Captain Hector MacNeal, a Scotsman who became an experienced captain in Bristol's Atlantic seafaring community in the eighteenth century. Mr and Mrs Charles Bright of Melbourne were similarly helpful in talking to me about their family papers, already mentioned above. At the West London Institute, a college of Brunel University – my current academic base – David Abbott designed the maps, Janet MacPhail and Sandy Smith helped with typing, and Shirley Tubridy prepared computer printouts of the text. At Cambridge University Press, Richard Fisher has been a patient and helpful editor and Alison Gilderdale a meticulous copy-editor.

In addition to the libraries and archives listed in the bibliography – the list is too long to be repeated here – I am grateful for the use of facilities at Rhodes House Library, Oxford; at Senate House Library and the Institute of Historical Research, London University; at the Baillieu Library, University of Melbourne; at the Firestone Library, Princeton University; at Van Pelt Library, the University of Pennsylvania; at the Milton S. Eisenhower Library, Johns Hopkins University; and at Northwestern University Library. I should like to acknowledge, in particular, the courtesy and help given by the Society of Merchant Venturers, Bristol, for allowing me extended periods of research in their private archives. It would also be remiss not to express gratitude to those librarians and archivists who assisted my research. Portions of this book were presented as papers at the annual colloquium of the Institute of United States Studies, London University, in May 1982; at the Fifth Anglo–French colloquium of the British and French Societies for Eighteenth-Century Studies, University of Bristol, September 1982; at the Economic History Society Conference, University of York, March 1985; at the British Association for Canadian Studies Annual Conference, University of Bristol, April 1986; at the Imperial History seminar of the Institute of Historical Research, London; and at seminars held at All Souls College, Oxford, the University of Melbourne, and the Philadelphia Center for Early American Studies. The comments made by the conveners and participants in these sessions have undoubtedly improved the calibre of this book.

Many friends have helped me indirectly to maintain momentum on what seemed at times a sprawling project and one that was slowed up by employment in a British system of higher education that has come to resemble a sweatshop rather than a profession. Those who have offered company and support include Daniel Barratt, Alan and Kate Beer, Kirk Brisacher, Steve and Lynne Coombs, Nigel Cousins, Laurence and Denis Fulbert, Glen Hayward, Tony, Maisie and Philip Marino, Richenda Milton-Thompson, Adrian Sandys-Wood, and Shandy (our late Irish setter). Lack of space precludes reference to their distinctive forms of help, but I would like to record a collective thank you. Elsie Walsh deserves thanks for her friendship and domestic support over the years. My late girlfriend Marie-Françoise Renault would have been proud to see this book in print. I owe much to her encouragement during difficult times. My partner Joyce Perry offered love, support and understanding in the final stages of the book. I must also thank her for undertaking the heroic task of helping to transcribe shipping statistics from records in the Public Record Office after my notes had gone missing via the postal network from Princeton to London. My final debts are to my family. My grandmother Gladys Morgan and my uncle and aunt Alfred and Janet Morgan – all now passed away – played a significant role in my education and cultural outlook. My brother, Philip, has always provided loyal support and has stimulated me with his own, somewhat Celtic, enthusiasm for history. My parents helped me to pursue the higher education that was unavailable to them when they were young, and provided the warmth and security of a happy childhood. They encouraged me to follow my academic interests, while gently reminding me that I should keep my feet on the ground. It is for their love and support that I dedicate this book to my parents and my brother.

Kenneth Morgan
November 1992

Note on textual conventions

Various technical features of the book should be mentioned here. All monetary figures are given in sterling unless otherwise stated. To convert eighteenth-century prices to their 1993 equivalent, the reader should multiply by fifty. Ships' tonnages are given in registered tons rather than measured tons, cargo tons or tons burden.[1] Sugar imports have been standardised by converting various containers into hogsheads. To make these calculations, I counted a tierce as three-quarters of a hogshead and a barrel as one-quarter.[2] Dates before 1752, when the calendar changed, are cited in New Style with 1 January rather than 25 March as the beginning of the year. Quotations from manuscript sources are transcribed verbatim except that contractions are expanded within square brackets. A fair amount of material is relevant to more than one chapter, so frequent cross references are used to avoid unnecessary repetition.

The following designations are used for geographical areas:
British America: the North American Colonies and the West Indian islands in the first British Empire;
Canada: Newfoundland, Nova Scotia, Quebec, Belle Isle, Labrador;
New England: Massachusetts, New Hampshire, Rhode Island, Connecticut;
Middle Colonies/States: New York, New Jersey, Pennsylvania;
Upper South: Virginia, Maryland;
Lower South: North Carolina, South Carolina, Georgia, Florida;

---

[1] John J. McCusker has shown that two registered tons were equivalent to three measured tons and to four cargo tons ('The tonnage of ships engaged in British Colonial Trade during the Eighteenth Century', *Research in Economic History*, 6 (1981), 73–105).

[2] This follows John J. McCusker, 'The Rum Trade and the Balance of Payments of the Thirteen Continental Colonies, 1650–1775' (University of Pittsburgh Ph.D. dissertation, 1970), app. C, p. 795. McCusker provides better evidence on this point than Richard Pares who considered that 'a tierce can be reckoned at two-thirds of a hogshead and a barrel as one-quarter' (*West-India Fortune*, p. 88). W. E. Minchinton understates Bristol's sugar imports in the late eighteenth century by failing to add in tierces and barrels with hogsheads (*Trade of Bristol in the Eighteenth Century*, p. xiii).

Other West Indies: Barbados, St Kitts, Nevis, Antigua, Montserrat,
   Grenada, St Vincent, Dominica, Tortola, Tobago, the Bahamas, Gua-
   deloupe, Martinique, Anguilla;
Wine Islands: Madeira, the Azores, the Cape Verdes.

Abbreviations

Add. MS	Additional Manuscript
ADM	Admiralty
Alderman Library, UVA	Alderman Library, University of Virginia
ACRL	Avon County Reference Library, Bristol
BL	British Library
BRO	Bristol Record Office
BHR	*Business History Review*
CO	Colonial Office
Davis, *Rise of the English Shipping Industry*	Ralph Davis, *The Rise of the English Shipping Industry in the Seventeenth and Eighteenth Centuries* (London, 1962)
EcHR	*Economic History Review*
FFBJ	*Felix Farley's Bristol Journal*
HSP	Historical Society of Pennsylvania, Philadelphia
JEcH	*Journal of Economic History*
Latimer, *Annals of Bristol*	John Latimer, *The Annals of Bristol in the Eighteenth Century* (Bristol, 1893)
LC	Library of Congress
McGrath, ed., *Bristol in the Eighteenth Century*	Patrick McGrath, ed., *Bristol in the Eighteenth Century* (Newton Abbot, 1972)
McGrath, *Merchant Venturers of Bristol*	Patrick McGrath, *The Merchant Venturers of Bristol; A History of the Society of Merchant Venturers of the City of Bristol from its Origin to the Present Day* (Bristol, 1975)

MacInnes, *Bristol: A Gateway of Empire* — C. M. MacInnes, *Bristol: A Gateway of Empire* (Bristol, 1939)

Massachusetts HS — Massachusetts Historical Society, Boston

Maryland HS — Maryland Historical Society, Baltimore

Minchinton, ed., *Trade of Bristol in the Eighteenth Century* — W. E. Minchinton, ed., *The Trade of Bristol in the Eighteenth Century* (Bristol Record Society's *Publications*, 20, 1957)

Minchinton, ed., *Politics and the Port of Bristol* — W. E. Minchinton, ed., *Politics and the Port of Bristol in the Eighteenth Century: The Petitions of the Society of Merchant Venturers 1698–1803* (Bristol Record Society's *Publications*, 23, 1963)

Morgan, 'Bristol Merchants and the Colonial Trades' — Kenneth Morgan, 'Bristol Merchants and the Colonial Trades, 1748–1783' (Oxford University D.Phil. thesis, 1984)

MSS — Manuscripts

New England HGS — New England Historic Genealogical Society, Boston

New Hampshire HS — New Hampshire Historical Society, Concord

New York HS — New York Historical Society

New York PL — New York Public Library

Pares, *West–India Fortune* — Richard Pares, *A West-India Fortune* (London, 1950)

Pennsylvania MHC — Pennsylvania Museum and Historical Commission, Harrisburg

PRO — Public Record Office, London

RO — Record Office

SHC — Southern Historical Collection, University of North Carolina at Chapel Hill

SMV — Society of Merchant Venturers, Bristol

TBGAS — *Transactions of the Bristol and Gloucestershire Archaeological Society*

TRHS — *Transactions of the Royal Historical Society*

UL	University Library
UMA	University of Melbourne Archives, Parkville, Victoria
Virginia HS	Virginia Historical Society, Richmond
VMHB	*Virginia Magazine of History and Biography*
Virginia SL	Virginia State Library and Archives, Richmond
WMQ	*William and Mary Quarterly*

Introduction

Favoured with a long history of maritime commerce and a westward geographical outlook, Bristol played a significant role in the exploration, colonisation and trade of the New World from the time of the Cabot voyages onwards. In the late sixteenth and seventeenth centuries, Bristol's main commercial interests in the Atlantic were the search for the Northwest Passage, involvement in the fisheries off Newfoundland and New England, and early trade connections with the Chesapeake and the Caribbean. Between 1660 and 1700, trading links with the colonies grew apace and helped Bristol and England to gain access to a wider commercial world.[1] But it was during the eighteenth century that Bristol became a bustling gateway of empire trading with all the British colonies in North America and the West Indies, with the slave coast of West Africa, and with the Atlantic wine islands and the Iberian peninsula (which were integral parts of the transatlantic shipping network).[2] Burgeoning

[1] On these developments see especially C. M. MacInnes, *Bristol: A Gateway of Empire*, chs. 1–6; 'Bristol and Overseas Expansion' in C. M. MacInnes and W. F. Whittard, eds., *Bristol and its Adjoining Counties* (Bristol, 1955), pp. 219–30; Patrick McGrath, ed., *Merchants and Merchandise in Seventeenth-Century Bristol* (Bristol Record Society's *Publications*, 19, 1955); 'Bristol and America, 1480–1631' in K. R. Andrews, Nicholas P. Canny and P. E. H. Hair, eds., *The Westward Enterprise: English Activities in Ireland, the Atlantic, and America 1480–1650* (Liverpool, 1978), pp. 81–102; David H. Sacks, *Trade, Society and Politics in Bristol circa 1500–circa 1640* (New York, 1985), pp. 401–17; *The Widening Gate: Bristol and the Atlantic Economy, 1450–1700* (Berkeley and Los Angeles, 1991); and G. D. Ramsay, *English Overseas Trade during the Centuries of Emergence: Studies in Some Modern Origins of the English Speaking World* (London, 1957), pp. 134–51.

[2] Previous studies which discuss aspects of Bristol's eighteenth-century Atlantic trade include MacInnes, *Bristol: A Gateway of Empire*, chs. 7–14; W. E. Minchinton, 'The Port of Bristol in the Eighteenth Century' in McGrath, ed., *Bristol in the Eighteenth Century*, pp. 127–60; *Trade of Bristol in the Eighteenth Century*; 'The Slave Trade of Bristol with the British Mainland Colonies in North America, 1699–1770' in Roger Anstey and P. E. H. Hair, eds., *Liverpool the African Slave Trade and Abolition* (Historic Society of Lancashire and Cheshire, Occasional Series, 2, 1976), pp. 39–59; Pares, *West-India Fortune*, ch. 9; David Richardson, 'The Bristol Slave Trade in the Eighteenth Century' (University of Manchester MA thesis, 1969); *The Bristol Slave Traders: A Collective Portrait* (Bristol Branch of the Historical Association, pamphlet no. 60, 1985); and Morgan, 'Bristol Merchants and the Colonial Trades'.

oceanic commerce helped to develop wealth and prosperity in the Bristol mercantile community. It was a major impetus behind the investment of merchants in banking in the city after 1750 and in their participation in various industrial enterprises. It also enabled many of them to acquire country estates, fine Georgian town houses and urban residences among the terraces and crescents of Clifton.[3]

Bristol's increasing commercial connections with North America and the West Indies reflected a similar shift in the overall pattern of British overseas trade. Though English domestic exports and retained imports both quadrupled in value during the eighteenth century, the transatlantic sector expanded while trade with Europe experienced relative decline. In 1700–1, English colonies in the New World accounted for 11 per cent of the value of English exports and for 20 per cent of imports. By 1772–3, they took 38 per cent of exports and were the source of 39 per cent of imports. By 1797–8, North America and the Caribbean received 57 per cent of British exports and supplied 32 per cent of imports. Many re-exported goods also consisted of colonial commodities.[4] British exports sent across the Atlantic were mainly finished manufactured wares, while imports from the Americas were dominated by sugar, tobacco, rice, coffee, naval stores, dyestuffs and other products increasingly in demand with British and European consumers.

Bristol was not the only west-coast outport to benefit from this 'Americanisation' of British foreign trade. The economic development of Liverpool, Glasgow and Whitehaven was also stimulated to varying degrees by the same phenomenon. Though the metropolis nearly always accounted for around two-thirds of the value of exports and imports in English transatlantic trade during the eighteenth century, and also dominated overseas commerce as a whole, the west coast outports reduced the relative share of London's visible trade and shipping activity by the time of the American Revolution.[5] They also contributed to the relative commercial decline of Bristol. In 1700 Bristol was the third largest town

---

[3] C. H. Cave, *A History of Banking in Bristol from 1750 to 1899* (Bristol, 1899); W. E. Minchinton, 'The Merchants of Bristol in the Eighteenth Century' in *Sociétés et groupes sociaux en Aquitaine et en Angleterre*, Fédérations Historiques du Sud-Ouest (Bordeaux, 1979), pp. 185–200.

[4] For overviews of these changing trade patterns see Ralph Davis, 'English Foreign Trade, 1700–1774', *EcHR*, 2nd Series, 15 (1962–3), 285–303, and *The Industrial Revolution and British Overseas Trade* (Leicester, 1979).

[5] W. E. Minchinton, ed., *The Growth of English Overseas Trade in the Seventeenth and Eighteenth Centuries* (London, 1969), pp. 33–42; Christopher J. French, ' "Crowded with Traders and a Great Commerce": London's Dominion of English Overseas Trade, 1700–1775', *The London Journal*, 17 (1992), 27–35. The rise of Glasgow in the half century before 1776 means, of course, that London had a lower share of British, as distinct from English, transatlantic trade during the eighteenth century.

in England and the second largest port; by 1800 she was ranked fifth among towns and ninth among ports.[6] Bristol was not seriously challenged by Whitehaven, which was prominent in Atlantic trade only in the 1740s before fading away (largely through lack of an extensive hinterland for the collection and distribution of consumer goods).[7] But Glasgow and Liverpool provided stiffer competition. Glasgow outstripped Bristol and all other British ports in the tobacco trade between the 1740s and the late 1770s, and rose to become a thriving commercial city in the eighteenth century largely because of expanding overseas trade.[8] From small beginnings in 1700, Liverpool rose to become the leading British outport a century later. Liverpool overhauled Bristol in the volume of overseas trade conducted at both ports in the 1740s, in the shipping tonnage owned at British ports in 1751, and in population size in the late 1780s.[9]

The chief aims of this book are to analyse the commercial organisation of Bristol's Atlantic trade during its 'golden age' in the eighteenth century, and to examine the performance of Bristol as a port in an international trading world that was becoming more sophisticated, specialised and complex. This is not virgin territory. Historians have examined various themes relevant to my investigation: the place of Bristol as 'metropolis of the west' in the eighteenth century; her role in the Atlantic slave trade; the contribution of the Society of Merchant Venturers to the port and trade of the city; the development of the port of Bristol; the main characteristics of the Bristol merchant community; the nature of the sugar trade and the sugar market at Bristol; and the main trends in Bristol's overseas trade.[10] The reasons why eighteenth-century Bristol experienced relative decline as a port have also attracted analysis. It has

[6] Minchinton, ed., *Trade of Bristol in the Eighteenth Century*, p. ix.

[7] J. V. Beckett, *Coal and Tobacco: The Lowthers and the Economic Development of West Cumberland, 1660–1760* (Cambridge, 1981), pp. 108, 120, 121, 143; J. E. Williams, 'Whitehaven in the Eighteenth Century', *EcHR*, 2nd Series, 7 (1956), 393–404.

[8] See especially, among a large literature, Jacob M. Price, 'The Rise of Glasgow in the Chesapeake Tobacco Trade, 1707–1775', *WMQ*, 3rd Series, 11 (1954), 179–99; T. M. Devine, *The Tobacco Lords: A Study of the Tobacco Merchants of Glasgow and their Trading Activities, c.1740–1790* (Edinburgh, 1975); W. R. Brock, *Scotus Americanus: A Survey of Sources for Links between Scotland and America in the Eighteenth Century* (Edinburgh, 1982), ch. 3.

[9] P. J. Corfield, *The Impact of English Towns, 1700–1800* (Oxford, 1982), pp. 35–6, 39–40. See also F. E. Hyde, *Liverpool and the Mersey: An Economic History of a Port, 1700–1970* (Newton Abbot, 1971), chs. 2–3, and Paul G. E. Clemens, 'The Rise of Liverpool, 1665–1750', *EcHR*, 2nd Series, 29 (1976), 211–25.

[10] See especially the studies listed in note 2 above plus the following: W. E. Minchinton, 'Bristol – Metropolis of the West in the Eighteenth Century', *TRHS*, 5th Series, 4 (1954), 69–89; David Richardson, ed., *Bristol, Africa and the Eighteenth-Century Slave Trade to America*, 3 vols. (Bristol Record Society's *Publications*, 38, 39, 42, 1986–90); McGrath, *Merchant Venturers of Bristol*, chs. 6, 8–10; Alan F. Williams, 'Bristol Port Plans

been suggested that sluggish improvement of port facilities placed strain on Bristol's shipping by the late eighteenth century; that some leading merchants at the port had complacent business attitudes; that Bristol and her hinterland suffered from lack of industrial development after 1760 comparable to that of south Lancashire; that canal construction in the north Midlands after 1770 helped to channel export goods to Liverpool rather than to Bristol; that Bristol was over-committed to West India trade by 1800; and that heavy port dues drove shipping away from Bristol.[11] These points, however, have never been analysed with reference to the full range of sources available on Bristol's Atlantic trading connections in the eighteenth century, or with close attention to the entrepreneurial practices of merchants in the city. This book seeks to redress the situation.[12]

The discussion below falls into seven topical chapters. Chapter 1 traces the chronological development of Bristol's Atlantic trade during the eighteenth century, with particular attention to periods of war and peace. It analyses the commercial problems experienced by Bristol merchants from the 1740s onwards and examines the pressures placed on port facilities at Bristol by an increased volume of shipping. Chapter 2 looks at the characteristics of the vessels used in Bristol's transatlantic trade – their size, armaments, manning, place of build and place of ownership. It also considers the varied productivity trends for ships trading with Virginia and Jamaica. Chapter 3 explores the nature of shipping patterns to show that, by mid-century, Bristol merchants increasingly favoured regular, direct routes instead of multilateral voyage patterns. The remaining chapters concentrate on four major trades. Chapter 4 investigates the structure and organisation of the export trade. It highlights various business problems including over-extension of credit, lack of full remittances, difficulties in the supply network, and problems in filling up space on board ship on outward voyages. Chapter 5 is devoted to the problems

and Improvement Schemes of the Eighteenth Century', *TBGAS*, 81 (1962), 138–88; I. V. Hall, 'A History of the Sugar Trade in England with Special Attention to the Sugar Trade of Bristol' (University of Bristol M.A. thesis, 1925); Ronald H. Quilici, 'Turmoil in a City and an Empire: Bristol's Factions, 1700–1775' (University of New Hampshire Ph.D. dissertation, 1976), chs. 4–5. For an assessment of MacInnes' work see Alan F. Williams, 'Bristol and C. M. MacInnes: The Canadian Dean of Gateway of Empire', *British Journal of Canadian Studies*, 1 (1986), 307–17.

11 Minchinton, 'Port of Bristol in the Eighteenth Century', pp. 153–8; *Trade of Bristol in the Eighteenth Century*, pp. xv–xvi; Williams, 'Bristol Port Plans and Improvement Schemes', pp. 138–88; McGrath, *Merchant Venturers of Bristol*, pp. 150–67; Corfield, *Impact of English Towns*, pp. 41–2; William Hunt, *Bristol* (Bristol, 1895), pp. 208–9.

12 For an overview of the main argument advanced in this book see Kenneth Morgan, 'Bristol and the Atlantic Trade in the Eighteenth Century', *English Historical Review*, 107 (1992), 626–50.

experienced by Bristolians in the slave trade: a falling share in the slave markets of the Americas from the 1730s onwards, high shipping costs, and diversion into privateering activity during wartime. Throughout the book special attention is given to the West Indies and the Chesapeake, the two most lucrative regions in the Atlantic basin for Bristol merchants. Thus chapters 6 and 7 conclude the book with an examination of the contrasting fortunes of the Bristol sugar and tobacco trades with regard to levels of imports and customs duties, marketing, and business organisation.

My analysis draws on an extensive range of manuscript and printed sources on Bristol's Atlantic trade plus printed material on Liverpool, Whitehaven and Glasgow. I have cast my net as widely as possible: whatever its deficiencies, this book is based on all the relevant data I could find for Bristol for the entire eighteenth century. For this period, Bristol has better surviving statistics on shipping and trade than any other British port. This study therefore draws on quantitative material included in the Port Books, Wharfage Books, Ships' Muster Rolls, Colonial Naval Officers' Returns and Mediterranean Passes.[13] Other documents proved more elusive to track down. The Bristol customs records were burned in the Reform Bill riots of 1831. The in- and out-letter books at the other end were similarly destroyed along with the London Custom house in 1814.[14] Bristol itself contains relatively few merchants' business records – the material is much thinner, for instance, than for eighteenth-century Philadelphia merchants.[15] Very few merchants' ledgers, articles of partnership or balance sheets are still available for Bristol merchants. Tantalising glimpses of what was once, but no longer, in existence are given in some surviving sources.[16] What still survives sometimes turns up in unexpected places: the only relevant documents in private possession that came to light during my research were found in Kintyre, Scotland; and the fullest merchants' papers for Georgian Bristol are deposited in Melbourne.[17]

Fortunately, much useful documentation on the activities of Bristolians engaged in Atlantic trade can be gleaned from archives in Great Britain, Europe, the West Indies, the United States, and Australia. This

---

[13] The data given in these sources are outlined in the appendix, pp. 225–9.

[14] Rupert C. Jarvis, ed., *Customs Letter-Books of the Port of Liverpool, 1711–1813* (Chetham Society's Publications, 3rd Series, 6, Manchester, 1954), p. v.

[15] Cf. Thomas M. Doerflinger, *A Vigorous Spirit of Enterprise: Merchants and Economic Development in Revolutionary Philadelphia* (Chapel Hill, NC, 1986).

[16] E.g. the merchants' papers listed in PRO, T 79/30 and in ACRL, List of Deeds in the possession of Henry Bengough, Apr. 1818, Acc. B4942.

[17] See entries in the bibliography of manuscript sources under MacNeal of Losset, by Campeltown, and the University of Melbourne Archives.

information is fairly sparse for the period before 1740 but abundant thereafter.[18] It is also fuller on some aspects of Atlantic trade than on others (as will be apparent from my discussions of the Bristol sugar and tobacco markets). Much of the primary material has been under-researched by previous historians, perhaps because it requires extensive digging in archives. But I hope that my book demonstrates the veins of gold that can be uncovered. My aim is to interweave material from these various sources into an analysis that will interest historians of eighteenth-century Britain, of Colonial American history, and of business and maritime history. Throughout emphasis lies on the entrepreneurial decline of Bristol merchants in the eighteenth century and the interdependence of the Atlantic trading world of that era.[19] If the book contributes to a deeper understanding of the complex interrelationship between different economic sectors in a century when Britain became the centre of an Atlantic economy, it will have succeeded.

[18] Transcripts of selected documents will appear in Kenneth Morgan, ed., *Bristol's Transatlantic Commerce in the Eighteenth Century* (Bristol Record Society's *Publications*, forthcoming).
[19] On the latter theme see Jacob M. Price, 'What Did Merchants Do? Reflections on British Overseas Trade, 1660–1790', *JEcH*, 49 (1989), 267–84.

1 Atlantic trade and the port of Bristol

Bristol was a place of bustling commercial activity in the early eighteenth century. Merchants, shipowners, manufacturers, packers, hauliers, shipwrights, sailors and customs officers jostled one another in the centre of what was still largely a medieval walled city. Business vitality was most evident in the centre of Bristol where a spacious quay, about a mile in length, was surrounded by wooden ships, merchants' counting houses, shops and warehouses, sugar refineries and glasshouses, taverns and coffee houses, all clustered by the rivers Avon and Frome. Commercial affairs were also conducted by merchants at the Tolzey, a covered walkway in Corn Street, and, from 1745 onwards, at the Exchange in the same street, designed by John Wood the Elder. By the 1760s, many an hour was whiled away with talk of the Atlantic trading world at the Exchange coffee house and at the American and West Indian coffee houses. Trade and shipping were regularly discussed by the Bristol Corporation, which met at the Council House in a square at the intersection of Broad, Corn, High and Wine Streets. Politics and commerce were also intertwined in the lobbying activities of the Society of Merchant Venturers, founded in 1552 and based at Merchants' Hall, King Street, and in the work of Bristol's MPs. Through these influential channels, the city's trading interests were represented to Parliament and government departments. Commerce also received the close attention of local port officials – the haven master, quay wardens and water bailiffs – and of customs officers based at the Custom House in Queen Square, a group that included the Customer, Controller, Collector and Searcher, plus lesser officials such as the landwaiters and weighers.[1]

The main commercial features of Bristol, illustrated in map 1, attracted

---

[1] This paragraph is based on W. E. Minchinton, 'The Port of Bristol in the Eighteenth Century' in McGrath, ed., *Bristol in the Eighteenth Century*, pp. 141, 146–8; Ronald H. Quilici, 'Turmoil in a City and an Empire: Bristol's Factions, 1700–1775' (University of New Hampshire Ph.D. dissertation, 1976), ch. 1; Marcus Rediker, *Between the Devil and the Deep Blue Sea: Merchant Seamen, Pirates, and the Anglo–American Maritime World, 1700–1750* (Cambridge, 1987), pp. 42–3; Winslow C. Watson, ed., *Men and Times of the Revolution; or, Memoirs of Elkanah Watson* ... (2nd edn., New York, 1856), p. 197;

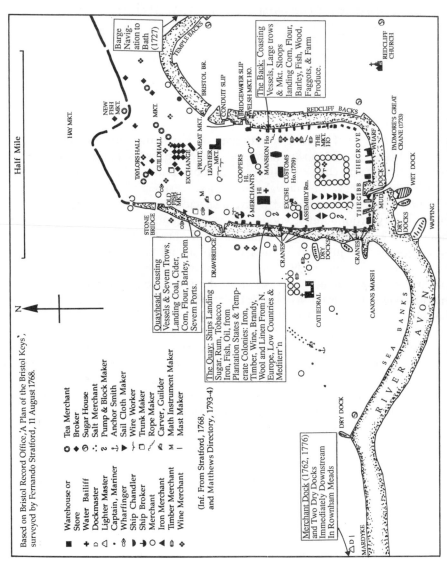

Map 1   Port area installations, trades and industries for Bristol

the notice of many visitors to the city. 'The streets here are but narrow and populous', one visitor noted in 1705, '& everywhere appears an air of Business & Vivacity'.[2] Though later observers voiced some harsh criticisms of the dirt and squalor of the city, all were impressed by the attention paid to trade.[3] Bristol was 'the greatest, the richest, and the best port of Trade in Great Britain, London only excepted', and traded 'with more entire independency upon London than any other town in Britain'.[4] Bristolians were remarkable 'for early enquiries into the character of all strangers for commercial motives' and 'for sharp and hard dealings'.[5] Even the clergy, it was claimed, 'talk of nothing but trade and how to turn a penny . . . all are in a hurry, running up and down with cloudy looks and busy faces, loading, carrying and unloading goods and merchandises of all sorts from place to place; for the trade of many nations is drawn hither by the industry and the opulency of the people'.[6] Eighteenth-century historians of Bristol agreed with visitors that the growth of the city and the port stemmed from trading advantages found in her citizens and her location.[7] To contemporaries and modern historians, Bristol at that time was a 'metropolis of the west' acting as a magnet for the economic life of her region.[8]

During the eighteenth century, Bristolians formed business connections with an Atlantic community of traders as the circulation of people, commodities and exchange drew merchants and markets together. The growing interdependence of the Atlantic trading world led some people from Bristol to set up as merchants in Philadelphia and Jamaica, to settle at Harbour Grace, Newfoundland, and to establish storchouses throughout the West Indies.[9] Bristol ships and seamen could be found from Labrador to Angola, from Curaçao to the Cape Verde islands, and from

---

Nicholas Rogers, *Whigs and Cities: Popular Politics in the Age of Walpole and Pitt* (Oxford, 1989), ch. 8; McGrath, *Merchant Venturers of Bristol*, ch. 8; and *FFBJ*, 23 Nov. 1765.

[2] Bristol UL, Samuel Gale, 'A Tour Through Several Parts of England, A.D. 1705' (n.p.).

[3] For contrasting contemporary impressions of Bristol see Peter T. Marcy, 'Eighteenth Century Views of Bristol and Bristolians' in McGrath, ed., *Bristol in the Eighteenth Century*, pp. 11–40.

[4] Daniel Defoe in *A Tour Thro' the Whole Island of Great Britain* (1724–6), as quoted in *ibid.*, p. 14.

[5] *The Journal of Samuel Curwen, Loyalist*, 6 Sept. 1777, as quoted in *ibid.*, p. 36.

[6] Thomas Cox, *Magna Britannia et Hibernia: Somersetshire* (1720–31), as quoted in Minchinton, 'Port of Bristol in the Eighteenth Century', *ibid.*, p. 129.

[7] Jonathan Barry, 'The Cultural Life of Bristol, 1640–1775' (Oxford University D.Phil. thesis, 1985), pp. 301–2.

[8] W. E. Minchinton, 'Bristol – Metropolis of the West in the Eighteenth Century', *TRHS*, 5th Series, 4 (1954), 69–89.

[9] Gary B. Nash, 'The Early Merchants of Philadelphia: The Formation and Disintegration of a Foundling Elite' in Richard S. Dunn and Mary Maples Dunn, eds., *The World of*

Virginia to Amsterdam. There was also an influx of commercial knowledge, for an increasing minority of Bristol merchants were born or
trained overseas in Boston, New York, Philadelphia, Virginia, South
Carolina, Nevis, Barbados and Jamaica.[10] The transatlantic flow of business information was further sustained by visits of American merchants
to Bristol.[11] The Bristol–American connection reached its height in the
generation before the American Revolution. Bristol became the leading
English provincial subscription town to successive editions of John
Wright's *American Negotiator* (1761–5), a reference work on the various
coins and moneys of account used in the American colonies.[12] In 1775
John Adams, the future second president of the United States, coupled
Bristol with Philadelphia as the greatest commercial cities of the British
Empire after London.[13] The American links of Bristol were even obvious
in the city during the War of Independence, owing to the presence of a
small community of Massachusetts Loyalists at Bristol.[14]

William Penn (Philadelphia, 1986), pp. 339, 346, 356–7, 360–1; UMA, Henry Bright to
Richard Meyler, Sr, 16 Mar. 1740, Henry Bright Letterbook (1740–8); Francis Bright to
Richard Meyler, Sr, 16 July 1751, Francis Bright Letterbook (1752–3); and Lowbridge
Bright to Henry Bright, 28 June 1765, Lowbridge Bright Letterbook (1765–73); Bright
Family Papers, and below, p. 145; W. Gordon Handcock, 'An Historical Geography of
the Origins of English Settlement in Newfoundland: A Study of the Migration Process'
(University of Birmingham Ph.D. thesis, 1979), p. 21; *Memoirs of the Life and Travels of
the late Charles MacPherson Esq., in Asia, Africa, and America . . .* (Edinburgh, 1800),
pp. 59–60; BL, Add. MS 34, 181: Abstracts of Wills relating to Jamaica, 1625–1792, fo.
174 (will of Samuel Delpratt).

10 Philip M. Hamer *et al.*, eds., *The Papers of Henry Laurens* (Columbia, SC, 1968–), II, p.
212; South Caroliniana Library, Elias Ball to Elias Ball, Jr, 28 May 1788, Ball Family
Papers, and Isaac King to Nathaniel Russell, 2 Sept. 1785, and to Joshua Ward, 12 Mar.
1788, Isaac King Letterbook (1783–98); Vere Langford Oliver, ed., *Caribbeana: Miscel-
laneous Papers relating to the History, Genealogy, Topography and Antiquities of the
British West Indies*, 6 vols. (London, 1911–12), II, pp. 80, 172, VI, p. 116; Latimer,
Annals of Bristol, p. 462; W. E. Minchinton, 'The Merchants of Bristol in the Eighteenth
Century' in Paul Butel, ed., *Sociétés et groupes sociaux en Aquitaine et en Angleterre*,
Fédérations Historiques du Sud-Ouest (Bordeaux, 1979), p. 189; and below, pp. 168,
185.

11 E.g. Kenneth Morgan, ed., *An American Quaker in the British Isles: The Travel Journals
of Jabez Maud Fisher, 1775–1779* (Oxford, 1992), pp. 112–15, 282–3; HSP, Diary of
Henry Drinker (1759); Dickinson College, Thomas Fisher Journals (1762–4); Swarthmore College, Samuel Rowland Fisher Journals (1767–8, 1783–4).

12 Jacob M. Price, 'Who Cared about the Colonies? The Impact of the Thirteen Colonies on
British Society and Politics, circa 1714–1775' in Bernard Bailyn and Philip D. Morgan,
eds., *Strangers within the Realm: Cultural Margins of the First British Empire* (Chapel
Hill, NC, 1991), p. 409.

13 John Adams to the Inhabitants of the Colony of Massachusetts Bay, 6 Feb. 1775, in
Robert J. Taylor, ed., *Papers of John Adams, vol. 2, December 1773–April 1775*
(Cambridge, MA, 1977), p. 250.

14 Wilbur H. Siebert, 'The Colony of Massachusetts Loyalists at Bristol, England', *Proceedings of the Massachusetts Historical Society*, 45 (1912), 409–14; Peter Marshall, 'A
Refuge from Revolution: The American Loyalists' Residence in Bristol' in Patrick
McGrath and John Cannon, eds., *Essays in Bristol and Gloucestershire History* (Bristol,
1976), pp. 200–16.

Bristol's major Atlantic markets in the eighteenth century are shown on map 2. These point to a far-flung commercial network that linked three continents. The commercial vitality of this trade is reflected in shipping statistics: North America and the West Indies each accounted for between one quarter and one third of all the shipping tonnage arriving at Bristol in every decade down to the American Revolution.[15] All of this trade was conducted within the protectionist framework of the Navigation Acts. These laws specified that the ships, masters and three-quarters of the crew engaged in British transatlantic trade had to be English. They also required most colonial goods to be shipped directly to England or an English colony.[16] On outward Atlantic crossings Bristol ships carried packages of textiles, metalware and hardware for sale to colonists, and filled up excess cargo space by taking voluntary and involuntary passengers, in the form of indentured servants and convicts, and by picking up provisions in southern Ireland.[17] On homeward-bound voyages the same ships brought back cargoes that included tobacco, wheat and iron from Virginia and Maryland, deerskins, rice and indigo from South Carolina, naval stores (pitch, tar, turpentine) from New England and New York, and sugar, rum, pimento and ginger from the Caribbean islands.[18]

This long-distance trade was interrupted by five international wars, which accounted for nearly half of the years in the eighteenth century. During these conflicts European powers tried to establish naval and imperial supremacy and British maritime commerce in the Atlantic, the Mediterranean and the English Channel was subject to attacks by French, Spanish or American vessels. This chapter traces the chronological development of Bristol's Atlantic trade within this overall context. My discussion pays particular attention to fluctuations in the volume and value of trade during war and peace years, and to the impact of commerce on the port of Bristol. Emphasis falls on the relative decline in the city's transatlantic trade flows and shipping services when compared with the

---

[15] Quilici, 'Turmoil in a City and an Empire', tables H 1–7, pp. 325–38. Quilici based his tables on Bristol's civic year, which ran from late September to late September.

[16] The legislation is summarised in Lawrence A. Harper, *The English Navigation Laws: A Seventeenth-Century Experiment in Social Engineering* (New York, 1939), pp. 387–414.

[17] Bristol's transatlantic export trade is analysed below in ch. 4, pp. 89–127.

[18] Bristol's sugar and tobacco trades are examined below in chs. 6 and 7, pp. 152–218. The organisation of iron imports into Bristol is discussed in Keach Johnson, 'The Baltimore Company seeks English Markets: A Study of the Anglo–American Iron Trade, 1731–1755', *WMQ*, 3rd Series, 16 (1959), 48–9. For Bristol's imports from South Carolina see Converse D. Clowse, *Measuring Charleston's Overseas Commerce, 1717–1767: Statistics from the Port's Naval Lists* (Washington, DC, 1981), tables B-22, B-26 and C-54, pp. 59, 63, 134, and Kenneth Morgan, 'The Organization of the Colonial American Rice Trade' (Paper presented to the Organization of American Historians' Conference, Washington, DC, 1990).

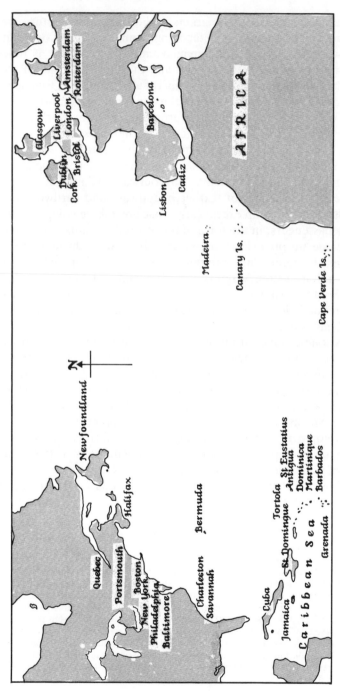

Map 2 Bristol's major Atlantic markets in the eighteenth century

performance of rival west-coast outports. But evidence is also produced to show that Bristol's overseas commerce remained more valuable than Liverpool's for most of the eighteenth century.[19]

The best index of the overall development of Bristol's Atlantic trade consists of incoming shipping tonnage figures in the Wharfage Books kept by the Society of Merchant Venturers (supplemented, where necessary, with other sources). These data are presented in table 1.1.[20] They show that the volume of transatlantic shipping arriving at Bristol more than doubled between the beginning and the end of the eighteenth century. For the period 1729–97, the table indicates that 59 per cent of this tonnage came from the Caribbean and 41 per cent from the North American mainland. The regional breakdown was as follows: some 36.8 per cent of the tonnage came from Jamaica, 22.3 per cent from the other West Indian islands, 11.7 per cent from the Upper South, 10.7 per cent from the Middle colonies and states, 8.0 per cent from the Lower South, 5.3 per cent from New England, and 5.2 per cent from Canada. These percentages understate the role of Newfoundland and the Carolinas in Atlantic commerce because the cargoes of cod and rice often picked up respectively in those areas found markets in continental Europe, and many vessels in those trades therefore appear in the Wharfage Books as entering Bristol from a European port. But this does not detract from the two major points that stand out from the percentages: that the Caribbean sector of Bristol's Atlantic trade was more substantial than the American mainland portion, and that three-quarters of the tonnage arriving at Bristol from American regions came from the Caribbean and the Chesapeake alone. Though the volume of shipping arriving at Bristol increased in the first three-quarters of the century, the distribution of tonnage entering from Europe and from British America remained fairly steady: the European proportion of the total tonnage only fluctuated between 43 and 56 per cent, while the proportion from North America and the West Indies ranged from 45 to 55 per cent.[21]

In 1700 the shipping tonnage entering Bristol was evenly divided between ships coming from Europe and those coming from British America. The most important European markets for Bristol vessels were, in descending order of importance, Southern Europe, the Baltic, and Ireland – though, in terms of vessels rather than tonnage, Ireland was well ahead of the rest. Some 26 per cent of the tonnage entering Bristol

---

[19] Two previous discussions of the trends in Bristol's eighteenth-century Atlantic trade are Quilici, 'Turmoil in a City and an Empire', pp. 102–23, and Minchinton, 'Port of Bristol in the Eighteenth Century', pp. 128–32.

[20] Any undocumented figures in the discussion below are taken from this table.

[21] Quilici, 'Turmoil in a City and an Empire', tables H 1–7, pp. 325–38.

Table 1.1. *Ships entering Bristol from transatlantic destinations, 1700–1797 (annual averages)*

	Canada		New England		Middle Colonies/States		Upper South		Lower South		Jamaica		Other West Indies		Totals	
	N	Tons	N	Tons	N	Tons	N	Tons	N	Tons	N	Tons	N	Tons	N	Tons
1700	a	a	a	a	0	0	29	4,270	a	a	18	2,060	37	3,110	93[b]	9,830
1713–17	7	n.a.	7	n.a.	7	n.a.	26	n.a.	7	n.a.	31	n.a.	52	n.a.	137	n.a.
1718–21	6	n.a.	10	n.a.	8	n.a.	45	n.a.	13	n.a.	41	n.a.	47	n.a.	170	n.a.
1723–7	10	n.a.	12	n.a.	7	n.a.	31	n.a.	15	n.a.	38	n.a.	49	n.a.	162	n.a.
1729–32	9	430	8	597	7	2,495	18	1,918	12	1,011	56	5,508	37	3,102	147	15,061
1733–7	8	372	8	554	9	734	22	2,426	17	1,523	43	4,392	23	1,913	130	11,914
1738–42	9	462	12	909	8	529	16	1,854	16	1,329	41	4,742	34	2,931	136	12,756
1743–7	9	576	6	584	2	161	15	1,748	10	860	31	3,826	20	1,778	93	9,533
1748–9	6	313	4	275	5	451	13	1,578	11	1,145	43	5,368	30	2,703	112	11,833
1754–7	8	474	5	418	8	728	23	2,888	14	1,201	34	4,064	38	3,098	130	12,871
1758–62	12	752	5	424	12	1,079	18	2,611	15	1,608	26	3,506	29	2,583	117	12,563
1763–7	13	788	13	1,164	15	1,452	16	2,251	23	2,247	31	4,348	44	4,470	155	16,720
1768	11	595	12	1,250	30	3,080	13	1,603	30	3,511	45	6,006	37	4,507	178	20,552
1773–7	17	1,216	4	534	21	2,501	20	2,788	14	1,538	49	7,623	40	5,002	165	21,202
1778–80	11	828	0	0	2	320	1	30	1	123	42	7,257	29	3,768	86	12,326
1785	21	1,529	1	200	7	1,010	12	1,730	7	935	38	7,480	28	3,950	114	16,834
1788–90	26	2,435	9	1,317	15	2,807	15	2,978	10	1,727	41	11,057	23	4,930	139	27,251
1792	15	1,538	21	4,430	24	5,543	6	1,205	4	991	45	12,069	36	7,333	151	33,109
1797	13	901	5	943	18	4,412	9	2,132	3	531	22	6,720	21	4,851	91	20,490

Notes: [a] In 1700, 9 ships with a combined capacity of 390 tons entered Bristol from Newfoundland, New England, the Carolinas and Bermuda. But there is no breakdown available of the proportion of ships and tonnage arriving from each colony.

[b] Includes ships and tonnage noted in a.

[c] The headings in the table include the following colonies: Canada: Newfoundland, Nova Scotia, Quebec, Belle Isle, Labrador. New England: Massachusetts, New Hampshire, Rhode Island. Middle Colonies/States: New York, New Jersey, Pennsylvania. Upper South: Virginia, Maryland. Lower South: North Carolina, South Carolina, Georgia, Florida. Other West Indies: Barbados, St Kitts, Nevis, Antigua, Montserrat, Grenada, St Vincent, Dominica, Tortola, Tobago, the Bahama Islands, Guadeloupe, Martinique, Anguilla.

Sources: (i) 1700, 1789–90: W. E. Minchinton, ed., *The Trade of Bristol in the Eighteenth Century* (Bristol Record Society's *Publications*, 20, 1957), pp. 5, 53–5. (ii) 1713–27: Public Record Office, London, Bristol Port Books, Inwards, E 190/1173/1–1200/1. (iii) 1729–88, 1792, 1797: Society of Merchant Venturers, Bristol, Wharfage Books.

from the colonies came from the Caribbean, while 23.5 per cent came from North America. Of this latter group, 4,270 out of 4,660 tons arrived from Virginia and Maryland alone – a reflection of the importance of the Chesapeake tobacco trade to Bristol's transatlantic commerce.[22]

During the War of the Spanish Succession, shipping lanes were dislocated and Bristol shipowners therefore needed convoy protection for their transoceanic vessels.[23] Some Bristolians turned to privateering while the conflict continued. Woodes Rogers' cruising voyage from Bristol around the world, a venture that accounted for twenty Spanish prizes between 1708 and 1711, including the richly laden Manila galleon that sailed annually to Acapulco, no doubt inspired a good many of these ventures.[24] Certainly Bristol was notably successful in privateering voyages, sending out 157 vessels armed with letters of marque (a higher number than any other outport) and taking 85 prizes.[25] A few years later Bristolians sent out seventeen commissioned vessels during the brief War of the Quadruple Alliance (1718–20).[26] But privateering only brought short-term financial gains. As soon as peace was restored, Bristol merchants reverted to their normal commodity trade. Fierce competition among different shippers in the Bristol tobacco trade points to considerable trading vitality at this time.[27] The volume of overseas trade also suggests a buoyant commercial situation. Thus by the late 1720s Bristol's incoming tonnage had increased by some 54 per cent since 1700. Of the trading areas in Europe, only tonnage entering Bristol from the Baltic experienced a decline. War and political difficulties affecting trade with that region contributed to this slump.[28] There was, in addition, a shift in trade from the Baltic towards the American mainland for pitch, tar and turpentine for masts and naval stores, these commodities being available

[22] Data from *ibid.*, table H 1, p. 325, and from Minchinton, ed., *Trade of Bristol in the Eighteenth Century*, p. 5.

[23] Lists of Bristol ships bound to British America under convoy for the years 1703–6 are given in BRO, Miscellaneous letters and other documents relating to Bristol, 1679–1742, fos. 41, 46–8, 50, 51.

[24] W. R. Meyer, 'English Privateering in the War of the Spanish Succession, 1702–13', *The Mariner's Mirror*, 69 (1983), 441; Donald Jones, *Captain Woodes Rogers' Voyage Round the World 1708–1711* (Bristol Branch of the Historical Association, pamphlet no. 79, Bristol, 1992).

[25] David J. Starkey, *British Privateering Enterprise in the Eighteenth Century* (Exeter, 1990), tables 1 and 5, pp. 88–9, 101–2. For a detailed discussion of Bristol privateering in the eighteenth century see J. W. Damer Powell, *Bristol Privateers and Ships of War* (Bristol, 1930), pp. 91–102, 131–4, 135–320. Letter-of-marque vessels were armed trading ships carrying a privateer's commission. During wartime, they supplemented earnings from trade with this prize-taking facility.

[26] Starkey, *British Privateering Enterprise*, table 6, p. 113.

[27] Virginia HS, John Tayloe to Samuel Jacob & Co., 20 Apr. 1717, Account Book and Letterbook (1714–78) of John Tayloe (1687–1747) and John Tayloe (1721–79).

[28] Quilici, 'Turmoil in a City and an Empire', tables H 1–7, pp. 325–38.

in abundance in colonies with substantial acreages of forest (such as New Hampshire and the Carolinas).[29]

Between 1700 and 1729–32, shipping entering Bristol from the West Indies increased in volume by 59.3 per cent and improved its share of all incoming tonnage from transatlantic regions from 52.0 to 57.2 per cent. During the same period, the North American portion of Bristol's Atlantic trade experienced relative decline: its percentage share of transatlantic tonnage entering Bristol fell from 47.4 to 42.8 per cent, though the volume of its tonnage rose by 44.6 per cent. The slight decline in the share of tonnage entering Bristol from the continental colonies partly reflects the depressed state of the tobacco trade in the 1720s, while the increase in total tonnage trading with the American mainland was aided by the growth of commerce with areas such as the Carolinas, New England, New York and Pennsylvania.[30] During the 1720s Bristol outpaced Liverpool, Glasgow and Whitehaven in the volume of trade with British America, and was second only to London among major British ports engaged in this commerce (see tables 1.2 and 1.3). Bristol vessels sailed safely on most shipping lanes at this time. Occasional depredations by Spanish *guarda costas* were nevertheless a reminder of the ever-present international rivalry on the high seas. Between March 1728 and June 1730, for example, eight Bristol ships were taken by the Spanish while sailing in the Caribbean; their computed loss ranged from £100 to £7,000.[31] Altogether, it was claimed, some twenty Bristol ships worth more than £60,000 had been captured by the Spanish during peacetime years in the 1720s.[32]

Most sectors of Bristol's overseas shipping declined in the early 1730s. The volume of overseas shipping entering the port in 1734–5 was 25,865 tons, whereas in 1727–8 it had been 30,655 tons – a fall of 15.6 per cent.[33] The contraction in tonnage was unevenly distributed among various

[29] Joseph J. Malone, 'England and the Baltic Naval Stores Trade in the Seventeenth and Eighteenth Centuries', *The Mariner's Mirror*, 58 (1972), 388.

[30] The best detailed discussion of this depression in the tobacco trade is in John M. Hemphill, 'Virginia and the English Commercial System, 1689–1733: Studies in the Development and Fluctuations of a Colonial Economy under Imperial Control' (Princeton University Ph.D. dissertation, 1964), ch. 2. On the trading relationship between Bristol and New York see Lawrence J. Bradley, 'The London/Bristol Trade Rivalry: Conventional History and the Colonial Office 5 Records for the Port of New York' (Notre Dame University Ph.D. dissertation, 1971).

[31] Cambridge UL, 'List of Bristol Ships taken by the Spaniards, March 1728–June 1730', section 13, Cholmondeley (Houghton) MSS. For another example of a Bristol vessel taken by Spanish marauders see ACRL, Case of Lyonel Lyde *et al.*, Mar. 1725, Braikenridge Collection, VI.

[32] Memorial of the Merchants of Bristol to Lord Townshend, n.d. but *c*.1721–30, in Minchinton, ed., *Politics and the Port of Bristol*, p. 22.

[33] Quilici, 'Turmoil in a City and an Empire', tables H2 and H3, pp. 327–30.

Table 1.2. *Number and tonnage of ships entering selected British ports from the American mainland colonies, 1721–1730*

	London		Bristol		Liverpool		Whitehaven		Glasgow & Greenock	
	N	Tons	N	Tons	N	Tons	N	Tons	N	Tons
1721	129	14,359	53	4,355	32	2,616	19	1,809	38	2,860
1722	126	14,465	42	3,775	31	2,535	19	2,008	47	3,691
1723	139	16,605	44	3,860	19	1,625	10	1,061	43	3,331
1724	121	14,545	38	3,007	19	1,570	14	1,342	23	2,100
1725	136	15,055	55	4,417	15	1,175	11	819	29	1,625
1726	140	15,381	54	4,822	22	1,464	19	2,014	36	2,762
1727	141	13,250	66	5,780	34	2,858	14	1,612	42	3,716
1728	169	19,046	56	5,110	29	2,205	14	1,313	36	3,325
1729	164	20,608	33	3,081	36	2,840	15	1,445	35	3,135
1730	158	17,290	40	3,650	24	1,780	17	2,132	22	2,095
Totals	1,423	160,604	481	41,857	261	20,668	152	15,555	351	28,640

Source: Public Record Office, London, T64/276A no. 272.

Table 1.3. *Number and tonnage of ships entering selected British ports from the British Caribbean, 1721–1730*

	London		Bristol		Liverpool		Whitehaven		Glasgow & Greenock	
	N	Tons	N	Tons	N	Tons	N	Tons	N	Tons
1721	115	13,973	66	5,615	21	1,300	3	245	9	506
1722	150	18,550	70	7,065	29	1,996	3	144	11	810
1723	206	23,184	64	5,975	33	2,000	3	174	9	520
1724	193	22,040	79	7,070	33	2,105	2	157	13	735
1725	219	24,883	88	8,400	41	2,505	3	198	15	855
1726	175	20,078	82	7,713	33	2,065	0	0	11	780
1727	187	21,357	53	4,900	29	1,595	1	60	7	470
1728	249	27,235	92	8,054	42	2,443	1	60	10	705
1729	260	28,506	78	7,229	39	2,270	3	205	6	420
1730	235	28,266	100	8,733	62	3,781	2	130	13	1,055
Totals	1,989	228,072	722	70,754	362	23,060	21	1,373	104	6,856

Source: Public Record Office, London, T 64/276A no. 271.

regions. There were increases in tonnage only for ships coming from Ireland, the Baltic and the American mainland colonies. All other regions in Europe and British America lost ground.[34] Shipping in the

[34] *Ibid.*

West India trade was hit hardest; the tonnage arriving at Bristol from the Caribbean fell from 8,610 to 6,305 tons – a 26.8 per cent drop – between 1727–32 and 1733–7. This large dip in the volume of Bristol West India trade resulted from a decline in the production and British importation of sugar at that time.[35]

Bristol's Atlantic trade experienced additional problems by the 1730s. Already by the early part of that decade, rival outports were encroaching on her commerce with the Americas. Thus the Bristol merchant Richard Meyler noted that 'the Liverpoole & Scotch vessels that saile cheap and pay out Little Commission & no more charges than are actually needfull . . . drive all our Ships out of the Trade & can by that means Dispose of their Sugar in London or in Bristol on Lower Terms than we can and gett some profitt'. He added that 'by degrees' they take 'that trade from our City'.[36] To compound this difficulty it was acknowledged by the late 1730s that Bristol was the worst market in Britain for sales of tobacco.[37] The reasons for this situation are unclear, but they were probably connected to Bristol confining itself largely to sweetscented tobacco for snuff takers rather than to coarser leaf for pipe smokers.[38]

These problems were multiplied by the middle of the next decade. For nine years after 1739, oceanic shipping lanes were severely disrupted by the international hostilities that occurred during the War of Jenkins's Ear and the War of the Austrian Succession. Bristol was clearly undergoing a trade recession by the mid-1740s. The volume of shipping arriving at Bristol from transatlantic areas fell by a quarter from 12,756 tons in 1738–42 to 9,533 tons in 1743–7 – the lowest figure since the beginning of the century (see table 1.1). The traffic between Bristol and the North American colonies also declined from the position achieved in the mid-1730s (the same was true, incidentally, of trade between Bristol and Europe).[39] The one exception to this pattern of contraction was in Caribbean trade, for the West Indian share of transatlantic shipping tonnage entering Bristol rose from 52.9 per cent in 1733–7 to 58.8 per cent in 1743–7. That even such a modest increase happened at a time of intense naval warfare in the West Indies – the cockpit of European maritime rivalry in the eighteenth century – is testimony to renewed growth in sugar production and British demand for sugar and other groceries.[40]

Spanish depredations on Bristol-based shipping began before the out-

---

[35] This decline is discussed below on pp. 187, 191.
[36] UMA, Richard Meyler to William Wells, 3 Dec. 1732, Bright Family Papers.
[37] LC, John Custis to Mr Loyd, 1736 and n.d. (but c.1739), John Custis Letterbook (1717–42), Custis Family Papers.
[38] See below, pp. 169–70, 177–9.
[39] Quilici, 'Turmoil in a City and an Empire', pp. 118–19.
[40] For further discussion of this point see below, pp. 184, 187.

break of war, but the situation deteriorated between 1739 and 1741 when at least seventeen Bristol vessels were captured by Spanish privateers.[41] These marauders were particularly active in the chops of the Bristol Channel and there was little naval protection against them.[42] They undoubtedly contributed to what one merchant referred to in 1742 as 'the decline of trade' being 'so great in Bristol' – a comment echoed by others at the time.[43] Several Bristol merchants preferred to lay up their ships rather than venture to sea while this threat to their trade continued.[44] By the mid-1740s, more Bristolians cut back on shipping and the number of vessels paying anchorage at the port fell significantly.[45]

Bristol merchants petitioned Parliament to seek naval protection for their vessels in the English Channel and near the African coast.[46] They even wanted Lundy Island annexed to the Crown and a garrison of forty men kept there to deal with French privateers, which frequented nearby sheltered waters.[47] But by 1745 so many French and Spanish privateers were cruising in the English Channel that ships could scarcely pass to the African coast. The result was that 'all trade to ye Coast & other places is Laid aside' at Bristol and 'the most is privateering'.[48] These privateers had a fair amount of success. The commissioned fleet of 132 vessels accounted for 82 condemnations, which made Bristol the leading British

41 Minchinton, ed., *Trade of Bristol in the Eighteenth Century*, p. 152; BL, Add. MS 32,800, fos. 79, 81–5: George Packer, Richard Farr, Thomas Ross and Thomas Roach to the Duke of Newcastle, 3 Jan. 1739, and depositions; Petitions of the Society of Merchant Venturers on Spanish attacks on trade, 3 Mar. 1738, 23 Feb. 1739, in Leo Francis Stock, ed., *Proceedings and Debates of the British Parliaments respecting North America*, 5 vols. (Washington, DC, 1924–41), IV, pp. 358, 667. For a vivid account of a ship taken by a Spanish privateer on her homeward voyage from Charleston to Bristol see J. H. Bettey, 'The Capture of the *Baltick Merchant*, 1740', *The Mariner's Mirror*, 76 (1990), 36–9.
42 UMA, Richard Meyler to Henry Bright, 21 Nov. 1741, box 6, Bright Family Papers; Hector MacNeale to Neal MacNeal, 1 Dec. 1740, bundle 5, Family Papers of MacNeal of Tirfergus, Ugadale and Losset.
43 UMA, Henry Bright to Allen Bright, 15 Apr. 1742, Henry Bright Letterbook (1739–48), *ibid.* (from which the quotation is taken); ACRL, George Blake to Edward Southwell, 28 Mar. 1744, Southwell Papers, VIII (B11159); Arthur Pierce Middleton, *Tobacco Coast: A Maritime History of Chesapeake Bay in the Colonial Era* (Newport News, VA, 1953), p. 342.
44 Hector MacNeale to Neal MacNeal, 1 Dec. 1740, bundle 5, Family Papers of MacNeal of Tirfergus, Ugadale and Losset.
45 Minchinton, ed., *Trade of Bristol in the Eighteenth Century*, p. x and app. A, p. 177.
46 Petition of Bristol merchants to the Privy Council, 2 Apr. 1744; Petition of Bristol merchants to the House of Commons, 4 Mar. 1746; and Walter Lougher to Members of Parliament, 27 Feb. 1745, in Minchinton, ed., *Politics and the Port of Bristol*, pp. 57, 60–1, 63–4.
47 Petition of Bristol merchants to the Privy Council, 26 Mar. 1743, in *ibid.*, p. 56.
48 UMA, Richard Meyler to Henry Bright, 11 June 1745, box 7, Bright Family Papers. By 1747, French cruisers were also roaming the West African coast (SMV, Abraham Saunders to Philip Protheroe & Co., 19 Oct. 1747, Letters received by the Society of Merchant Venturers).

outport in privateering ventures.[49] Lucrative captures from the French included the *St Philip* in 1747 (valued at £30,000) and the *Santa Theresa* in 1748 (valued at £40,000).[50] Many Bristol slave traders converted their ships into privateers during the war years of the 1740s. They found it easy to fit out ships for such cruises, since both types of voyages were essentially organised on an *ad hoc* basis.[51]

Attention to privateering coupled with a marked cutback in normal trading voyages meant, however, that Bristol's transatlantic shipping lost vital ground in the 1740s to that of Liverpool, whose geographical location was more distant from the sea passages frequented by enemy men-of-war. Liverpool merchantmen evaded foreign *corsaires* by taking the route around the north of Ireland on their Atlantic crossings.[52] Masters of French privateers avoided sailing into the Irish Sea, regarding navigation there as dangerous without a pilot. Liverpool's relative safety from attack enabled her to emerge from the War of the Austrian Succession with a greater share of the trades in slaves and Caribbean produce.[53] Glasgow merchants also benefited from the lack of enemy privateers in northerly waters. They were able to reduce voyage times (and, hence, freight charges and insurance costs too), and this enabled them to forge ahead of Bristol and other ports further south in the tobacco trade.[54] There was another, more speculative, reason why Bristol's trade declined in the mid-1740s. If Bristolians had been willing to help man their convoys, one contemporary suggested, they might have been more certain of gaining defence for their merchant shipping and therefore might have maintained a higher level of trading voyages during wartime.[55]

The fall in the volume of incoming tonnage at Bristol was checked at the end of the 1740s. This was a time when peace was restored with Europe, when rapid growth occurred in the British economy, and when exports to the American colonies increased both in quantity and value.[56] Bristol's overseas shipping began to recover in this buoyant economic

---

[49] Starkey, *British Privateering Enterprise*, tables 7 and 12, pp. 121, 141.

[50] Powell, *Bristol Privateers and Ships of War*, p. 136.

[51] See below, p. 141.

[52] Paul G. E. Clemens, 'The Rise of Liverpool, 1665–1750', *EcHR*, 2nd Series, 29 (1976), 219. Apparently, Liverpool also had the advantage over Bristol of having half or more of her sailors as apprentices and the others 'married in a manner to their ships' through long service (Somerset RO, Caleb Dickinson Diary (1740), Dickinson Papers, DD/DN 230).

[53] Patrick Crowhurst, *The Defence of British Trade, 1689–1815* (Folkestone, 1977), p. 66; Starkey, *British Privateering Enterprise*, pp. 247, 271.

[54] Crowhurst, *Defence of British Trade*, pp. 151–2.

[55] ACRL, Edward Southwell to the Master of the Society of Merchant Venturers, 15 Feb. 1746, Southwell Papers, IX (B11160).

[56] See below, pp. 92, 110.

climate. This can be seen from comparison of the figures in table 1.1 for 1743–7 and 1754–7. The annual average of shipping tonnage arriving at Bristol from transatlantic areas rose by 35.0 per cent between those two sets of years. The upsurge in the volume of shipping was fairly evenly spread among different regions in British America, but a particularly marked growth occurred in tonnage entering Bristol from the Windward and Leeward Islands. This rise in the volume of trade enabled Bristol to maintain its lead over Liverpool in terms of the value of commodity trade. Between 1750 and 1757 average annual gross customs receipts in the two ports were £289,365 and £201,862 respectively, while average net remittances amounted to £155,190 for Bristol and £51,136 for Liverpool.[57] Bristol still led Liverpool, in terms of the value of trade, throughout the latter part of the Seven Years War. Between 1759 and 1763, Bristol's annual customs receipts amounted to £299,000 while Liverpool's were £252,000.[58]

Nevertheless, the general recovery of Bristol's transatlantic shipping in the late 1740s and early 1750s slowed down with the coming of the Seven Years War. Though Bristol's trade was protected by convoys, after consultation between the Admiralty and the Society of Merchant Venturers, sixty-eight ships sailing to the colonies were taken by French and Spanish privateers on outward voyages and fifty-five on homeward runs.[59] Many of the losses occurred in the Windward Islands.[60] One result was a higher incidence of bankruptcies among Bristol merchants than at any previous time during the century.[61] To counter these difficulties, many Bristolians converted their trading vessels into letter-of-marque ships.[62] They also turned, once again, to privateering. Their record was successful. Bristol fitted out more commissioned vessels (253 in all) and claimed more prize condemnations (81) than any other British outport during the war. Of all eighteenth-century conflicts, the Seven Years War

---

[57] William Barrett, *The History and Antiquities of the City of Bristol* (Bristol, 1789; facs. repr. 1982), p. 187.

[58] William Enfield, *An Essay Towards the History of Liverpool* (London, 1774), p. 70.

[59] R. P. Crowhurst, 'British Oceanic Convoys in the Seven Years' War, 1756–1763' (University of London Ph.D. thesis, 1970), pp. 80, 123–9, and Morgan, 'Bristol Merchants and the Colonial Trades', p. 80, which gives full statistics on losses of Bristol vessels during the war.

[60] UMA, Meyler, Hall & Torry to Henry Bright, 27 Jan. 1760, box 40, Bright Family Papers.

[61] Minchinton, ed., *Trade of Bristol in the Eighteenth Century*, pp. G(i), app. 184–6.

[62] Shipping articles for two Bristol vessels (the *Planter* and the *True Patriot*) bound to Virginia, but empowered to seize French and Spanish ships, are given in Somerset RO, Graham-Clarke (Hestercombe) MSS, DD/GC/73.

was the one in which Bristol's cruising voyages reached their peak.[63] Concentration on privateering, however, deflected investment from normal trading voyages. 'I fear the great Attention to Privateering out of your City has much hurted the Trade of it', a Bristolian based in Jamaica noted, 'for there is Ten Times the Business carried on from Liverpool to this Island than from your City, & a great trade from London in the Linen way'.[64] Given those developments, it is not surprising that the shipping tonnage entering Bristol from British America slipped slightly from an annual average of 12,871 tons in 1754–7 to 12,563 tons per year in 1758–62.

Yet the Seven Years War exercised only a temporary brake on the growth of Bristol's Atlantic trade. Despite political difficulties affecting trade in the 1760s and early 1770s – notably the non-importation measures practised by some North American ports in response to British imperial policies – incoming tonnage at Bristol from transatlantic areas was 68.8 per cent higher in 1773–7 than in 1758–62 (21,202 as opposed to 12,563 tons).[65] Between the Peace of Paris and the outbreak of the American War of Independence, Bristol's European trade flourished[66] but her transatlantic trade grew more rapidly than at any other time during the century. Significant increases were particularly evident in the number and tonnage of vessels arriving at Bristol from the Middle Colonies, the Lower South and Jamaica. The jewel in the crown of Bristol's commercial connections with the colonies was Jamaica where, by 1773, Bristol merchants had business contacts all over the island (in harbours such as Morant Bay, Savanna-la-Mar, Montego Bay, Green Island, Kingston, Lucea, Old Harbour, Martha Brae and Port Antonio, and in areas such as St James and Westmoreland parishes and the north side of

---

[63] Starkey, *British Privateering Enterprise*, tables 13 and 18, pp. 165, 181; John Latimer, *The History of the Society of Merchant Venturers of the City of Bristol* (Bristol, 1903), pp. 202–3. For sales of six prizes taken by a Bristol vessel see William L. Clements Lib., Accounts of the *Tryall* (1757–8), Bristol Shipping Account Books, I.

[64] UMA, Jeremiah Meyler to Richard Meyler, Sr, 29 Sept. 1759, box 23, Bright Family Papers.

[65] For the effect of political difficulties on Bristol's Atlantic commerce at this time see W. R. Savadge, 'The West Country and the American Mainland Colonies, 1763–1783, with special reference to the Merchants of Bristol' (University of Oxford B.Litt. thesis, 1952); Peter T. Underdown, 'The Parliamentary History of the City of Bristol, 1750–1790' (University of Bristol MA thesis, 1948), pp. 117–27, 154–8; W. E. Minchinton, 'The Stamp Act Crisis: Bristol and Virginia', *VMHB*, 73 (1965), 145–55, and 'The Political Activities of Bristol Merchants with Respect to the Southern Colonies before the Revolution', *VMHB*, 79 (1971), 167–89; PRO, HO 55/6/8: Petition from the Citizens of Bristol condemning the actions of the present government, 25 July 1769; MacInnes, *Bristol: A Gateway of Empire*, pp. 263–306.

[66] Quilici, 'Turmoil in a City and an Empire', tables H6 and H7, pp. 335–8.

the island).[67] Jamaica was the largest sugar-producing island in the British Caribbean and her dominance of Bristol's West India trade at this time is clearly shown in map 3.

The growth of Bristol's colonial shipping reflected the general rise of the English shipping industry plus the strong boost created by demand within Britain and American demand for exports, slaves and sugar.[68] The value of produce entering the port was considerable. By 1770 – and for several years beforehand – annual customs receipts at Bristol amounted to £200,000 per annum; the excise contributed a further £100,000 per year.[69] Clearly, Bristol still had a lot at stake in foreign trade. As the Anglo–American political relationship deteriorated, there was much heated discussion in Bristol over the merits and demerits of British government policies towards the colonies.[70] Some Bristolians criticised government ministers for destroying 'a lucrative trade' while others hoped for a healing reconciliation with the colonies.[71] Bristol merchants obviously wished to keep the wheels of commerce turning. They agitated for measures that would promote Atlantic commerce by campaigning for the repeal of the Stamp Act, for modifications to the Sugar Act, and for the establishment of a free port in Dominica.[72] When the Stamp Act was repealed, several houses in Bristol were illuminated, including the American coffee house, from whose windows merchants trading across the Atlantic 'generously threw money to the populace'.[73] But the rejoicing was only temporary; over the next decade the political rifts were not resolved. In 1775, Bristol's exports to the American mainland were severely cut back because of non-importation policies in the colonies.[74] Later in the year her merchants scrambled to get as many of their 'effects'

---

[67] UMA, Lowbridge Bright to Bright, Milward & Duncomb, 24 Sept. 1773, Lowbridge Bright Letterbook (1765–73), Bright Family Papers.

[68] See below, chs. 4, 5, 7, plus Davis, *Rise of the English Shipping Industry*, pp. 41–2, and David Richardson, 'The Slave Trade, Sugar, and British Economic Growth, 1748–1776', *Journal of Interdisciplinary History*, 18 (1987), 739–69.

[69] Barrett, *History and Antiquities*, p. 186.

[70] P. T. Underdown, 'Bristol and Burke' in McGrath, ed., *Bristol in the Eighteenth Century*, pp. 46–56; James E. Bradley, *Popular Politics and the American Revolution in England: Petitions, the Crown and Public Opinion* (Macon, GA 1986), pp. 22–4, 69–70, 110; and the studies cited in note 65.

[71] E.g. New York PL, Richard Champion to Willing, Morris & Co., 30 Sept. 1774, Richard Champion Letterbook (1773–5), from which the quotation is taken; PRO, HO 55/11/64: the humble petition of the merchants, traders, manufacturers and others, citizens of Bristol, ?1776; Petition to the House of Commons on American trade, 18 Jan. 1775, in Minchinton, ed., *Politics and the Port of Bristol*, pp. 130–2.

[72] Savadge, 'West Country', pp. 198ff; Petition to the House of Commons on American Trade, 6 Jan. 1766, and Petition to the House of Lords on American Trade, 3 Mar. 1766, in Minchinton, ed., *Politics and the Port of Bristol*, pp. 103–5.

[73] *FFBJ*, 1 Mar. 1766.

[74] See the list in Minchinton, ed., *Trade of Bristol in the Eighteenth Century*, pp. 48–50.

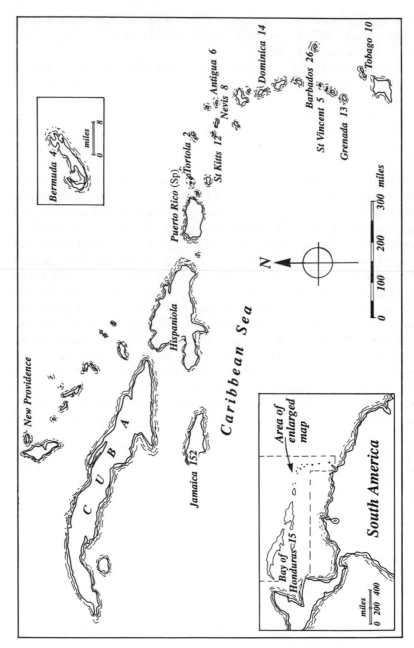

Map 3   Vessels entering Bristol from the West Indies, 1773–1775

out of North America before Congress's adoption of non-exportation came into effect in September 1775. No less than 270 vessels – including 68 from the Middle Colonies and 59 from the Chesapeake – entered the port of Bristol from British America in 1775, many of them carrying grain cargoes.[75]

By the end of 1776, Bristolians fully supported the policies of George III's government against the American colonists.[76] Edmund Burke, one of the two MPs for Bristol, realised the significance of this decision. In *A Letter to the Sheriffs of Bristol* (1777), he noted that 'this great city, a main pillar in the commercial interest of Great Britain, must totter on its base by the slightest mistake, with regard to our American measures'.[77] Bristol merchants in fact paid a heavy price, for the American War of Independence seriously disrupted the patterns of imperial commerce. At Bristol the volume of incoming shipping from transatlantic regions fell from an annual average of 21,202 tons in 1773–7 to 12,326 tons per year in 1778–80 – a 41.8 per cent drop to the lowest level of trade since the War of the Austrian Succession. The closure of North American markets to British shipping was a particularly hard blow. Bristolians, it is true, continued a modest traffic with New York City, Philadelphia and Charleston while those cities were occupied by British forces.[78] Nevertheless, a mere fifteen ships arrived at Bristol from the rebellious colonies between 1776 and 1780.[79]

Some Bristol merchants tried to sustain Atlantic trading links during the war by sending cargoes on indirect routes (an example being Richard Champion, who tried to dispatch porcelain to the American mainland via Amsterdam and St Eustatius).[80] Other merchants either ceased trading (such was the fate of the Farrs and of John Mallard) or avoided financial

[75] For the organisation of large shipments of wheat and corn to Bristol at this time see Maryland HS, John Smith & Sons to Joseph Jones & Sons, 5 Nov., 3 Dec. 1774, 6 Jan. 1775, John Smith & Sons Letterbook (1774–86), and various letters from Richard Champion to Willing & Morris of Philadelphia in George H. Guttridge, ed., *The American Correspondence of a Bristol Merchant, 1766–1776: Letters to Richard Champion*, University of California Publications in History, 22 (Berkeley, CA, 1934), pp. 23, 25–9, 38–42, 44, 47, 55–7.
[76] PRO, HO 55/11/9, Condemnation of the American Rebellion by the Mayor and inhabitants of Bristol, 28 Sept. 1775; MacInnes, *Bristol: A Gateway of Empire*, pp. 296–7.
[77] Quoted in G. E. Weare, *Edmund Burke's Connection with Bristol, from 1774 till 1780: With a Prefatory Memoir of Burke* (Bristol, 1894), p. 46.
[78] Savadge, 'West Country', pp. 514–20; New York HS, Frederick & Philip Rhinelander to Vigor & Stevens, 7 June 1777, 21 Mar., 17 May 1778, Frederick & Philip Rhinelander Letterbook (1774–83). Full details of ships and cargoes entering New York City from Bristol during the War of Independence are given in Robert M. Dructor, 'The New York Commercial Community: The Revolutionary Experience' (University of Pittsburgh Ph.D. dissertation, 1975), app. F, pp. 519–76.
[79] SMV, Wharfage Books.
[80] Guttridge, ed., *American Correspondence*, p. 7.

catastrophe by securing military contracts to supply rum and bread (the strategy pursued by Samuel Span and Joseph Jones & Son).[81] Still others never recovered the debts owed to them by correspondents in places such as Virginia, Maryland and South Carolina.[82] Small wonder that many Bristol merchants found the war a severe ordeal, and that some turned to West Indian commerce to compensate for the cessation of trade with the American mainland.[83] Those who continued trade with North America faced the threat of attack from enemy privateers.[84] This created great resentment in Bristol. 'Who could have thought', the Bristol merchant Thomas Griffiths wrote in 1777, 'that the People of America w[oul]d be so infamous as to fit out Cruizers to take the Ships & properties of people of this country who had no hand with their quarrell with Gover[n]m[en]t many of whom had been the means of their riseing into Consequence by giveing them unlimitted Credit? Such base treatment is not in the power of words to describe.'[85]

Not all of Bristol's transatlantic trade suffered so much during the revolutionary war. Between 1778 and 1780, eleven ships with a volume of 828 tons entered Bristol from the fisheries off Newfoundland and seventy-one ships of 11, 025 tons arrived at Bristol from the Caribbean (though the proportion coming from the West Indian islands other than Jamaica was smaller than just before the war). Some of these vessels snapped up temporary supplies of tobacco in the Caribbean better than ships from Liverpool and Lancaster (see table 1.4). This tobacco was mainly available through clandestine trade with the Danish islands of St Thomas and St Croix and with the Dutch island of St Eustatius, to which a considerable amount of British manufactured goods were sent in 1779–80 to assist in purchasing leaf there.[86] But this is not to suggest that Bristol's West India trade experienced comfortable trading conditions throughout the war. Bristolians expressed concern about convoy provision to protect the West India fleet against enemy privateers. There is also evidence of

---

[81] Peter Marshall, *Bristol and the American War of Independence* (Bristol Branch of the Historical Association, pamphlet no. 41, Bristol, 1977), pp. 13–14.

[82] See below, pp. 163–4, and SHC, Miscellaneous Papers: Indenture Tripartite: An Instrument of Assignment by Christopher Rolleston, London, surviving partner of the late Edward Neufville, Bristol, 29 Apr. 1789: this shows that, at 31 Dec. 1788, some £86,229 4s. 3d. was still owed to Neufville & Rolleston, a firm that traded between Bristol and Charleston before the American Revolution.

[83] Savadge, 'West Country', pp. 502–4.

[84] For a list of Bristol ships taken by American privateers in the early war years (down to 27 Jan. 1777) see BL, Lansdowne MS 1,219, fos. 18–30.

[85] Massachusetts HS, Thomas Griffiths to Silvester Gardiner, 26 Apr. 1777, Gardiner, Whipple & Allen Papers, II.

[86] ACRL, *Bristol Presentments*, Imports, 1779 and 1780; William Miles to Edmund Burke, 20 May 1780, cited in Savadge, 'West Country', p. 516. Glasgow merchants also took much tobacco during the war from the same islands (T. M. Devine, *The Tobacco Lords:*

Table 1.4. *Tobacco imports at selected English ports from the British West Indies, 1777–1780 (in lb.)*

	1777	1778	1779	1780
Bristol	1,979	0	1,029,202	2,580,490
Lancaster	0	24,683	40,243	54,756
Liverpool	0	193,299	334,141	1,326,080
London	78,847	138,137	1,516,866	2,489,341
Totals	80,826	356,119	2,920,452	6,450,667

Source: Public Record Office, London, T 64/276B: 'An Account of all the British Plantation Tobacco which has been imported into the several ports of south Britain from the
British West India islands which appear by the clearances not to have been of the growth or
produce of those islands nor prize tobacco for 1777–1780.'

falling sugar imports, losses of sugar ships, increasing wage, freight and
insurance rates, and a decline in the slave trade at Bristol in these years.[87]
One solution to disruptions in overseas trade, as in previous wars, was for
Bristol shipowners to convert vessels into privateers and letter-of-marque
ships. This they did with alacrity, fitting out 203 commissioned vessels
between 1777 and 1783 (or 7.6 per cent of all British privateers) and
taking 88 prize captures. Bristol's level of privateering activity did not
reach the peak achieved during the Seven Years War, but it put idle
vessels to productive use when major transatlantic shipping lanes were
effectively closed.[88]

Despite commercial difficulties during the War of Independence, Bristol remained the leading British outport in terms of the value of cargoes
received. Thus average annual gross receipts of customs at Bristol for
1771–80 amounted to £252,631. The second outport, Liverpool, amassed
a sum of £239,879 in annual customs revenue in the same years.[89] In 1781
gross customs receipts at Bristol and Liverpool were £243,370 and
£241,587 respectively.[90] Large sums of money continued to be earned in
Bristol's overseas trade. In the late 1780s it was claimed that customs

A *Study of the Tobacco Merchants of Glasgow and their Trading Activities, c. 1740–1790*
(Edinburgh, 1975), pp. 130–1).
[87] See below, pp. 133, 201–14.
[88] Starkey, *British Privateering Enterprise*, tables 20 and 25, pp. 200, 221. Starkey effectively rebuts the assertion that the War of Independence witnessed 'disastrous losses' for
Bristolians engaged in privateering, a view advanced by Latimer in *Annals of Bristol*,
p. 436.
[89] E. E. Hoon, *The Organization of the English Customs System, 1696–1786* (2nd edn.,
Newton Abbot, 1968), p. 192.
[90] Liverpool Central Library, Holt and Gregson Papers, X, fos. 276–7, duplicated in XIX,
fos. 99–100.

duties at Bristol had fluctuated for several years past from between £350,000 and £400,000 per annum.[91] By 1787, the estimated value of ships and exports sent from Bristol to Africa and the West Indies amounted to £240,000 and £459,000 respectively; imports from Africa and the Caribbean together were worth £789,000; and the gross commercial value of ships and cargoes in Bristol's other overseas trades was assessed at £900,000.[92]

Tonnage figures reflect this substantial level of trade. During the peacetime decade from the end of the war with America until the outbreak of conflict with revolutionary France, the volume of transatlantic shipping entering Bristol rose to unprecedented levels of 27,251 tons per year in 1788–90 and of some 33,109 tons in 1792. In 1791, according to the *Bristol Mercury*, 'the trade of this city notwithstanding the astonishing growth of its rival Liverpool was never at any former period at the height to which it has lately attained'.[93] But to regard this upsurge of commerce as simply a boom is chimerical when a broader perspective is taken. In the period 1783–93 Liverpool took more advantage of the substantially increased production of export goods, partly because of improved transport links with the industrial Midlands. She also outpaced Bristol in the slave trade and almost caught up with her West-Country rival in the sugar trade.[94] Bristol's trade with the American mainland also failed to match the performance of London and Liverpool at this time.[95] The Bristol tobacco trade was much reduced from its pre-revolutionary level – a result mainly of heavy import duties, poor sales, and an inelastic home market for tobacco.[96] Less hardware and pottery was now exported from Bristol to North America and exports of glass to New York faced great competition from Ireland.[97] This all suggests that a Virginia merchant visiting Bristol in 1783 was prescient in concluding that 'Am[erican] trade to that port will not be of sufficient importance to take the attention of a

---

[91] BRO, [Richard Bright], 'Draft of Particulars of the Trade of Bristol, 1788' (n.p.), Bright MSS, Acc. 11168/2c.

[92] Marshall, 'The Anti-Slave Trade Movement in Bristol' in McGrath, ed., *Bristol in the Eighteenth Century*, p. 198.

[93] A notice for 14 Nov. 1791 quoted in Minchinton, ed., *Trade of Bristol in the Eighteenth Century*, p. xi.

[94] See below, pp. 106–7, 132–3, 140–1, 143–5, 188–90. A detailed descriptive account of Liverpool's commerce at this time is given in D. J. Pope, 'Shipping and Trade in the Port of Liverpool, 1783–1793' (University of Liverpool Ph.D. thesis, 1970).

[95] BRO, [Richard Bright], 'Draft of Particulars of the Trade of Bristol, 1788'.

[96] See below, p. 179.

[97] BRO, [Richard Bright], 'Draft of Particulars of the Trade of Bristol, 1788' (n.p.); New York HS, Stewart & Jones to Stevens, Cave & Co., 10 May 1794, Stewart & Jones Letterbook (1786–95).

Capital House'.[98] Other merchant observers, around the same time, also felt that Bristol traders were content to rest on their laurels.[99]

In 1793 Bristol suffered a severe economic crisis in which mercantile credit was curtailed, banks collapsed, and merchants went bankrupt. At this time no less than nineteen Bristol commercial houses failed for a grand total of £1,110,000.[100] In the remaining years before the end of the century, Bristol's commerce declined as a result of renewed international maritime warfare. In 1797, ninety-one ships with a total volume of 20,490 tons entered Bristol from transatlantic areas – a drop of 38.1 per cent from the peak achieved five years earlier.[101] It was abundantly clear by this time that Bristol's physical capacity as a port was too limited to cope with even a reduced level of overseas trade.

Bristol's situation as a port, illustrated in map 4, contributed to these problems. For many years, the winding nature of the Avon gorge, the extremely wide tidal range of forty-five feet, and the spillage of industrial waste into the River Avon from glass houses, sugar houses and other works, all hindered the navigation of ocean-going vessels plying between the centre of Bristol and the anchorages seven miles downstream where the Avon flows into the Bristol Channel. Ships were damaged by grounding on mud banks at low tides, or immobilised by lack of water at neap tides. They had particular difficulty in negotiating the tortuous bends of the Avon near St Vincent's Rock. Vessels greater than 150 tons rarely ventured even this far up river. Pilots and towboats were needed to help large ships pass up and down the Avon. By the 1780s, only a maximum of twenty vessels could lie safely at Kingroad, a roadstead off Portishead, near the mouth of the Avon, where ships dropped anchor in sheltered waters. Facilities for discharging cargoes onto rafts and lighters at Hungroad, another anchorage about three miles up river from Kingroad, also needed improvement.[102] In addition, congestion occurred in the city

---

[98] LC, J. Heron to Nicholas Low, 4 Dec. 1783, box 3, Nicholas Low Papers.

[99] See below, pp. 217–18.

[100] Marshall, 'Anti-Slave Trade Movement', pp. 212–13; L. S. Pressnell, *Country Banking in the Industrial Revolution* (Oxford, 1956), pp. 457–8 and app. 28, pp. 546–7. Cf. Minchinton, *Trade of Bristol in the Eighteenth Century*, app. G(ii), p. 190.

[101] The berthing locations of vessels using the port of Bristol in 1791 and 1795 are shown in Alan F. Williams, 'Bristol Port Plans and Improvement Schemes of the Eighteenth Century', *TBGAS*, 81 (1962), fig. 6, p. 173.

[102] Among the extensive contemporary commentary on these problems see especially SMV, Petition of John Bowman, 4 Nov. 1784, Docks: Miscellaneous Papers, 1784–92; Henry West to the Master of the SMV, 13 Aug. 1761, and John Shaw to Henry Cruger, 24 June, 20 September 1782, Letters received by the Master of the SMV, bundles 6 and 24; John Shaw to Edward Brice, 19 July 1787, box of Papers on the Quays and Docks of Bristol; BRO, 'General View of the question respecting the improvement of the harbour of Bristol', n.d. but probably c. early 1790s, Bright MSS, Acc. 11168/5f; PRO,

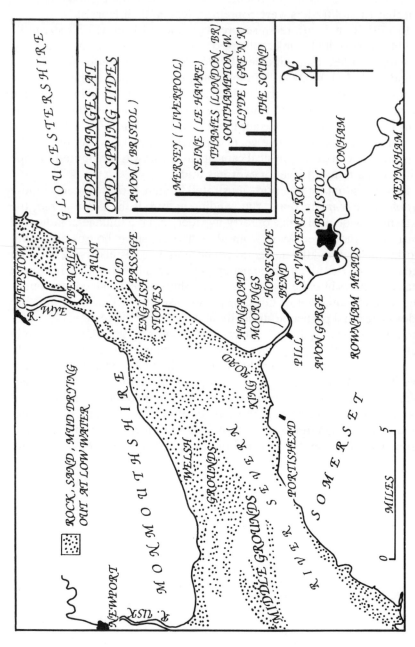

Map 4   The situation of Bristol as an eighteenth-century port

docks with the increase in the number and size of ships using the port. This problem was partly caused by vessels trading with the colonies: ships in the Bristol–Jamaica trade, for instance, grew from an average of 123 tons in the late 1740s to over 200 tons by the mid-1780s.[103]

Between 1660 and 1700 the Society of Merchant Venturers, who leased the quays from the city, was already active in improving port facilities at Bristol.[104] During the eighteenth century, they continued this work. They drew up petitions about the need for port improvements; they installed new cranes, wharves, quays and moorings; they also took over Champion's wet dock in 1770 (the largest one in Bristol at that time). By 1800, accommodation at the quays was over a mile in extent. Yet commercial quayage had extended little from the sites used in the Middle Ages and there was insufficient space for large ships, which took a considerable time to load and unload. Improvements to port facilities were sluggish for several reasons. The Bristol City Council baulked at the sums proposed for various schemes; the Merchant Venturers' finances were stretched by contributions to the upkeep of the port; and delays occurred because of conflicting advice from engineers.[105] The slow improvement to port facilities at Bristol reflected the business conservatism of the leading mercantile lobby and the city's politicians. It was not the result of lack of capital. On the contrary, there was plenty of money available for investment in trade, canals, housing and other types of economic enterprise in Georgian Bristol.[106] The situation at Liverpool was very different because the city corporation there invested large sums of money in port development during the eighteenth century, and many of the major docks

T 1/523: Memorial of William Jones and Samuel Worrall, 13 Feb. 1776, fos. 6–7; Petition to the House of Commons on the Port of Bristol, 5 Feb. 1776, in Minchinton, ed., *Politics and the Port of Bristol*, pp. 137–8; and New York HS, William Bedlow Journal (1759), 14 Mar. 1759. See also Latimer, *History of the Society of Merchant Venturers*, pp. 206–14; Minchinton, 'Port of Bristol in the Eighteenth Century', pp. 135, 138–41, 146; and Grahame Farr, 'Bristol Channel Pilotage: Historical notes on its administration and craft', *The Mariner's Mirror*, 39 (1953), 27–44.

103 See below, table 2.3, p. 43.

104 Patrick McGrath, 'The Society of Merchant Venturers and the Port of Bristol in the Seventeenth Century', *TBGAS*, 72 (1953), 114–18.

105 Minchinton, 'Port of Bristol in the Eighteenth Century', pp. 153–7; F. Walker, 'The Port of Bristol', *Economic Geography*, 15 (1939), 108–10; Williams, 'Bristol Port Plans', 138–88; McGrath, *Merchant Venturers of Bristol*, pp. 150–67; James Bird, *The Major Seaports of the United Kingdom* (London, 1963), pp. 187–8.

106 See below, pp. 162–3, 185–6, and Jacob M. Price, *Capital and Credit in British Overseas Trade: The View from the Chesapeake, 1700–1776* (Cambridge, MA, 1980), pp. 101, 189 note 17; J. R. Ward, *The Finance of Canal Building in Eighteenth-Century England* (Oxford, 1974), pp. 47–8, 92–4, 138–40, and 'Speculative Building at Bristol and Clifton, 1783–1793', *Business History*, 20 (1978), 3–18.

on the Mersey were first erected in that period.[107] These developments were paralleled at Glasgow where, from the late seventeenth century onwards, considerable expense and civic initiative led to the improvement of docks at Port Glasgow, then the head port and principal customs station on the Clyde.[108]

A satisfactory solution to Bristol's port development did not emerge until a private company built the Floating Harbour, a huge dock of seventy acres with an artificial cut, in the first decade of the nineteenth century. Even then, it did not solve all of the problems. It tended to silt up, which led to the expense of regular dredging.[109] It also represented the limit of possible port development on the Bristol Avon; further elaboration only came with the construction of docks at Avonmouth and Portishead in the 1870s. The difficulties were compounded by heavy dock dues which, by the early nineteenth century, were much greater than corresponding taxes paid at London or Liverpool. Port dues at Bristol were levied on all ships coming within the jurisdiction of the port of Bristol and not just on vessels using dock facilities. When one considers that the boundaries of the port of Bristol extended down the Avon to the Bristol Channel and to part of that channel, it is not difficult to imagine the complaints that ensued.[110] All in all, Bristol's indecision and delays over port improvement were singularly unhelpful for the expansion of her trading activity at the close of the eighteenth century. Better organisation and finance of the docks at Liverpool stimulated the rise of Merseyside even if they cannot be claimed as indispensable to the growth of Liverpool's trade.[111]

[107] F. E. Hyde, *Liverpool and the Mersey: An Economic History of a Port, 1700–1970* (Newton Abbot, 1971), pp. 10–15, 72–7; Gordon Jackson, 'The Ports' in Derek H. Aldcroft and Michael J. Freeman, eds., *Transport in the Industrial Revolution* (Manchester, 1983), pp. 200–1.

[108] J. R. Kellett, 'Glasgow' in M. D. Lobel, ed., *Historic Towns of the British Isles* (London, 1969), I, p. 9.

[109] R. A. Buchanan, 'The Construction of the Floating Harbour in Bristol, 1804–9', *TBGAS*, 88 (1969), 184–204.

[110] Bird, *Major Seaports of the United Kingdom*, p. 188; B. W. E. Alford, 'The Economic Development of Bristol in the Nineteenth Century: An Enigma?' in Patrick McGrath and John Cannon, eds., *Essays in Bristol and Gloucestershire History* (Bristol, 1976), pp. 259–60; B. J. Atkinson, 'An Early Example of the Decline of the Industrial Spirit? Bristol Enterprise in the First Half of the Nineteenth Century', *Southern History*, 9 (1987), 73–4; A. J. Pugsley, 'Some Contributions towards the Study of the Economic History of Bristol in the Eighteenth and Nineteenth Centuries' (University of Bristol MA thesis, 1921), ch. 2.

[111] Cf. Gordon Jackson, *The History and Archaeology of Ports* (Tadworth, Surrey, 1983), pp. 47–8.

2 Shipping

The considerable demand for shipping services in eighteenth-century Bristol meant that the wharves and quays in the centre of the city were thronged with many different types of wooden sailing ships – Severn trows, coasters, lighters, towboats and ocean-going vessels of various rigs and sizes. The miscellany of vessels can be glimpsed in Peter Monamy's contemporary painting of Broad Quay (now in the Bristol City Art Gallery) or in the marine scenes painted by Nicholas Pocock, who had served as a master on several transatlantic voyages from Bristol.[1] The striking visual effect of so many ships clustered together caught the attention of the poet, Alexander Pope. In 1739, on a visit to Bristol, he observed that on the quay there were 'as far as you can see, hundreds of ships, their Masts as thick as they can stand by one another, which is the oddest and most surprising sight imaginable'.[2] By mid-century, the port of Bristol was congested with vessels. The regular sale of ships by auction added to the air of commercial bustle.[3] The shipping involved in Bristol's Atlantic trade during the eighteenth century is the focus of this chapter. The analysis concentrates, first of all, on the ownership of vessels, the places where ships were built, and the size of ships. It then examines selected features of Bristol's shipping in the Virginia and Jamaica trades, which carried the bulkiest and most valuable cargoes. Particular emphasis is given here to productivity trends in order to determine what gains in

---

[1] Some of Pocock's scenes of maritime life in Bristol are reproduced in Francis Greenacre, *Marine Artists of Bristol: Nicholas Pocock (1740–1821), Joseph Walter (1783–1856)* (Bristol, 1982). Original sketches by Pocock are available in National Maritime Museum, Logbooks of the *Lloyd* (1767–9); BRO, Logbooks of the *Lloyd* (1771–2); Mariners' Museum, Newport News, VA, Logbooks of the *Minerva* (1772, 1776). See also David Cordingly, 'Nicholas Pocock's Voyages from Bristol' in *Sea Studies: Essays in Honour of Basil Greenhill on the Occasion of his Retirement* (Greenwich, 1983), pp. 27–32.

[2] Quoted in Peter T. Marcy, 'Eighteenth Century Views of Bristol and Bristolians' in McGrath, ed., *Bristol in the Eighteenth Century*, p. 20.

[3] See the following advertisements for auctions of ships: *FFBJ*, 27 Dec. 1755 (the *Betsey*), 28 Apr. 1759 (the *Prince Ferdinand*), 3 July 1762 (the *Bacchus*), 23 Oct. 1762 (the *America*), 25 Feb. 1764 (the *Duke of York*), and 22 Feb. 1766 (the *Peace and Plenty*, the *Sally*, and the *Cornell*). Hundreds of other examples could be supplied.

efficiency were achieved over time in these major staple trades. The shipping data deployed here have a close bearing on the performance of Bristol as a port and, therefore, on the themes of the book as a whole.

For most of the eighteenth century, shipping firms did not exist even though there were trades – such as the slave trade – in which the shipowning and trading groups coincided.[4] During this period there was also no occupational group of businessmen calling themselves 'shipowners'. Merchant ships were owned by one or several investors (often merchants) who used the vessels for their own transport requirements or who hired and chartered out cargo space to non-owners.[5] The managing owner was known as the ship's husband, purser or agent. Table 2.1 shows the place of ownership of ships arriving at Bristol from North America and the West Indies between 1729 and 1797. In each set of years covered, Bristol ownership accounted for over three-fifths of the vessels. Bristol's dominance here is not surprising, and seems not to have been adversely affected by the incidence of war. Apart from Bristol itself, the next two areas of importance for shipownership were the North American mainland and miscellaneous ports in the British Isles – London, Topsham, Dublin, Cork, Ross, Plymouth, Glasgow and so on. That ships owned in mainland North America were significant in Bristol's Atlantic trade is not surprising, since this was the one area where American-owned shipping predominated on routes between Britain and the New World.[6] As for ownership at British ports outside Bristol, one noteworthy feature not apparent from table 2.1 is that two-thirds of the vessels were involved in the Newfoundland cod trade and were owned at the regional British centres of that commerce: Poole in Dorset or various Devon ports such as Dartmouth, Teignmouth, Bideford and Barnstaple.[7]

Some idea of the trades in which ships were jointly owned by personnel in different ports can be gleaned from figures compiled by Thomas Irving, who was Inspector General of Imports and Exports and Registrar General of Shipping for North America from 1768 to 1774. These data point

---

[4] This phenomenon in the Bristol slave trade is discussed in David Richardson, 'The Bristol Slave Trade in the Eighteenth Century' (University of Manchester MA thesis, 1969), ch. 3. For an example of co-owners taking shares in the outset, cargo and proceeds of a Bristol slaving voyage see BRO, Account book of the snow *Molly* (1750–2), Bright Papers.

[5] Davis, *Rise of the English Shipping Industry*, ch. 5; 'Maritime History: Progress and Problems' in Sheila Marriner, ed., *Business and Businessmen: Studies in Business, Economic and Accounting History* (Liverpool, 1978), p. 171.

[6] For the rise of American shipowning see John J. McCusker, 'The Shipowners of British America before 1775' (unpublished typescript, 1985).

[7] This evidence refutes Minchinton's suggestion that 'almost all the shipping connecting Bristol with ... Newfoundland was Bristol-owned' (*Trade of Bristol in the Eighteenth Century*, p. xviii). The prominent position of Dorset and Devon in the Newfoundland cod trade is analysed in G. J. Davies, 'England and Newfoundland: Policy and Trade, 1660–1783' (University of Southampton Ph.D. thesis, 1980), ch. 6.

Table 2.1. *Ships entering Bristol from North America and the West Indies, 1729–1797, arranged by place of ownership (percentages in brackets)*

	Bristol		Other British ports		Ireland		Europe		West Indies		Canada		Northern American Colonies		Southern American Colonies	
1729–38	1,082	(81.1)	97	(7.3)	38	(2.8)	0	(0.0)	17	(1.3)	2	(0.1)	81	(6.1)	17	(1.3)
1739–48	731	(69.5)	104	(9.9)	78	(7.4)	0	(0.0)	25	(2.4)	4	(0.4)	90	(8.6)	20	(1.9)
1749–55	275	(70.5)	45	(11.5)	11	(2.8)	0	(0.0)	13	(3.3)	0	(0.0)	38	(9.7)	28	(2.1)
1756–63	663	(68.6)	85	(8.8)	27	(2.8)	1	(0.1)	33	(3.4)	9	(0.9)	123	(12.7)	25	(2.6)
1764–75	861	(61.0)	168	(11.9)	18	(1.3)	0	(0.0)	39	(2.8)	3	(0.2)	248	(17.6)	74	(5.2)
1776–83	368	(77.6)	60	(12.7)	16	(3.4)	0	(0.0)	23	(4.9)	2	(0.4)	2	(0.4)	3	(0.6)
1785–97	314	(63.8)	49	(10.0)	15	(3.0)	0	(0.0)	6	(1.2)	1	(0.2)	92	(18.7)	15	(3.0)

Source: Society of Merchant Venturers, Bristol, Wharfage Books. I have only included years for which full lists of shipping entering the port of Bristol are available. I have assumed that the column headed 'Of What Place' in the Wharfage Books specifies the home port of ships as declared by masters to wharfage collectors and/or that this is also the residence of the managing owner(s).

to striking differences in the geographical distribution of shipownership for vessels sailing on various routes between the continental colonies and Britain on the eve of the American Revolution. Irving reckoned that three-quarters of the ships clearing from the Chesapeake to Britain and 62.5 per cent of the vessels leaving the Carolinas for Britain were British-owned. The proportions of British-owned shipping sailing on homeward-bound voyages from other continental colonies were smaller – 37.5 per cent for New York, 25.0 per cent for Pennsylvania, and only 12.5 per cent for New England.[8] My own calculations, based on ships entering certain colonial ports from Bristol, suggest slightly different shares. They indicate that the proportion of Bristol-owned ships entering various colonies from Bristol was 92.6 per cent for York River, Virginia, 25.8 per cent for New York, and 18.4 per cent for Philadelphia.[9]

Despite the differences between Irving's calculations and my own – a consequence of the shares being worked out from different sources for various periods – both sets of percentages reveal that British- and Bristol-owned ships were especially prominent in trade with the tobacco colonies, whereas ships trading with the Northern continental colonies were much more likely to be owned in North America. Bristol shipowners in the Chesapeake trade were usually tobacco merchants. They included John Perks, Thomas Knox, Joseph Farell, Leighton Wood, John Lidderdale and Thomas Griffiths.[10] By owning most of their ships in the Chesapeake trade, Bristol tobacco merchants maintained a fair degree of control over the seasonal shipping of this staple commodity. The predominance of American owners in trade between Bristol and the Northern continental colonies stemmed from inelastic demand within Britain for many products shipped from those areas. Merchants in New England and the Middle colonies/states were better placed to match products for

---

[8] John J. McCusker and Russell R. Menard, *The Economy of British America 1607–1789* (Chapel Hill, NC, 1985), table 9.1, p. 192.

[9] Based on eighty-one ships entering York River, Virginia directly from Bristol for 1749–69, given in PRO, CO 5/1444, 1447–50; on thirty-two ships entering New York from Bristol for 1748–64, given in PRO, CO 5/1226–8; and on eighty-seven ships entering Philadelphia from Bristol for 1766–76, given in HSP, Custom House Tonnage Books (1765–75), Thomas Cadwallader Section, Cadwallader Collection, and Pennsylvania, Records of the Office of the Comptroller General, Record Group 4: Register of Vessels: Duty on Tonnage (1775–6). Many of these ships were owned by several individuals. Where the sources do not indicate the proportion owned by each person, I have divided the shares equally among the owners. A similar procedure is used in studies such as Rupert C. Jarvis, 'Eighteenth-Century London Shipping' in A. E. J. Hollaender and William Kellaway, eds., *Studies in London History presented to Philip Edmund Jones* (London, 1969), pp. 415–16, and John J. McCusker, 'Sources of Investment Capital in the Colonial Philadelphia Shipping Industry', *JEcH*, 32 (1972), 148–9.

[10] Cf. PRO, CO 5/1444, 1447–8 with the names given in Morgan, 'Bristol Merchants and the Colonial Trades', app. B, pp. 325–35.

shipment with specific markets and so they regularly owned ships in these trades.[11]

Most vessels trading between Bristol and the Caribbean were owned in Bristol. The Naval Officers' Returns for Jamaica in the 1760s list sugar commission merchants who were also shipowners – men such as Robert Gordon, Mark Davis and William Miles – while similar sources for Barbados for the 1770s list sugar merchants such as David Parris, Richard Farr and Samuel Munckley among owners of ships.[12] As with the tobacco trade, sugar merchants who were also shipowners hoped to exercise control over shipment of the staple crop and to guarantee regular consignments of sugar. Pinney & Tobin of Bristol explained this well in their comment that 'shipowning at this port is a much more *serious affair* than it is in London, where the merchant seldom holds more than a 16th, and often no part at all; whereas our ships are entirely owned by ourselves, which in the first place ties up a large sum of money which might be more profitably employed in procuring consignments and in the next place makes it absolutely necessary that we should find freight both out and home for them, without which they must prove very sinking funds indeed'.[13]

The number of owners on Bristol–West India vessels was usually between 1 and 7. The average number of owners on letter-of-marque ships sailing between Bristol and the Caribbean during the American War of Independence was 2.8.[14] Ownership was often spread among several people partly because the risks and depreciation in handling ships could be high, and partly because some shareholders were 'sleeping partners'. The proportion of shares held by investors varied from ship to ship and sometimes from voyage to voyage. Shares were usually owned in binary divisions down to 64ths but could be held in any convenient fraction.[15] Thus the division of shares on two voyages of the *Kingston Packet* between Bristol and Jamaica in 1775 and 1776 was as follows: Bright, Milward & Duncomb held two-sixths; Bush & Elton also held two-sixths; and Lowbridge & Richard Bright and Henry Bright each held

[11] See below, pp. 75, 78.
[12] Cf. PRO, CO 142/17 and T 64/48–9 with the names given in Morgan, 'Bristol Merchants and the Colonial Trades', app. C, pp. 336–66.
[13] Quoted in Pares, *West-India Fortune*, p. 209.
[14] Based on a sample of forty-three ships listed in PRO, HCA 25/56–75 and HCA 26/60. I have only included ships that intended to trade solely with the West Indies. Vessels for which only the principal owner is named are also excluded. For purposes of comparison, the average number of owners for thirty-seven ships registered at Philadelphia but owned at Bristol was 3.8: see John J. McCusker, compiler, 'Ships Registered at the Port of Philadelphia before 1776: A Computerized Listing' (on deposit at HSP).
[15] Rupert C. Jarvis, 'Fractional Shareholding in British Merchant Ships with Special Reference to 64ths', *The Mariner's Mirror*, 45 (1959), 310.

one-sixth.[16] Sometimes one shareholder – invariably the managing partner – held a larger share in a vessel than his co-owners. This was true of
the snow *Fanny*, which sailed on eleven consecutive annual voyages
between Bristol and Barbados between 1777 and 1788.[17] On the first
seven crossings the division of shares was as follows: Samuel Munckley
held a half share, while George Gibbs, James Richards, Richard Twine
and Thomas Richards (the captain of the vessel) each held one-eighth
shares. A change occurred only on the eighth voyage when Thomas
Richards ceased to be master and his one-eighth share was split between
George Gibbs and James Richards, who now each held three-sixteenths
shares. The rest of the ownership stayed the same, suggesting that continuity of ownership was valued in the West India trade.[18] A similar
division of ownership was common in the Bristol slave trade.[19]

Table 2.2 shows the percentage distribution of ships and tonnage
clearing the port of Bristol for transatlantic destinations between 1730
and 1799. Three broad areas of build – Great Britain, the Americas and
foreign areas – are separated in the table, as are war and peace years and
the regions to which ships were bound.[20] Some interesting patterns
emerge. First of all, it is clear that prize captures contributed to the
number of Bristol's colonial ships in wartime. Bristol privateers captured
at least 209 prizes during the Seven Years War and a further 173 prizes
during the American War of Independence.[21] These were mainly French,
Spanish and American vessels. After being condemned in the Admiralty
court, they could be freed and registered as British ships. The table
shows, however, that foreign-built prizes were the least important source
of ships for Bristolians. Before 1783, prize vessels always comprised less
than 10 per cent of the ships and tonnage engaged in Bristol's Atlantic
trade during peacetime but made a more significant contribution in
wartime. After the American Revolution prize vessels were more widely
used, however, in trade between Bristol and the North American mainland. The percentages in table 2.2 suggest that this was related to a drop in

---

[16] William L. Clements Library, 8th and 9th voyages of the *Kingston Packet*, Bristol
  Shipping Account Books, III.
[17] For the organisation of some of these voyages see below, pp. 198–9.
[18] BRO, Account Book of the *Fanny*.
[19] Examples of the binary division of shares in the Bristol slave trade are given below on p.
  142. For a detailed account of shipping in the Bristol slave trade see D. Gareth Rees,
  'The Role of Bristol in the Atlantic Slave Trade, 1710–1769' (University of Exeter MA
  thesis, 1970). A fair amount of data from this study is reproduced in W. E. Minchinton,
  'The British Slave Fleet, 1680–1775: The Evidence of the Naval Office Shipping Lists' in
  Serge Daget, ed., *De la traite à l'esclavage*, 2 vols. (Nantes, 1988), I, pp. 395–427.
[20] For the coverage of Mediterranean Passes see below, app., pp. 228–9.
[21] Jonathan Press, *The Merchant Seamen of Bristol 1747–1789* (Bristol Branch of the
  Historical Association, pamphlet no. 38, 1976), p. 15.

Table 2.2. *Percentages of ships and tonnage clearing Bristol for North America and the West Indies, 1730–1799, according to place of build*

	Thirteen Mainland American Colonies/States						Canada						West Indies					
	British built		American built		Foreign built		British built		American built		Foreign built		British built		American built		Foreign built	
	% Ships	% Tons	% Ships	% Tons	% Ships	% Tons	% Ships	% Tons	% Ships	% Tons	% Ships	% Tons	% Ships	% Tons	% Ships	% Tons	% Ships	% Tons
1730–8	46	52	54	48	0	0	35	34	65	66	0	0	45	47	55	53	0	0
1739–47	28	35	68	59	4	6	33	32	46	39	21	29	46	48	44	40	10	12
1748–55	45	50	51	44	4	6	35	30	61	67	4	3	58	65	40	32	2	3
1756–63	38	40	53	47	9	13	32	34	54	48	14	18	51	55	35	26	14	19
1764–75	29	37	70	62	1	1	20	18	76	79	4	3	47	55	50	43	3	2
1776–83	40	44	50	48	10	8	34	38	51	45	15	17	59	65	35	28	6	7
1784–92	65	71	18	14	17	15	53	55	32	30	15	15	89	92	5	3	6	5
1793–9	75	78	0	0	25	22	57	64	32	26	11	10	92	94	4	3	4	3

Note: Percentages were calculated for each of the three areas. Data were only used for direct voyages, not multilateral voyages, using the definitions of those terms outlined on p. 58. Ships touching at more than one port in each broad region were excluded in compiling the table, as were ships calling at ports in more than one of the three broad regions.

Source: Public Record Office, London, Mediterranean Passes, ADM 7/77–116.

the use – and possibly the availability – of vessels built in Canada and the United States in the late eighteenth century.

Table 2.2 shows, secondly, that British-built ships were always prominent in trade between Bristol and the Caribbean. British-built vessels always contributed at least 45 per cent of both the tonnage and ships in the Bristol West India trade before the American War of Independence and over 85 per cent thereafter. The use of home-built vessels dramatically increased in this particular trade during the late eighteenth century. This was undoubtedly connected to the concentration of Britain's imperial economy on the West Indies in that period. Most of these ships were built in Bristol itself. This is true, for instance, of forty-six of the fifty-four British-built ships entering Jamaica from Bristol between 1762 and 1768.[22] No doubt many of these vessels had been constructed ship-shape and Bristol fashion; in other words, with sufficient strength for them to withstand the strain of lying aground between tides even when laden with goods.[23] They were built at various sites situated on the banks of the Avon, the best-known yards being at Hotwells, Dean's Marsh, Redcliff Backs and Wapping.[24] Much of this shipbuilding and its related activities took place in St Augustine's parish in the centre of the city. There, in the heart of Bristol's extensive seafaring community, shipwrights and related craftsmen, such as anchorsmiths, sailmakers and porters, plied their trade.[25]

A third main point can be discerned from table 2.2. Before 1783, the proportion of American-built ships and tonnage sailing between Bristol and two areas – the thirteen American colonies/states and Canada – was often higher than the proportion of British-built ships and tonnage.[26] Ships constructed in North America were particularly prominent in the Bristol trade with these two areas from 1764 to 1775. This was a phenomenon common to all British ports at that time: nearly 40 per cent of the

---

[22] PRO, CO 142/16–18. These figures were compiled only from ship entrances where a specific port in Britain or Ireland was named.

[23] The earliest reference to this phrase is in Scott's *Chronicles of Canongate* (1829).

[24] W. E. Minchinton, 'The Port of Bristol in the Eighteenth Century', in McGrath, ed., *Bristol in the Eighteenth Century*, p. 134; Grahame Farr, *Shipbuilding in the Port of Bristol* (National Maritime Museum Monographs and Reports, no. 27, Greenwich, 1977); and John Lord and Jem Southam, *The Floating Harbour: A Landscape History of Bristol City Docks* (Bristol, 1983), pp. 21–7. See map 1 for the location of some of these shipbuilding sites.

[25] Ronald H. Quilici, 'Turmoil in a City and an Empire: Bristol's Factions, 1700–1775' (University of New Hampshire Ph.D. dissertation, 1976), pp. 53–4, 75, 78–9, examines this point in more detail.

[26] The only exception to this is the colonial-built tonnage sailing to the American colonies in the periods 1730–8 and 1748–55.

British-owned tonnage listed in the shipbuilding sites section of *Lloyd's Register* for 1776 was colonial-built.[27] Bristol merchants purchased such vessels in two ways. One method was to commission American shipbuilders to construct them and to send detailed instructions about the intended dimensions of the ship to be built, the time allowed for completion of construction, the expected cost, and so forth.[28] The second way was to buy one of the many ships dispatched from the American mainland for sale on arrival in Britain. Sales of colonial-built ships by this method increased during wartime in the first half of the eighteenth century. The period from 1764 to 1775, however, was the first time that a considerable peacetime demand occurred.[29] This trend was probably linked to the qualities of middle-sized brigs and snows in particular trades, for these were the main types of colonial-built ships sold in Britain.[30] With plentiful supplies of timber and a thriving shipping industry by 1776, the colonists were generally able to construct such vessels at lower costs than in Britain.[31] Thus Richard Champion estimated that, during the eighteenth century, ships built in North America for use in British transatlantic trade were 30 per cent cheaper than those constructed in Britain.[32]

Bristol's Atlantic trading vessels were built with various rigs; they included ships, schooners, brigs, snows and sloops.[33] These vessels usually had a maximum of two decks: the first triple-decked ship was not

[27] Joseph A. Goldenberg, 'An Analysis of Shipbuilding Sites in *Lloyd's Register* of 1776', *The Mariner's Mirror*, 59 (1973), 422.

[28] W. E. Minchinton, 'Shipbuilding in Colonial Rhode Island', *Rhode Island History*, 20 (1961), 119–24, and *Trade of Bristol in the Eighteenth Century*, pp. 93–101, both print examples of such orders written by Bristol merchants in the early eighteenth century. For further correspondence about ships built in America for Bristol merchants see ACRL, Samuel Weekes to Isaac Hobhouse, 13 Jan. 1723, Thomas Gunter to Isaac Hobhouse, 3 Sept., 23 Nov. 1736, Jefferies MSS, XIII; New York PL, Thomas Moffatt to Stephen Perry, 22 Nov. 1715, Thomas Moffatt Letterbook (1714–16); HSP, Jonathan Dickinson to Jonathan Gale, 30 Apr. 1715, Jonathan Dickinson Letterbook (1715–21); James & Drinker to Nehemiah Champion, 20 Dec. 1756, 20 Apr., 7 May, 28 June, 13 Sept. 1757, James & Drinker Letterbook (1756–9), Henry Drinker Papers.

[29] Ralph Davis, 'Untapped Sources and Research Opportunities in the Field of American Maritime History from the Beginning to about 1815' in *Untapped Sources and Research Opportunities in the Field of American Maritime History: A Symposium ...* (Mystic Seaport, CT, 1966), pp. 17–19. See also Jacob M. Price, 'A Note on the Value of Colonial Exports of Shipping', *JEcH*, 36 (1976), 704–24, and Joseph A. Goldenberg, *Shipbuilding in Colonial America* (Charlottesville, VA, 1976), pp. 99–106.

[30] Davis, 'Untapped Sources and Research Opportunities', p. 18.

[31] Alan McGowan, *The Ship: The Century before Steam: The Development of the Sailing Ship, 1700–1820* (London, 1980), p. 27.

[32] Richard Champion, *Considerations on the Present Situation of Great Britain and the United States of America ...* (2nd edn., London, 1784), p. 24.

[33] For useful illustrations and descriptions of these different types of vessels see W. E. Minchinton, 'Characteristics of British Slaving Vessels, 1698–1775', *Journal of Interdisciplinary History*, 20 (1989), app. 2, 77–81.

constructed at Bristol until 1781.[34] Newspaper advertisements suggest
that vessels were generally constructed with regard to their carrying
capacity for trades in which volume was important. For instance, the
Manchester was described in 1764 as having 'excellent dimensions for the
African or any other Trade where Dispatch is required'.[35] Similarly, the
Elizabeth was advertised in the same year as 'very fit for the West India,
Virginia, or any Trade where room and burthen are required'.[36] Evidence of the use of vessels in the tobacco and sugar trades indicates that
many ships, though not initially built for a specific trade, were deployed
increasingly by mid-century on fixed shipping routes.[37]

During the eighteenth century, the size of vessels in Bristol's ocean-
going commerce grew at varying rates. Table 2.3 gives the average size of
ships entering Bristol from seven regions in the Americas. Apart from the
American War of Independence – where data for the rebellious colonies
are based on a very small number of ships – vessels in most trades
increased slightly in size in the mid-eighteenth century and became
significantly larger after the mid-1780s.[38] The largest ships, predictably,
were those arriving from Jamaica and the Upper South. That these
vessels were usually twenty to thirty tons larger than those trading with
other regions was related to the need for sufficient cargo space to carry
the bulky staple crops, sugar and tobacco.[39] Thus ships arriving at Bristol
from Jamaica or the Chesapeake were normally between 100 and 270
registered tons in size. Ships coming from other regions were smaller,
with those entering Bristol from Canada being the smallest of all at
between 45 and 90 tons.

Data on the average size of vessels trading with different colonial
regions according to the place of build of a ship re-emphasise the general
growth in size of Bristol vessels in all transatlantic trades (see table 2.4).
British-built vessels trading with the American mainland and the West

---

[34] Entry for 18 Oct. 1781 in Kenneth Morgan, ed., 'Calendar of Correspondence from
William Miles, a West Indian Merchant in Bristol, to John Tharp, a Planter in Jamaica,
1770–1789' in Patrick McGrath, ed., *A Bristol Miscellany* (Bristol Record Society's
Publications, 37, 1985), p. 99.

[35] *FFBJ*, 22 Dec. 1764.

[36] *Ibid.*, 29 Dec. 1764.

[37] See below, pp. 84–7.

[38] A *caveat* is in order here. In the late 1780s both Britain and the United States revised their
formulas for measuring the size of ships. John J. McCusker estimates that tonnages for
the post-1786 period may therefore inflate the size of vessels by one-third ('The Tonnage
of Ships engaged in British Colonial Trade during the Eighteenth Century', *Research in
Economic History*, 6 (1981), 91). This *caveat* applies to several other tables in this
chapter: namely 2.4, 2.6 and 2.8.

[39] Cf. Davis, *Rise of the English Shipping Industry*, pp. 183–4.

Table 2.3. *Average tonnage of ships entering Bristol from transatlantic regions, 1729–1797*

Year	Canada	New England	Middle Colonies/States	Upper South	Lower South	Jamaica	Other West Indies
1729–38	48	77	83	110	89	101	83
1739–48	58	84	71	118	83	123	88
1749–55	60	81	82	121	89	117	81
1756–63	60	82	97	138	101	128	89
1764–75	65	103	108	141	106	145	113
1776–83	76	65	160	90	83	170	127
1784–97	89	174	209	199	172	265	200

Sources: 1789, 1790: W. E. Minchinton, ed., *The Trade of Bristol in the Eighteenth Century* (Bristol Record Society's *Publications*, 20, 1957), pp. 5, 53–5. All other years: Society of Merchant Venturers, Bristol, Wharfage Books. The figures were compiled for the same years represented in table 1.1.

Table 2.4. *Average tonnage of ships clearing from Bristol to Africa, North America and the West Indies, 1730–1799, according to place of build*

	British built				American built				Foreign built			
	Africa	Thirteen Mainland American Colonies/States	Canada	West Indies	Africa	Thirteen Mainland American Colonies/States	Canada	West Indies	Africa	Thirteen Mainland American Colonies/States	Canada	West Indies
1730–8	95	132	61	116	79	106	63	107	—	—	—	—
1739–47	101	158	83	129	88	103	75	111	106	183	120	156
1748–55	101	125	59	118	100	99	74	86	123	170	60	166
1756–63	109	139	95	135	110	117	79	90	117	199	114	175
1764–75	120	159	81	159	99	115	93	119	113	123	65	103
1776–83	129	150	136	178	96	129	108	130	152	110	146	192
1784–92	150	200	120	244	127	151	109	174	190	155	124	187
1793–9	160	211	181	282	194	227	138	181	245	205	148	216

Source: Public Record Office, London, ADM 7/77–116. Apart from slave vessels, these percentages were calculated only for direct voyages.

Indies were usually 20 to 30 tons larger than colonial-built vessels bound to the same regions. This difference in tonnage was also present in the Bristol slave trade.[40] Vessels in the latter trade were more modest in size than some older studies suggest.[41] Table 2.4 also shows that they were smaller than vessels trading directly with the thirteen American colonies or the Caribbean but larger than ships bound to Canada. Foreign-built vessels were quite large in wartime; but this is perhaps to be expected with the miscellaneous capture of prizes.

Two general points emerge from this discussion of ship size. Firstly, all of the transatlantic ships trading at Bristol in the eighteenth century were modest in size, the average being under 200 registered tons. This is much smaller than the London–Jamaica traders or the English East India Company ships of the same period but these, of course, were always the largest in the English merchant service.[42] Secondly, the vessels in Bristol's Atlantic trades, though relatively small, still grew in size during the mid-eighteenth century. This seems linked, especially in the Bristol–Jamaica trade, to the growth in volume and value of commerce.[43] It therefore seems that ship size increased, not so much because technical obstacles in shipbuilding were overcome, but because over time there were lower risks of under-capacity loading.[44]

The final section of this chapter examines available data on productivity trends in ocean-going shipping trading from Bristol between 1700 and 1800. The analysis is confined to ships in the Virginia and Jamaica trades, the two most important sectors of Atlantic trade for Bristolians.[45] Historians have disagreed about the contributory factors to productivity gains in oceanic shipping. The work of Gary M. Walton and others suggests that such gains were achieved in the century before the American Revolution. Defining these advances as the increase in quantity (shipping per ton) per pound sterling (in real terms) that could be shipped over the period, Walton argued that in this century the average yearly compounded rate of productivity change was approximately 0.8 per cent.[46] This gain in efficiency, which helped to reduce transport costs, was apparent in various quantifiable areas. Between 1675 and 1775

---

[40] Richardson, 'Bristol Slave Trade in the Eighteenth Century', pp. 59–60.

[41] Minchinton, 'British Slave Fleet', p. 405.

[42] Davis, *Rise of the English Shipping Industry*, pp. 261, 280–1.

[43] See above, pp. 13–14, and below, pp. 190, 196–7.

[44] Davis, *Rise of the English Shipping Industry*, pp. 72–3, 281.

[45] It is worth noting that New York is the only other colony in British America for which the data are full enough for a similar analysis of productivity trends in shipping.

[46] Gary M. Walton, 'Obstacles to Technical Diffusion in Ocean Shipping, 1675–1775', *Explorations in Economic History*, 8 (1970–1), 124–5.

freight rates generally fell by a half and insurance rates experienced a modest fall. The elimination of piracy led to greater safety on the oceans and so merchants were able to use less armaments and fewer crew on their ships. There was also a decrease in round-trip voyage times – the result not of increased sailing speed but of improvements in market organisation leading to reduced turn-around in port, both at home and in the colonies.[47] Economies of scale in ship size or technological change seem to have been largely unimportant as sources of productivity change, though possibly the reduction of crew size on larger vessels – an important technical advance – was assisted by the adoption of the steering wheel and the use of fore-and-aft sails (which could receive the wind on either side).[48] These interpretative points have not commanded unqualified acceptance, however. Nathan Rosenberg and John J. McCusker and Russell R. Menard consider that technological improvements did affect the productivity of shipping.[49] And R. C. Nash thinks that freight rates did fall before 1720 but that thereafter the pace of improvements in the rates slowed down.[50]

Tables 2.5–2.12 present data on productivity trends among ships trading between Bristol and Virginia and Bristol and Jamaica during the eighteenth century.[51] Most of the shipping characteristics recorded in tables 2.5 and 2.6 reflect the impact of war.[52] The age of ships in both the Bristol–Virginia and the Bristol–Jamaica trades rose during the War of

---

[47] For fuller details on these points see *ibid.*, *passim*; Gary M. Walton, 'Sources of Productivity Change in American Colonial Shipping, 1675–1775', *EcHR*, 2nd Series, 20 (1967), 67–78; 'A Measure of Productivity Change in American Colonial Shipping', *EcHR*, 2nd Series, II (1968), 268–82; all summarised in James F. Shepherd and Gary M. Walton, *Shipping, Maritime Trade, and the Economic Development of Colonial North America* (Cambridge, 1972), pp. 60, 73, 75–7, 80–5 and app. 3, pp. 188–203.

[48] McGowan, *The Ship: The Century before Steam*, pp. 31, 36. See also Davis, *Rise of the English Shipping Industry*, pp. 75–6.

[49] Nathan Rosenberg, 'Factors affecting the Diffusion of Technology', *Explorations in Economic History*, 10 (1972), 29–33; McCusker and Menard, *Economy of British America*, p. 266; and Russell R. Menard, 'Transport Costs and Long-Range Trade, 1300–1800: Was there a European "Transport Revolution" in the Early Modern Era?' in James D. Tracy, ed., *The Political Economy of Merchant Empires* (Cambridge, 1991), pp. 257–63.

[50] Robert C. Nash, 'English Transatlantic Trade, 1660–1730: A Quantitative Study' (University of Cambridge Ph.D. thesis, 1982), pp. 265–71.

[51] Evidence for London is assessed in Christopher J. French, 'Productivity in the Atlantic Shipping Industry: A Quantitative Study', *Journal of Interdisciplinary History*, 17 (1987), 613–38.

[52] The only ships considered for inclusion in tables 2.5 and 2.6 were those sailing on direct round-trip voyages (apart from prize vessels, which were excluded). As in ch. 3 below, ships first touching at Irish ports before entering Virginia or Jamaica were counted as direct traders. The calculations for Virginia include ships moving between individual customs districts in the colony. Where entrance and clearance lists give slightly different data, I have averaged the totals.

the Austrian Succession and the Seven Years War, but then fell after the Peace of Paris in 1763. On average most vessels in these trades were under ten years old, which suggests that the use of worn and old ships was the exception rather than the rule. The perennial difficulty of teredo worms fouling the hull of vessels probably set constraints on the seaworthiness of older ships before the diffusion of copper sheathing in the merchant fleet towards the end of the eighteenth century.[53] Some of Bristol's Atlantic trading ships, it seems, had been sheathed by the 1760s.[54] But the lack of longevity of vessels in the Bristol–Virginia and Bristol–Jamaica trades did not aid shipping productivity at this time. It must have led, on the contrary, to capital depreciation and substantial replacement costs for individual vessels.[55]

Any increases in tons-per-gun and tons-per-man ratios would indicate a productivity gain, for fewer crew and armaments would then be necessary on ships in these staple trades. Tons-per-gun ratios lowered in wartime, as one might expect: about twice as many guns were carried on Bristol–Virginia and Bristol–Jamaica ships in the Seven Years War than in the seven previous peace years. But there was a sharp drop in the number of guns carried between 1764 and 1776. In the case of Jamaica, the tons-per-gun ratio rose more than sixfold in these years; in the case of Virginia, not a single gun was carried by any of the ships that provided the data. Predictably, the number of guns carried on Bristol–Jamaica ships increased appreciably during the American Revolution and then decreased drastically in the peace years of the 1780s. Tons-per-man ratios in tables 2.5 and 2.6 also reflect the impact of war. This was especially the case with Bristol–Virginia traders, where the ratios fell by 40 per cent in the Seven Years War. Significant productivity gains in the level of crew were achieved, however, on both Bristol–Virginia and Bristol–Jamaica vessels sailing in peacetime. Between the two periods 1749–55 and 1764–76, the number of tons-per-man increased by 10 per cent and 17.7 per cent for Bristol–Virginia and Bristol–Jamaica vessels respectively.[56] Since these improvements occurred at a time when the average ship size in Bristol's Atlantic trade was increasing,[57] considerable economies in running costs must have been made. After 1783, as table 2.6 shows,

[53] Gareth Rees, 'Copper Sheathing: An Example of Technological Diffusion in the English Merchant Fleet', *Journal of Transport History*, New Series, 1 (1971/2), 85–94.

[54] E.g. Advertisements for the *Elizabeth*, the *Little Jerry*, the *Jeremiah and Elizabeth*, and the *Elizabeth*, in *FFBJ*, 29 Dec. 1764, 8 Feb. 1766, 25 Apr. 1767 and 25 June 1768.

[55] For the situation at London see Christopher J. French, 'The Longevity of Ships in Colonial Trade: Some Further Evidence', *International Journal of Maritime History*, 3 (1991), 155–63.

[56] To make these calculations, I averaged the tons-per-man-in and tons-per-man-out figures for Virginia and Jamaica.

[57] See above, pp. 42–3.

Table 2.5. *Characteristics of ships trading on direct routes between Bristol and Virginia, 1725–1776*

	Average tonnage	Average age (years)	Tons per gun	Tons per man in	Tons per man out
1725–38	120	9	32	10	10
1739–48	145	11	20	9	9
1749–55	129	4	47	10	10
1756–63	150	7	21	6	6
1764–76	135	6	*a*	11	11

Note: *a* = no guns carried at all.
Sources: Public Record Office, London, CO 5/1442–50, T 1/488, 498.

Table 2.6. *Characteristics of ships trading on direct routes between Bristol and Jamaica, 1712–1798*

	Average tonnage	Average age (years)	Tons per gun	Tons per man in	Tons per man out
1712–13	137	n.a.	14	n.a.	n.a.
1714–20	119	4	26	n.a.	n.a.
1743–8	141	9	15	5	6
1749–55	126	5	67	9	9
1756–63	152	10	23	7	8
1764–75	155	9	145	10	10
1776–83	198	9	19	8	10
1784–8	244	6	725	14	14
1796–8	306	8	44	16	18

Sources: Public Record Office, London, CO 142/14–23, BT 6/186.

productivity gains in manning ratios were increased in the Bristol–Jamaica trade.

Bristol's slaving vessels did not comprise a separate slave fleet; nor were many of these ships employed continually in the slave trade.[58] But they were sufficiently numerous for one to calculate productivity trends for Bristol's slaving voyages with Virginia and Jamaica. The results, presented in tables 2.7 and 2.8, are similar to those outlined for direct voyages between Bristol and the same areas. Slaving vessels in both the Bristol–Virginia and Bristol–Jamaica trades were nevertheless slightly

[58] See the evidence cited in Minchinton, 'Characteristics of British Slaving Vessels', pp. 53–81, a discussion confined to slaving vessels trading with the American mainland colonies.

Table 2.7. *Characteristics of ships engaged in slaving voyages between Bristol and Virginia, 1725–1776*

	Average tonnage	Average age (years)	Tons per gun	Tons per man in	Tons per man out
1725–38	91	9	15	4	5
1739–48	86	10	11	4	4
1749–55	118	13	23	4	4
1756–63	128	14	18	4	4
1764–76	140	n.a.	30	5	5

Sources: Public Record Office, London, CO 5/1442–50, T 1/488, 498.

Table 2.8. *Characteristics of ships engaged in slaving voyages between Bristol and Jamaica, 1712–1788*

	Average tonnage	Average age (years)	Tons per gun	Tons per man in	Tons per man out
1712–13	132	n.a.	11	n.a.	n.a.
1714–20	93	5	n.a.	n.a.	n.a.
1742–8	94	13	12	4	5
1749–55	112	10	26	4	5
1756–63	118	13	12	3	3
1764–75	118	11	40	5	7
1776–83	128	16	9	3	5
1784–8	160	8	48	5	10

Sources: Public Record Office, London, CO 142/14–22, BT 6/186.

older on average than direct traders.[59] This seems to reflect the continued employment of older ships during periods of high demand for slaves.[60] Productivity gains in the level of armaments were achieved during peacetime on slave ships trading with Virginia and Jamaica. But in wartime tons-per-gun ratios usually fell, since swivel and carriage guns were necessary to combat the threat posed by enemy privateers.[61] Reductions in manning were always hard to achieve on slave vessels because of the

[59] D. Gareth Rees shows that British-built vessels in the Bristol slave trade with Virginia were older than American-built ships in the same trade ('Role of Bristol in the Atlantic Slave Trade', pp. 13, 20). Cf. Herbert S. Klein, 'Slaves and Shipping in Eighteenth-Century Virginia', *Journal of Interdisciplinary History*, 5 (1975), table 11, 403–4, 407.

[60] Minchinton, 'Characteristics of British Slaving Vessels', p. 65.

[61] On the disruptions to Bristol's transatlantic commerce by foreign privateers see above, pp. 15, 19–22, 26.

Table 2.9. *Tobacco hogsheads per ton on ships clearing from Virginia to Bristol, 1725–1776*

Trade pattern	1725–38	1739–48	1749–55	1756–63	1764–76
Bristol/Virginia/Bristol	2.6	2.6	2.5	2.4	2.2
Other British Port/Virginia/Bristol	2.1	2.5	3.6	—	—
Europe/Virginia/Bristol	1.8	—	3.5	3.3	—
Africa/Virginia/Bristol	0.6	1.3	1.0	1.2	0.8
West Indies/Virginia/Bristol	2.0	2.8	2.2	2.5	2.6
Other American Colony/ Virginia/Bristol	2.3	2.0	2.2	2.3	2.6
Overall average	1.9	2.2	2.7	2.3	2.0

Sources: Public Record Office, London, CO 5/1442–50, T 1/488, 498.

need to employ sufficient seamen to control the slaves.[62] Evidence for Bristol suggests that productivity advances in crew size only happened in both sets of slaving voyages in the peace years after 1763, when they were particularly noticeable on Bristol slaving voyages with Jamaica.

Another quantitative measure of productivity gains in shipping consists of loading efficiencies. Tables 2.9 and 2.10 examine this matter by tabulating hogshead-per-ton ratios for ships carrying tobacco and sugar from Virginia and Jamaica to Bristol on different routes. Before discussing the implications of these data, a word of caution is necessary. Loading efficiencies are difficult to pinpoint exactly because the size of tobacco and sugar hogsheads probably trebled between 1670 and 1770; the weight of these containers also increased over the same timespan.[63] Since the average size of ocean-going vessels increased during the eighteenth century, any increase in hogshead-per-ton ratios may indicate either that larger ships had more cargo space or that there was greater efficiency in loading and packaging – the two cannot be separated from the available data.[64] One has to assume also that improved loading efficiencies for sugar and tobacco reflect the priority given by shipowners to these com-

[62] David Richardson, 'The Costs of Survival: The Transport of Slaves in the Middle Passage and the Profitability of the 18th-Century British Slave Trade', *Explorations in Economic History*, 24 (1987), 188–90.

[63] See the discussions in Davis, *Rise of the English Shipping Industry*, pp. 282–4, 288–9; John J. McCusker, 'The Rum Trade and the Balance of Payments of the Thirteen Continental Colonies, 1650–1775' (University of Pittsburgh Ph.D. dissertation, 1970), app. C, pp. 778–811; and Helen L. Klopfer, 'Statistics of the Foreign Trade of Philadelphia, 1700–1860' (University of Pennsylvania Ph.D. dissertation, 1936), ch. 2.

[64] Christopher J. French, 'The Trade and Shipping of the Port of London, 1700–1776' (University of Exeter Ph.D. thesis, 1980), pp. 294–303.

Table 2.10. *Sugar hogsheads per ton on ships clearing from Jamaica to Bristol, 1712–1788*

Trade pattern	1712–13	1714–20	1743–8	1749–55	1756–63	1764–75	1776–83	1784–8
Bristol/Jamaica/Bristol	1.3	1.2	1.6	1.4	1.6	2.0	1.8	1.6
Other British Port/Jamaica/Bristol	—	1.0	1.2	1.5	2.1	2.1	2.4	2.2
Europe/Jamaica/Bristol	—	—	—	0.9	—	—	—	—
Africa/Jamaica/Bristol	1.6	0.9	1.1	1.0	1.5	1.1	0.2	0.1
Central America/Jamaica/Bristol	—	—	—	—	—	1.0	—	—
Other West Indian Island/Jamaica/Bristol	—	—	—	1.2	2.4	1.9	2.6	1.6
American Colony/Jamaica/Bristol	1.2	—	1.0	1.1	1.7	1.4	0.6	1.4
Overall average	1.4	1.0	1.2	1.2	1.9	1.6	1.5	1.4

Note: The figures for sugar exports in the Naval Officer's Returns are given in various containers. I have converted the quantities into hogsheads using the procedure outlined on p. xvi.
Sources: Public Record Office, London, CO 142/14–23, BT 6/186.

Table 2.11. *Voyage and turn-around times on direct voyages in the Bristol–Virginia trade, 1749–1770*

	Average turn-around in Bristol (days)	Average turn-around in Virginia (days)	Average round-trip time (days)
1749–55	146	100	209
1756–63	144	122	241
1764–70	151	111	218

Sources: Society of Merchant Venturers, Bristol, Annual List of Ships, 1748–69, and Muster Rolls, 1769–70; Public Record Office, London, CO 5/1444, 1446–50.

Table 2.12. *Voyage and turn-around times on direct voyages in the Bristol–Jamaica trade, 1749–1770*

	Average turn-around in Bristol (days)	Average turn-around in Jamaica (days)	Average round-trip time (days) (direct)	Average round-trip time (days) (via Ireland)
1749–55	102	68	262	277
1756–63	106	71	253	281
1764–70	108	120	250	268

Sources: Society of Merchant Venturers, Bristol, Annual List of Ships, 1748–69, and Muster Rolls, 1769–70; Public Record Office, London, CO 142/15–18.

modities rather than to supplementary goods when filling ships' holds. Despite these problems, it is accepted here that a rise in the number of hogsheads carried per ton represents a productivity advance, for more of the staple commodity can be fitted into the same volume of space. It is also assumed that a reasonably stable hogsheads-per-ton ratio also points to more efficient loading, because of the increase in size of the hogshead in this period.

Tables 2.9 and 2.10 reveal that Bristol slave vessels trading with Virginia and Jamaica respectively carried home less tobacco and sugar per ton than shuttle ships trading with the same regions. This is not surprising, for direct traders were more likely than slavers to arrive at American destinations in seaworthy condition and to be better suited to the carriage of tropical produce.[65] Thus Bristol slave ships trading with Jamaica carried less and less sugar in relation to their carrying capacity as the

---

[65] Henry A. Gemery and Jan S. Hogendorn, 'Technological Change, Slavery, and the Slave Trade' in Clive Dewey and A. G. Hopkins, eds., *The Imperial Impact: Studies in the Economic History of Africa and India* (London, 1978), p. 257.

eighteenth century progressed. The figures also show that, in most cases, direct traders were loaded more efficiently than ships following any of the other shipping patterns specified. Ships plying shuttle routes often had several advantages over ships sailing on more diverse tracks, including better timing in seasonal trades, regular annual voyages and close commercial contacts with colonial agents.[66] Tables 2.9 and 2.10 also indicate that, between 1748 and 1776, ships trading directly between Bristol and Jamaica were loaded more efficiently, with a 33 per cent rise in the hogsheads-per-ton ratio between the periods 1748–55 and 1764–76, while ships trading directly between Bristol and Virginia were loaded less efficiently, with a 10.2 per cent fall in the equivalent ratio between the same two periods. These findings are probably related to the contrast between a buoyant Bristol–Jamaica trade and a stagnant Bristol–Virginia trade, as measured by level of imports, by the mid-eighteenth century.[67]

Tables 2.11 and 2.12 present material on voyage and turn-around times for direct voyages in the Bristol–Virginia and Bristol–Jamaica trades between 1749 and 1770. Mixed conclusions arise from examination of the productivity trends shown here. From 1749 to 1770, turn-around times at Bristol rose slightly for ships trading with both Virginia and Jamaica. Turn-around times in both colonies increased in the same period, with a very large rise in the time spent by ships in Jamaican harbours in the years 1764–70. The time taken for round-trip voyages increased in the Seven Years War for direct traders between Bristol and Virginia and for ships sailing from Bristol to Ireland and Jamaica. But there was an average reduction in passage time of 7.3 per cent for ships trading directly between Bristol and Jamaica during the same war. Quicker ocean passages on the latter route were maintained after 1763 even though, as noted above, the time spent loading in colonial waters rose considerably. Thus there was a saving of twelve days (a 9.5 per cent reduction) in overall passage time on direct voyages between Bristol and Jamaica between the periods 1748–55 and 1764–70. Perhaps too much should not be made of increased efficiency in passage times, however, since only one voyage per year was possible in most transatlantic trades.[68]

The overall evidence for the Bristol–Virginia and Bristol–Jamaica trades suggests that productivity gains were only partially achieved during the eighteenth century.[69] The same holds true for Bristol slaving vessels engaged in trade with those two colonies.[70] The above discussion

[66] For a definition of shuttle voyages see below, p. 58.
[67] See below, pp. 155, 172, 196–7.
[68] See below, p. 55.
[69] See below, pp. 84–7.
[70] For more general analysis of lack of productivity gains in the sugar and slave trades see Menard, 'Transport Costs and Long-Range Trade', p. 271.

nevertheless omitted one further way of improving productivity on trading ventures: the establishment of ships on fixed direct routes year after year. Here the available data indicate that Bristolians made improvements in efficiency on shuttle voyages with both Virginia and Jamaica, as regular voyages and regular ships became increasingly the norm in the generation before the American Revolution.[71] This phenomenon is discussed in the next chapter, which offers a full analysis of the shipping routes followed by Bristol ships in the Atlantic trading world of the mid-eighteenth century.

[71] See below, pp. 85–7.

3 Shipping patterns

Shipping was the lifeblood of the Atlantic economy in the eighteenth century; shipping patterns were the arteries through which the merchants and commodities of the North Atlantic trading world were drawn together into an international commercial network. Ships making trans-atlantic voyages from British ports picked up the northeast trade winds around the latitude of Madeira and sailed three thousand miles to their destinations. This was the first leg of a passage that involved unloading and reloading cargoes, time spent in colonial waters, a complex shipping schedule, and possibly multilateral trading connections before vessels caught the prevailing southwesterlies near Newfoundland back to Europe.[1] This long haul on 'the busiest ocean highway in the world in the mid-eighteenth century',[2] was dominated by problems of time and space – time, because ships usually took the best part of a year to make a round-trip; space, because markets around the North Atlantic were decentralised and fragmented. Atlantic crossings were also partly con-strained by the Navigation Acts, which not only confined trade within the empire to British and colonial ships and seamen but 'enumerated' certain commodities produced in British colonies that could not be shipped directly to foreign countries. Among these products were sugar, tobacco, indigo, furs, and naval stores. Because the Navigation Acts allowed free and equal competition for shipping services between individual parts of

---

[1] For good black-and-white maps of the major Atlantic currents and the main sailing routes from Britain to the Caribbean, the Chesapeake and Newfoundland see Arthur Pierce Middleton, *Tobacco Coast: A Maritime History of the Chesapeake Bay in the Colonial Era* (Newport News, VA, 1953), p. 5, and Ian K. Steele, *The English Atlantic, 1675–1740: An Exploration of Communication and Community* (Oxford, 1986), pp. 8, 22, 46, 80. A good colour map of the Atlantic trade routes is in Christopher Lloyd, *Atlas of Maritime History* (London, 1975), pp. 48–9.

[2] D. A. Farnie, 'The Commercial Empire of the Atlantic, 1607–1783', *EcHR*, 2nd Series, 15 (1962), 213.

the empire, merchants had many possible options with regard to shipping patterns.[3]

Despite their importance, the Atlantic shipping routes of the eighteenth century have never received the attention they deserve.[4] Historians have noted that transatlantic voyages from British ports sometimes followed multilateral rather than bilateral routes, and that circuitous voyages were common in the African slave trade and in the Newfoundland cod trade.[5] Others have deployed literary evidence, culled from business letters, on shipping patterns between the American mainland and the West Indies.[6] Still others have taken statistics from the Naval Officers' Returns, which record the ports from which ships entered colonial waters and the areas to which they cleared, and have used these data to discuss the distribution of shipping on various Atlantic routes.[7]

[3] Ralph Davis, 'Untapped Sources and Research Opportunities in the Field of American Maritime History from the Beginning to about 1815' in *Untapped Sources and Research Opportunities in the Field of American Maritime History: A Symposium* ... (Mystic Seaport, CT, 1966), p. 19.

[4] Curiously, there is no detailed consideration of shipping routes in J. H. Parry, 'Transport and Trade Routes' in E. E. Rich and C. H. Wilson, eds., *The Cambridge Economic History of Europe, IV: The Economy of Expanding Europe in the Sixteenth and Seventeenth Centuries* (Cambridge, 1967), pp. 155–219. For descriptive accounts of direct transatlantic trade routes see Middleton, *Tobacco Coast*, pp. 5–8; Susan E. Hillier, 'The Trade of the Virginia Colony, 1606–1660' (University of Liverpool Ph.D. thesis, 1971), pp. 105–15; and especially Steele, *English Atlantic*, pp. 21–93.

[5] Davis, *Rise of the English Shipping Industry*, p. 188; K. G. Davies, *The Royal African Company* (London, 1957), pp. 185–90; Christopher J. French, 'The Role of London in the Atlantic Slave Trade, 1680–1776' (University of Exeter MA thesis, 1970), pp. 41–53; B. K. Drake, 'Continuity and Flexibility in Liverpool's Trade with Africa and the Caribbean', *Business History*, 18 (1976), 85–97; W. E. Minchinton, 'The Triangular Trade Revisited' in Henry A. Gemery and Jan S. Hogendorn, eds., *The Uncommon Market: Essays on the Atlantic Slave Trade* (New York, 1979), pp. 331–52; G. J. Davies, 'England and Newfoundland: Policy and Trade, 1660–1783' (University of Southampton Ph.D. thesis, 1980), pp. 275–81.

[6] C. M. Andrews, 'Colonial Commerce', *American Historical Review*, 20 (1914–15), 58–61; Herbert C. Bell, 'The West India Trade before the American Revolution', *ibid.*, 22 (1917), 276–7; Bruce M. Bigelow, 'The Commerce of Rhode Island with the West Indies before the American Revolution' (Brown University Ph.D. dissertation, 1930), pt. 2, ch. 2; Byron Fairchild, *Messrs. William Pepperrell: Merchants at Piscataqua* (Ithaca, NY, 1954), pp. 65–9; W. T. Baxter, *The House of Hancock: Business in Boston, 1724–1775* (Cambridge, MA, 1945), ch. 2; Thomas M. Doerflinger, *A Vigorous Spirit of Enterprise: Merchants and Economic Development in Revolutionary Philadelphia* (Chapel Hill, NC, 1986), pp. 116–22; Dale Miquelon, *Dugard of Rouen: French Trade to Canada and the West Indies, 1729–1770* (Montreal, 1978), app. C, pp. 191–5.

[7] Murray G. Lawson, 'The Routes of Boston's Trade, 1752–1765', *Transactions of the Colonial Society of Massachusetts*, 38 (1947–51) (Boston, 1959), 81–120; William I. Davisson, 'The Philadelphia Trade', *Western Economic Journal*, 3 (1965), 310–11; William I. Davisson and Lawrence J. Bradley, 'New York Maritime Trade: Ship Voyage Patterns, 1715–1765', *New York Historical Society Quarterly*, 55 (1971), 309–17; W. A. Claypole and D. J. Buisseret, 'Trade Patterns in Early English Jamaica', *Journal of Caribbean History*, 5 (1972), 1–19; Robert C. Nash, 'English Transatlantic Trade, 1660–1730: A Quantitative Study' (University of Cambridge Ph.D. thesis, 1982), pp. 217–29.

Gary M. Walton, in particular, has employed this material to argue that shuttle routes were the norm between ports in the North Atlantic trading world and that multilateral routes, though they did exist, were uncommon.[8] The two attempts that have been made to provide figures on shipping routes for transatlantic voyages begun in British ports in the eighteenth century lend support to Walton's conclusion. Christopher J. French has analysed the Naval Officers' Returns to show that the majority of London vessels trading with three colonies – New York, Virginia, and Jamaica – mainly pursued direct shipping patterns, though more complicated tracks were sometimes followed.[9] Elaine G. Cooper has used statistics from Mediterranean Passes (see the appendix) to demonstrate that shuttle routes were followed by 56 per cent of British ships sailing in the Atlantic during the American War of Independence.[10]

A major problem for these discussions is that no single quantitative source provides all the information necessary for assessing the prevalence of some shipping routes over others. The two sources used in the most effective studies to date – the Naval Officers' Returns and Mediterranean Passes – are serviceable but are hampered by significant omissions.[11] Furthermore, historians who have used them to analyse shipping routes have tended to base their conclusions on a slender sample. Thus Walton's data consist of merely one half of the ships entering Barbados and Jamaica in a handful of years in the late seventeenth and eighteenth centuries.[12] Reliance on one set of records for statistical information is bound to yield limited data and can be misleading, for individual sources

---

[8] Gary M. Walton, 'New Evidence on Colonial Commerce', *JEcH*, 28 (1968), 363–89. The findings of this article are incorporated into James F. Shepherd and Gary M. Walton, *Shipping, Maritime Trade, and the Economic Development of Colonial North America* (Cambridge, 1972), pp. 49–51, 53, 156–7. Walton has also noted, without presenting detailed evidence, that there was an important multilateral shipping route in the eighteenth century between Great Britain, the West Indies and the southern American colonies, and that the 'triangular trade in colonial waters' at this time 'resulted mainly from the movements of British vessels' ('Trade Routes, Ownership Proportions, and American Colonial Shipping Characteristics' in *Les Routes de l'Atlantique: travaux de neuvième colloque international d'histoire maritime*, Seville, 1967 (Paris, 1969), especially p. 479 from which the quotation is taken). Most of this article, apart from the point mentioned here and one or two others, is substantially the same as the paper cited at the head of this note.

[9] Christopher J. French, 'The Trade and Shipping of the Port of London, 1700–1776' (University of Exeter Ph.D. thesis, 1980), pp. 252–65.

[10] Elaine G. Cooper, 'Aspects of British Shipping and Maritime Trade in the Atlantic, 1775–1783' (University of Exeter MA thesis, 1975), table 12, p. 40.

[11] See the appendix, pp. 228–9, for a discussion of this problem.

[12] Walton, 'New Evidence on Colonial Commerce', p. 370. The years chosen for analysis were Barbados: 1697, 1698, 1716, 1729–31, 1736, 1773; Jamaica: 1685–8, 1764. Cf. Davisson and Bradley, 'New York Maritime Trade', p. 317, which is based on only 11.6 per cent of the vessels entering and clearing the port of New York in the period covered (1715–65).

often suggest direct routes simply because they do not list all the colonial ports of call for specific voyages.[13] Such difficulties can engender doubts about the findings of historians who have conducted their research along these lines.

This chapter overcomes these problems by drawing on a variety of sources and by reconstructing all round-trip transatlantic voyages beginning at Bristol from 1749 through to 1770 – 2,223 in all.[14] The time-consuming nature of research for this topic precluded covering the entire eighteenth century. The period selected was chosen because it included both war and peace years and because the English shipping industry's involvement in the first British Empire was then at its height.[15] By using multiple sources of data on the names of ships, their masters and tonnage, and the dates when they left Bristol, called at colonial ports, and arrived home, a voyage-by-voyage account of Bristol's transatlantic trading patterns has been established. The sources are described in the appendix.

This inquiry has two chief aims. The first is to use the reconstructed voyages to establish the routes and to discover how many voyages were of the shuttle variety and how many were multilateral. Although these terms do scant justice to the multifaceted nature of shipping patterns, they are used here in a specific sense for analytical clarity. Throughout this chapter two broad types of Atlantic crossing are distinguished: shuttle or direct voyages, in which ships touched at only one colony in the New World, and multilateral or circuitous voyages, in which vessels called at two or more colonies or at a combination of colonial and European ports.[16] The second aim is to discuss the reasons why ships followed some types of routes rather than others. This involves assessing

[13] Cf. Davies, 'England and Newfoundland', pp. 275–7.

[14] It must be emphasised that *only* round-trip transatlantic voyages beginning and ending at Bristol are included. This means that ocean passages ending in shipwreck or capture, one-way Atlantic crossings, and voyages terminating at British ports other than Bristol have been excluded from consideration.

[15] The importance of transatlantic voyages to the English shipping industry in the mid-eighteenth century is brought out in Davis, *Rise of the English Shipping Industry*, pp. 40–1.

[16] Several points need to be made here about the allocation of vessels to the shuttle and multilateral categories. First, ports of call where freight was usually not unloaded were not considered to be similar to entries and clearances at ports on the American mainland or in the Caribbean. Thus voyage patterns such as Bristol–Cork–Jamaica–Bristol or Bristol–Madeira–Barbados–Bristol (both fairly common) were counted as direct crossings. Secondly, ships entering more than one port within a single colony were also classified as following shuttle routes. These included voyages such as Bristol–York River, Virginia–Upper James River, Virginia–Bristol and Bristol–Kingston, Jamaica–Falmouth, Jamaica–Bristol. Thirdly, the European continent was considered in working out circuitous voyages because it was an important constituent part of some major transatlantic trades. So Bristol–Newfoundland–Cadiz–Bristol voyages or Bristol–South Carolina–Lisbon–Bristol crossings are counted as multilateral voyages.

the importance of risk in determining shipping routes; it also requires delving into merchants' correspondence to discover the business decisions behind the choice of routes. The findings show that the distinction between shuttle and multilateral routes reflects different patterns of shipowning in particular trades, varying levels in the volume of European demand for colonial commodities, and the problems of coping with the risks of oceanic commerce. This analysis should interest historians studying the 'invisibles' in the current account of the balance of payments between Britain and the colonies, that is, the foreign earnings not covered by the official English trade statistics.[17]

Table 3.1 presents the overall picture of Bristol's transatlantic voyage patterns between 1749 and 1770. The figures show that just over three-fifths of the total ship tonnage was engaged in shuttle routes (39.6 per cent directly to the West Indies and back; 21.3 per cent to the thirteen American mainland colonies; 1.9 per cent to Canada), while the rest was distributed over multilateral routes. Of this latter group, 16.9 per cent of the tonnage belonged to slaving voyages and 20.3 per cent to other polyangular routes. If the figures for slavers are omitted from table 3.1, then 24.4 per cent of the remaining tonnage was bound up in circuitous routes. The table also reveals that the Seven Years War had an effect on whether ships followed shuttle or multilateral routes, the increase in the percentage of direct voyages to the American colonies and the corresponding decrease in the number of slaving and other roundabout voyages being most noticeable in this regard.

A further significant point is that the majority of multilateral voyages touched at only two or three ports. Among the variety of tracks, the patterns of Bristol–Newfoundland–Europe–Bristol and Bristol–Leeward Islands–Chesapeake *or* South Carolina–Bristol were prominent, involving several ships in most years on a regular basis.[18] Two types of multilateral voyages resulted in pentagonal, hexagonal, or even more complex routes. In one type, vessels called at several different ports or islands in rapid succession; for example, the *Wennie* sailed from Bristol to Lisbon, Madeira, Barbados, Martinique, St Kitts, St Eustatius, Charleston, Cape Fear and Hampton, Virginia, between November 1765 and June 1766.[19]

---

[17] The importance of this issue is brought out in Shepherd and Walton, *Shipping, Maritime Trade*, pp. 44, 57, 116–36, 139, and John J. McCusker and Russell R. Menard, *The Economy of British America, 1607–1789* (Chapel Hill, NC, 1985), pp. 36–7, 72, 74–6, 81–2, 109–10, 198.

[18] This is partly revealed in tables 3.1, 3.5–3.7 below. Examples of these types of voyages are described in Morgan, 'Bristol Merchants and the Colonial Trades', p. 56, and app. A (nos. 21 and 25), pp. 320, 322.

[19] Newberry Library, Chicago, Logbook of the snow *Wennie*, Edward E. Ayer Manuscripts, MS 817.

Table 3.1. *Distribution of Bristol ships completing round-trip transatlantic voyages, 1749–1770*

| | Direct voyages | | | | | | | | | Multilateral voyages | | | | | |
| | Thirteen Mainland American Colonies | | | West Indies | | | Canada | | | Slaving | | | Other | | |
	N	Tons	% Tons	N	Tons	% Tons	N	Tons	% Tons	N	Tons	% Tons	N	Tons	% Tons
1749–55	106	13,399	16.4	296	32,562	40.0	13	835	1.0	149	16,825	20.7	178	17,802	21.9
1756–63	158	23,803	26.3	266	35,795	39.5	20	1,511	1.7	105	13,052	14.4	144	16,407	18.1
1764–70	152	20,778	20.7	290	39,644	39.4	35	2,722	2.7	139	16,285	16.2	172	21,061	21.0
Totals	416	57,980	21.3	852	108,001	39.6	68	5,068	1.9	393	46,162	16.9	494	55,270	20.3

Sources for Tables 3.1–3.11

[a] Society of Merchant Venturers, Bristol, Annual List of Shipping (1748–87), Ships' Muster Rolls (1747–94), Wharfage Books (1748–9, 1754–68).
[b] Public Record Office, London, Bristol Port Books, Outwards, E 190/1217/1–1228/2 (1752–3, 1755–67, 1770); Mediterranean Passes, ADM 7/86–96 (1748–60, 1764–70); Naval Officers' Returns, CO 221/30–31, Nova Scotia (1760, 1763), CO 5/967–968, New Hampshire (1749–69), CO 5/849–51, Massachusetts (1752–65), CO 5/1226–8, New York (1751–5, 1763, 1764), CO 5/1036, New Jersey (1755), CO 5/750, Maryland (1754–9, 1761–4), T 1/355/58–60, and T 1/374/50–9, Maryland (1754, 1756–7), CO 5/1444, 1446–50, Virginia (1749–69), CO 5/510–11, South Carolina (1752–3, 1757–60, 1762–7), CO 5/709–710, Georgia (1763–6), CO 142/15–18, Jamaica (1749, 1753–7, 1762–9), CO 7/6/4, Dominica (1763), CO 106/1, Grenada (1765–7).
[c] Historical Society of Pennsylvania, Custom House Tonnage Books (1765–70), Thomas Cadwallader Section, Cadwallader Collection.
[d] Maryland Hall of Records, Annapolis, Entrances and Clearances (1748–59), Port of Annapolis.
[e] Maryland Historical Society, Baltimore, Entrances and Clearances (1756–70), MS 21, Port of Annapolis.
[f] Georgia Historical Society, Savannah, Port Records of Savannah (1767).
[g] Arquivo Nacional da Torre do Tombo, Lisbon, Junta do Comercio, Maço 311, ord. 442.
[h] Bristol Record Office, Daybook of Richard Neale (1761–4), Acc. 04399.

i Bristol newspapers: *Bristol Oracle* (1749), *Bristol Weekly Intelligencer* (1750–1), *Felix Farley's Bristol Journal* (1752–70).

j American newspapers: *Boston Evening-Post* (1749–66), *Boston Gazette or Weekly Journal* (1749–70), *Boston Weekly Newsletter* (1749–70), *Massachusetts Gazette and Boston News-Letter* (1764), *New-York Gazette* (1760), *Weyman's New-York Gazette* (1765–7), *New-York Gazette or Weekly Post-Boy* (1759), *New-York Mercury* (1756–7, 1763–4), *New-York Weekly Journal* (1749–50), *Pennsylvania Gazette* (Philadelphia) (1749–70), *Pennsylvania Journal and Weekly Advertiser* (Philadelphia) (1763–6), *Maryland Gazette* (Annapolis) (1749–70), *Virginia Gazette* (Williamsburg) (1749–66), Purdie and Dixon's *Virginia Gazette* (1766–70), Rind's *Virginia Gazette* (1766–70), *South Carolina Gazette* (Charleston) (1749–70).

k West Indian newspaper: *Barbados Mercury* (1766).

l Printed sources: Bristol *Presentments*, Imports (1770) available at the Avon County Reference Library, Bristol; Lloyd's Shipping List (1749–70), available at the Guildhall Library, London; Walter Minchinton, Celia King and Peter Waite, eds., *Virginia Slave-Trade Statistics, 1698–1775* (Richmond, VA, 1984).

In the other, ships interspersed several calls at a transatlantic destination with trips to other suitable markets. Thus the *Dispatch*, which left Bristol on 5 July 1756, made two separate calls at Trinity, Newfoundland (in October 1756 and October 1757), as well as visits to Cadiz, Malaga, Gibraltar and Cartagena, before returning to Bristol on 26 July 1758.[20] Nevertheless, both sorts of tramping voyage were the exception rather than the rule.

Breaking down the routes of vessels trading with eight colonial areas reveals significant trends in the patterns of Bristol's transatlantic trade. The statistical results, shown in tables 3.2–3.9, highlight four main points.[21] The first is that the Seven Years War had a considerable impact on shipping routes, for one finds an increase in the percentage of tonnage sailing on direct routes in wartime to and from six of the regions.[22] This rise was especially large for trade with Philadelphia and with Charleston, South Carolina. The percentage of total tonnage on shuttle routes between Bristol and Philadelphia rose from zero in 1749–55 to 48.9 in 1756–63, while the percentage for Bristol–Charleston rose from 14.7 to 40.3. The prevalence of direct voyages during the Seven Years War, for six of the eight regions, probably reflects efforts to reduce the risks incurred in operating multilateral voyages, for no fewer than sixty-eight ships on transatlantic voyages from Bristol were captured by French privateers on their outward crossing during the war and a further forty-five were taken on the return voyage.[23] This suggests that the convoy

---

[20] Details taken from SMV, List of Shipping (1747–87), Muster Roll no. 181 (1757–8), and Wharfage Books (1757–8).

[21] The areas were chosen to represent different regions of the British mainland and Caribbean colonies. The headings of the tables refer to ports or to colonies or islands in accordance with the designation usually given to these transatlantic destinations in the shipping records referred to in the appendix. 'Ireland' refers to southern Irish ports such as Dublin, Cork and Waterford; the 'Wine Islands' are Madeira, the Azores and the Cape Verdes; 'Other Colony' indicates any North American or West Indian colony other than the one around which each table is based; 'Combination' refers to more than one colony; and 'Europe' refers to one or more ports on the European continent. In table 3.6 'Europe' includes vessels first touching at Cowes, on the Isle of Wight, before continuing on to a northern European port. It should be remembered that, as mentioned above, all ships trading at Irish ports and one colonial region are considered to be pursuing shuttle voyages, and that individual ships are sometimes included in more than one table in this group.

[22] That St Kitts and Barbados are the two odd-men-out can probably be attributed to the proximity of the British colonies in the Lesser Antilles and to opportunities for trade with Guadeloupe and Martinique, which were briefly in British hands towards the end of the Seven Years War before being handed back to the French in 1763.

[23] Calculated from shipping news in *FFBJ* (1756–63). For a statistical breakdown of the places of loss of ships trading between Bristol and the New World, 1750–68, see Morgan, 'Bristol Merchants and the Colonial Trades', pp. 79–81.

provision procured after requests to the Admiralty from the Society of Merchant Venturers in Bristol was not particularly effective.[24]

The second point is the general decline in the total tonnage of slavers trading with Virginia, South Carolina and Jamaica. Comparison of the two peace periods, 1749–55 and 1764–70, shows that slavers declined from 13.8 to 1.8 per cent of the total tonnage trading between Bristol and Virginia; the figures for South Carolina and Jamaica show falls, respectively, from 27.6 to 8.3 per cent and from 24.8 to 17.8 per cent. These reductions reflect the general decline of the Bristol slave trade after the 1740s as Liverpool rose to become the leading slave trading port in the world.[25]

Third, with the exception of St Kitts, all the tables reveal increases in the proportion of total tonnage sailing on direct routes in peacetime. Comparing again the periods 1749–55 and 1764–70, one finds that the percentage of shipping tonnage involved in direct trade rose from 13.8 to 40.2 for Newfoundland, from 7.6 to 23.1 for Boston, from zero to 27.3 for Philadelphia, from 67.4 to 76.7 for Virginia, from 14.7 to 32.9 for South Carolina, from 66.5 to 76.1 for Jamaica, and from 62.5 to 72.7 for Barbados.[26] All this suggests that most vessels continued to sail directly to Virginia, Jamaica and Barbados, but that shuttle voyages with Newfoundland, Boston, Philadelphia and South Carolina also increased substantially between 1749 and 1770. The analysis below should indicate that this trend reflects the difficulties encountered by shipowners in maintaining multilateral voyages with these areas.

The fourth point is that some American regions were foci for shuttle routes from Bristol while others served as entrepôts for multilateral voyages. More than half the shipping tonnage trading between Bristol and Newfoundland, Boston, Philadelphia, Charleston, and St Kitts usually followed circuitous routes in each group of years, whereas 60–80 per cent of the tonnage linked with Virginia, Jamaica and Barbados sailed on direct tracks. This important difference stemmed from the unbalanced

---

[24] On convoy protection for Bristol–West India Vessels see W. E. Minchinton, ed., *Politics and the Port of Bristol*, pp. xxix, 62–6; McGrath, *Merchant Venturers of Bristol*, pp. 173–4; Patrick Crowhurst, *The Defence of British Trade, 1689–1815* (Folkestone, 1977), pp. 62–3, 66; R. P. Crowhurst, 'British Oceanic Convoys in the Seven Years' War, 1756–1763' (University of London Ph.D. thesis, 1970), pp. 42, 76–80, 123–9.

[25] For the decline of the Bristol slave trade from the 1740s see below, pp. 132–3, 140–51, and David Richardson, 'The Bristol Slave Trade in the Eighteenth Century' (University of Manchester MA thesis, 1969).

[26] As with table 3.1, the percentages on direct traders extracted from tables 3.2–3.9 include ships touching at Ireland or the Wine islands.

Table 3.2. *Shipping routes followed by ships trading between Bristol and Newfoundland, 1749–1770*

Shipping routes	1749–55			1756–63			1764–70		
	N	Tons	% Tons	N	Tons	% Tons	N	Tons	% Tons
Bristol–Newfoundland–Bristol	8	495	9.8	13	855	19.6	19	1,139	18.0
Bristol–Ireland–Newfoundland–Bristol	3	200	4.0	5	576	13.2	15	1,403	22.2
Bristol–Newfoundland–Europe–Bristol	29	2,500	49.8	13	1,360	31.1	24	2,181	34.6
Bristol–Newfoundland–other Colony–Bristol	0	0	0.0	5	388	8.9	1	120	1.9
Bristol–other Colony–Newfoundland–Bristol	2	110	2.2	0	0	0.0	1	100	1.6
Bristol–other Colony–Newfoundland–Europe–Bristol	3	140	2.8	3	260	5.9	4	460	7.3
Bristol–Ireland–Newfoundland–Europe–Bristol	11	830	16.5	5	490	11.2	3	324	5.1
Bristol–Europe–Newfoundland–Europe–Bristol	1	80	1.6	0	0	0.0	1	60	1.0
Others	8	670	13.3	5	440	10.1	8	525	8.3

Table 3.3. Shipping routes followed by ships trading between Bristol and Boston, 1749–1770

Shipping routes	1749–55			1756–63			1764–70		
	N	Tons	% Tons	N	Tons	% Tons	N	Tons	% Tons
Bristol–Boston–Bristol	1	100	7.6	2	340	20.6	4	340	23.1
Bristol–Boston–other Colony–Bristol	4	355	27.1	8	920	55.8	3	330	22.4
Bristol–Boston–Europe–Bristol	3	175	13.3	0	0	0.0	2	200	13.6
Bristol–other Colony–Boston–Bristol	0	0	0.0	0	0	0.0	0	0	0.0
Bristol–Boston–Combination–Bristol	4	500	38.2	1	150	9.1	2	204	13.8
Bristol–Boston–other Colony–Europe–Bristol	1	60	4.6	1	100	6.1	2	200	13.6
Bristol–Europe–Boston–other Colony–Bristol	1	120	9.2	0	0	0.0	0	0	0.0
Bristol–other Colony–Boston–other Colony–Bristol	0	0	0.0	0	0	0.0	1	100	6.8
Others	0	0	0.0	1	140	8.5	1	100	6.8

ratio of exports to imports in many Atlantic trades. Some bilateral commodity routes were only semi-productive, consisting of bulk and mixed cargoes carried one way and mainly ballast in return.[27] Many colonies in British America produced primary products that were never in sufficient demand in Britain for ships' holds to be fully laden with them on homeward-bound voyages. Such commodities included forest products, deerskins, and the range of foodstuffs respectively produced by, and exported from, New England, the Carolinas, and the Middle Colonies. Other products, such as fish from Newfoundland or rice from South Carolina, found their natural markets more in continental Europe and the West Indies than in Britain.[28] The varying volume of European demand for staple products strongly influenced the type of shipping route followed: uncertain demand within Britain for particular commodities often necessitated the choice of multilateral routes, whereas a dependable home market for certain goods, such as sugar and tobacco, led to the pursuit of direct shipping tracks. As we shall see, changing levels of demand also had a significant bearing on shipownership in Bristol's trade with different Atlantic regions.

The reasons why some ships followed shuttle routes and others multilateral routes need to be explained more fully. In the absence of runs of voyage accounts giving details of costs and profits, one may assume that shipowners were anxious to gain maximum returns and that voyage patterns therefore reflect the relative profitability of routes. Shipping routes, however, were also dominated by risk and uncertainty in the practice of navigation, the nature of prices and markets, and the means of commercial communication. To some extent, it is true, these problems associated with Atlantic shipping were being overcome. By the mid-eighteenth century, the diffusion of maps, globes, marine atlases, octants and printed guides for master mariners improved the accuracy of navigation; Atlantic trade routes provided frequent opportunities for dissemination of commercial intelligence on a year-round rather than a seasonal basis; information began to travel more rapidly as the time ships spent at sea increased in relation to time spent in port; and the circulation of the posts, packets and newspapers aided the efficient spread of business information.[29] By 1747, for instance, *Felix Farley's Bristol Journal* re-

---

[27] Douglass C. North, 'Sources of Productivity Change in Ocean Shipping, 1600–1850', *Journal of Political Economy*, 76 (1968), 962. For ways in which Bristol merchants filled up excess space on outward transatlantic voyages see below, pp. 123–7.

[28] These points are stressed in Shepherd and Walton, *Shipping, Maritime Trade*, p. 45.

[29] Steele, *English Atlantic*, pp. 213–28; Ian K. Steele, 'Moat Theories and the English Atlantic, 1675 to 1740', *Canadian Historical Association Papers* (1978), 27–8; Robin Craig, 'Printed Guides for Master Mariners as a Source of Productivity Change in Shipping, 1750–1914', *Journal of Transport History*, 3rd Series, 3 (1982), 23–35.

ceived news directly via ships arriving from British America.[30] By the same time, several Bristol newspapers also printed detailed information on the progress of Bristol voyages as well as lists of shipping arrivals and departures. These developments, along with talk at Bristol's Exchange and coffee houses, helped to spread information about events in the Atlantic world with minimum delay.

Despite these improvements in communications, it was not until the late eighteenth century that improved navigational techniques were fully co-ordinated or that sailing in coastal waters was made safer by lights, buoys and the dredging of estuaries.[31] It was also not until then that navigation by compasses and by parallel sailing along the latitudes was improved by the diffusion of the chronometer, which helped to find longitude at sea.[32] The vagaries of the weather – fogs, winds, periods of calm or storm, hurricanes, ice – were always a threat to sailing vessels in the Atlantic and skilful navigation was required to avoid rocks, shoals, and running ships aground.[33] Wartime, as noted above, brought the additional problem of enemy privateers. Further risks lay in the inability of shipowners to predict accurately the level of prices and the state of markets in a large Atlantic trading bowl. Commodity prices fluctuated between and within ports and regions, and shifts in exchange rates were common in a commercial world where many metallic currencies were used and where the depth of exchange markets varied. Great distances between producing and consuming markets also led quite frequently to disequilibrium between supply and demand, and to uncertainty at the time of shipment about the best market in which to sell.[34] Since trade was

---

[30] R. M. Wiles, *Freshest Advices: Early Provincial Newspapers in England* (Columbus, OH, 1965), p. 206.

[31] Ralph Davis, 'Maritime History: Progress and Problems' in Sheila Marriner, ed., *Business and Businessmen: Studies in Business, Economic and Accounting History* (Liverpool, 1978), pp. 180–1.

[32] J. H. Parry, *Trade and Dominion: the European Oversea Empires in the Eighteenth Century* (London, 1971), ch. 12; J. B. Hewson, *A History of the Practice of Navigation* (Glasgow, 1951), pp. 104, 106, 153.

[33] The ways in which navigators coped with these natural hazards are discussed at length in E. G. R. Taylor, *The Haven-Finding Art: A History of Navigation from Odysseus to Captain Cook* (London, 1956).

[34] For useful commentary on the risk environment of the early modern period see Stuart Bruchey, 'Success and Failure Factors: American Merchants in Foreign Trade in the Eighteenth and Nineteenth Centuries', *BHR*, 32 (1958), 272–92, and *The Roots of American Economic Growth, 1607–1861* (London, 1965), pp. 55–60; Barry Supple, 'The Nature of Enterprise' in E. E. Rich and C. H. Wilson, eds., *The Cambridge Economic History of Europe, V: The Economic Organization of Early Modern Europe* (Cambridge, 1977), pp. 396, 407–10; K. N. Chaudhuri, *The Trading World of Asia and the English East India Company, 1660–1760* (Cambridge, 1978); and Frank C. Spooner, *Risks at Sea: Amsterdam Insurance and Maritime Europe, 1766–1780* (Cambridge, 1983). Suggestive studies dealing with similar problems for different trades and areas of the

Table 3.4. *Shipping routes followed by ships trading between Bristol and Philadelphia, 1749–1770*

Shipping routes	1749–55			1756–63			1764–70		
	N	Tons	% Tons	N	Tons	% Tons	N	Tons	% Tons
Bristol–Philadelphia–Bristol	0	0	0.0	7	870	48.9	9	1,090	27.3
Bristol–Philadelphia–Europe–Bristol	0	0	0.0	0	0	0.0	2	300	7.5
Bristol–Philadelphia–other Colony–Bristol	3	405	22.8	4	470	26.4	13	1,936	48.5
Bristol–Philadelphia–Combination–Bristol	1	180	10.1	0	0	0.0	0	0	0.0
Bristol–other Colony–Philadelphia–Bristol	0	0	0.0	0	0	0.0	2	260	6.5
Bristol–Ireland–other Colony–Philadelphia–other Colony–Bristol	2	190	10.7	0	0	0.0	0	0	0.0
Bristol–Europe–Philadelphia–Europe–Philadelphia–Bristol	1	250	14.0	0	0	0.0	0	0	0.0
Bristol–other Colony–Philadelphia–other Colony–Bristol	3	275	15.4	1	100	5.6	2	234	5.9
Others	4	480	27.0	3	340	19.1	2	171	4.3

Table 3.5. *Shipping routes followed by ships trading between Bristol and Virginia, 1749–1770*

Shipping routes	1749–55			1756–63			1764–70		
	N	Tons	% Tons	N	Tons	% Tons	N	Tons	% Tons
Bristol–Virginia–Bristol	66	9,720	67.4	78	12,817	79.5	57	8,511	76.7
Bristol–Ireland–Virginia–Bristol	0	0	0.0	1	80	0.5	0	0	0.0
Bristol–Wine Islands–Virginia–Bristol	0	0	0.0	1	90	0.6	0	0	0.0
Bristol–Africa–Virginia–Bristol	18	1,990	13.8	7	1,030	6.4	2	204	1.8
Bristol–other Colony–Virginia–Bristol	15	2,125	14.7	12	1,860	11.5	12	2,016	18.2
Bristol–Ireland–other Colony–Virginia–Bristol	0	0	0.0	0	0	0.0	1	160	1.4
Bristol–other Colony–Virginia–other Colony–Bristol	1	140	1.0	0	0	0.0	0	0	0.0
Bristol–Combination–Virginia–Bristol	1	180	1.3	0	0	0.0	1	200	1.8
Others	3	260	1.8	2	240	1.5	0	0	0.0

a prominent sector of the English economy for bankrupts in the eighteenth century, business failure was an ever-present possibility for merchants who did not overcome these risks.[35]

Bearing in mind these considerations, one may view circuitous shipping routes as an attempt by Bristol merchants to make efficient use of their ships in trades where bilateral routes could not provide suitable goods to fill shipping space on both outward and return voyages. Merchants adopted rational and flexible business arrangements to organise roundabout routes: they relied on a network of ship captains and overseas factors, plus the spread of mercantile letters and shipping news in the newspapers, to co-ordinate commercial knowledge. Overseas correspondents, in particular, were used extensively. They handled business for British merchants at low cost and, unlike employees permanently maintained abroad, they could always be changed if they proved unreliable.[36] Shipowners, in their letters to correspondents, were especially anxious that their vessels should not be idle or merely trading in ballast. Henry Cruger, Jr, a New York-born merchant resident in Bristol, highlighted this problem when he noted, in relation to the return voyage of one of his vessels from Boston, that 'to be obliged to go away in ballast, unable to procure a freight for Love or Money is the very Devil – the loss of time is what a Ship cannot nowadays support'.[37] Besides time lags, the costs of sending ships deadfreighted were high. Thus in 1757 Austin & Laurens of Charleston, annoyed at the arrival of a ship with nothing on freight, remarked to Richard Meyler, Sr of Bristol that 'tis bad . . . ships should

world are Robert G. Albion, 'Sea Routes' in Critchell Rimington, ed., *Merchant Fleets: A Survey of the Merchant Navies of the World* (New York, 1944), pp. 19–39; Niels Steensgaard, *The Asian Trade Revolution of the Seventeenth Century: The East India Companies and the Decline of the Caravan Trade* (Chicago, 1974); and Christian Koninckx, *The First and Second Charters of the Swedish East India Company (1731–1766)* (Korkrijk, Belgium, 1980), pp. 119–44. The fluctuating nature of exchange rates is well documented in John J. McCusker, *Money and Exchange in Europe and America, 1600–1775: A Handbook* (Chapel Hill, NC, 1978), which also discusses the coins used in the North Atlantic trading world.

35 Julian Hoppit, *Risk and Failure in English Business, 1700–1800* (Cambridge, 1987), especially ch. 5.

36 Jacob M. Price, 'Transaction Costs: A Note on Merchant Credit and the Organization of Private Trade' in James D. Tracy, ed., *The Political Economy of Merchant Empires* (Cambridge, 1991), p. 279.

37 Houghton Library, Henry Cruger, Jr to William Palfrey, 1 Aug. 1772, Palfrey Papers. For further insight into the 'heavy work' of sending a vessel on 'so long a voyage in ballast' see a letter dealing with a ship plying between Bristol, Philadelphia and Charleston: Henry Laurens to William Freeman, 9 Oct. 1767, in Philip M. Hamer *et al.*, eds., *The Papers of Henry Laurens* (Columbia, SC, 1968–), V, p. 347.

move from place to place now their Expenses run high without carrying some thing to defray it'.[38]

Colonial agents who were on their toes would, of course, take the initiative to avoid trading in ballast and keeping ships anchored in port. In October 1753, for example, a Jamaican firm connected with John Curtis, a leading Bristol sugar merchant, informed a mutual Philadelphia correspondent that one of Curtis's vessels had 'fallen in too late in the year to be dispatched from hence with a load of Sugars &c. of the last crop', so they had, 'in order to pass the time till the next crop, thought proper to address her to you [that is, in Philadelphia] for a load of Lumber'.[39] This shows that even an experienced merchant like Curtis could get the timing of voyages wrong, but on this occasion he could thank the quick decision made by his Jamaican factors.

To avoid the problems of idle time and trading in ballast, Bristol merchants frequently reassessed the commodity and market options for the return voyages of their vessels using roundabout routes. Thus in 1752 Francis Bright suggested several alternatives for a return voyage of the *Pelham*; these included sailing from Jamaica, the outward-bound destination of the vessel, to Charleston and then either back to Jamaica or to New York, Philadelphia or Bristol.[40] And in 1766 a Quaker merchant, William Reeve, instructed a Boston correspondent either to load his ship back to Bristol with a freight of oil 'or in default thereof to load her with a lumber cargoe suteable for the L[eewar]d Islands or Barbados of w[hi]ch the Captain have [*sic*] some directions regarding the sorts'.[41] In letters of instruction to ship captains, some Bristol merchants provided assistance by listing their business connections in ports of the North Atlantic with a view to reliable commercial contacts where ships might need to call. In 1763 a Bristol firm advised a correspondent in Portsmouth, New Hampshire, to send a consignment of fish to named agents in either Lisbon, Cadiz, Malaga, Oporto, Alicante, Barcelona, Leghorn or Naples.[42] And the instructions to the master of the *Kingston Packet* in 1775 listed

---

[38] Austin & Laurens to Richard Meyler, Sr, 10 Jan. 1757, in Hamer *et al.*, eds., *Papers of Henry Laurens*, II, p. 405.

[39] HSP, Bayly, Elworthy & Bayly to John Reynell, 15 Oct. 1753, Reynell Papers.

[40] UMA, Francis Bright to Austin & Laurens, 15 Dec. 1752, Francis Bright Letterbook (1752–3), Bright Family Papers.

[41] Boston Public Library, William Reeve to John Hancock, 14 Oct. 1766, in the Chamberlain Collection of Autographs, II, Hancock Papers (1763–1816).

[42] Portsmouth Athenaeum, Devonsheir & Reeve to Hugh Hall Wentworth, 12 Sept. 1763, Larkin Papers.

Table 3.6. *Shipping routes followed by ships trading between Bristol and South Carolina, 1749–1770*

Shipping routes	1749–55			1756–63			1764–70		
	N	Tons	% Tons	N	Tons	% Tons	N	Tons	% Tons
Bristol–South Carolina–Bristol	13	1,125	14.7	28	3,592	40.3	30	4,345	32.9
Bristol–Africa–South Carolina–Bristol	15	2,110	27.6	16	1,830	20.5	11	1,102	8.3
Bristol–South Carolina–Europe–Bristol	4	450	5.9	2	195	2.2	18	3,000	22.7
Bristol–South Carolina–other Colony–Bristol	1	70	0.9	3	200	2.2	4	600	4.5
Bristol–other Colony–South Carolina–Bristol	8	920	12.0	18	2,266	25.4	23	2,907	22.0
Bristol–other Colony–South Carolina–other Colony–Bristol	3	355	4.6	1	50	0.6	2	222	1.7
Bristol–other Colony–South Carolina–Europe–Bristol	7	737	9.6	0	0	0.0	2	180	1.4
Bristol–Combination–South Carolina–Bristol	5	610	8.0	0	0	0.0	1	120	0.9
Others	15	1,280	16.7	8	790	8.9	7	740	5.6

Table 3.7. Shipping routes followed by ships trading between Bristol and Jamaica, 1749–1770

Shipping routes	1749–55			1756–63			1764–70		
	N	Tons	% Tons	N	Tons	% Tons	N	Tons	% Tons
Bristol–Jamaica–Bristol	104	13,850	44.0	103	16,460	54.0	110	16,971	54.7
Bristol–Ireland–Jamaica–Bristol	51	7,068	22.5	48	7,672	25.2	47	6,635	21.4
Bristol–Africa–Jamaica–Bristol	66	7,805	24.8	35	4,518	14.8	43	5,530	17.8
Bristol–other Colony–Jamaica–Bristol	8	1,210	3.8	10	1,090	3.6	6	720	2.3
Bristol–Jamaica–other Colony–Bristol	0	0	0.0	2	190	0.6	3	348	1.1
Bristol–Ireland–other Colony–Jamaica–Bristol	2	480	1.5	1	200	0.7	2	254	0.8
Bristol–Jamaica–other Colony–Europe–Bristol	1	170	0.6	0	0	0.0	0	0	0.0
Bristol–Combination–Jamaica–Bristol	1	90	0.3	0	0	0.0	0	0	0.0
Others	6	775	2.5	3	336	1.1	4	570	1.8

factors in no less than ten places: Milford, Cork, Waterford, St Kitts, Grenada, St Vincent, Nevis, South Carolina, New York, and Norfolk, Virginia.[43]

To maximise opportunities arising in particular markets, colonial agents sometimes used their initiative in selecting a different route for a vessel than the one intended by the owner. In 1765 James & Drinker of Philadelphia received instructions from Devonsheir & Reeve of Bristol to load wheat on the *Bristol Packet* for Cadiz, but instead they directed the ship to a more promising market in St Kitts.[44] Such changes sometimes resulted from poor information about the possible destinations for a ship. In 1756 Austin & Laurens complained to Richard Meyler that his ship *Brislington* had arrived at their wharves from Antigua without 'one Line from any one of the Gentlemen Concern'd to Let us know their Opinion what you would Choose to have done with the Ship'.[45] The master had orders to load rice for Oporto, but, since a great deal of rice had already been sent from Charleston to Oporto that year, Austin & Laurens dispatched the *Brislington* to Lisbon, with instructions to await further advice from merchant correspondents in Oporto before selecting another port in the Iberian peninsula for disposal of the cargo.[46] The rapid business decisions made necessary by such contingency arrangements led some colonial merchants to complain that British shipowners often failed to provide sufficient information on the number and expected arrival dates of their ships.[47]

Owners of Bristol slaving vessels had to exercise particular care in providing captains and agents with a range of options in order to seek the best possible markets for selling Negroes and picking up return cargoes. This is well illustrated by a voyage of the *Swift* in 1759. The master of this ship was instructed to barter his export cargo for 280–300 slaves in Bonny, in West Africa, and to transport them across the Atlantic to Austin & Laurens at Charleston. But the owners requested that if the vessel was

[43] William L. Clements Library, Bush & Elton and Lowbridge & Richard Bright to Capt. William Mattocks, 23 Dec. 1775, 9th voyage of the *Kingston Packet*, Bristol Shipping Account Books, III. For examples of letters of instruction to masters and factors connected with Bristol–Jamaica ships that occasionally followed roundabout routes see BRO, Account Book of the *Ruby* (1758–63).

[44] HSP, James & Drinker to Devonsheir & Reeve, 16 Dec. 1765, James & Drinker Letterbook (1764–6), Henry Drinker Papers.

[45] Austin & Laurens to Richard Meyler & Co., 17 Jan. 1756, in Hamer *et al.*, eds., *Papers of Henry Laurens*, II, p. 70.

[46] *Ibid.*; Austin & Laurens to Thompson, Croft & Mitchell, 2 Feb. 1756, *ibid.*, p. 86.

[47] Joseph A. Goldenberg, *Shipbuilding in Colonial America* (Charlottesville, VA, 1976), pp. 117–18.

unlikely to reach that destination by 20 October 1759 – as a result, say, of sickly slaves, delays, or the need for extra provisions – the master should sail instead to Antigua or St Kitts and apply to John and William Halliday for sale of the slaves on specified terms. If the Hallidays would not accept the conditions, the captain should sail on to Jamaica and put the same terms to William and John Miles, merchants in Kingston.[48] Two additional letters were sent giving further instructions. Austin & Laurens were advised what cargo they should load if the vessel ended up at Charleston.[49] The Hallidays were informed that, if the *Swift* reached the Leeward Islands, the captain could, if he wished, sell the slaves at Guadeloupe, which had just been captured by the British from the French.[50] (In the event, none of these options fell out, for the *Swift* was taken by a French privateer on her middle passage, retaken by HMS *Arundell*, and sold at salvage in Antigua.)[51] Such detailed instructions, giving great flexibility to agents and ship captains, were common in the Bristol slave trade.[52]

Flexibility and options were crucial in arranging other types of multilateral voyages. That is why Bristol shipowners sometimes sounded out colonial correspondents to see whether they were interested in sending their own vessels on roundabout routes. For instance, in 1765 Henry Cruger, Jr wondered if a fellow merchant in Rhode Island would care 'to keep one, or more Ships in this trade, load them with the most valuable Cargo Rhode Island produced, send them some times to Carolina, or the West Indies, etc., etc., the Produce of these places always meet a ready sale here'.[53] Suggestions often went further by proposing that Bristol and colonial merchants might own vessels jointly, so that shipping routes could be determined by whichever owner had the most up-to-date information on particular markets.[54] The initiative for such ventures could come from either side of the Atlantic. In 1766, for example, Stephen Apthorp of Bristol suggested to a merchant house in Portsmouth, New Hampshire, that such an arrangement might be suitable for dispatching a brig they were building on a Bristol–New England–Barbados–Bristol

[48] BRO, Henry Bright & Co. to Capt. James McTaggart, 5 Mar. 1759, Account Book of the *Swift* (1759), Ships' Account Books.

[49] BRO, Henry Bright & Co. to Austin & Laurens, 5 Mar. 1759, *ibid*.

[50] BRO, Henry Bright & Co. to John and William Halliday, 1 Nov. 1759, *ibid*.

[51] BRO, Account Book of the *Swift*, *ibid*.

[52] See below, pp. 138–9.

[53] Henry Cruger, Jr to Aaron Lopez, 4 Oct. 1765, in Worthington C. Ford *et al*., eds., *The Commerce of Rhode Island, 1726–1800*, 2 vols. Massachusetts HS, *Collections*, 7th Series, 9 (Boston, 1914), I, p. 126.

[54] For the ownership of vessels arriving at Bristol from North America and the West Indies see above, pp. 34–8.

Table 3.8. *Shipping routes followed by ships trading between Bristol and St Kitts, 1749–1770*

Shipping routes	1749-55			1756-63			1764-70		
	N	Tons	% Tons	N	Tons	% Tons	N	Tons	% Tons
Bristol–St Kitts–Bristol	28	2,165	23.0	11	940	11.8	15	1,830	17.4
Bristol–Ireland–St Kitts–Bristol	6	480	5.1	5	480	6.0	3	340	3.2
Bristol–Africa–St Kitts–Bristol	31	2,900	30.9	22	2,488	31.3	32	3,742	35.5
Bristol–St Kitts–other Colony–Bristol	20	2,745	29.2	14	2,160	27.2	14	2,064	19.6
Bristol–other Colony–St Kitts–Bristol	2	200	2.1	5	510	6.4	9	1,177	11.2
Bristol–Ireland–St Kitts–other Colony–Bristol	6	480	5.1	5	590	7.4	6	804	7.6
Bristol–other Colony–St Kitts–other Colony–Bristol	1	80	0.9	0	0	0.0	1	200	1.9
Bristol–Combination–St Kitts–Bristol	0	0	0.0	1	100	1.3	1	50	0.5
Others	2	350	3.7	3	680	8.6	3	320	3.0

Table 3.9. *Shipping routes followed by ships trading between Bristol and Barbados, 1749–1770*

Shipping routes	1749–55			1756–63			1764–70		
	N	Tons	% Tons	N	Tons	% Tons	N	Tons	% Tons
Bristol–Barbados–Bristol	42	3,546	52.7	35	3,570	47.1	44	5,192	52.4
Bristol–Ireland–Barbados–Bristol	8	660	9.8	7	610	8.0	2	270	2.7
Bristol–Wine Islands–Barbados–Bristol	0	0	0.0	3	270	3.6	12	1,740	17.6
Bristol–Africa–Barbados–Bristol	7	650	9.6	3	370	4.9	9	1,091	11.0
Bristol–Barbados–other Colony–Barbados–Bristol	1	100	1.5	1	120	1.6	1	120	1.2
Bristol–other Colony–Barbados–other Colony–Bristol	3	470	7.0	0	0	0.0	1	120	1.2
Bristol–Barbados–other Colony–Bristol	4	250	3.7	15	1,420	18.7	6	690	7.0
Bristol–other Colony–Barbados–Bristol	3	405	6.0	9	788	10.4	5	630	6.4
Others	8	650	9.7	3	436	5.7	1	50	0.5

voyage.[55] Similarly, in 1760, a Boston merchant tried to attract Devonsheir, Reeve & Lloyd of Bristol into joint ownership of a ship plying
between Bristol, Boston and Oporto.[56] Henry Cruger, Jr explained the
significance of such jointly owned ships when he remarked to John
Hancock of Boston that 'the *more* owners you have of your side the water
the better on account of their orders for goods to promote her Freight'.[57]

The trading connections of some Bristol and Philadelphia merchants
illumine the difficulties involved in organising multilateral shipping
routes. During the 1760s and early 1770s, for instance, the Bristol merchant John Noble sent at least one ship a year via New York or Philadelphia to the Newfoundland Banks, where it took a cargo of fish for
southern Europe.[58] Noble was a substantial merchant, 'much respected
by every body reckon'd rich & in good business'.[59] He acquired significant interests in Newfoundland and Labrador but did not normally export
goods to the American colonies.[60] His speculative ventures in an irregular
shipping route avoided trading in ballast on the first leg of a voyage to
Newfoundland by sending a ship to pick up a cargo of provisions in the
Middle Colonies. Noble relied on commission agents in Philadelphia for
accurate information on exchange rates and current prices for provisions,
and he expected his factors to dispatch his vessels from that city in time to
reach Newfoundland before the fishing season ended in mid-Sep-
tember.[61] But he found that cargoes of cod sometimes ended up in
European markets that were already glutted. On one occasion he tried to
skirt this problem by ordering his agents to sell their fish when prices were
high in Newfoundland and by getting them to load a wheat cargo for the

[55] Portsmouth Athenaeum, Stephen Apthorp to Montgomery & Wentworth, 31 May 1766,
Larkin Papers.
[56] Baker Library, John Rowe to Devonsheir, Reeve & Lloyd, 10 June 1760, John Rowe
Letterbook (1759–62).
[57] New England HGS, Henry Cruger, Jr to John Hancock, 18 Mar. 1771, John Hancock
Foreign Letters, 1764–91, box 27, folder 3, Hancock Papers. Joint ownership of ships
spread the risks and costs of multilateral voyages but could still lead to many difficulties.
This is well illustrated by the problems experienced in settling a newly built ship (the
Ann) in trade between Bristol, Philadelphia and Charleston: see Henry Laurens to
William Freeman, 9 Oct., 21 Dec. 1767, to William Cowles & Co., 26 Dec. 1767, and to
Cowles & Co. and Freeman, 21 Jan. 1768, in Hamer *et al.*, eds., *Papers of Henry
Laurens*, V, pp. 347, 523, 532, 557.
[58] LC, Samuel Smith to John Smith, (?) Apr. 1774, Samuel Smith Letterbook (1772–4), box
7, Samuel Smith Papers; Pennsylvania MHC, John Noble to Baynton & Wharton, 9 June
1764, Baynton-Wharton-Morgan Papers.
[59] LC, Quotation (n.d.) in Samuel Smith Letterbook (1772–4), box 7, Samuel Smith
Papers.
[60] Keith Matthews, 'A History of the West of England-Newfoundland Fishery' (University
of Oxford D.Phil. thesis, 1968), p. 423; C. Grant Head, *Eighteenth-Century Newfoundland: A Geographer's Perspective* (Toronto, 1976), p. 181; Pennsylvania MHC, John
Noble to Baynton & Wharton, 9 June 1764, Baynton-Wharton-Morgan Papers.
[61] Pennsylvania MHC, John Noble to Baynton & Wharton, 5 Mar. 1765, *ibid.*

Mediterranean.[62] Unfortunately, these orders arrived too late, and Noble noted in exasperation that he would lose £1,000 in profits.[63] Noble attempted to retrieve matters quickly by offering to adventure a cargo of best red wheat to Cadiz, Barcelona and Leghorn, using a ship owned by his Philadelphia agents, but this scheme did not bear fruit.[64] He therefore decided to drop these circuitous voyages for, as he put it to Baynton, Wharton & Morgan of Philadelphia, 'so many gentlemen at your place adventure on their own accounts and my orders last year could not be executed, I have dropp'd all thoughts of the same as I make no doubt but that they will be fully supply'd soon after the demand is known at your place'.[65]

Thus even in the peak period of the Newfoundland fishery in the eighteenth century there were serious problems in arranging a regular multilateral route involving perishable foodstuffs as well as highly fluctuating markets and prices.[66] Other Bristolians trading with Philadelphia from the 1750s to the 1770s tried to fix their ships in roundabout routes via the West Indies, but after a few years this proved unsuccessful (for reasons similar to those defeating Noble's ventures). The experiment was therefore cast aside.[67] Lowbridge Bright, a leading West India merchant at Bristol, later summarised succinctly the difficulties of operating multilateral crossings when he responded to a request to send a ship on a Bristol–Nova Scotia–Jamaica–Bristol voyage. 'Most of the West Indian Merch[an]ts have at times tried the No[rth] American voyage', he commented, 'but are so sick of it as not to be dispos'd to attempt a renewal. The additional Wages, Port Charges, Insurance, renewal of Ships Comp[lemen]ts & in particular the *wear & tear* of the Ships & their materials in such long Circuitous Voyages are a bar to the continuance of that branch being carried on ... There is little or no outw[ar]d freight hence for

---

[62] Pennsylvania MHC, John Noble to Baynton, Wharton & Morgan, 31 Oct. 1765, *ibid.*
[63] *Ibid.*
[64] *Ibid.*
[65] Pennsylvania MHC, John Noble to Baynton, Wharton & Morgan, 25 Aug. 1766, *ibid.* For further details on Noble's trade with Newfoundland and Europe see Somerset RO, Letterbook of R. Anstice of Bridgwater (1769–81), Stradling MS, DD/ST 23.
[66] Head, *Eighteenth-Century Newfoundland*, ch. 7. For an analysis of risks and uncertainties in the foodstuffs trade between Newfoundland and Portugal see H. E. S. Fisher, *The Portugal Trade: A Study of Anglo–Portuguese Commerce, 1700–1770* (London, 1971), pp. 69–76.
[67] For details on such voyages see HSP, Michael Atkins to John Reynell, 30 June 1737, 23 Feb. 1749, 5 July 1751, 8 Oct. 1755, Reynell Papers; University of the West Indies Library, Mona, Jamaica, Account Book of the *Sarah* (1753–8); UMA, Francis Bright to Bright, Whatley & Co., 3 Mar. 1753, Francis Bright Letterbook (1752–3), Bright Family Papers; and Marc Egnal, 'The Changing Structure of Philadelphia's Trade with the British West Indies, 1750–1775', *Pennsylvania Magazine of History and Biography*, 99 (1975), 169–79.

transient Vessells. The Station'd Ships take it all as the Goods tho Valluable are not bulky and the middle freight generally neats but little while the expenses of such a Voyage are enormous.'[68]

The need to make full use of ships on all legs of voyages, to co-ordinate shipping movements with colonial agents, to time voyages to coincide with the availability of seasonal crops, and to cope with the irregularity of many markets and the instability of prices posed ever-present problems that made multilateral routes more speculative than bilateral routes. These are probably the reasons why Captain Hector MacNeal, after sailing on several circuitous voyages from Bristol, informed his brother that 'there is but Little gott by running to Different Ports every Voyage; a Constant trade of any kind is more advantagious than running to and fro every voyage'.[69] But there were important additional reasons why out-and-back voyages predominated over diverse shipping tracks. These will be considered in relation to ships sailing to Virginia and Jamaica. The justification for looking at shuttle voyages with these two regions lies in the value of trade and volume of shipping involved. In the eighteenth century Chesapeake tobacco was the most valuable British import from the American mainland, and Caribbean sugar was the most lucrative commodity shipped to Britain from any overseas area.[70] Between 1749 and 1770, almost three-quarters of the shipping tonnage entering Bristol from transatlantic destinations came from the Chesapeake and the West Indies, and direct shipping lanes accounted for over two-thirds of the tonnage travelling between Bristol and Virginia and Bristol and Jamaica.[71]

One important reason why Bristolians dispatched ships on direct voyages to these colonies was that the high volume of European demand for sugar and tobacco led to the establishment of close commercial ties with planters and agents over a period of years.[72] Such links were encouraged partly by the need to maintain trust and one's business reputation in the credit and debt arrangements of Atlantic commerce, and partly by the seasonal rhythm of trade. Bristol merchants bought goods on credit to supply their colonial correspondents; in return they expected punctual

[68] UMA, Lowbridge Bright to David Duncombe, 6 Apr. 1791, 14 Mar. 1793, box 20, Bright Family Papers.
[69] Hector MacNeal to Neal MacNeal, 4 May 1736, Family Papers of MacNeal of Tirfergus, Ugadale and Losset.
[70] Ralph Davis, 'English Foreign Trade, 1700–1774,' EcHR, 2nd Series, XV (1962), 300–1, and The Industrial Revolution and British Overseas Trade (Leicester, 1979), pp. 43–4, 110, 112.
[71] Calculated from SMV, Annual List of Shipping (1747–87) and the Wharfage Books (1748–9, 1754–68); see also tables 3.5 and 3.7 above, pp. 69, 73.
[72] This point is illustrated below on pp. 170, 173–6, 203–4, 209–14.

and full remittances.[73] Manufactured exports were either 'spring' or 'fall' goods, and tobacco and sugar were shipped after yearly harvests.[74] The bulk of the tobacco crop was gathered in between October and December. The sugar harvest was concentrated in the first five months of the year. Ships in the tobacco and sugar trades accordingly followed distinct seasonal rhythms.[75] By the mid-eighteenth century, three-quarters of the Bristol vessels entering naval districts in Virginia did so in the first six months of the year. During the same period, some 72 per cent of the Bristol ships entering Kingston, Jamaica arrived between December and April.[76]

The easiest and most secure way of coping with these financial and seasonal demands was for Bristol merchants trading with Virginia or Jamaica to own shares in ships sailing on direct routes and consigned to familiar colonial agents.[77] These considerations explain why there was a reluctance to sever individual commercial ties unless unsolvable business problems occurred and why colonial correspondents favoured regular traders. Thus in 1758, at the time of a small tobacco crop, a Virginia planter advised Farell & Jones, a leading Bristol tobacco firm, that they should not send a second ship to the York River in Virginia, because 'your interest here is not yet good enough to load two vessels in our river for people can't so suddenly break off their Engagements'.[78] A similar fate befell William Clutsam, master of the *Hope*, on a round-trip voyage between Bristol and Jamaica in 1760. Clutsam could not secure a sugar cargo at Kingston and so he proceeded westward along the southern coast of Jamaica to Old Harbour. But he found that the factors there were used to dealing with Michael Atkins – the premier Bristol sugar merchant at

---

[73] On the interrelationship of credit and debt in Bristol's eighteenth-century Atlantic trade see below, pp. 109–18, 146–9, 161–5.

[74] Morgan, 'Bristol Merchants and the Colonial Trades', pp. 158–9; Shepherd and Walton, *Shipping, Maritime Trade*, pp. 107–8; Davis, *Rise of the English Shipping Industry*, pp. 279, 285. For 'spring' and 'fall' goods see below, pp. 118–19.

[75] Cf. Davis, *Rise of the English Shipping Industry*, pp. 279, 281, 285.

[76] Based on 127 Bristol ships entering Virginia in 1737–45, 1758, 1761 and 1762, and on 142 Bristol vessels arriving at Kingston, Jamaica in 1752–5, 1762–5 and 1767 (PRO, CO 5/1444–9 and CO 142/15–18). The years covered are those in which all quarterly entrances are given in the Naval Officers' Returns. The Virginia totals exclude one naval district – Accomac – with which Bristol did not trade.

[77] The involvement of these merchants in shipownership can be established by comparing the names of owners in Bristol–Virginia and Bristol–Jamaica vessels in PRO, CO 5/1444, 1446–50, and CO 142/15–18, with the importers of sugar and tobacco listed in Morgan, 'Bristol Merchants and the Colonial Trades', apps. B and C, pp. 325–66.

[78] Virginia SL, John Syme to Farell & Jones, 19 May 1758, US Circuit Court, Virginia District, Ended Cases, Record Book 5, E (1796).

that time – and that they insisted in waiting for his ships, which were expected soon, before committing freight to the *Hope*.[79]

A second major reason for the prevalence of shuttle routes in Bristol's trade with Virginia and Jamaica lay in the role of ship captains in such commerce. Shipowners knew that the success or failure of voyages often hinged on masters' judgement in navigation, supervision of crew and cargo, observation (where relevant) of charter parties, and other related matters; accordingly, they frequently tried to maximise the expertise of ship captains by settling them in regular direct shipping routes.[80] This gave masters time to absorb the intricate business procedures of trades where they were in control of an owner's ship and freight for long stretches of time. Captains on Bristol–Virginia vessels needed a thorough knowledge of the consignment system long used in British–Chesapeake trade, whereby planters shipped their leaf to British merchants who sold it on commission; of the newer 'cargo' trade, in which Chesapeake merchants remitted either tobacco or bills of exchange to British merchants in payment for manufactured goods; and of the direct purchase system, where tobacco was bought in the Chesapeake by resident professional buyers acting on behalf of British principals.[81]

Masters in the tobacco trade also needed familiarity with the river network of the Chesapeake Bay, so that tobacco planters received goods with certainty at the place where they carried on business. That this was a problem was well expressed by the Scots merchant, William Allason, who traded on the Rappahannock River. Attempting to re-establish connections with Henry Lippincott & Co. after the American Revolution, Allason commented that he was 'long acquainted with the great inconveniency attending Goods for this, being first sent into another River. It frequently happened that al[though] they were nearer, yet they were

---

[79] BRO, Capt. William Clutsam to Samuel Munckley & Co., 16 Feb. 1760, Samuel Munckley Papers, AC/MU/1(11c), Ashton Court MSS. For an example of a West Indian factor refusing to withdraw sugar consignments 'without ... particular reason for so doing' from a Bristol commission agent who 'treats me with every Civility and Respect, as well as the greatest punctuality' see Bristol UL, John Pinney to Simon Pretor, 26 July 1771, Letterbook of John Frederick Pinney and John Pinney (1761–75), Pinney Papers. Richard Pares provides an illuminating discussion of the relationship between shipowners and captains in the Bristol–West India trade in the late eighteenth and early nineteenth centuries in his *West-India Fortune*, pp. 207–38.

[80] Whether or not to charter out a ship was one of the most important decisions that managing owners of vessels had to make. Masters had to comply in all respects with the charter party, which would usually specify the ports to be visited, the agents from whom instructions should be taken, and the agreed procedures on unloading and loading. For a clear discussion of chartering and an overview of the relations between owners and masters in seaborne trade see Davis, *Rise of the English Shipping Industry*, pp. 159–74.

[81] For the organisation of Bristol's sugar and tobacco trades see below, pp. 165–83, 193–217.

as long in getting to hand as if they had been in Britain in a vessell just about leaving it and bound to the River for what the Goods were intended.'[82]

Masters of Bristol–Jamaica vessels, for their part, had to understand the workings of the commission system, in which planters consigned their crops to British commission agents, and of the direct purchase method, which involved either the captains themselves or colonial factors buying sugar on the spot on the account of British firms.[83] They needed expertise in handling ships in Caribbean waters to avoid natural hazards such as coral cays and reefs and to ensure that anchors were hoisted for the return voyage before the start of the hurricane season on 1 August. Captains used their experience to gauge the correct return route via either the Leeward Passage (around the west of Cuba to the Florida Channel) or the Windward Passage (between Cuba and St Domingue, a haven for privateers during wartime).[84] They played the major part in ensuring that ships reached their markets ahead of their competitors.[85] Masters trading to Virginia and Jamaica also had to assess the quality of the staple produce they loaded aboard ship, especially the sweet-scented tobacco and the various grades of muscovado sugar that generally sold well in the Bristol market.[86]

The skills required for command of these aspects of business organisation came only with experience. That they were invaluable was realised both in the colonies and at Bristol. This is why, in 1766, John Snelson, a tobacco planter in Hanover County, Virginia, advised a long-standing correspondent, Edward Harford, Jr, of Bristol, that the Chesapeake friends of Captain David Mcriwether, an experienced master, 'would ship you a good deal of Tob[acc]o another year if you would give him the

---

[82] Virginia SL, William Allason to Henry Lippincott & Co., 20 Nov. 1783, Allason Letterbook (1770–89), Allason Papers. For other examples of ships and goods from Bristol ending up in the wrong river in Virginia see Virginia SL, John Syme to Farell & Jones, 27 May 1754, 9 Feb. 1757, US Circuit Court, Virginia District, Ended Cases, Record Book 5, E (1796); Swem Library, Francis Jerdone to Farell & Jones, 10 Mar. 1761, Francis Jerdone Letterbook (1756–63), Jerdone Papers; George Braxton to Lidderdale & Co., 28 July 1757, in Frederick Horner, *A History of the Blair, Banister, and Braxton Families* (Philadelphia, 1898), p. 144.
[83] Some of these concerns are aired in BRO, Thomas Harris & Henry Bright to Robert Wallace, 10 Aug. 1758, Account Book of the *Ruby* (1758–63).
[84] UMA, Lowbridge Bright to Capt. William Mattocks, 10 May 1770, Lowbridge Bright Letterbook (1765–73), Bright Family Papers.
[85] See below, pp. 175, 199.
[86] See below, pp. 169, 205–7.

command of your ship York'.[87] The value of a proficient captain was also stressed by William Miles, an important Bristol West India merchant, when he expressed a preference for keeping his sugar in Jamaica 'a Year Round, rather than ship my Goods on Ships and with masters I know nothing of'.[88] The use of tried and trusted masters on direct routes is borne out by the fact that, between 1749 and 1770, only forty-two captains sailed on 143 regular voyages between Bristol and Virginia, and only seventy-one masters were employed on 308 regular Bristol–Jamaica voyages.[89] Once owners settled such captains into fixed shuttle routes they were often able to repeat their written instructions verbatim from year to year, making the organisation of Atlantic crossings much easier.[90]

A third and final reason why Bristol merchants favoured direct routes in trade with Virginia and Jamaica was their desire to cut costs by achieving productivity gains in shipping. Advances in economic efficiency could be made by reducing the number of guns and crew, improving loading efficiencies for staple crops, and cutting transit and turn-around times.[91] The evidence for the Bristol–Virginia and the Bristol–Jamaica trades suggests that such gains were only partially achieved in the mid-eighteenth century.[92] However, the productivity of trading ventures could also be promoted by establishing vessels on fixed direct routes year

---

[87] SHC, John Snelson to Edward Harford, Jr, 27 Aug. 1766, John Snelson Letterbook (1757–75), Frederick's Hall Plantation Books. David Meriwether was the master of ten Bristol–Virginia voyages between 1749 and 1770 (see entries in SMV, Annual List of Shipping (1747–87), and in PRO, E 190/1217/1–1228/2, ADM 7/86–96, and CO 5/1444, 1446–50). The success of captains in promoting a firm's interest often hinged on a record of profitable tobacco sales in Britain. This is why a Virginia planter noted that masters had little influence over planters even 'with all their rhetorick to continue their favours' where losses had previously occurred, for the dispatch ships are to meet with here is done in your counting houses: & not at our Court houses': Swem Library, Francis Jerdone to Thomas, Griffiths & Thomas, 10 Sept. 1762, Francis Jerdone Letterbook (1756–63).

[88] Quoted in Kenneth Morgan, ed., 'Calendar of Correspondence from William Miles, a West Indian Merchant in Bristol, to John Tharp, a Planter in Jamaica, 1770–1789' in Patrick McGrath, ed., A Bristol Miscellany (Bristol Record Society's Publications, 37, 1985), p. 97.

[89] Calculated from SMV, Annual List of Shipping (1747–87), PRO, E 190/1217/1–1228/2, and ADM 7/86–96.

[90] E.g. ACRL, Owners' letters of instruction to Capt. John Lorain of the Milford, engaged on Bristol–Jamaica–Bristol voyages, 8 Sept. 1761, 22 Nov. 1763, (?) Dec. 1764, (?) Jan. 1766, 23 Feb. 1767, and 4 Feb. 1768, Papers of the Milford. The first of these letters is transcribed (with an error in listing the owners) in Minchinton, ed., The Trade of Bristol in the Eighteenth Century, pp. 162–4.

[91] For disagreement among historians over the contributory factors to productivity advances in oceanic shipping see above, pp. 45–6.

[92] The relevant statistical data are analysed on pp. 46–53 above.

after year.[93] Tables 3.10–3.11 demonstrate that Bristol shipowners were able to improve productivity on shuttle voyages with both Virginia and Jamaica.[94] Table 3.10 shows that regular voyages normally dominated the direct shipping lanes between Bristol and Virginia from 1749 to 1770. Among the prominent ships were the *True Patriot* with fifteen voyages in twenty-one years, the *Virginia Packett* with eleven in ten years, the *Planter* with ten in fourteen years, and the *Ann* with ten in ten successive years.

Table 3.11 reveals that constant traders also dominated the shuttle routes between Bristol and Jamaica. Occasional crossings outnumber regular sailings only in the first year covered by the table. The most prominent ships included the *Milford* with seventeen voyages in twenty years, the *Eagle* with nineteen in nineteen years, the *Lucea* with nineteen in twenty years, and the *St James* with eighteen in eighteen years.[95] The greater efficiency owners hoped to achieve on these ventures was vital because of the substantial amounts of capital tied up in running these ships. One Bristol sugar commission house later pinpointed this need by stating that the large investment made in ships on direct routes made it 'absolutely necessary that we should find freight both out and home for them, without which they must prove very sinking funds indeed'.[96] Since outward freight earnings were trifling on ships bound from British ports to the West Indies, profitability for shipowners in the trade came from

[93] Ralph Davis hints that regular ships were a significant feature of transatlantic trade in the mid-eighteenth century (*Rise of the English Shipping Industry*, p. 273). The deployment of regular vessels in the Bristol–West India trade after 1783 is discussed in Pares, *West-India Fortune*, pp. 207–8.

[94] Regular traders in tables 3.10 and 3.11 are considered to be ships making either four or more consecutive direct voyages to the colony listed or six or more such trips in a decade. All other vessels are classified as occasional traders. Obviously, the near coincidence between regular voyages and regular ships in each year indicates that most vessels only made one annual round-trip voyage. My procedure in classifying voyages follows Richard F. Dell, 'The Operational Record of the Clyde Tobacco Fleet, 1747–1775', *Scottish Economic and Social History*, 2 (1982), 4–5. For discussion of the balance between constant and casual traders in another branch of oceanic commerce see David M. Williams, 'The Shipping of the North Atlantic Cotton Trade in the Mid-Nineteenth Century' in David Alexander and Rosemary Ommer, eds., *Volumes not Values: Canadian Sailing Ships and World Trades* (St John's, Newfoundland, 1979), pp. 311–23. It is possible that tables 3.10 and 3.11 slightly understate the number of regular traders, for the names of vessels were sometimes changed and one cannot always spot the alterations in the sources.

[95] Calculated from the sources used to construct tables 3.1–3.11. A list of the arrival dates at Bristol of some regular traders on direct routes with Virginia and Jamaica is included in Morgan, 'Bristol Merchants and the Colonial Trades', pp. 103–5. For the dominance of regular ships in the Glasgow tobacco trade see Dell, 'Record of the Clyde Tobacco Fleet', pp. 5–6.

[96] Pinney & Tobin to Ulysses Lynch, Nov. 20, 1789, as quoted in Pares, *West-India Fortune*, p. 209.

Table 3.10. *Distribution of regular and occasional ships sailing on direct routes between Bristol and Virginia, 1749–1770*

	Total inwards voyages	Total inwards ships	Regular voyages	Regular ships	Occasional voyages	Occasional ships
1749	11	8	8	5	3	3
1750	5	5	4	4	1	1
1751	6	5	6	5	0	0
1752	9	8	9	8	0	0
1753	11	11	10	10	1	1
1754	13	11	10	9	3	2
1755	12	11	9	9	3	3
1756	12	11	10	10	2	1
1757	19	18	13	12	6	6
1758	13	13	7	7	6	6
1759	10	10	5	5	5	5
1760	10	10	6	6	4	4
1761	6	6	5	5	1	1
1762	4	4	4	4	0	0
1763	7	6	2	2	5	4
1764	6	6	3	3	3	3
1765	9	9	5	5	4	4
1766	10	9	7	6	3	3
1767	10	9	8	7	2	2
1768	8	8	5	5	3	3
1769	7	7	5	5	2	2
1770	7	7	7	7	0	0

Table 3.11. *Distribution of regular and occasional ships sailing on direct routes between Bristol and Jamaica, 1749–1770*

	Total inwards voyages	Total inwards ships	Regular voyages	Regular ships	Occasional voyages	Occasional ships
1749	16	16	7	7	9	9
1750	26	23	17	14	9	9
1751	23	21	14	13	9	8
1752	25	24	16	15	9	9
1753	29	28	17	16	12	12
1754	21	21	15	15	6	6
1755	15	15	11	11	4	4
1756	24	22	16	15	8	7
1757	16	16	10	10	6	6
1758	22	22	11	11	11	11
1759	29	29	16	16	13	13
1760	9	9	7	7	2	2
1761	22	16	17	11	5	5
1762	9	9	6	6	3	3
1763	21	18	15	12	6	6
1764	16	15	13	12	3	3
1765	21	20	15	14	6	6
1766	19	19	15	15	4	4
1767	23	22	14	13	9	9
1768	21	19	16	15	5	4
1769	29	26	21	18	8	8
1770	25	24	17	16	8	8

sugar and other produce brought home – and that could be achieved more rapidly and frequently on shuttle routes rather than via multilateral crossings.[97]

The overall evidence on Bristol's shipping patterns shows that slaving and other multilateral voyages were important parts of the Atlantic trade, but that shipowners were increasingly turning towards direct shipping routes by the mid-eighteenth century. This was particularly the case in trade with colonies such as Virginia and Jamaica, whose staple produce was always keenly in demand in Britain. The preponderance of shuttle voyages among the Bristol ships stemmed from the greater certainty this practice afforded in overcoming time and communication lags, seasonal shifts in prices and markets, and disruptions caused by war, as well as from the opportunities that direct routes provided for establishing close contacts with colonial factors and for settling masters and vessels in regular annual voyages. Direct shipping routes were the safest way to deal with the risks and costs of long-distance seaborne trade a century before oceanic shipping was transformed by the electric cable, the telegraph, and the introduction of steamships into international commerce.

---

[97] This is emphasised in Richard Champion, *Considerations on the Present Situation of Great Britain and the United States of America* . . . (2nd edn., London, 1784), pp. 158–9.

4 The export trade

On outward transatlantic voyages the holds of Bristol vessels were laden with an infinite variety of export wares. These cargoes became an increasingly significant feature of overseas commerce, for English domestic exports quadrupled in value and increasingly found transatlantic markets during the eighteenth century. North America and the West Indies received 11 per cent of English exports in 1700–1 and 16 per cent in 1750–1; they then took 38 per cent of British exports in 1772–3 and 57 per cent in 1797–8.[1] The burgeoning American market for English exports mainly stemmed from rising demand for finished manufactured wares (mainly dry goods and hardware) rather than for crude raw materials and foodstuffs (which were produced either in individual colonies or imported coastwise by one colony from another). In the quarter century before the American Revolution, the range of exports widened to include not only textiles – the major component of export cargoes for centuries – but a variety of manufactures that were probably concentrated at the top and bottom ends of the price range.[2] By 1770 about half of all English exports of ironware, copperware, earthenware, glassware, window glass, printed cotton and linen goods, silk goods and flannels were sent to the colonies plus two-thirds or more of all exports of cordage, sailcloth, iron nails, beaver hats, wrought leather, linen, and Spanish cloth woollen goods.[3] After 1783 textiles renewed their dominance in export cargoes:

[1] Phyllis Deane and W. A. Cole, *British Economic Growth, 1688–1959* (2nd edn., Cambridge, 1967), p. 87. These percentages are based on 'official prices' for exports in the PRO Customs ledgers. Re-exports did not undergo this shift in geographical direction; they were mainly channelled to European markets throughout the eighteenth century. For a summary of the main trends in British exports during the eighteenth century see P. K. O'Brien and S. L. Engerman, 'Exports and the Growth of the British Economy from the Glorious Revolution to the Peace of Amiens' in Barbara L. Solow, ed., *Slavery and the Rise of the Atlantic System* (Cambridge, 1991), pp. 182–7.

[2] Ralph Davis, *A Commercial Revolution: English Overseas Trade in the Seventeenth and Eighteenth Centuries* (London, 1967), pp. 4, 18–20; Jacob M. Price, 'The Transatlantic Economy' in Jack P. Greene and J. R. Pole, eds., *Colonial British America: Essays in the New History of the Early Modern Era* (Baltimore, 1984), p. 35.

[3] John J. McCusker and Russell R. Menard, *The Economy of British America, 1607–1789* (Chapel Hill, NC, 1985), table 13.2, p. 284, and PRO, Customs 3/70.

by 1801 cottons and woollens comprised some 39 per cent of total exports to American markets and 56 per cent of British exports as a whole.[4] Though Britain did not possess 'a fully-fledged export economy' until the mid-Victorian period,[5] the rise of manufactured exports, especially to transatlantic destinations, became a significant feature of British economic growth in the early stages of industrialisation.[6]

The substantial increase in commodities shipped across the Atlantic was fuelled by rapid population growth, rising living standards and changing tastes in America and the West Indies, and by increased purchasing power in both Britain and the Western Hemisphere. Between 1700 and 1800, the population of those parts of North America that became the United States multiplied twenty-fold from 275,000 to 5.3 million people and the per capita income of white settlers rose at an annual rate of between 0.3 and 0.6 per cent (which was comparable to growth rates in Britain and France at that time).[7] Between 1700 and 1790 the predominantly black population of the British Caribbean quadrupled from 148,000 to 570,000 people, while by the 1770s the net worth of white settlers in Jamaica amounted to £1,200 per person.[8] Rising prosperity enabled white colonists to buy a wide array of British exports in what amounted to an Atlantic extension of the consumer revolution of eighteenth-century Britain.[9] The commodities in demand were increasingly fashionable, high quality wares. This was recognised by William Reeve of Bristol. During the Stamp Act crisis, he was asked whether lack of access to British manufactured goods would lead the colonists to abandon their opposition to government revenue measures. He replied, significantly,

[4] N. F. R. Crafts, *British Economic Growth during the Industrial Revolution* (Oxford, 1985), p. 143.
[5] François Crouzet, 'Toward an Export Economy: British Exports during the Industrial Revolution', *Explorations in Economic History*, 17 (1980), 92.
[6] For a more detailed discussion of this theme see Kenneth Morgan, 'Atlantic Trade and British Economic Growth in the Eighteenth Century' in Peter Mathias and John A. Davis, eds., *International Trade and British Economic Growth since the Eighteenth Century* (Oxford, 1994).
[7] US Department of Commerce, Bureau of the Census, *Historical Statistics of the United States: Colonial Times to 1970*, 2 vols. (Washington, DC, 1975), I, Series A 6–8, p. 8, II, Series Z 1–19, p. 1168; McCusker and Menard, *Economy of British America*, pp. 55–60, 268.
[8] McCusker and Menard, *Economy of British America*, table 7.2, p. 154; John J. McCusker, 'Growth, Stagnation or Decline? The Economy of the British West Indies, 1763–1790' in Ronald Hoffman et al., eds., *The Economy of Early America: The Revolutionary Period, 1763–1790* (Charlottesville, VA, 1988), table 1, pp. 277–9, 301 note 29.
[9] For elaboration of this theme see T. H. Breen, 'An Empire of Goods: The Anglicization of Colonial America, 1690–1776', *Journal of British Studies*, 15 (1986), 467–99, and '"Baubles of Britain": The American and Consumer Revolutions of the Eighteenth Century', *Past and Present*, 119 (1988), 73–104; Thomas M. Doerflinger, 'Farmers and Dry Goods in the Philadelphia Market Area, 1750–1800' in Hoffman et al., eds., *The Economy of Early America: The Revolutionary Period, 1763–1790* (Charlottesville, VA, 1988), pp. 166–95.

that 'they can do without some of our coarse manufactures but the fine manufactures they cannot do without'.[10] John Wayles, the father-in-law of Thomas Jefferson, made the same point to the Bristol–Virginia merchants, Farell & Jones. 'In 1740', he commented, 'I don't remember to have seen such a thing as a turkey carpet in the country except a small thing in a bedchamber. Now nothing are so common as Turkey or Wilton Carpets, the whole furniture of the Roomes Elegant & every appearance of opulence.'[11]

Exports undoubtedly comprised a valuable portion of Bristol's transatlantic trade. By the late eighteenth century, contemporaries estimated that a single cargo of goods from Bristol to Boston was worth £40–50,000 and that Bristol ships carried supplies to the West Indies amounting to £250–300,000 per annum.[12] Yet it is virtually impossible to analyse the trends in Bristol's export trade either by volume or by value. For one thing, no annual series of the value of exports exists for any British port in the eighteenth century other than for London; the customs records lump together all other ports under the heading 'outports'. For another, the hundreds of goods and diverse weights and measures listed in the Port Books and *Bristol Presentments* almost defy analysis.[13] Given a lifetime in which to conduct an investigation, it would be possible to use these sources for selected years to calculate the volume of Bristol's exports and then to convert quantities into prices by using the Book of Rates. No historian has attempted this task for any port, and so the export performance of Bristol, Liverpool and Glasgow cannot be compared in any precise statistical way.

Nevertheless, customs records chart the growth of exports and the proportion of English manufactured goods and foreign merchandise in the trade. Table 4.1 indicates the rising value of exports from the outports to transatlantic markets in the first eighty years of the eighteenth century. It shows that most commodities sent to transatlantic markets were

---

[10] 'Testimony of British Merchants on Colonial Trade and the Effects of the Stamp Act, 1766' in Merrill Jensen, ed., *English Historical Documents, IX: American Colonial Documents to 1776* (London, 1955), p. 689.

[11] PRO, T 79/30, John Wayles to Farell & Jones, 30 Aug. 1766, as quoted in Jacob M. Price, *Capital and Credit in British Overseas Trade: The View from the Chesapeake, 1700–1776* (Cambridge, MA, 1980), p. 18.

[12] UMA, Lowbridge Bright to Bright & Milward, 21 Mar. 1771, Lowbridge Bright Letterbook (1765–73), Bright Family Papers; BRO, [Richard Bright], 'Draft of Particulars of the Trade of Bristol, 1788', Bright MSS, Acc. 11168/2c. See also HSP, Thomas Clifford, Jr to John Clifford, 5 Apr. 1785, Clifford Correspondence, VII (1783–5), Pemberton Papers, which reports the loss in the River Severn of a trow with export goods valued at £30–40,000.

[13] The sheer miscellany of commodities exported from Bristol can be seen in the invoices reprinted in Philip L. White, ed., *The Beekman Mercantile Papers, 1746–1799*, 3 vols. (New York, 1956), III, pp. 1404–11.

Table 4.1. *Exports and re-exports sent to North America and the West Indies from the outports of England and Wales, 1700–1780 (annual averages)*

	North America				British West Indies			
	English manufactures		Foreign merchandise		English manufactures		Foreign merchandise	
	£	%	£	%	£	%	£	%
1700–2	64,063	(68.9)	28,945	(31.1)	52,065	(76.0)	16,440	(24.0)
1703–4	54,520	(74.5)	18,655	(25.5)	50,373	(81.7)	11,281	(18.3)
1706–7	69,609	(80.5)	16,904	(19.5)	32,962	(83.5)	6,511	(16.5)
1708–11	64,180	(74.1)	22,400	(25.9)	69,981	(69.4)	30,861	(30.6)
1713–17	88,593	(69.6)	38,668	(30.4)	78,123	(79.8)	19,802	(20.2)
1718–22	92,345	(68.8)	41,923	(31.2)	75,914	(83.3)	15,261	(16.7)
1723–7	106,849	(67.2)	52,077	(32.8)	86,631	(76.1)	27,245	(23.9)
1728–32	109,086	(69.8)	47,100	(30.2)	76,135	(73.9)	26,941	(26.1)
1733–7	120,907	(70.0)	51,833	(30.0)	63,884	(73.5)	23,012	(26.5)
1738–42	154,642	(74.3)	53,350	(25.7)	101,420	(79.8)	25,677	(20.2)
1743–7	139,399	(78.8)	37,405	(21.2)	120,295	(85.0)	21,168	(15.0)
1748–52	187,671	(78.2)	52,172	(21.8)	137,241	(84.6)	24,925	(15.4)
1753–7	214,800	(80.4)	52,233	(19.6)	130,763	(83.6)	25,644	(16.4)
1758–62	247,818	(90.1)	27,296	(9.9)	183,879	(87.1)	27,334	(12.9)
1763–7	374,749	(85.1)	65,519	(14.9)	205,216	(89.0)	25,319	(11.0)
1768–72	494,762	(87.4)	71,354	(12.6)	251,873	(90.1)	27,830	(9.9)
1773–7	297,554	(75.7)	95,472	(24.3)	370,943	(89.4)	43,874	(10.6)
1778–80	205,617	(64.8)	111,264	(35.2)	352,519	(86.5)	55,133	(13.5)

Source: Public Record Office, London, Customs 3/4–80, 82.

English manufactured wares, with re-exports fluctuating from 10 to 35 per cent of English exports to the North American mainland and from 10 to 31 per cent of English exports to the West Indies. The regional distribution of exports was affected by yearly fluctuations, especially at the beginning of wars, and by non-importation measures adopted on three separate occasions in the 1760s and 1770s by Boston, New York and Philadelphia.[14] The overall regional pattern (shown in table 4.2) reveals that between one-third and one-half of English exported wares were always sent to the Caribbean in the eighteenth century. The most notable patterns for mainland America were the increase in goods dispatched to the Middle Colonies in the 1760s and early 1770s, the prominence of English manufactures sent to the Chesapeake until the mid-1770s, and the swift rise in the value of English goods bound for Canada after 1776 when most other American mainland areas, involved in the struggle for independence, stopped being markets for English commodities.

How many Bristolians were involved in the export trade, and how far did they specialise in terms of the goods handled and the geographical areas with which they traded? These matters can best be analysed by breaking down the quantity and destination of exports for a sample year. I have selected 1773 for this exercise partly because it was a peace year in which normal trading conditions prevailed, and partly because exporters named in the *Bristol Presentments* for 1773 can be compared with the names and occupations of tradesmen listed in Bristol's first printed commercial directory, produced by James Sketchley in 1775.[15] The *Bristol Presentments* reveal that 247 people exported goods to the North American/West Indian trading complex in 1773, a higher figure than Sketchley gives for the total number of merchants in Bristol.[16] This apparent discrepancy is not difficult to explain: eighteenth-century business descriptions were often imprecise and few acted only in the capacity in which they described themselves. Sketchley's *Bristol Directory* thus describes many exporters as soap makers, tallow chandlers, wholesale linendrapers, sugar refiners, tobacconists, snuff makers, druggists, owners of glass warehouses, ropemakers, ironmongers and shoemakers,

---

[14] T. S. Ashton, *Economic Fluctuations in England, 1700–1800* (Oxford, 1959), pp. 64, 154. Charleston joined in the second non-importation boycott.

[15] The following section is based on ACRL, *Bristol Presentments*, Exports, 1773, and James Sketchley, *Bristol Directory* (Bristol, 1775; facs. repr., Bath, 1971). Only two of the 49 weekly Presentments are missing for 1773. My figures include details of cargoes taken on ships that touched at ports of call, such as Cork or Madeira, before sailing on to transatlantic destinations. Cf. Joanne Pickering, 'The Bristol–American Export Trade, 1773–1775' (University of Exeter MA thesis, 1983).

[16] Sketchley lists 4,400 tradesmen, including 167 merchants who, together with bankers, were considered of sufficient commercial importance to be also listed separately at the end of the directory (Sketchley's *Bristol Directory* (1775), pp. 111–16).

Table 4.2. *Percentage distribution of exports from the outports of England and Wales to regions of North America and the British West Indies, 1700–1780*

Year	Canada	New England	Middle Colonies/States	Upper South	Lower South	Jamaica	Other West Indies
1700–2	12	6	3	41	1	15	22
1703–4	4	4	1	40	2	20	29
1706–7	7	14	3	42	2	20	22
1708–11	6	7	6	24	4	34	19
1713–17	2	12	10	24	5	20	27
1718–22	3	17	10	22	3	22	23
1723–7	4	18	9	19	4	21	25
1728–32	5	17	12	17	8	17	24
1733–7	9	13	10	23	10	14	21
1738–42	8	8	10	22	13	15	24
1743–7	8	9	5	24	8	19	27
1748–52	11	7	8	24	8	21	21
1753–7	8	5	10	31	8	19	19
1758–62	9	4	9	29	6	17	26
1763–7	9	7	17	24	7	13	23
1768–72	8	4	24	24	6	14	20
1773–7	18	2	12	8	4	25	31
1778–80	23	0	10	0	4	27	36

Source: Public Record Office, London, Customs 3/48–80, 82.

to cite only the most commonly recurring occupations, rather than as merchants. Roger North wrote of Bristol in the late seventeenth century that 'all men that are dealers even in shop trades launch into adventures by sea chiefly to the West India plantations. A poor shopkeeper that sells candles will have a bale of stockings or a piece of stuff for Nevis or Virginia &c.'[17] The same situation obtained at Bristol on the eve of the American Revolution: many exporters listed by Sketchley were small men who had only a minor interest in sending goods across the Atlantic. In 1773 more than half of the Bristol exporters across the Atlantic (135 out of 247) contributed to just one or two export cargoes. They belonged to the artisan classes that accounted for nearly half of Bristol's population at that time.[18]

Four categories of exporters, of varying numerical importance, emerge from the data for 1773.[19] The first group were fifty-three tradesmen who specialised in sending specific products to various colonial destinations. Often these exporters were as much shopkeepers as merchants, and they played little or no part in the major import trades. They included John Powell, George Fownes, William King and Samuel Child, all of whom specialised in the shipment of bottled beer, cider and, in some cases, Hotwell water; Fry, Fripp & Co., Thomas Shapland, and Benjamin Watkins, who concentrated on the export of soap and tallow candles; Booth, Champion & Co., Peach & Henderson, Pope, Munckley & Co. and several other firms dealing in small quantities of refined sugar; Stephen Bagg, a specialist in the export of saddlery and leatherware; Perry & Hayes, who dispatched anvils, pots and wrought iron; and Bence & Lock, who exported shoes. These businessmen tended to dabble in colonial markets where their specialised wares could be sold with profit. Some of them, though operating on a small scale, had wide geographical connections. In 1773 Stephen Bagg provided saddlery and leatherware for no less than twenty-four vessels, including five shipments to Jamaica, five to Virginia, ten to the Carolinas, and two each to Newfoundland and Quebec. In the same year John Freeman & Copper Company, though engaged in less shipments, had even wider geographical connections, sending thirteen small cargoes of metalware to seven destinations: four cargoes to Philadelphia, three to New York, two to Boston, and one each to Grenada, Barbados, Jamaica and St Kitts.

[17] Augustus Jessopp, ed., *The Lives of the Right Hon. F. North ... Hon. Sir D. North*, 3 vols. (London, 1890), I, p. 156.
[18] Elizabeth Baigent, 'Economy and Society in Eighteenth-Century English Towns: Bristol in the 1770s' in Dietrich Denecke and Gareth Shaw, eds., *Urban Historical Geography: Recent Progress in Britain and Germany* (Cambridge, 1988), p. 116.
[19] The following discussion is confined to the 112 men who contributed to more than two transatlantic export cargoes.

A second group of exporters also dispatched specialised commodities but did not distribute them widely; instead they tended to concentrate on just one colony. There were only seven of these tradesmen altogether, and their shipments were very small. At least four seem to have been ironmongers. Thus in 1773 J. Hall sent four small cargoes of different ironwares to the Carolinas, his only other export cargo in that year being a few jars of sun raisins dispatched to Jamaica. In the same year, Robert Rogers sent small quantities of wrought iron on five ships bound to Philadelphia; his only other export shipment in 1773 was a consignment of wrought iron to New York. Thirdly, thirty-eight exporters were relatively unspecialised in the regions with which they traded and in the type of goods they handled. They were virtually all merchants operating, it seems, on a more substantial scale than tradesmen in the first two groups. Two firms sending mixed cargoes to miscellaneous areas in 1773 were Cruger & Mallard and Joseph Smith, Jr. Cruger & Mallard contributed to ten large shipments in all – three each to New York and Philadelphia, and one each to Boston, Piscataqua, Tortola and St Kitts. Smith provided sixteen separate consignments: six to Philadelphia, four to New York, two to Jamaica, and single shipments to Maryland, Virginia, Boston and St Kitts. Similar individual instances could be cited.

Finally, fourteen exporters assembled varied cargoes intended for one or two colonies. They were nearly all merchants, and most handled large shipments. Apart from Lancelot Cowper, who sent six cargoes of metalware to Philadelphia and one shipment to Maryland, and Neufville & Rolleston, whose total exports comprised six mixed cargoes for South Carolina, this group consisted of merchants whose trade centred on the import of valuable staple commodities such as tobacco and sugar. Most leading Bristol sugar merchants, including Robert Lovell, Meyler & Maxse and William Miles, only traded with islands from which they received sugar. Their exports consisted entirely of provisions, plantation equipment and supplies. Leading tobacco merchants also tended to send exports just to the Chesapeake. The only exceptions consisted of very small shipments of tobacco re-exported to Newfoundland by merchants such as Edward Harford, Jr, Farell & Jones, and Lippincott & Brown. This suggests that ancillary exports to areas other than those normally traded with developed from the specialised commodities usually handled by such merchants.[20]

Exporters gathered wares for shipment from Bristol itself, from the wide hinterland of the city, and from the West Midlands and even more

---

[20] Cf. D. W. Jones, 'London Overseas Merchant Groups at the End of the Seventeenth Century and the Moves against the East India Company' (Oxford University D.Phil. thesis, 1970), p. 173.

distant areas. The supply network was highly varied. A number of flourishing industries in Bristol provided goods for export to the colonies as well as for domestic consumption. Among the industries which made Georgian Bristol 'not more a commercial than a manufacturing town' were sugar refining, rum distilling, and smaller enterprises in bricks and tiles, soap, leather, earthenware, chocolate, porter brewing, ceramics, and clay-tobacco pipe making.[21] Those industries all appear in Sketchley's *Bristol Directory* (1775), in which twenty-one breweries are listed as well as eleven soap makers and chandlers, fifteen tanners and leather-dressers, and twenty sugar bakers and refiners.[22] Glass manufacture and the copper and brass industry also supplied many export wares to America and other overseas areas, and thus deserve more detailed attention.

Copper and brass were two of the most important industrial products available in Bristol and its vicinity. The Bristol Brass Wire Company began operations in the city at Baptist Mills in 1702. It later extended its business by establishing warehouses not just locally but also in Birmingham and London. By the 1720s two important copper works at Bristol, situated upstream of the city at Conham and Crew's Hole, were exclusively concerned with brass production. Thirty years later notable copper companies in the city included John Freeman & Copper Company and William Champion's Warmley Company. The latter works pioneered copper smelting, the production of brass and the new process of making zinc all on the same premises. In 1767 the Warmley Company had a capital of £200,000 and employed 2,000 people. Before Champion went bankrupt in 1769, it was apparently the most up-to-date establishment of its kind in England.[23] Today there are still visual reminders in the landscape around Bristol of the once-flourishing industries in copper and brass, with over thirty sites where industrial archaeologists have located copper works, many of which were in operation in the eighteenth century.[24] The *Bristol Presentments* show that many items of brass and

---

[21] F. M. Eden, *The State of the Poor*, 3 vols. (London, 1797), II, p. 183; W. E. Minchinton, 'The Port of Bristol in the Eighteenth Century' in McGrath, ed., *Bristol in the Eighteenth Century*, p. 133; W. J. Pountney, *Old Bristol Potteries* (Bristol, 1920); Iain C. Walker, *The Bristol Clay Tobacco-Pipe Industry* (Bristol, 1971), and *Clay Tobacco-Pipes, with particular reference to the Bristol Industry*, 4 vols. (Ottawa, 1977), vol. B, pp. 451–759.

[22] Sketchley, *Bristol Directory* (1775), pp. 1–110.

[23] Henry Hamilton, *The English Brass and Copper Industries to 1800* (2nd edn., London, 1967), pp. 108–10, 154–6, 300; Arthur Raistrick, *Quakers in Science and Industry* (London, 1950), p. 196; Joan Day, *Bristol Brass: A History of the Industry* (Newton Abbot, 1973); Rhys Jenkins, 'The Copper Works at Redbrook and at Bristol', *TBGAS*, 63 (1942), 145–67.

[24] Day, *Bristol Brass*, pp. 204–19.

copper manufacture, including copper stills and heads for West Indian plantations, were sent to the colonies by Lancelot Cowper, Cruger & Mallard and John Freeman & Copper Company.[25]

Glass manufacture was at least as important as the making of copper and brass in Georgian Bristol. The staple products of the industry in Bristol were flint glass, crown (or window) glass, and ordinary bottles (either dark or pale) rather than decorative glassware.[26] In 1739 Alexander Pope, on a visit to the city, referred to the 'twenty odd pyramids smoking over the town'[27] – that is, the large cones of the glasshouses that dominated the skyline of Bristol. Matthews' *Bristol Directory* of 1793/4, which included a longer entry for glass manufacture than for any other industry, recorded twelve glasshouses in the city and commented on the significance of the industry for Bristol: 'the great demand for glass bottles for the Bristol water, for the exportation of beer, cider and perry; for wine, and for the use of town and country keep the various bottle warehouses here constantly at work. The call for window glass at home, at Bath and in the towns about Bristol in the Western Counties, Wales and from North to South wherever Bristol trade extends, and the great quantities sent to America, employ several houses for this article.'[28]

Glass manufacturers played an important role in Bristol's transatlantic exports. By the 1750s several owners of glass warehouses exported bottled mineral water from the Hotwell spa, sending half the total quantity to Jamaica.[29] By the 1770s glass manufacturers were more frequently exporters of beer to the colonies than were brewers, probably because the glasshouses produced the bottles that contained the beer.[30] Crates of bottles and barrels of beer served as ballast to fill up excess shipping space on outward voyages, while Bristol beer, Bath porter and Taunton ale were in demand in many American markets.[31] Among the exporters of

[25] ACRL, *Bristol Presentments*, Exports, 1773.
[26] For detailed commentary on glassmaking at Bristol see A. C. Powell, 'Glassmaking in Bristol,' *TBGAS*, 47 (1925), 211–57; Francis Buckley, 'The Early Glasshouses in Bristol', *Journal of the Society for Glass Technology*, 9 (1925), 36–61; and Cleo Witt, Cyril Weeden and Arlene Palmer Schwind, *Bristol Glass* (Bristol, 1984).
[27] Quoted in M. D. Lobel and E. M. Carus-Wilson, *Bristol: Historic Towns Atlas* (London, 1975), p. 21.
[28] W. Matthews, *The New History, Survey and Description of the City of Bristol, or Complete Guide and Bristol Directory for the Year 1793–4* (Bristol, 1794), p. 40. A glasshouse, in eighteenth-century usage, was a glass-making kiln.
[29] Sylvia McIntyre, 'The Mineral Water Trade in the Eighteenth Century', *Journal of Transport History*, New Series, 2 (1973–4), 13.
[30] Peter Mathias, *The Brewing Industry in England, 1700–1830* (Cambridge, 1959), pp. 193–4.
[31] *Ibid.*, p. 172; HSP, Waring & Fry to Richard Waln, 3 Oct. 1783, box 5, Richard Waln Papers; UMA, Lowbridge Bright to Bush & Elton, 6, 24 July 1765, Lowbridge Bright Letterbook (1765–73), Bright Family Papers.

bottled beer and cider to the colonies in 1773 were Thomas Lucas, Bush & Elton and John Clark, and among those sending out window glass and other glass wares were Warrens, Cannington & Co., Coghlan, Peach & Co., and Samuel Taylor & Sons.[32]

Bristol's geographical situation and prominent situation in overseas trade made her 'the metropolis of the West' in the eighteenth century.[33] By 1760 the dominance of Bristol over her hinterland was such that Thornbury, a market town a few miles north-west of the city, was 'of no great trade, or business; being swallowed up by the neighbourhood of Bristol'.[34] Waterborne communications were vitally important to the commercial prosperity of the port. The Bristol Avon flowed into the Bristol Channel, which linked the city in a southerly direction with small coastal ports in Somerset, Devon, Cornwall and South Wales, and in a northerly direction with the rivers Severn and Wye, serving both the Welsh Marches and the West Midlands.[35] There was a busy coasting trade – in 1735 alone, for instance, Bristol sent 477 coastwise cargoes to fifty-five ports, especially to Gloucester and Swansea.[36] On the Severn many craft plied their trade to and fro, with trows, of about eighty tons, mainly carrying iron and general cargoes, and the much smaller wherries, only about five or six tons each, carrying bulk cargoes, especially coal.[37] Benjamin Martin stressed the importance of this waterborne carriage of goods when he observed, in 1759, that 'by the Severn and the Wye, the Inhabitants of this City have almost the whole trade of South Wales'. He also underscored the significance of road traffic by adding that 'by land carriage they send goods to Exeter, Bath, Wells, Frome, and all the principal Townes from Southampton to the Banks of the Trent'.[38] By 1750 ninety-six separate road carriers were based in Bristol. They operated from twenty-two locations in the city, mainly inns, and sent waggons to one hundred and seventeen different towns and cities via the turnpike

---

[32] ACRL, *Bristol Presentments*, Exports, 1773.

[33] W. E. Minchinton, 'Bristol – Metropolis of the West in the Eighteenth Century', *TRHS*, 5th Series, 4 (1954), 70–1.

[34] Quoted in John A. Chartres, 'The Marketing of Agricultural Produce in Metropolitan Western England in the Late Seventeenth and Eighteenth Centuries' in M. A. Havinden, ed., *Husbandry and Marketing in the South-West, 1500–1800*, Exeter Papers in Economic History, 8 (Exeter, 1973), p. 65.

[35] Minchinton, 'Bristol – Metropolis of the West', p. 71; T. S. Willan, 'The River Navigation and Trade of the Severn Valley, 1600–1750', *EcHR*, 8 (1937–8), 68–79.

[36] T. S. Willan, *The English Coasting Trade, 1600–1750* (Manchester, 1938), p. 173.

[37] Barrie Trinder, *The Industrial Revolution in Shropshire* (London and Chichester, 1973), p. 105; Grahame Farr, 'Severn Navigation and the Trow', *The Mariner's Mirror*, 32 (1946), 66–95.

[38] Benjamin Martin, *The Natural History of England* (London, 1759), as quoted in Peter T. Marcy, 'Bristol's Roads and Communications on the Eve of the Industrial Revolution, 1740–1780', *TBGAS*, 87 (1968), 149.

roads.[39] Preference between road and water carriage oscillated according to the degree of risk and level of costs, but both modes of transport could be used for single transactions. In 1755, for example, a Bristol firm, buying Yorkshire cloths for shipment to New York, paid for land carriage from Wakefield to Manchester and Bewdley and then hired a trow to bring the goods down the Severn to Bristol.[40]

With these land and water communications, Bristol served as the metropolitan market for the agricultural produce of its hinterland and for industrial raw materials such as timber, tinplate and wool, intended both for local industries and for distribution elsewhere.[41] Many of these products were sold at the two large annual fairs held in Bristol – one beginning on 1 March in Temple Street, the other on 1 September in St James's churchyard.[42] On these occasions 'home manufactures of every description poured in by means of wagons and pack horses, and London mercers and milliners eagerly hired shops in the oddest localities . . . in order to dazzle provincial eyes with their fashionable wares'.[43] Welsh and Midlands ironmasters also visited the Bristol fairs to settle accounts with fellow tradesmen; woollen manufacturers from the provinces were often present; and many local people found the fairs were suitable open marketplaces where they could pay their debts.[44] One merchant noted that goods for export from Bristol were purchased on the best terms before or during these fairs, presumably because competitive prices prevailed at such times.[45] In 1757, for instance, Peach & Pierce of Bristol regretted that orders from an American correspondent had arrived late, 'as our Faire (at which time we can generally with most articles do better) was over before they came to hand'.[46] Yet by the 1790s the fairs had declined and the author of a *Bristol Directory* of 1791 commented that 'in

---

[39] *Ibid.*, pp. 158, 171–2.
[40] New York HS, Thomas Penington & Son, Invoice dated 10 Sept. 1755, David Clarkson Invoices (1751–5).
[41] Minchinton, 'Bristol – Metropolis of the West', pp. 73–6.
[42] These were the times of the two fairs after 1770; before then they were held in January and July.
[43] Latimer, *Annals of Bristol*, pp. 173–4. For an example of an advertisement announcing the forthcoming presence of London businessmen at Bristol fairs see *FFBJ*, 27 Feb. 1773.
[44] Marie B. Rowlands, *Masters and Men in the West Midland Metalware Trades before the Industrial Revolution* (Manchester, 1975), p. 74; Jacob M. Price, ed., *Joshua Johnson's Letterbook, 1771–1774: Letters from a Merchant in London to his Partners in Maryland* (London Record Society, 15, 1979), no. 14, p. 15.
[45] American Philosophical Society, Israel Pemberton, Jr to John Southall, 7 Nov. 1746, Israel Pemberton, Jr Letterbook (1744–7).
[46] Peach & Pierce to James Beekman, 14 Apr. 1757, in White, ed., *Beekman Mercantile Papers*, II, p. 609.

all probability in a very few years, the Bristol fairs, once so famed, will be entirely set aside'.[47]

Besides fairs, export merchants bought goods in Bristol from other outlets. The proliferation of shopkeepers, which accompanied the rise of Bristol as a wholesale centre, provided plenty of wearing apparel, consumable household goods, furnishings and hardware for sale.[48] Linendrapers, haberdashers, mercers and woollen drapers attracted business from merchants and other customers by advertising the wares available in their shops near the centre of the city.[49] Some extended sales by operating warehouses. Already by the 1720s there was a Norwich warehouse at the Sun Inn, outside Lawford's Gate, which sold all sorts of Norwich goods at low rates, plus a warehouse at the upper end of St James's churchyard, where John Shirtcliffe of Sheffield retailed goods from Sheffield and Birmingham.[50] By 1785 silver and plated goods, including knives, forks, jewellery and japanned ware from London, Sheffield and Birmingham, were sold at a warehouse in the Cooper's Hall, King Street at 20 per cent under the usual prices. There were ten thousand articles on display at these premises.[51] Auctions of goods bought from distressed or deceased tradesmen were another way of buying export wares.[52] Auction rooms enabled traders to buy and sell all kinds of commodities on commission. Thus James Bullin's auction room at 37 Bridge Street, Bristol had woollen drapery, hosiery, Kidderminster, Scotch, Yorkshire, Birmingham and other goods on display.[53] Tradesmen also visited provincial towns to investigate wares available outside Bristol, and followed up their trips by ordering goods. For instance, Joseph Shepard, a stocking maker and hosier, travelled to Nottingham in early 1788 and, on his return, received from that city a large and fashion-

[47] *Bristol Directory* (1791), pp. 123–4.
[48] Hoh-Cheung Mui and Lorna H. Mui, *Shops and Shopkeeping in Eighteenth-Century England* (London, 1989), pp. 11, 19, 67–9.
[49] E.g. *Bristol Weekly Intelligencer*, 5 Nov. 1757 (advertisement for Simeon Cox); *Bonner and Middleton's Bristol Journal*, 30 Dec. 1775, 25 June 1785 (advertisements for H. Toye and William & Thomas Chilcott).
[50] *Farley's Bristol Newspaper*, 13 Nov. 1725, 23 Apr. 1726 (advertisements for John Steward and John Shirtcliffe).
[51] *Bonner and Middleton's Bristol Journal*, 6 Aug. 1785 (advertisement for the Cooper's Hall). For further evidence of Bristol warehouses selling textiles see *FFBJ*, 13 Mar. 1790 (advertisements for Hughes & Co. and J. Wright & Co.), and Bailey's *Western and Midland Directory: or Merchant's and Tradesman's Useful Companion for the year 1783*, p. 91.
[52] E.g. *The Bristol Oracle*, 10 Apr. 1742 (advertisement for John Clark); *FFBJ*, 9 Feb. 1788 (advertisement for James Cumming) and 13 Feb. 1790 (advertisement for J. Cowie).
[53] *Bonner and Middleton's Bristol Journal*, 7 May 1785 (advertisement for James Bullin).

able assortment of silk, cotton and hosiery, which he advertised for sale at his premises in Corn Street.[54]

These examples suggest that many goods exported from Bristol did not originate from the city itself but from its hinterland. Access to such wares was aided by capital investment by Bristol merchants in this hinterland, especially in various mining and metal enterprises in South Wales.[55] Bristol merchants helped to finance new ironworks at Abercarn, Cardiff, and Dowlais, near Merthyr Tydfil in the mid-eighteenth century.[56] They also provided capital for the copper industry in South Wales – for the establishment of the White Rock Copper Company in 1737, and for the running of the Longurelach Copper Works, Swansea, around 1780.[57] Most tinplate centres in South Wales were also connected with Bristol in the eighteenth century, and much of the tinplate was exported.[58] Richard Reynolds, James Harford, Richard Summers, William Cowles, James Getley and Edward Garlick, all Bristol merchants, were partners in the Melingriffith tinplate works, near Cardiff, the largest works of its kind anywhere in the world by the late eighteenth century.[59] Some of these merchants can be traced as exporters to the colonies in the 1770s: Reynolds, Getley & Co., for instance, dispatched tinplate and wrought iron to South Carolina, Boston and Philadelphia in 1773 and 1774.[60] All in all, the industrial links between Georgian Bristol and South Wales were extensive enough for Cardiff to become virtually an economic suburb of 'the metropolis of the West'.[61]

Capital investment by Bristolians outside South Wales seems to have been limited, with the important exception of the Coalbrookdale iron-works in Shropshire. Bristol merchant involvement in this famous site, eighty miles up the Severn from Bristol, was substantial. Abraham Darby I, a Bristol Quaker ironfounder, leased a blast furnace there in 1708 and became the first person to introduce the smelting of iron with coke rather

[54] *FFBJ*, 9 Feb. 1788 (advertisement for Joseph Shepard).
[55] Minchinton, 'Bristol – Metropolis of the West', pp. 82–4; A. H. John, *The Industrial Development of South Wales, 1750–1850* (Cardiff, 1950), pp. 8, 25, 31–2.
[56] John, *Industrial Development*, pp. 8, 31–2; Madeleine Elsas, ed., *Iron in the Making: Dowlais Iron Company Letters, 1782–1860* (Cardiff, 1960), p. vii.
[57] John, *Industrial Development*, p. 8; A. H. John, 'Iron and Coal on a Glamorgan Estate, 1700–1740', *EcHR*, 13 (1943), 94; Raistrick, *Quakers in Science and Industry*, pp. 213–14.
[58] W. E. Minchinton, *The British Tinplate Industry: A History* (Oxford, 1957), pp. 18–19; L. J. Williams, 'A Carmarthenshire Ironmaster and the Seven Years' War', *Business History*, 2 (1959), 39.
[59] Minchinton, *British Tinplate Industry*, pp. 20–4; Raistrick, *Quakers in Science and Industry*, pp. 148–51.
[60] ACRL, *Bristol Presentments*, Exports, 1773 and 1774.
[61] Philip Jenkins, 'The Tory Tradition in Eighteenth-Century Cardiff', *Welsh History Review*, XII (1984), 193–5.

than charcoal, a crucial step forward in the production of iron. Other Bristol Quakers, such as the Goldneys and Richard Reynolds, took shares in Coalbrookdale a little later in the eighteenth century. There were also several Bristol partners in five new ironworks opened in Shropshire in the mid-1750s.[62] Nearly all the Bristol merchants concerned with the metal industries in South Wales and Shropshire were Quakers – a reflection of the dominance of this close-knit sect in the ownership and management of ironworks in eighteenth-century Britain.[63] Of the merchants mentioned above, Thomas Goldney sent transatlantic consignments of guns, shot, iron and copper goods from Coalbrookdale via Bristol, and William Reeve, Son & Hill exported ironware to various colonies.[64] Graffin Prankard, another Quaker merchant resident in Bristol, received cast iron pots and kettles from Coalbrookdale for export across the Atlantic.[65]

Bristol merchants also gathered export goods from areas where they did not have any capital investment. This was particularly the case in the cloth trade. Various woollen and worsted goods were exported from Bristol to North America, including camblets, shalloons, tammies, callimancoes, plains, duffils, serges, short cloths, sagathies, single and double bays, duroys, everlastings, minikin bays, penistones, perpets, Barnstaple bays, fearnoughts and harrateens.[66] In 1716 alone Bristol sent 1,410 pieces of kerseys, 14,612 lbs. of serge, 1,067 cwt. of worsted stuffs, 2,906 lbs. of silk and worsted stuffs, and 616 pieces, 115 ells and 1,959 ends of fustians to British colonies in North America and the West Indies.[67] Bristol was in the midst of clothiers, and her merchants bought woollens

---

[62] Wiltshire RO, Thomas Goldney Account Book (1741–68); Trinder, *Industrial Revolution*, pp. 8, 20, 36, 44, app. 1; Arthur Raistrick, *Dynasty of Ironfounders: The Darbys and Coalbrookdale* (London, 1953).

[63] Charles K. Hyde, *Technological Change in the British Iron Industry, 1700–1870* (Princeton, NJ, 1977), p. 16.

[64] Wiltshire RO, Thomas Goldney Account Book (1741–68), fos. 16, 18, 23, 71; ACRL, *Bristol Presentments*, Exports, 1773. William Reeve was a partner in the New Willey ironworks in Shropshire.

[65] J. H. Bettey, 'Graffin Prankard, an Eighteenth-Century Bristol Merchant', *Southern History*, 12 (1991), 35–6.

[66] E.g. PRO, E 190/1179/1, fos. 51v, 54r, 55v, 56v, 57r, 61r and v, 71v; E 190/1211/4, fos. 11r, 23v, 30r, 35v, 41v, 50r, 52r; E 190/1218/2, fos. 8r, 11r, 12r, 13v, 16r, 19v, 37v, 40v, 47v, 48v, 59r; E 190/1225/5, fos. 4r, 8v, 9v, 14r, 15r, 24r, 28r, 38v, 49v, 52v. For descriptions of these textiles see Kenneth Morgan, ed., *An American Quaker in the British Isles: The Travel Journals of Jabez Maud Fisher, 1775–1779* (Oxford, 1992), app. II, pp. 329–34.

[67] Calculated from PRO, E 190/1179/1.

in the West Country and places farther afield.[68] Every Spring one Bristol merchant house usually purchased 3,000 pieces of stuff from makers in Wiveliscombe, Somerset, for export across the Atlantic.[69] Bristol merchants also acquired kerseys, blankets and other woollen goods intended for American markets from Dunster, Exeter, Warminster and Shrewsbury (respectively in Somerset, Devon, Wiltshire and Shropshire).[70] The livelihood of a good many rural clothiers partly depended on export opportunities: trade was stagnant in Chippenham and Devizes in the autumn of 1774, we are told, 'chiefly owing to the merchants in Bristol not making their usual provision for America'.[71]

Bristol exporters to America had particularly close contacts in and around Birmingham and other manufacturing towns in the West Midlands. Though most Birmingham firms produced goods mainly for the home market, a petition of 1766 from manufacturers in the city stated 'that $\frac{3}{4}$ of the Iron Manufactures of this neighbourhood, which are made for exportation, are sent to America, besides great Quantitys of Metal toys, & other articles, to a very considerable amount.'[72] Bristol received significant amounts of bar iron, tinplate and nails from Warwickshire and Worcestershire for export to America.[73] During the 1760s and 1770s Laugher & Hancox of Dudley, Perry & Hayes of Wolverhampton, and three Birmingham firms – Joseph Rabone & Co., Welch, Wilkinson & Startin, and Smith, Son & Russell – were among the businessmen who

---

[68] New England HGS, Henry Cruger, Jr to John Hancock, 18 Mar. 1771, John Hancock Foreign Letters (1764–91), box 27, Hancock Papers; HSP, Thomas Frank to Thomas Clifford & Sons, 11 Sept. 1772, Clifford Correspondence, V (1766–77), Pemberton Papers.

[69] Latimer, *Annals of Bristol*, p. 414.

[70] New Hampshire HS, Invoices nos. 20, 40, 68, 73, 128, 139, John Moffatt Invoice Book (1737–55), box 2, Moffatt-Whipple Papers; HSP, John Reynell Invoice Book (1736–58), fos. 75, 92, 105, 138, 292; Julia de Lacy Mann, ed., *Documents illustrating the Wiltshire Textile Trades in the Eighteenth Century* (Wiltshire Record Society, 19, Devizes, 1964), pp. xiv–xv, xix, 31; South Caroliniana Library, Elias Ball to [?Elias Ball], 21 June 1786, folder 3, Ball Family Papers.

[71] Julia de Lacy Mann, *The Cloth Industry in the West of England from 1640 to 1880* (Oxford, 1971), p. 45.

[72] D. E. C. Eversley, 'The Home Market and Economic Growth in England, 1750–1780' in E. L. Jones and G. E. Mingay, eds., *Land, Labour and Population in the Industrial Revolution: Essays presented to J. D. Chambers* (London, 1967), p. 238; SMV, 'To the Honourable the Commons of Great Britain in Parliament Assembled the humble Petition of the Merchants, Factors & Manufacturers of Birmingham in the County of Warwick . . .', January 1766, bundle 10, Miscellaneous Correspondence (1765–6). For an example of a Bristol merchant travelling to Birmingham to inspect goods there see UMA, Lowbridge Bright to Bright & Milward, 1 Sept., 4 Oct. 1769, Lowbridge Bright Letterbook (1765–73), Bright Family Papers.

[73] Minchinton, ed., *Politics and the Port of Bristol*, p. 134; Kidderminster Public Library, Stour Works General Account, 1772–3, fo. 6, and Brindgwood Iron Works Accounts, 1753–4, fo. 18, Knight MSS.

sent goods to Bristol for export to the colonies.[74] They were all connected with the metal industries or the hardware trades. Laugher & Hancox were ironmongers; Joseph Rabone was a button and 'toy' maker; the three others were merchants.[75] Family ties linked some Midlands manufacturers with Bristol exporters; Joseph Turton, for instance, was an agent for his brothers John Turton & Co. of Birmingham.[76] Some businessmen also maintained warehouses both in Bristol and in the Midlands. Edward and William Gravenor, manufacturers of ribbons at Coventry, kept a warehouse at Bristol in the 1760s. A few years later, William Freeman and Joseph Waldo had warehouses at Birmingham and Bristol.[77] It was not until the very late eighteenth century, however, that manufacturers began to bypass overseas merchants on a significant scale by maintaining depots in ports through which to export goods.[78]

Bristol merchants did not merely acquire goods from the West Country woollen industry and from the Birmingham area; they also tapped a network of suppliers throughout Britain to acquire varied export cargoes. They ordered buttons from the north of England for dispatch to Boston, and took wares from Leeds for shipment to Pennsylvania.[79] They also procured cotton goods from Kendal, Westmorland, for customers in Maryland, and received carpeting and buttons from Scotland plus cotton

[74] HSP, James & Drinker to Laugher & Hancox, 26 Aug. 1773, James & Drinker Foreign Letterbook (1772–85), Henry Drinker Papers; New York HS, Entry of 13 Jan. 1766, Waste book of Henry & John Cruger (1762–8); Maryland HS, John Smith & Sons to Thomas Frank, 23 Mar. 1775, Smith Letterbook (1774–86); Baker Library, Invoices for 1772, Foreign Invoices, 1757–74, box 12, Samuel Abbot Papers (1732–1812); New York HS, Frederick & Philip Rhinelander to Smith, Son & Russell, 7 Nov. 1776, Frederick & Philip Rhinelander Letterbook (1774–83); American Antiquarian Society, Welch, Wilkinson & Startin to Samuel & Stephen Salisbury, 13 Feb. 1773, box 2 folder 5, Salisbury Family Papers.

[75] Bailey's *Western or Midland Directory . . . 1783*, pp. 167, 226; *Sketchley's and Adams's Tradesman's True Guide: Or an Universal Directory for the Towns of Birmingham, Wolverhampton, Walsall, Dudley . . .* (1770), pp. 41, 88.

[76] New Hampshire HS, Woodbury Langdon to Capt. John Langdon, 28 Apr. 1766, box 2, John Langdon Papers (1716–1841).

[77] Baker Library, List of Prices by Edward & William Gravenor, 30 Sept. 1765, box 14 file 22: Prices Current, Bristol, 1765–72, Samuel Abbot Papers; LC, William Freeman to Stephen Collins, 20 Feb. 1772, XIII, Stephen Collins Papers; American Antiquarian Society, Joseph Waldo to Samuel & Stephen Salisbury, 19 March 1773, box 2 folder 5, Salisbury Family Papers.

[78] Stanley D. Chapman, 'British Marketing Enterprise: The Changing Roles of Merchants, Manufacturers, and Financiers, 1700–1860', *BHR*, 53 (1979), 209.

[79] Massachusetts HS, William Wansey to Samuel P. Savage, 17 Aug. 1742, Samuel P. Savage Papers, I (1702–50); Bucks County HS, Kuhn & Risberg to George Ormiston, 28 Feb. 1785, Kuhn & Risberg Letterbook (1785–8).

goods from Manchester for the New York market.[80] These transactions were usually carried out by agents who earned a 5 per cent commission for their services.[81] The way in which particular goods were matched with specialisation in regional manufacturing is illustrated in an order for sundry merchandise drawn up by a Bristol-based firm trading with Philadelphia immediately after the American Revolution. This order included gathering calimancoes from Leeds, Coventry and Halifax; plain cyprus gauze, India persians, satins, callicoes and chintz from London; Manchester tapes, India dimities, drawboys and bobbins from Manchester; cotton and thread hose from Leicester or Nottingham; mittens from Worcester; dark coloured crapes from Norwich; scarf twist from Macclesfield and Leek; and knives, forks and scissors from Sheffield.[82] Evidence from Whitehaven and Glasgow suggests that it was not uncommon for other eighteenth-century merchants to draw on such a wide catchment area for export wares.[83]

Bristol competed with other British ports in the supply of exports to American markets. During the second half of the eighteenth century, when such competition increased, it seems that Liverpudlians gained the edge over Bristolians in the trade. This was particularly the case with textiles. The weaving trade in Bristol seems to have declined during the eighteenth century. In 1722 some 119 weavers lived in St Philip's and the area south of the Avon. By 1784, the number had fallen to twenty-two.[84] Moreover, the West Country woollen industry was generally in decline after the American Revolution. By the 1790s the production of woollen textiles in North Somerset suffered from foreign and regional competition, a failure by entrepreneurs to persist with machinery, inadequate marketing and salesmanship, and an inability to improve transport links

---

[80] Maryland HS, Sedgley, Hilhouse & Berry to Charles Carroll, 1 May 1755, box 7, Carroll-MacCubbin Papers; Peach & Pierce to James Beekman, 1 June 1758, 14 May 1771, in White, ed., *Beekman Mercantile Papers*, II, pp. 612, 886. For the supply of Manchester materials to Bristol see also Beverly Lemire, *Fashion's Favourite: The Cotton Trade and the Consumer in Britain, 1660–1800* (Oxford, 1991), pp. 116–17, 119.

[81] Houghton Library, Henry Cruger, Jr to Nathaniel Carter, 15 July 1771, Palfrey Papers; New York PL, Stewart & Jones to Henry Cruger, Jr, 5 Oct. 1784, Stewart & Jones Letterbook (1784–6).

[82] HSP, Order for sundry merchandise shipped by Thomas Clifford & Co. of Bristol on the account and risque of John Clifford of Philadelphia, n.d. [but *c*.Dec. 1783/Jan. 1784], Clifford Correspondence, VII (1783–5), Pemberton Papers.

[83] J. V. Beckett, *Coal and Tobacco: The Lowthers and the Economic Development of West Cumberland, 1660–1760* (Cambridge, 1981), p. 142; Jacob M. Price, 'Buchanan & Simson, 1759–1763: A Different Kind of Glasgow Firm Trading to the Chesapeake', *WMQ*, 3rd Series, 40 (1983), 35.

[84] Bryan Little, *The City and County of Bristol: A Study in Atlantic Civilization* (London, 1954), p. 173.

to local coalfields.[85] The production of West Country woollens such as druggets, half says and shalloons also diminished at this time. These staple textiles among Bristol's exports were increasingly regarded as unsuitable for wear in the hot climate of the tropical colonies.[86]

Liverpool merchants, by contrast, dealt in cheaper woollens from the West Riding of Yorkshire, which comprised a growing proportion of English woollen exports after 1750. They bought mixed cottons, linens and woollens from Manchester, which were considered superior as articles of everyday clothing on the plantations to serges, baizes and other lighter woollens handled by Bristol merchants.[87] They also tapped the supply of Manchester checks, stripes, osnaburghs and handkerchiefs to monopolise the provision of coarse textiles to West Indian markets, and by this means ousted Bristol's trade in re-exported linen from Germany and France.[88] These developments were already advanced by 1770, the one year in the second half of the eighteenth century for which direct quantitative comparisons are possible. In that year Liverpool dispatched 641,931 yards of British linen plus 42,711 pieces of cotton and linen checks to the colonies, whereas Bristol sent a mere 559 bales of linen to transatlantic markets and no cotton goods whatsoever.[89] By the 1780s Liverpool had added advantages over Bristol in the textile trade, including closer proximity to the burgeoning cotton mills of south Lancashire and more reliable internal communications via the canal network.[90] By linking a well-connected hinterland to a burgeoning Atlantic entrepôt, Liverpudlians were better placed than Bristolians to capitalise on the commercial opportunities made possible by the growth of both home and foreign demand in the early industrial revolution.[91]

[85] B. J. Buchanan, 'Aspects of Capital Formation: Some Insights from North Somerset, 1750–1830', *Southern History*, 8 (1986), p. 88.

[86] BRO, [Richard Bright], 'Draft of Particulars of the Trade of Bristol, 1788', Bright MSS; Thomas Baines, *History of the Commerce and Town of Liverpool* (Liverpool, 1852), pp. 692–3.

[87] Baines, *History of the Commerce and Town of Liverpool*, pp. 692–3; Crouzet, 'Toward an Export Economy', pp. 87–9; R. G. Wilson, 'The Supremacy of the Yorkshire Cloth Industry in the Eighteenth Century' in N. B. Harte and K. G. Ponting, eds., *Textile History and Economic History: Essays in Honour of Miss Julia de Lacy Mann* (Manchester, 1973), pp. 230, 243–4.

[88] *The Stranger in Liverpool; or an Historical and Descriptive View of the Town of Liverpool and its Environs* (Liverpool, 1820), p. 29; J. A. Picton, *Memorials of Liverpool, Historical and Topographical*, 2 vols. (London, 1875), I, p. 168.

[89] PRO, E 190/1228/2; William Enfield, *An Essay Towards the History of Liverpool* (London, 1774), pp. 73–4.

[90] See below, p. 121.

[91] John Langton, 'Liverpool and its Hinterland in the Late Eighteenth Century' in B. L. Anderson and P. J. M. Stoney, eds., *Commerce, Industry and Transport: Studies in Economic Change on Merseyside* (Liverpool, 1983), pp. 1–25.

Bristol exporters faced further problems mainly connected with extension of credit, timing of payments, and impediments to the supply of exports. Bristol merchants earned a $2\frac{1}{2}$ per cent commission for gathering export cargoes and sending goods to their American colleagues.[92] In working out satisfactory commercial procedures, they paid particular attention to the means of payment: goods were either sold at a discount for ready money or on credit for varying periods. The offer of discounts for remittance on receipt of the invoice helped merchants to settle accounts quickly with suppliers, enabled tradesmen to pay their workers' wages, and allowed American merchants to sell goods at competitive prices. Bristol merchants offered cash for coloured plains and duffel blankets from Shropshire for discounts of 5 and $2\frac{1}{2}$ per cent respectively, and purchased cotton goods from Manchester for a 10 per cent deduction.[93] They allowed American merchants a 7–$7\frac{1}{2}$ per cent discount on orders of nails purchased with ready money or with bills at thirty or forty days' sight.[94] An American visitor to Bristol in 1772 suggested that 5 per cent was the maximum discount available there for pewter, tin and other goods, and evidence from mercantile letters indicates that this was generally true.[95] But the situation probably became more flexible after the

[92] E.g. Virginia SL, Lippincott & Brown to William Allason, 22 June 1771, box 6, Allason Papers; New York HS, Invoice no. 9, Barent, Robert & John Sanders: Invoice Book of imported goods (1737–49), and Invoices for Bristol, 17 Feb. 1767, 29 July 1768, Evert Bancker Invoice Book (1764–74); New England HGS, Invoices of sundries bought by Devonsheir & Reeve, 30 Aug. 1764, John Hancock Foreign Invoices: 1764–92, box 28, Hancock Papers; Baker Library, William Reeve, Son & Hill to Samuel Abbot & Co., 8 Sept. 1773, Foreign Letters and Accounts, 1757–87, box 5, Samuel Abbot Papers; HSP, John Reynell Invoice Book (1736–58), Reynell Papers, and Invoices of goods shipped by Freeman & Oseland, 20 Aug. 1760, and Devonsheir, Reeve & Lloyd, 15 Aug. 1760, Jones & Wister Invoice Book (1759–62), Owen Jones Papers; New Hampshire HS, Invoices nos. 10, 17, 20, John Moffatt Invoice Book (1737–55), box 2, Moffatt-Whipple Papers; Scottish RO, Invoices of Devonsheir & Reeve, 20 Nov. 1759, 26 Mar. 1760, 13 Oct., 14 Nov. 1761, Unextracted Processes, CS 237/T4/1; Bristol UL, Invoice of sundries shipped by Evan Baillie & Co., 15 Sept. 1798, box F (1796–1800), Pinney Papers; Somerset RO, Abraham Birkin to Thomas Whitson, 18 Aug. 1701, DD/WHh/1090 pt. 3, Helyar Muniments.
[93] South Caroliniana Library, Invoice of sundry merchandise shipped by Vanderhorst & Davis to Elias Ball, Jr, 2 July 1787, folder 4, Ball Family Papers; PRO, C 107/7: William Rawlinson to Richard Fydell & Co., 23 Feb. 1788, James Rogers Papers.
[94] New England HGS, William Jones to Thomas Hancock, 15 Mar. 1764, Thomas Hancock Foreign Letters (1728–64), box 7, Hancock Papers; Invoice of William Jones, 25 Jan. 1771, and William Jones to Thomas Hubbard, 8 Apr. 1768, Thomas Hubbard Papers; American Antiquarian Society, William Jones to Samuel & Stephen Salisbury, 8 Apr. 1768, box 1 folder 3, Salisbury Family Papers.
[95] LC, Samuel Smith to John Smith, 5 Sept. 1772, Samuel Smith Letterbook (1772–4), box 7, Samuel Smith Papers; William Freeman to Stephen Collins, 27 Dec. 1769, and Lucas, Porter & Coathupe to Stephen Collins, 16 May 1790, X and XLI, Stephen Collins Papers; New York PL, Malcolm Ross to Stewart & Jones, 3 Nov. 1789, box 1, Stewart & Jones Papers.

American Revolution. Some Bristol firms then offered a $7\frac{1}{2}$ per cent discount for the export of glassware paid with ready money and a 10 per cent deduction for Queensware (or, in the latter case, 5 per cent if paid in six months).[96]

The availability of discounts for prompt payment was a major attraction for Bristol merchants buying goods in Birmingham for export to American markets.[97] Welch, Wilkinson & Startin of Birmingham, a leading firm of metal 'toy' manufacturers, offered discounts to Bristol exporters that amounted to $7\frac{1}{2}$ per cent on buckles, 10 per cent on buttons, buckles and links, $12\frac{1}{2}$ per cent on buttons, 15 per cent on links and tea tongs, and 20 per cent on boxes.[98] Another Birmingham firm allowed a $14\frac{1}{2}$ discount on the sale of guns.[99] By the 1770s, Birmingham manufacturers usually offered Bristol tradesmen discounts of 10 to 20 per cent on the price of goods in return for cash payment.[100] This stimulated sales and suited the needs of small manufacturers in the Midland city, who could not afford to trade on credit.[101] To take advantage of such competitive devices, Bristolians needed to be good judges of the price and quality of metalware and hardware for, according to one observer, 'even the Merch[an]t[s] here are afraid & keeps Agents who buy their goods from them'.[102]

Buying and selling goods on credit, however, was a more common commercial practice for Bristol exporters than paying cash for commodities at discounted prices. Credit was already a binding force in the Bristol

96 New York HS, Stewart & Jones to Stevens, Randolph & Co., 26 Nov. 1790, Stewart & Jones Letterbook (1786–95); HSP, Thomas Clifford, Jr to John Clifford, 29 Sept. 1783, Clifford Correspondence, VI (1778–83), Pemberton Papers.
97 Henry Laurens to James Cowles, 7 Mar. 1749, in Philip M. Hamer et al., eds., *The Papers of Henry Laurens* (Columbia, SC, 1968–), I, p. 220.
98 Baker Library, Invoice of hardware sent by Welch, Wilkinson & Startin via George Watson, Jr to Samuel Abbot & Co., 3 Mar. 1772, box 12, Samuel Abbot Papers. Cf. HSP, Invoice of orders addressed by Welch, Wilkinson & Startin via George Watson to Richard Waln, 29 Feb. 1772, Foreign Correspondence: 1761–90, box 5, Richard Waln Papers; LC, Order of goods from Welch, Wilkinson & Startin . . . , 15 Apr. 1767, Stephen Collins Letterbook (1760–73), XVII, Stephen Collins Papers; Baker Library, Invoice of goods addressed by Welch, Wilkinson & Startin via William Seede to Reynell & Coates, 5 Aug. 1770, Reynell & Coates Collection, I (1744–85).
99 PRO, C 107/9: John Whately to Rogers, Blake & Co., 22 Oct. 1789, James Rogers Papers.
100 LC, Samuel Smith to John Smith, 5 Sept. 1772, Samuel Smith Letterbook (1772–4), box 7, Samuel Smith Papers.
101 American Antiquarian Society, Joseph Waldo to Samuel & Stephen Salisbury, 7 Sept. 1773, box 2 folder 5, Salisbury Family Papers.
102 LC, Samuel Smith to John Smith, 5 Sept. 1772, Samuel Smith Letterbook (1772–4), box 7, Samuel Smith Papers. For further contemporary comment on buying goods in Birmingham at a discount see Price, ed., *Joshua Johnson's Letterbook*, no. 41c, p. 39.

merchant community in the Tudor and Stuart periods.[103] This was still true during the eighteenth century. Short-term credit was then 'the most efficient and the most mobile factor of production', while long-term credit underpinned the finance of British foreign trade.[104] Commercial credit had three chief functions for merchants in a trading world with an inadequate money supply. First, many business transactions could be carried out by debit or credit entries in open accounts, thus dispensing with the need for hard or paper money. Secondly, the circulation of bills of exchange from one person to another increased the money supply. Thirdly, credit made use of resources which might otherwise have remained dormant.[105]

An expansion of credit accompanied the rapid increase in British transatlantic exports in the 1750s. Credit terms were enlarged to well-established American merchants, with twelve months being the upper limit. Credit was extended to small, sometimes fledgling, merchants and to shopkeepers. Large numbers of stores or credit outlets were also established, especially in the Chesapeake.[106] These developments occurred as the British economy expanded between 1745 and 1760. When economic growth slackened after 1760, exporters did not extend the length of credit beyond twelve months.[107] Bristol merchants kept within the maximum credit period when dealing with American correspondents, though they offered individual terms as they saw fit. William Reeve gave different credit to different traders – usually six, nine or twelve months – but considered 'nine months good payment'.[108] William Jones, Thomas Frank and Perry & Hayes allowed nine months' credit to individual traders in North America.[109] Stephen Apthorp granted six months' credit to some correspondents and nine months to others, but noted that most

[103] David Harris Sacks, *The Widening Gate: Bristol and the Atlantic Economy, 1450–1700* (Berkeley and Los Angeles, 1991), p. 72.
[104] Peter Mathias, *The Transformation of England: Essays in the Economic and Social History of England in the Eighteenth Century* (London, 1979), p. 98; Price, *Capital and Credit*, p. 117.
[105] Price, *Capital and Credit*, p. 121.
[106] Joseph Ernst, '"Ideology" and an Economic Interpretation of the Revolution' in Alfred F. Young, ed., *The American Revolution: Explorations in the History of American Radicalism* (De Kalb, II, 1976), p. 173.
[107] Marc Egnal, 'The Economic Development of the Thirteen Continental Colonies, 1720–1775', *WMQ*, 3rd Series, 32 (1975), 204, 215–16.
[108] 'Testimony of British Merchants on Colonial Trade . . .' in Jensen, ed., *English Historical Documents, IX*, p. 690.
[109] New England HGS, William Jones to Thomas Hancock, 15 Mar. 1764, Thomas Hancock Foreign Letters (1728–64), box 7 folder 2, Hancock Papers; HSP, Thomas Frank to Joseph Stansbury, 3 Feb. 1773, Coates-Reynell Correspondence (1729–84); Pennsylvania MHC, Entry for Nov. 1796, Joshua Gilpin Journals, XXVIII.

Bristol merchants allowed six months before payment.[110] Thomas Clifford & Co. shipped goods on twelve months' credit.[111]

Secure credit terms were a major priority for colonial merchants. It is therefore not surprising that many American traders opened their correspondence with a new Bristol merchant contact by inquiring about the credit available. Philip Cuyler of New York followed this procedure when he began to deal with Devonsheir, Reeve & Lloyd. In his first letter he asked what credit terms they offered, whether the length of credit varied on different goods, and, if so, on what sort.[112] Similarly, the Bostonian Thomas Hancock, when striking up trade with Morgan Thomas of Bristol, first wanted to know the credit terms on which the latter traded.[113] Presumably commercial arrangements worked out satisfactorily in these two cases since mutual correspondence continued.

Arrangement of credit terms with a new merchant contact did not always proceed so smoothly, however. This can be seen in letters written by Jackson & Bromfield of Newburyport, Massachusetts to two sets of Bristol merchants. Jonathan Jackson, in his first letter as an independent merchant, requested a small cargo of English goods from Devonsheir & Reeve, but specified his intention to conduct 'a cash trade entirely'.[114] Jackson soon changed his mind: he considered that a 5 per cent discount offered by the Bristol firm on cash purchases was insufficient compensation for the loss of a year's credit. One year after his first request, Jackson, now in partnership with Bromfield, announced a change of policy, finding it 'more for our advantage to take your usual credit than to make prompt payment for disco[unt], unless on those articles where the disco[unt]s are pretty large'.[115] Yet this resort to credit transactions presented difficulties, for at this time William Reeve faced financial problems. Reeve had been concerned in transatlantic trade for thirty years, trading with a turnover he himself estimated at 'something less than £100,000 per annum', but he now found, while English exports to

110 Baker Library, Stephen Apthorp to Samuel Abbot, 21 Aug. 1764, 26 Feb., 20 Apr. 1765, Foreign Letters and Accounts, 1757–87, box 5, Samuel Abbot Papers.
111 HSP, Thomas Clifford & Co. to John Clifford, 13 Nov. 1783, Clifford Correspondence, VI (1778–83), Pemberton Papers.
112 New York PL, Philip Cuyler to Devonsheir, Reeve & Lloyd, 15 Aug. 1758, Philip Cuyler Letterbook (1755–60).
113 New England HGS, Thomas Hancock to Morgan Thomas, 12 July 1752, Thomas Hancock Letterbook (1750–62), Hancock Papers.
114 Jonathan Jackson to Devonsheir & Reeve, 13 Feb. 1765, in Kenneth Wiggins Porter, ed., *The Jacksons and the Lees: Two Generations of Massachusetts Merchants*, 2 vols. (Cambridge, MA, 1937), I, p. 157.
115 Jonathan Jackson to Devonsheir & Reeve, 21 Mar. 1766, in *ibid.*, I, pp. 164–5.

America stagnated during the Stamp Act crisis, that American merchants owed him over £150,000.[116] Reeve therefore considered cutting back his business with North America.

Jackson & Bromfield now needed a new correspondent in Bristol. By 1767 they increased their merchant contacts in English ports and were more expert in judging the price and quality of English goods. They now contacted Stephen Apthorp of Bristol and informed him that they wanted to establish a steady correspondence in Bristol; to receive an assortment of dry goods in the correct season; and to pay for the goods on nine months' credit. Once again they inquired what discounts were allowed for payment with ready money, since it would encourage them to send cash with their next orders.[117] This is a good example of colonial merchants becoming more precise and bold in their requests once experience of credit terms granted and dealings with a variety of English businessmen had been established. It also reminds us that, since credit terms were set by English tradesmen, colonial merchants had to shop around for the best suppliers.

Many British merchants over-extended credit to their colonial counterparts. Often the result was large-scale indebtedness by colonial merchants to British suppliers. This became probably the most serious problem encountered by exporters in transatlantic trade. Generous extension of credit was partly caused by over-confidence on the part of British exporters, who granted credit to consolidate and expand trade connections in a competitive commercial world. American merchants fully realised the extent of the problem. This was particularly true of large, well-established firms. One such concern claimed that liberality of credit prevented good colonial correspondents from extending orders to British exporters and that the trade, to be worthwhile, must be concentrated in fewer hands.[118] The difficulty lay mainly in credit being allowed indiscriminately 'to people of little or no capital' so 'that it discourages a man of property from Importing Goods; as it is impossible to sell them whilst the Cr[edit] your side the water is so general'.[119] In 1767 a New

---

[116] 'Testimony of British Merchants on Colonial Trade . . .' in Jensen, ed., *English Historical Documents, IX*, pp. 688–9. The merchant house of William Reeve, Son & Hill was declared bankrupt in 1774 (Minchinton, ed., *Trade of Bristol in the Eighteenth Century*, p. 189; Haverford College Quaker Collection, William Miles *et al.* to Joshua Fisher & Sons, 5 Mar. 1774, box 3-A, Edward Wanton Smith Collection).

[117] Jackson & Bromfield to Stephen Apthorp, 16 Apr. 1767, in Porter, ed., *The Jacksons and the Lees*, I, pp. 178–9.

[118] New England HGS, John Hancock to William Reeve, 3 Sept. 1767, John Hancock Letterbook (1762–83), Hancock Papers.

[119] New Hampshire HS, George Boyd to Cruger & Mallard, 15 Sept. 1773, George Boyd Letterbook (1773–5), Boyd Papers (1773–1821).

England merchant firm noted that 'the English Merchants in general have nobody but themselves to blame for their losses here' because they extended credit to unsound people.[120]

British exporters were fully aware of this precarious situation; some, indeed, tried to deal with the problem. In 1766, Henry Cruger, Jr refused to extend the period of credit to a Rhode Island correspondent, Aaron Lopez, because of the slow remittances he had received. The following year Cruger stated that Lopez owed him £10,500 and that he did not wish to send more exports to North America until his debts were reduced.[121] But Cruger was unable to gather his debts. He had nearly £100,000 owed to him in the colonies in 1772 and £200,000 in 1785.[122] In 1772 Cruger became desperate for remittances shortly after a major credit crisis hit London. 'The late failures in London', he wrote to John Hancock of Boston, 'have given a sensible shock to Credit in this Country. People dun with more than usual earnestness. Wherefore I must request the favor of you to let my linens and other Goods . . . be sold immediately on receipt of this letter, *for the most they will yield* in order that I may without loss of time, *receive a Remittance for the N[et] Proceeds.*'[123] Similar business problems were experienced by other Bristol merchants trading with the American colonies during the financial crisis of 1772–3.[124] One leading Bristol merchant firm noted that the low ebb of credit and uncommon scarcity of money at that time had given them greater business inconvenience than they had ever known.[125] Such financial crises

---

[120] Jackson & Bromfield to William Reeve, 15 Apr. 1767, in Porter, ed., *The Jacksons and the Lees*, I, p. 177.

[121] Henry Cruger, Jr to Aaron Lopez, 30 July 1766, 20 Feb. 1767, in Worthington C. Ford, ed., *The Commerce of Rhode Island, 1726–1800*, 2 vols. (Massachusetts HS Collections, 7th Series, 9, Boston, 1914), I, pp. 169, 188–9.

[122] New England HGS, Henry Cruger, Jr to John Hancock, 1 Aug. 1772, John Hancock Foreign Letters, 1764–91, box 27, Hancock Papers; Thomas Blount to John Gray Blount, 5 Sept. 1785, in Alice Barnwell Keith, ed., *The John Gray Blount Papers*, 2 vols. (Raleigh, NC, 1952, 1959), I, p. 214.

[123] New England HGS, Henry Cruger, Jr to John Hancock, 1 Aug. 1772, John Hancock Foreign Letters, 1764–91, box 27, Hancock Papers. Cf. New York HS, Henry Cruger, Jr to Joshua Delaplaine, 13 July 1772, Joshua Delaplaine Papers. On the credit crisis of 1772 see Price, *Capital and Credit*, ch. 7, and Richard B. Sheridan, 'The British Credit Crisis of 1772 and the American Colonies', *JEcH*, 20 (1960), 164–73. For Cruger's exports to the United States see New York Genealogical and Biographical Society, Bristol Account with Cruger & Co., 1784–9.

[124] American Antiquarian Society, Joseph Waldo to Samuel & Stephen Salisbury, 19 Mar. 1773, and William Jones to Samuel & Stephen Salisbury, 22 Mar. 1773, box 2 folder 5, Salisbury Family Papers; Peach & Pierce to James Beekman, 24 Jan. 1773, in White, ed., *The Beekman Mercantile Papers*, II, p. 891.

[125] Farell & Jones to Richard Randolph, 10 Dec. 1773, in Julian P. Boyd, ed., *The Papers of Thomas Jefferson, vol. 15: 27 March 1789 to 30 November 1789* (Princeton, NJ, 1958), p. 665.

were nerve-wracking because the credit worthiness of even large merchants could 'fall to pieces at once' without them even 'being suspected
till the day they shutt up'.[126]

Facing the possibility of large unpaid debts in the colonies, some
Bristol firms tried to conduct business more prudently. William Freeman,
after the dissolution of his partnership with John Oseland, was advised to
trade with Philadelphia in future by confining business to a few good
houses.[127] Possibly over-extension of credit played some part in this
decision and in the ending of the partnership. Devonsheir & Reeve
resolved, around the time of the Stamp Act crisis, to cut back on trade
with various New England ports, 'as we now (tho very late) Plainly see
that we are hurting you & some other people of Capitall by sending
Inferior People & Crediting Them'.[128] But pruning business built up
gradually via transatlantic letters took time. In 1768 William Reeve, Son
& Hill were still trying to reduce their commercial connections with New
England; they no longer shipped goods to people incapable of furnishing
punctual remittance 'for we can at all times do better with our Capital
than receive 5 p[er] cent [interest] for the over time taken beyond the
credit of 9 Mo[nth]s'.[129]

Most of the above examples on the interrelatedness of credit and debt
in Atlantic trade are taken from commerce with New England, but the
problem was even more serious in the tobacco colonies: planters and
merchants in Virginia, Maryland and North Carolina owed about £2
million to British creditors by 1776.[130] One Bristol merchant partnership
that incurred debts in the Chesapeake was Stevenson, Randolph &
Cheston. This firm experienced such difficulty in collecting debts from
Maryland customers that, in 1770, it proposed dropping the importation
of goods into that province altogether.[131] This drastic action never ma-
terialised, but by early 1774 the firm refused to take export orders from

[126] Hector MacNeal to Neal MacNeale, 22 Jan. 1761, bundle 5, Family Papers of MacNeal
of Tirfergus, Ugadale and Losset.
[127] HSP, James & Drinker to William Freeman, 18 May 1763, James & Drinker Letterbook
(1762–4), Henry Drinker Papers.
[128] Boston Public Library, Devonsheir & Reeve to John Hancock, 23 Oct. 1765, The
Chamberlain Collection of Autographs: The Hancock Papers, II (1763–1816).
[129] Baker Library, William Reeve, Son & Hill to Samuel Abbot, 20 June 1768, Foreign
Letters and Accounts, 1757–87, box 5, Samuel Abbot Papers.
[130] Price, *Capital and Credit*, p. 10. Ch. 2 of this book presents a full discussion of colonial
indebtedness to British merchants. For credit and debt in the Chesapeake in relation to
Bristol merchants see below, pp. 161–5.
[131] Maryland HS, James Cheston to Stevenson, Randolph & Cheston, 10 Oct. 1770, James
Cheston Letterbook (1768–71), box 8, Cheston-Galloway Papers.

new customers.[132] James Cheston, in Baltimore, explained to his partners in Bristol that he was 'really quite tired of Dunning for debts due for Goods shipp'd', adding that 'punctuality in this part of the world need never be expected, & the Merchant who keeps his Capital the most under his own command will in the end ... make the most money tho in the meantime he may not do so much business'.[133] By March 1775 only two or three men in Maryland had sufficient credit-worthiness to receive any goods at all from the Bristol firm. Even so, Stevenson, Randolph & Cheston still had £8,000 sunk in debts in Maryland by late 1775.[134]

'Quick remittance is the life of trade', one Bristol businessman averred, '& besides a Man unless he have [sic] a very great fortune can never ly out of his money'.[135] Bristol merchants needed punctual remittance from American correspondents to avoid outstanding debts in the colonies and to settle their own accounts with English suppliers. There was some variety in the amount of credit time allowed by suppliers to exporters. Among Bristol merchants, Thomas Frank purchased export goods either for cash or on three, six or twelve months' credit, while William Jones and Lowbridge Bright bought commodities on six or twelve months' credit.[136] Twelve months was probably the usual credit time specified by manufacturers before the American Revolution, though sometimes as much as fifteen or eighteen months was allowed.[137] For some articles, however, Bristol exporters were obliged to pay cash to suppliers.[138] This seems to have been the case when buying goods that were particularly subject to rapid price fluctuations.[139]

Bristol exporters tried to pay suppliers punctually in order to establish and maintain their business reputation – a paramount consideration in

[132] Maryland HS, James Cheston to George Maxwel, 20 Jan. 1774, James Cheston Letterbook (1772–6), ibid.
[133] Maryland HS, James Cheston to Stevenson, Randolph & Cheston, 31 Aug. 1774, ibid.
[134] Maryland HS, Stevenson, Randolph & Cheston to James Cheston, 11 Mar. 1775, and William Randolph to James Cheston, 24 Nov. 1775, James Cheston Incoming Letters (1775–82), box 15, ibid.
[135] UMA, Allen Bright to Sankey Hainsworth, 20 Jan. 1752, Allen Bright Letterbook (1751–62), box 25, Bright Family Papers.
[136] LC, Samuel Smith to John Smith, 5 Sept. 1772, Samuel Smith Letterbook (1772–4), box 7, Samuel Smith Papers; New England HGS, William Jones to Thomas Fayerweather, 25 Apr. 1762, John Fayerweather Papers; UMA, Lowbridge Bright to Bright & Milward, 1 Dec. 1769, Lowbridge Bright Letterbook (1765–73), Bright Family Papers.
[137] Price, Capital and Credit, p. 99.
[138] Bristol UL, Tobin & Pinney to Ulysses Lynch, 21 Dec. 1789, Tobin & Pinney Letterbook (1789–92), Pinney Papers.
[139] Rhode Island HS, Protheroe & Claxton to Christopher Champlin, 6 Mar. 1787, folder C-13, Champlin Papers.

eighteenth-century trade –[140] but slow remittances from colonial correspondents often thwarted these intentions. 'Be always punctual in your
payments as Goods become due', William Reeve, Son & Hill wrote to a
Boston merchant in 1773, 'otherwise it will not be in our power to execute
your orders. For as we buy the best Goods, & on the best terms, we are
oblig'd to pay our tradesmen punctually which cant be done without the
same punctuality in our correspondents.'[141] During the Seven Years
War, according to another Bristol firm, 'the payment for ye goods comes
round almost before they are gone from Kingroad & ye scarcity of Money
in England makes tradesmen very hungry for their money'.[142] Prompt
payment was therefore crucial for avoiding indebtedness. Bristolians
might allow nine months' credit on exports supplied to American merchants but only receive three or six months' credit from English manufacturers, who expected to be paid by Christmas for goods purchased in the
course of the year.[143] Moreover, a squeeze on credit occurred when
suppliers encountered hard times. In 1784 and 1785 small-scale manufacturers in the Bristol area were affected by the bankruptcy of some
London firms engaged in American trade, and by the increased need to
supply cash for raw materials and labourers' wages.[144] Bristol-based
exporters to America found, in this situation, that they obtained credit
only for six months at most and that, in some cases, suppliers allowed no
credit at all.[145]

American merchants were often responsible for the lack of remittance
that caused havoc for British exporters trying to pay off suppliers. But
payment for goods and provision of suitable commodities for the return
voyage could be difficult to secure, and lack of remittance was as much
the fault of British as of American merchants. Several regions of mainland North America produced goods that were never in sufficient demand
in Britain to enable ships' holds to be fully laden with those products on
homeward-bound voyages.[146] The Bristol market could only absorb a

---

[140] E.g. Maryland HS, William Stevenson to James Cheston, 15 July 1769, James Cheston
Incoming Letters, 1767–Apr. 1771, box 9, Cheston-Galloway Papers.
[141] Baker Library, William Reeve, Son & Hill to Samuel Abbot & Co., 25 May 1773,
Foreign Letters and Accounts, 1757–87, box 5, Samuel Abbot Papers.
[142] New England HGS, Thomas, Griffiths & Thomas to Thomas Hancock, 25 Feb. 1761,
Thomas Hancock Foreign Letters, 1728–64, box 7, Hancock Papers.
[143] American Antiquarian Society, Joseph Waldo to Samuel & Stephen Salisbury, 7 Sept.
1773, box 2 folder 5, Salisbury Family Papers.
[144] HSP, Thomas Clifford, Jr to John Clifford, 30 Aug. 1784, 27 Feb. 1785, and Bence &
Lock to John Clifford, 11 Feb. 1785, VII (1783–5), Clifford Correspondence, Pemberton Papers.
[145] HSP, Thomas Clifford, Jr to John Clifford, 10 July, 30 Nov. 1784, *ibid*.; Thomas Blount
to John Gray Blount, 5 Sept. 1785, in Keith, ed., *The John Gray Blount Papers*, I, p.
214.
[146] The importance of this point in relation to shipping routes is discussed on p. 66 above.

certain level of commodities that were never in great demand (such as pot ash, dyewoods and oil from New England or lumber and provisions from Pennsylvania).[147] Thus merchants in Philadelphia and New York occasionally sent to Bristol cargoes of mahogany gathered from the Bay of Honduras, Nicaragua wood brought from Curaçao, or wine purchased in Spain and Portugal simply because their own colonies had few commodities currently available that could serve as valuable remittances.[148]

When commodities for consignment to Britain were unavailable, some American merchants made rather desperate attempts to sell their ships abroad to raise money for remittance.[149] More often, however, lack of suitable cargoes also led many colonial merchants to remit bills of exchange to England in payment for goods. A typical example occurred when a Boston merchant sent remittance to Devonsheir & Reeve for goods received and requested that the Bristol firm draw on Barnards & Harrison of London, to whom he had written to honour the bill.[150] At times colonial merchants made more elaborate arrangements in an attempt to secure quick payment. For instance, in 1774 a Philadelphia merchant house enclosed bills of exchange for a Bristol firm 'which tho on Liverpool payable in London and at 90 days yet we were glad to give the money immediately for them at $167\frac{1}{2}$ Exchange in order to make a remittance'.[151] But remittance in bills was sometimes made difficult by the inadequate supply of money in the continental colonies.[152] There was the additional problem of American merchants occasionally supplying bills that could not be accepted.[153]

[147] New England HGS, Henry Cruger, Jr to John Hancock, 18 Mar. 1771, John Hancock Foreign Letters, 1764–91, box 27, Hancock Papers; HSP, James & Drinker to George Champion, 27 Nov. 1769, and to Lancelot Cowper, 11 Dec. 1769, James & Drinker Letterbook (1769–72), Henry Drinker Papers.

[148] HSP, James & Drinker to Lancelot Cowper, 13 Oct. 1770, James & Drinker Letterbook (1769–72), Henry Drinker Papers; New York HS, Henry & John Cruger to Henry Cruger, Jr, 22 Sept. 1766, Henry & John Cruger Letterbook (1766–7); Arthur L. Jensen, *The Maritime Commerce of Colonial Philadelphia* (Madison, WI, 1963), pp. 94–5.

[149] Burton Historical Collection, Detroit Public Library, John Moffatt to William Reeve, 9 Mar. 1768, John Moffatt Letterbook (1762–73).

[150] New England HGS, John Hancock to Devonsheir & Reeve, 7 Aug. 1765, John Hancock Letterbook (1762–83), Hancock Papers.

[151] HSP, James & Drinker to Lancelot Cowper & Co., 23 May 1774, James & Drinker Foreign Letterbook (1772–85), Henry Drinker Papers.

[152] John J. McCusker, *Money and Exchange in Europe and America, 1600–1775: A Handbook* (Chapel Hill, NC, 1978), pp. 117–19; James Beekman to Peach & Pierce, 24 Sept. 1767, in White, ed., *Beekman Mercantile Papers*, II, pp. 866–7; HSP, James & Drinker to Freeman & Oseland, 26 Sept. 1760, 29 May 1762, James & Drinker Letterbook (1759–62), Henry Drinker Papers.

[153] E.g. MacPhaedris-Warner House, Portsmouth, New Hampshire, Cruger & Mallard to Jonathan Warner, 8 Mar. 1775, MacPhaedris-Warner Papers. For an illuminating discussion of the role of bills of exchange in the Atlantic mercantile world of the early

The flow of remittances was hindered by the commercial policies of many British exporters. The expansion of British exports to North America after 1748 frequently led to flooding of the colonial market. Established merchants in North America were encouraged to take more goods by liberal offers of credit from British suppliers, many of whom, in the urge to dispose of their wares, increasingly entered into direct dealings with shopkeepers and other small importers in American ports.[154] Colonial merchants repeatedly complained about the glut of exports. They were particularly concerned when British merchants saddled them with unsolicited goods, a situation which could provoke a variety of responses. Jones & Wister of Philadelphia, after receiving such a cargo, put the goods on one side until Freeman & Oseland of Bristol arranged for disposal of the wares by another merchant in the Quaker city.[155] Another Philadelphian, on receipt of too much earthenware and glassware, found that much of the cargo remained unsold, which led him to consider changing his Bristol correspondent from Thomas Penington to Lancelot Cowper.[156] Thomas Willing, on receiving an unsolicited and unseasonal shipment of cloths from Bristol, hoped to sell the wares at vendue (or auction). He expected them to fetch 10 per cent less than they cost.[157] Yet vendue sales were a last resort for getting rid of unwanted goods, and often resulted in great losses.[158]

At least three other significant difficulties impeded the flow of exports. The first was a result of the seasonal rhythm of the trade. 'Spring goods' were shipped in the New Year to reach America in February or March, while 'Fall goods' were dispatched in June or July to arrive at their markets by September.[159] The following comment by a Philadelphia merchant indicates the types of wares suitable for each season: 'In the last of the winter or early in the Spring [we] choose to import our linens and

modern era see Jacob M. Price, 'Transaction Costs: A Note on Merchant Credit and the Organization of Private Trade' in James D. Tracy, ed., *The Political Economy of Merchant Empires* (Cambridge, 1991), pp. 283–8.

[154] Marc Egnal and Joseph A. Ernst, 'An Economic Interpretation of the American Revolution', *WMQ*, 3rd Series, 29 (1972), 15–16.

[155] HSP, Jones & Wister to Freeman & Oseland, 27 May 1761, Jones & Wister Letterbook (1759–70), Owen Jones Papers.

[156] HSP, Thomas Clifford to Thomas Penington, 14 June 1768, Clifford Letterbook (1767–73), Clifford Correspondence, XXVIII, Pemberton Papers.

[157] HSP, Thomas Willing to William Wansey, 2 June 1756, Willing Letterbook (1754–61).

[158] New England HGS, John Hancock to Henry Cruger, Jr, 7 July 1772, John Hancock Letterbook (1762–83), Hancock Papers. For commentary on vendue sales as a quick means of selling surplus goods for cash in Charleston, New York and Philadelphia in the 1760s and 1770s see Price, *Capital and Credit*, p. 145, and Thomas M. Doerflinger, *A Vigorous Spirit of Enterprise: Merchants and Economic Development in Revolutionary Philadelphia* (Chapel Hill, NC, 1986), p. 171.

[159] Price, ed., *Joshua Johnson's Letterbook*, p. xv.

other things fit for the summer, the latter end of which we should have our woolen goods of all kinds ready for the fall sale to use in winter. The Spring is the best time for ironmongery, cutleryware, furniture for furnishing houses, and all other brass and iron work.'[160] To generate successful sales, exports needed to arrive at their Atlantic destinations by the opening of the season. This was particularly true of woollens.[161] Goods which arrived either too early or too late for the spring or fall season led to complaints from North American merchants.[162] One Philadelphia merchant specifically stated that goods from Bristol were not to be shipped later than the beginning of October, for if they did not reach him by 10 December then they had to be kept until the next year.[163] Goods arriving out of season also forced colonial merchants to remit extra money to British suppliers. In 1759 Devonsheir, Reeve & Lloyd received a typical complaint about this problem from Philip Cuyler, a New York merchant. A large order of 'Fall goods' had not arrived until the end of March, within a month of warmer weather. Cuyler complained that nearly two-thirds of these goods would now lie on hand until next winter, and that this would debar him from paying his Bristol correspondents within the agreed credit period.[164]

Another commercial problem for Bristol exporters was unfavourable competition with London. American merchants quickly noticed price differences between similar goods offered by exporters in the two cities. Some claimed that Bristolians offered cheaper prices than Londoners for comparable types of goods.[165] In most cases, however, Bristol compared

160 Thomas Clifford to Abel Chapman, 25 July 1767, as quoted in James F. Shepherd and Gary M. Walton, *Shipping, Maritime Trade and the Economic Development of Colonial North America* (Cambridge, 1972), pp. 107–8.
161 Bucks County HS, Kuhn & Risberg to Henry Cruger, 22 May 1784, Kuhn & Risberg Letterbook (1779–85).
162 E.g. Montgomery Collection, Columbia University, John Ludlow to Peach & Pierce, 14 Jan. 1757, John Ludlow Letterbook (1752–63); HSP, Thomas Willing to William Wansey, 19 Aug. 1755, Willing Letterbook (1754–61); Thomas Rasberry to Devonsheir, Reeve & Lloyd, 27 Mar. 1759, in Hawes, ed., 'The Letterbook of Thomas Rasberry, 1758–1761', pt. 3, *Georgia Historical Quarterly*, 41 (1957), 66; New York PL, Thomas Moffatt to John Angier, 11 Oct. 1715, Thomas Moffatt Letterbook (1714–16).
163 HSP, John Kidd to John Perks, 24 July 1758, John Kidd Letterbook (1749–63).
164 New York PL, Philip Cuyler to Devonsheir, Reeve & Lloyd, 12 May 1759, Philip Cuyler Letterbook (1755–60). Colonial merchants also drew attention to goods that arrived in faulty condition: see, for instance, Austin & Laurens to Corsley Rogers & Son, 16 May 1755, in Hamer *et al.*, eds., *Papers of Henry Laurens*, I, p. 248, and HSP, James & Drinker to Freeman & Oseland, 6 Dec. 1760, James & Drinker Letterbook (1759–62), Henry Drinker Papers.
165 E.g. James Duncan Phillips Library, The Essex Institute, Samuel Curwen to Hayley & Hopkins, 25 Oct. 1771, Samuel Curwen Letterbook (1771–5); Massachusetts HS, Benjamin Dolbeare to Benjamin Henshaw, 23 June 1753, and to Tappenden & Hanbey, 7 Sept. 1764, Benjamin Dolbeare Letterbook (1739–67).

unfavourably.[166] In 1773 a merchant in Portsmouth, New Hampshire, observed that the price differences between London and Bristol 'would soon ruin a man that trades large Quantities of goods from Bristol all charg'd at such an extraordinary rate. People that Imports Stores from London can afford to sell them here, cheaper than yours are charg'd at Bristol.'[167] London also had access to a wider range and quantity of goods than Bristol, and therefore became a more reliable supplier of exports than 'the metropolis of the West'. In the early 1770s, a Savannah merchant explained that white plains were usually received from Bristol but that London was now a more certain source of supply for these woollens.[168] At the same time, a Bostonian noted to Henry Cruger, Jr that 'the trade of Your Place seems greatly Diminish'd. Many who were wont to send to Bristol for articles now import wholly from London.'[169] A decade later, an attorney on a sugar estate in Antigua claimed that plantation stores from London were superior to those from Bristol: temper lime from Bristol was not as good as it used to be and 'the copper from Bristol is soft, and soon burns out; the Nails are clumsy, and their threads break off in driving; and the Beans are seldom or never Kiln dried, and will not keep'.[170]

A final recurrent difficulty in the export trade consisted of problems arising in the inland supply network in Britain. Delays, labour shortages and poor co-ordination between packers, carriers, manufacturers and export merchants were three of the major obstacles.[171] Bristol merchants were often obliged to gather many goods from country areas, which unavoidably delayed shipment.[172] On some occasions carriers taking

---

[166] E.g. Montgomery Collection, Columbia University, John Ludlow to Peach & Pierce, 24 Nov. 1758, John Ludlow Letterbook (1752–62); HSP, James & Drinker to Freeman & Oseland, 6 Dec. 1760, James & Drinker Letterbook (1759–62), Henry Drinker Papers; Maryland HS, Samuel & John Smith to John Noble, 20 May 1784, John Smith & Sons Letterbook (1774–86), Smith Letterbooks.

[167] New Hampshire HS, George Boyd to Cruger & Mallard, 20 Aug. 1773, George Boyd Letterbook (1773–5), Boyd Papers (1773–1821).

[168] Georgia HS, Joseph Clay & Co. to Benjamin Stead, 23 Jan. 1773, Joseph Clay & Co. Letterbook (1772–4), Joseph Clay & Company Papers.

[169] New England HGS, John Hancock to Henry Cruger, Jr, 12 Dec. 1771, John Hancock Letterbook (1762–83), Hancock Papers.

[170] Somerset RO, Main Swete Walrond to [? Tudway], 30 Aug. 1785, box 11, bundle 6, Tudway MSS, DD/TD. A Bristol merchant house claimed, on the contrary, that plantation stores were sent on better terms from Bristol than from London (Bristol UL, Tobin & Pinney to Monsieur Dessalle, 18 Nov. 1794, Tobin & Pinney Letterbook (1792–6), Pinney Papers).

[171] The causes of delays are usefully discussed in Philip L. White, *The Beekmans of New York in Politics and Commerce, 1647–1877* (New York, 1956), pp. 368–72.

[172] Baker Library, Stephen Apthorp to Samuel Abbot, 30 Apr. 1767, Foreign Letters and Accounts, 1757–87, box 5, file 4, Samuel Abbot Papers.

inland goods to Bristol for exportation either lost the goods or delivered them to the wrong merchants. At other times inland wares arrived so late that there was no time for Bristol exporters to examine them before they were loaded on board ship.[173]

Delays were not entirely the fault of suppliers, for defects existed in Bristol's inland transport network in the early canal age. A Philadelphia merchant, writing in 1793 about increased exports of British hardware to the United States, and observing that the quantity sent from Bristol had diminished since the War of Independence, noted that 'the carriage of goods from Birmingham is less than from that place to Liverpool', and wondered 'why then should the latter have the preference?'[174] A contemporary description provided the answer. According to Richard Bright, the timing of sending hardware to Liverpool via the canal network from Staffordshire, Shropshire and Warwickshire was certain in all seasons whereas the carriage of goods from those counties to Bristol was hampered by frequent delays on the River Severn due to variable tides, lack of water in summer, and floods and bad weather in winter. Lower transport costs and a shorter distance from Birmingham and the Black Country were thus less significant than certainty of dispatch from the same area to Liverpool.[175]

Delays were sometimes exacerbated by labour shortages in wartime. In August 1759, in the middle of the Seven Years War, Thomas, Griffiths & Thomas noted that 'goods of all kinds are extremely scarce & dear oweing to great Demands & want of workmen'.[176] John Lidderdale, a Scotsman trading at Bristol, reported the same problem just a month later when he explained to a Virginia planter that 'the Laboring People are engag'd in the Land & Sea Service & in the national militia, in so much, that labor is dear & few Manufacturers to be employ'd w[hi]ch makes inland Manufactures scarce & dear'.[177] Even in the last year of the war, Peach & Pierce of Bristol had to delay sending cargoes of linen checks to New York because inland manufacturers, crippled by high prices, were forced to employ less weavers than usual.[178]

---

[173] Peach & Pierce to James Beekman, 1 Aug. 1765, 6 Apr. 1767, 25 July 1771, in White, ed., *Beekman Mercantile Papers*, II, pp. 860, 865, 888.

[174] HSP, John Clifford to Thomas Clifford, Jr, 27 Feb. 1793, Clifford Correspondence, X (1790–4), Pemberton Papers.

[175] BRO, [Richard Bright], 'Draft of Particulars of the Trade of Bristol, 1788', Bright MSS, Acc. 11168/2c. For delays on the Severn in winter see also UMA, Lowbridge Bright to Thompson & Whitlaw, 12 Feb. 1771, Lowbridge Bright Letterbook (1765–73), Bright Family Papers.

[176] New England HGS, Thomas, Griffiths & Thomas to Thomas Hancock, 20 Aug. 1759, Thomas Hancock Foreign Letters, 1728–64, box 7 folder 2, Hancock Papers.

[177] Virginia SL, John Lidderdale to Andrew Sprowl, 29 Sept. 1759, box 2, Allason Papers.

[178] Peach & Pierce to James Beekman, 12 Aug. 1763, in White, ed., *Beekman Mercantile Papers*, II, p. 620.

Sharp fluctuations in demand for labour (particularly at the time of the colonial non-importation agreements) could lead to significant losses of manufacturing 'hands' and thus restrict future production. During the Stamp Act crisis, William Reeve withdrew an export order for nails to the value of £16–20,000, with the result that 300 nailmakers were turned away in one day.[179] William Jones, writing to Boston during the non-importation agreement of 1769, explained how labour scarcity could be created by politics. He expected the unpopular Townshend duties to be repealed soon and considered that this would promote good orders for exports – especially nails and ironmongery – in the following Spring. He then referred to 'the great Scarcity of Workmen, the proper hands for Manufacturing our Exports having for want of Business in their own branches gone to the Canalls & other various works where they could get employ, from whence they will not return without great Expence. This circumstance will also render it very difficult to execute large orders & tho a Repeal takes place, yet in my opinion 'twill be some time before our Manufactories are again well settled.'[180]

Difficulties also arose between Bristol merchants and makers of goods. This is well illustrated in correspondence between Peach & Pierce of Bristol and James Beekman of New York. Beekman complained to the Bristol firm when he received unsatisfactory goods. Peach & Pierce admitted that they themselves were sometimes to blame because they placed too much confidence in the makers of some wares.[181] They tried to maintain good business relations with Beekman by allowing him to dispose of faulty goods on their account.[182] But sometimes the fault lay not with the Bristol firm but with manufacturers who failed to observe directions properly. Thus in 1767 Beekman's complaints about the colours of fustians and shalloons were attributed by Peach & Pierce to their dyers not keeping to their instructions.[183] Apart from carelessness, there was occasionally some justification for such errors – as, for instance, in 1772 when one supplier of export goods to the Bristol firm found that the great demand at that time prevented any control over his workmen.[184] Excessive demand for exports caused problems for other Bristol

---

[179] 'Testimony of British Merchants on Colonial Trade ... ' in Jensen, ed., *English Historical Documents, IX*, p. 689.

[180] New England HGS, William Jones to Thomas Hubbard, 19 Oct. 1769, Thomas Hubbard Papers. Cf. American Antiquarian Society, William Jones to Samuel & Stephen Salisbury, 19 Oct. 1769, box 2 folder 1, Salisbury Family Papers.

[181] Peach & Pierce to James Beekman, 8 Dec. 1759, in White, ed., *Beekman Mercantile Papers*, II, p. 616.

[182] Peach & Pierce to James Beekman, 8 Apr. 1760, in *ibid.*, p. 616.

[183] Peach & Pierce to James Beekman, 28 Aug. 1767, in *ibid.*, p. 866.

[184] Peach & Pierce to James Beekman, 6 Feb. 1772, in *ibid.*, p. 889.

merchants in dealing with suppliers. In such circumstances manufacturers found difficulty in maintaining the pace of production, workmen sometimes slighted their work to meet deadlines, and exporters often needed to place orders for goods at least a year ahead of their needs.[185]

Bristol merchants sometimes faced the additional difficulty of filling up excess cargo space on outward voyages, for goods shipped to transatlantic markets were usually relatively high in value but light in volume. One solution was to send ships to southern Irish ports, which were the last victualling points before the beginning of an Atlantic voyage. Provisions such as salt pork, beef, butter and herrings were thus frequently loaded at Cork, Waterford, Youghall and Kinsale, either as victuals for the crew or for sale primarily in the Caribbean and Newfoundland. This trade emerged out of long-standing commercial connections between Bristol and Ireland. Irish merchants transacted the business on behalf of merchant principals in Bristol and other British ports in return for a standard commission of $2\frac{1}{2}$ per cent for their services.[186] Sometimes Bristolians entered into elaborate commercial arrangements for such trade. For a voyage in 1719 of the *Sarah* from Bristol to Cork, Madeira, Barbados and the Leeward Islands, Richard Farr and John Stephens each took a one-third share in 300 barrels of herrings purchased at Cork from the firm of Falkner & Callwell. The captain of the vessel, Archibald MacPhaedris, held the other one-third share. The herrings were sold at Madeira and the proceeds taken in wine, which was exchanged for cotton and muscovado sugar in the Caribbean.[187]

Bristolians tended to send their West India vessels to Irish ports at the beginning of the slaughtering season.[188] They provided orders for ship

---

[185] South Caroliniana Library, Elias Ball to Elias Ball, 19 Jan. 1793, folder 13, Ball Family Papers; PRO, C 107/8: Robinson's & Heywood to James Rogers & Co., 13 May 1791, James Rogers Papers; New England HGS, William Jones to Thomas Hancock, 25 Apr. 1762, Thomas Hancock Foreign Letters (1728–64), box 7, Hancock Papers.

[186] F. G. James, 'Irish Colonial Trade in the Eighteenth Century', *WMQ*, 3rd Series, 20 (1963), 574–84; David Dickson, 'An Economic History of the Cork Region in the Eighteenth Century' (University of Dublin Ph.D. thesis, 1977), pp. 477–80; John Mannion, 'The Waterford Merchants and the Irish–Newfoundland Provisions Trade, 1770–1820' in Paul Butel and L. M. Cullen, eds., *Trade and Industry in France and Ireland in the Seventeenth and Eighteenth Centuries* (Paris, 1980), pp. 27–43; R. C. Nash, 'Irish Atlantic Trade in the Seventeenth and Eighteenth Centuries', *WMQ*, 3rd Series, 42 (1985), 329–56; Thomas M. Truxes, *Irish–American Trade, 1660–1783* (Cambridge, 1988), ch. 8.

[187] MacPhaedris-Warner House, Richard Farr & John Stephens to Archibald McFeders, 26 Oct. 1719, MacPhaedris-Warner Papers.

[188] Derbyshire RO, Mark Davis & Co. to W. P. Perrin, 19 Sept. 1774, Fitzherbert MSS: West Indian Papers, 239M/E19957.

captains to forward to Irish correspondents. For the voyage of the *Union* to Cork and Jamaica in 1778, for example, the Bristol owners instructed Richard Hare of Cork to procure extra freight because the ship was not full; to provide sundry provisions for the crew; to liaise with the captain and advance him any money needed for port charges and disbursements; and to ensure that the *Union* sailed with the convoy from Cork.[189] Hare, for his part, informed his Bristol correspondents about commodity prices at Cork, about livestock products he had bought for Bristol West Indiamen, and about bills he had drawn on Bristol merchants.[190] Dispatching Irish provisions to specific West Indian planters helped to secure return cargoes of tropical produce from the same people – an important consideration given the risks of trade in Caribbean waters.[191] But the Irish provisions trade only accounted, around 1770, for less than 9 per cent of the annual value of exports from England and Scotland.[192] Moreover Bristol merchants quickly cut back on shipping provisions from southern Ireland when high purchase prices seemed to preclude profits, except in cases where they felt confident in reaching West Indian markets expeditiously.[193]

Another solution to the imbalance of exports and imports in Atlantic trade consisted of shipping passengers to North America and the West Indies. Bristol merchants were fully involved in this traffic. They were particularly concerned with the recruitment of indentured servants and convicts. The trade in bonded servants was one where people wishing to emigrate to America, but unable to pay their passage, indentured themselves to a merchant or ship captain. In return for a free Atlantic crossing their masters were allowed to sell their labour for usually four, five or seven years to purchasers in the colonies. At the expiry of their service, indentured servants sometimes received freedom dues of land. At times this (more or less) voluntary form of migration led to forcible rounding up of young people by unscrupulous dealers desperate to fill up space on

---

[189] William L. Clements Library, Lowbridge & Richard Bright and Davis & Protheroe to Richard Hare, 26 July 1778, Voyage of the *Union*, Bristol Shipping Account Books, IV. For similar examples see Bristol UL, John Pinney to Peter Eaton, 3 June 1776, John Pinney Letterbook (1775–8), Pinney Papers; Cambridge RO, William Miles to John Tharp, 28 Sept. 1771, Tharp Papers.

[190] Cork Archives, Richard Hare to Robert Gordon, 29 July 1771, to Samuel Delpratt, 18 Oct. 1771, to William Miles, 24 Oct. 1771, and to Samuel Munckley, 7 Mar. 1772, Richard Hare Letterbook (1771–2).

[191] BRO, Thomas Harris & Henry Bright to Robert Wallace, 10 Aug. 1758, Voyage of the *Ruby*, Ships' Accounts, Acc. 39654(1).

[192] Shepherd and Walton, *Shipping, Maritime Trade*, pp. 111–12.

[193] UMA, Lowbridge Bright to Henry Bright, 11 Nov. 1765, and to Bright & Milward, 24 February 1767; Lowbridge Bright Letterbook (1765–73), Bright Family Papers.

board ship.[194] More commonly, though, Bristol traders advertised for servants in local newspapers and American merchants often specified in correspondence the expected age, sex, skills, price and anticipated season of arrival.[195] Sometimes attention was paid to the recruitment of servants in relation to the volume of a ship's export cargo: one Philadelphia merchant house requested servants from Bristol particularly if the ship should come out considerably short of a full freight with room to accommodate servants.[196] Another Philadelphia firm suggested that it might occasionally be worth omitting some export wares to create room for servants, and that chartered ships might remain at Bristol longer than specified if there was a possibility of taking servants.[197] Thus it was considered beneficial for ships to remain at Hungroad and Kingroad for some while to fill up with servants, even if this entailed extra expense for the lighterage of goods from the centre of Bristol to the vessels.[198]

The indentured servant trade fluctuated according to availability of servants and pressure of demand. Over time there was also a trend towards recruitment of more skilled servants.[199] The trade reached its height between 1654 and 1686, when over 10,000 indentured servants left Bristol for Virginia, Barbados, Nevis and other colonies, where they were snapped up by buyers in search of cheap white labour.[200] Improving economic opportunities and rising wage levels at home stemmed the flow of servants for many years thereafter, but the trade revived to some

---

[194] Latimer, *Annals of Bristol*, p. 153; H. B. Jameson, 'Bonded Servants on the North American Continent in the Eighteenth Century: Some New Evidence from Bristol', *TBGAS*, 99 (1981), 127–40.

[195] E.g. *FFBJ*, 6 Feb., 19 Mar., 29 Apr., 27 Aug. 1768; Maryland HS, John Smith & Sons to Daniel Lawrence, 3 Dec. 1774, Smith Letterbook (1774–86); HSP, Charles Willing & Son to John Perks, 2 Oct. 1754, Willing Letterbook (1754–61); MacInnes, *Bristol: A Gateway of Empire*, p. 160.

[196] HSP, James & Drinker to Lancelot Cowper & Co., 4 Aug. 1774, James & Drinker Foreign Letterbook (1772–85), Henry Drinker Papers.

[197] HSP, Thomas Clifford to Capt. Samuel Smith, 15 Nov. 1762, and to Lancelot Cowper, 17 May 1768, Clifford Letterbooks (1759–66, 1767–73), Clifford Correspondence, XXVII and XXVIII, Pemberton Papers. For detailed commentary on Clifford's importation of servants from Bristol see Grace Hutchison Larsen, 'Profile of a Colonial Merchant: Thomas Clifford of Pre-Revolutionary Philadelphia' (Columbia University Ph.D. dissertation, 1955), pp. 110–24.

[198] HSP, James & Drinker to Lancelot Cowper, 16 Sept. 1773, James & Drinker Letterbook (1772–85), Henry Drinker Papers.

[199] This is a major theme in David W. Galenson, *White Servitude in Colonial America: An Economic Analysis* (Cambridge, 1981).

[200] See especially *ibid.*; David Souden, '"Rogues, whores, and vagabonds"?: Indentured Servant Emigrants to North America and the Case of Mid-Seventeenth Century Bristol', *Social History*, 3 (1978), 23–41; James Horn, 'Servant Emigration to the Chesapeake in the Seventeenth Century' in Thad W. Tate and David L. Ammerman, eds., *The Chesapeake in the Seventeenth Century: Essays on Anglo–American Society* (Chapel Hill, NC, 1979), pp. 51–95; and Sacks, *Widening Gate*, pp. 251–303.

extent in the generation before the American Revolution. We know that 125 bonded servants left Bristol for the colonies between 1763 and 1768, and that 707 were shipped from Bristol to Maryland in the period 1749–75.[201] Printed notices and newspaper advertisements also record a regular flow of ships carrying servants from Bristol to Philadelphia in the half century before the American Revolution.[202] The overall number of servants carried is unavailable for most other eighteenth-century years, but it seems that the supply of indentured labour was always less elastic than that of another group of migrants dispatched from Bristol: convicts exiled to the colonies.

The convict trade was officially established in 1718 as an important secondary punishment for certain criminal offences, notably non-capital crimes against property such as grand larceny and petty larceny (defined respectively as theft of goods worth more than a shilling or less than a shilling). Convicts were sentenced to either seven or fourteen years' labour in the colonies, depending on the nature of their crime, though a minority, usually rapists or murderers, were sent for life.[203] This form of enforced migration was managed by a small group of exclusive operators who liaised closely with JPs and gaolers in order to gain access to felons. The supply of felons was steady and there was a constant demand for them in Virginia and Maryland, the chief dumping grounds for convicts. By the late 1760s, male convicts sold for about a third of the price of young male slaves in the Chesapeake, and were employed in plantation work, in the craft and construction trades, and at iron works. Some convicts were unskilled labourers but others had, or acquired, occupational skills as they served their sentences.[204]

[201] Jameson, 'Bonded Servants on the North American Continent', p. 128; Abbot Emerson Smith, *Colonists in Bondage: White Servitude and Convict Labor in America, 1607–1776* (Chapel Hill, NC, 1947), p. 325. For an analysis of indentured servants shipped from Bristol to North America between 1773 and 1775 see Bernard Bailyn, *Voyagers to the West: Emigration from Britain on the Eve of the American Revolution* (New York, 1986), pp. 114–18, 229, 289.

[202] E.g. ACRL, Jefferies MSS, VIII, fo. 3r; *American Weekly Mercury*, 25 Oct. 1722, 16 May 1723, 26 Dec. 1727, 16 May, 25 July, 17 Oct. 1728, 22 May 1729, 4 Jan. 1732, 26 Aug. 1736, 19, 26 Mar., 7 May 1741, 6 Sept. 1744; *Pennsylvania Gazette*, 23 Sept. 1742, 20 Sept. 1744, 22 Jan. 1745, 14 June 1750, 26 Sept. 1751, 21 May 1752, 1 Dec. 1768, 18 May, 12 Oct., 16 Nov. 1769, 3 May, 1 Nov. 1770, 1 Aug. 1771, 18 Nov. 1772. Sharon V. Salinger supplied me with the newspaper references.

[203] Smith, *Colonists in Bondage*, pp. 111–12.

[204] These aspects of the Bristol convict trade are analysed in Kenneth Morgan, 'The Organization of the Convict Trade to Maryland: Stevenson, Randolph & Cheston, 1768–1775', *WMQ*, 3rd Series, 42 (1985), 201–27, and 'Convict Transportation from Devon to America' in H. E. S. Fisher *et al.*, eds., *A New Maritime History of Devon*, 2 vols. (1993), I, pp. 121–2. See also George Lamoine, ed., *Bristol Gaol Delivery Fiats, 1741–1799* (Bristol Record Society's *Publications*, 40, 1989) and John F. Mackeson, *Bristol Transported* (Bristol, 1987), pp. 36–60.

A trickle of felons was conveyed from Bristol to the colonies on a voluntary basis before 1718.[205] But many more were transported between the latter date and 1775, when the traffic was cut off by war. During that period, probably about 10,000 of the 50,000 convicts sent from the British Isles to the Chesapeake sailed from Bristol.[206] The Bristol convict trade to Maryland was dominated by two firms in the years from 1746 to 1775 – Sedgley, Hilhouse & Randolph and Stevenson, Randolph & Cheston.[207] But though shipment of convicts and indentured servants provided useful extra earnings for Bristol merchants, neither trade was substantial enough to affect the overall performance of Bristol's Atlantic commerce in the eighteenth century. Another form of human cargo was much more important, as the next chapter shows: the traffic in slaves from West Africa to the New World plantations.

[205] Based on evidence in Peter Wilson Coldham, *Bonded Passengers to America, vol. V: Western Circuit, 1664–1775* (Baltimore, 1983).

[206] A conservative estimate of Bristol's share of the convict trade, inferred from A. Roger Ekirch, *Bound for America: The Transportation of Convicts to the Colonies, 1718–1775* (Oxford, 1987), pp. 23–7, 72–3.

[207] Smith, *Colonists in Bondage*, pp. 115–16, 126; Morgan, 'Organization of the Convict Trade', pp. 201–27.

5   The slave trade

Bristol's 'golden age' in the eighteenth century coincided with her participation in the Atlantic slave trade. Contemporaries emphasised the city's connection with this infamous branch of commerce by referring to Bristol as 'that rascally city' and as 'a dark den of slave traders'.[1] Their curiosity was aroused by the sight of slave ships in port, by the yarns of seamen with experience of Guinea voyages, and by the occasional presence in the city of blacks as personal servants.[2] In our own century, the Bristol slave trade has retained its fascination. Interest in the topic was stimulated by Marguerite Steen in her popular historical novel *The Sun is My Undoing* (1941). The slave trade has also become part of local folk wisdom. Bristolians today still associate the name of Blackboy Hill, Redland, and the grave of the African slave, Scipio Africanus, in Henbury churchyard, with the traffic in black cargoes. They recall that the Seven Stars pub, in the lane leading from St Thomas Street to Redcliff Street, was the place where the abolitionist Thomas Clarkson gained information about the conduct of the slave trade from local ship captains and seamen. Some Bristolians are also aware that leading charitable benefactors to their city, notably Edward Colston and the Society of Merchant Venturers, had strong links with the Guinea business. Modern historians have paid much attention to Bristol's role in this trade: several accounts describe the triangular trade from the 'metropolis of the west'. But though valuable work has appeared in print, especially recently, no one has investigated the rise and decline of Bristol's slave trade within the overall Atlantic trading context of the eighteenth century.[3] This chapter provides such an analysis.

The slave trade, as every schoolboy knows, operated in a triangular

---

[1] Charles James Fox and the Rev. Richard Watson, quoted in McGrath, ed., *Bristol in the Eighteenth Century*, p. 7.
[2] Latimer, *Annals of Bristol*, pp. 147–8.
[3] Previous accounts of the Bristol slave trade include A. M. Richards, 'The Connection of Bristol with the African Slave Trade, with some account of the currents of public opinion in the city' (University of Bristol MA thesis, 1923); MacInnes, *Bristol: A Gateway of Empire*, chs. 9 and 10; 'Bristol and the Slave Trade' in McGrath, ed., *Bristol in the*

way. Manufactured exports were supplied to the West African coast on the first leg of a voyage and exchanged for slaves; black cargoes were taken across the Atlantic on the second leg, the notorious 'middle passage'; and staple commodities, such as tobacco, rice and sugar, were loaded on board ship in the plantation colonies for the final leg of the voyage home. The slave trade stigmatised black Africans as racially inferior to white people and treated slaves as commodities that could be forced to work hard in tropical climates for the economic benefit of European empires. The Guinea business was vast in scope; it was the largest inter-continental movement of people in world history before the nineteenth century. Altogether, some 2.7 million African slaves were delivered by English vessels to American markets in the eighteenth century.[4] They were drawn from the main slaving areas of West Africa shown on map 5. Trade on these two thousand miles of coast was treacherous because of the disease environment. It was also internationally competitive: merchants from English ports competed not just with one another but with Spanish, Portuguese, French, Danish, Dutch and American traders.[5]

Bristol merchants fully entered the slave trade after the monopoly of the London-based Royal African Company was terminated in 1698. They remained in the trade until it was abolished by act of parliament in 1807. There were 2,114 slaving ventures in all from Bristol in these years (or

---

Eighteenth Century, pp. 161–84; David Richardson, 'The Bristol Slave Trade in the Eighteenth Century' (University of Manchester M.A. thesis, 1969); *The Bristol Slave Traders: A Collective Portrait* (Bristol Branch of the Historical Association, pamphlet no. 60, 1985); D. Gareth Rees, 'The Role of Bristol in the Atlantic Slave Trade, 1710–1769' (University of Exeter MA thesis, 1970); W. E. Minchinton, 'The Slave Trade of Bristol with the British Mainland Colonies in North America 1699–1770,' in Roger Anstey and P. E. H. Hair, eds., *Liverpool, the African Slave Trade, and Abolition* (Historic Society of Lancashire and Cheshire, Occasional Series, 2, 1976), pp. 39–59; and James A. Rawley, *The Transatlantic Slave Trade: A History* (New York, 1981), ch. 8. David Richardson has in progress a voyage-by-voyage reconstruction of the Bristol slave trade. Three volumes have appeared so far, each of which contains a valuable introduction: David Richardson, ed., *Bristol, Africa and the Eighteenth-Century Slave Trade to America, Vol. 1: The Years of Expansion 1698–1729, Vol. 2: The Years of Ascendancy 1730–1745, Vol. 3: The Years of Decline 1746–1769* (Bristol Record Society's *Publications*, 38, 39, 42, 1986–90).

[4] David Richardson, 'The Eighteenth-Century British Slave Trade: Estimates of its Volume and Coastal Distribution in Africa', *Research in Economic History*, 12 (1989), 158–9.

[5] The contribution of these different groups to the slave trade is discussed in Rawley, *Transatlantic Slave Trade*, and Philip D. Curtin, *The Atlantic Slave Trade: A Census* (Madison, WI, 1969). Many estimates in Curtin's pioneering study have been revised by subsequent scholarship. The best data on the number of slaves shipped from Africa during the eighteenth century are given in David Richardson, 'Slave Exports from West and West-Central Africa, 1700–1810: New Estimates of Volume and Distribution', *Journal of African History*, 30 (1989), 1–22.

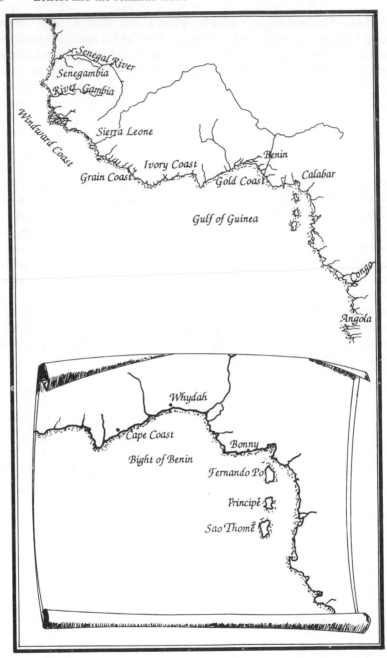

Map 5   The West African slave coast in the eighteenth century

19.3 per cent of all slaving voyages fitted out at British ports).[6] Though Bristol clearances in the slave trade accounted for only 4–9 per cent of all ships leaving the port in the eighteenth century,[7] the trade was more important than the percentages suggest. This was partly a matter of numbers: no less than 237 Bristolians were listed among the Company of Merchants trading to Africa in 1755.[8] But it was also due to the amount of capital invested in the trade. The fitting out of slaving vessels was very expensive: complete voyages usually lasted at least a calendar year and merchants often had to wait two years for returns on their investment. One contemporary estimate suggested that the value of Bristol's African trade between 1736 and 1744 was about £160,000 per year.[9] Another calculation claimed that the forty-seven ships and cargoes employed in the Bristol slave trade in 1749 were worth £260,800.[10] In 1769, the estimated cost of goods needed by a Bristol slaver to purchase 500 Negroes in Benin came to £1,605 6s. 6d. In the same year, the estimated outlay on goods loaded on the *Hungerford* to buy 400 slaves in New Calabar was £4,804 12s. 0d.[11] Overall, Bristolians may have invested at least £100,000 per year in slaving voyages during peacetime and more than £150,000 per annum when the Bristol slave trade was at its peak.[12] The size of that investment is readily apparent when one considers that multiplication by fifty is necessary to convert those amounts into today's money.[13]

The slave trade was also more important than the number of vessel clearances implies because it formed the apex of many other colonial trades with which Bristol was concerned. This was particularly true of the trades in plantation produce such as tobacco, sugar and rice. The capital amassed from selling black cargoes and staple commodities left its impact on Bristol. According to one annalist, there was 'not a brick in the city but what is cemented with the blood of a slave. Sumptuous mansions, luxurious living, liveried menials, were the produce of the wealth made from

---

[6] Richardson, 'Eighteenth-Century British Slave Trade', p. 169.

[7] Richardson, *Bristol Slave Traders*, p. 4.

[8] ACRL, Printed list of the Company of Merchants trading to Africa, 23 June 1755, XIII, Jefferies Collection.

[9] PRO, CO 388/43: Richard Henvill to the Lords Commissioners for Trade and Plantations, 12 Sept. 1744, which states that Bristol sent out forty slave ships per year during this period, each with goods on board worth £4,000.

[10] Minchinton, ed., *Trade of Bristol in the Eighteenth Century*, pp. 34–5. David Richardson considers that this source overstates the outfitting costs of these ships by at least 25 per cent: the amount of money involved is still very substantial (*Bristol, Africa and the Eighteenth-Century Slave Trade to America, Vol. 3*, pp. xv–xvi).

[11] Bristol UL, D. M. 15: Estimates of slave cargoes for 1769.

[12] Richardson, *Bristol Slave Traders*, p. 7.

[13] The ratio needed to convert eighteenth-century prices into today's money is based on work-in-progress by John J. McCusker.

the sufferings and groans of the slaves bought and sold by the Bristol merchants . . . In their childlike simplicity they could not feel the iniquity of the merchandise, but they could feel it lucrative.'[14] These comments are emotive, yet the sums cited above suggest that the sentiments were not entirely exaggerated. All in all, the significance of the slave trade to Bristol was such that the Society of Merchant Venturers acted as a persistent and well co-ordinated lobbyist of the Privy Council and both Houses of Parliament when plans were afoot to raise duties for the benefit of the Royal African Company rather than the separate traders, when taxes were imposed on Negroes imported into the plantation colonies, when the export of small arms and gunpowder to Africa was prohibited during the Seven Years War, and when the campaign began for the abolition of the British slave trade.[15]

Table 5.1 shows, however, that Bristol's share in the slave trade fluctuated considerably. Her merchants only sent out a handful of slaving vessels in most years during the War of the Spanish Succession, but by the early 1720s they had increased their level of activity to twenty-four annual ships. Bristol was then the second slave trading port in England. In 1724, for instance, London dispatched forty-nine Guinea ships carrying 13,670 slaves, Bristol sent out forty-five ships that took 11,850 slaves, and Liverpool accounted for eighteen ships that carried 3,710 slaves.[16] By 1728–32 Bristol was the premier slave trading port in Britain. In those years she dispatched an average of forty-eight annual ships on slaving voyages whereas London and Liverpool sent out forty and forty-four slave vessels respectively. But Bristol was overhauled by Liverpool in the slave trade in the 1740s and never recovered her former eminence. In the period 1738–42 Bristol ships supplied 42 per cent of the slaves delivered to the Americas by vessels from Bristol, Liverpool and London. Bristol's share of slave deliveries slumped thereafter from 24 per cent in 1753–7 to 10 per cent in 1773–7 and to a mere 1 per cent in 1803–7. Commercial competition did not come from Glasgow or Whitehaven, whose participation in the trade was negligible, but mainly from Liverpool, which rose to become the greatest slave trading port in the world between 1740 and 1807. In the final years of the trade more than 100 slave ships cleared out each year from Liverpool.[17]

The rise and fall of the Bristol slave trade is difficult to explain because

[14] Quoted in Eric Williams, *Capitalism and Slavery* (Washington, DC, 1944), p. 61.
[15] Minchinton, ed., *Politics and the Port of Bristol*, pp. 2–4, 7, 24–6, 37–9, 42–3, 67–9, 71–2, 74–5, 85–7, 129, 161–2, 165–6, 178–9; John Latimer, *The History of the Society of Merchant Venturers of the City of Bristol* (Bristol, 1903), pp. 179–80.
[16] BL, Add. MS 22, 676, fo. 41v.
[17] Cf. D. P. Lamb, 'Volume and Tonnage of the Liverpool Slave Trade 1772–1807' in Anstey and Hair, eds., *Liverpool, the African Slave Trade, and Abolition*, pp. 91–112.

Table 5.1. *Distribution of the slave trade from London, Bristol and Liverpool, 1699–1807 (annual averages)*

	London		Bristol		Liverpool	
	(1)	(2)	(1)	(2)	(1)	(2)
1699–1702	73	15,694	4	630	1	42
1703–7	42	9,002	5	806	0	0
1708–12	23	5,301	13	2,272	2	86
1713–17	31	7,567	20	3,596	9	1,205
1718–22	47	10,244	24	4,684	2	300
1723–7	56	12,430	34	7,224	11	1,749
1728–32	40	10,513	48	10,872	14	2,779
1733–7	27	6,987	34	8,044	22	4,620
1738–42	16	4,323	33	7,987	29	6,692
1743–7	6	1,879	20	5,161	31	7,497
1748–52	13	2,706	27	6,474	48	11,238
1753–7	15	2,535	20	4,594	53	12,122
1758–62	22	4,420	21	5,070	62	13,996
1763–7	39	8,499	28	6,881	72	16,967
1768–72	41	9,789	27	6,166	92	22,133
1773–7	31	10,350	14	3,091	73	17,763
1778–82	13	3,656	5	916	32	9,721
1783–7	24	7,269	14	3,830	81	26,260
1788–92	21	6,294	23	5,349	95	29,587
1793–7	13	3,835	7	1,680	83	25,276
1798–1802	18	5,105	4	841	135	37,086
1803–7	13	3,685	1	335	103	25,953

(1) Number of ships clearing to Africa for slaves.
(2) Estimated number of slaves delivered to the Americas.
Source: David Richardson, 'The Eighteenth-Century British Slave Trade: Estimates of its Volume and Coastal Distribution in Africa', *Research in Economic History*, 12 (1989), appendix, pp. 185–95.

only scattered and limited business material survives. Clearly, however, many fluctuations occurred due to the high degree of uncertainty in this riskiest form of Atlantic commerce. Each leg of the triangular voyage posed perennial problems for Bristol slave merchants. Export wares in the slave trade needed to be well sorted and suited to different consumption patterns at various parts of the West African coast. Firearms, beads, liquor and textiles were prominent among these wares.[18] East Indian

[18] David Richardson, 'West African Consumption Patterns and their Influence on the Eighteenth-Century English Slave Trade' in Henry A. Gemery and Jan S. Hogendorn, eds., *The Uncommon Market: Essays on the Atlantic Slave Trade* (New York, 1979), pp. 303–30; J. E. Inikori, 'The Import of Firearms into West Africa 1750–1807: A Quantitative Analysis', *Journal of African History*, 18 (1977), 339–68; BRO, Richard Meyler &

textiles were particularly important. They were the largest single item in the entire trade, comprising 27 per cent of the value of all goods shipped from England to Africa from 1699 to 1800.[19] Lack of the right assortment of goods caused serious commercial problems. One Bristol slave trader noted that the absence of India bafts ruined his purchase of slaves in West Africa.[20] Another found that chintz was not in demand for Negroes in Old Calabar after it had been 'the Commanding Article last voyage'.[21] Detailed instructions were given to captains of Bristol Guinea vessels to try to avoid such situations. They were advised to keep their best goods until they had purchased most of their slaves, so that they could then 'command the trade' with the correct assortment of commodities.[22] They were usually given several options about the parts of the African coast with which to trade. This was crucial for buying the best slaves – prime, healthy males and females aged between about ten and twenty-five rather than older, weaker Negroes.[23] Unfortunately, Bristol's main areas of slave purchase cannot be analysed with precision because the African destination is known for only 27 per cent of all her slaving voyages before 1769.[24]

Co. to Capt. John Fowler, 4 Jan. 1751, Account book of the snow *Molly*, Bright Papers. For exports of firearms in the Bristol slave trade see Birmingham Central Library, Samuel Galton to James Farmer, 12 Oct. 1751, and to John Parr, 20 May 1752, Samuel Galton Letterbooks (1741–55); Wiltshire RO, Account Book of Thomas Goldney (1741–68), fos. 16, 17, 22; and PRO, C 107/10: Samuel Galton to James Rogers, 15 June 1792, and to James Rogers & Co., 19 June 1792, James Rogers Papers. The quantity and value of goods exported from Bristol to Africa for the years 1772–87 inclusive is given in Sheila Lambert, ed., *House of Commons Sessional Papers of the Eighteenth Century* (Wilmington, 1975), LXVII, pp. 13–20, 41–3.

[19] Herbert S. Klein, 'Economic Aspects of the Eighteenth-Century Atlantic Slave Trade' in James D. Tracy, ed., *The Rise of Merchant Empires: Long-Distance Trade in the Early Modern World, 1350–1750* (Cambridge, 1990), p. 292.

[20] PRO, C 107/6: Edward Taylor to James Rogers, 2 July 1792, James Rogers Papers.

[21] PRO, C 107/12: Richard Rogers to James Rogers, 10 Nov. 1787, *ibid*.

[22] UMA, Richard Meyler, Henry Bright & Co. to Capt. John Brown, 1747, the snow *Bristol Merchant's* Book, box 36, Bright Family Papers; BRO, Henry Bright *et al.* to Capt. James McTaggart, 5 Mar. 1759, Voyage Accounts: the *Swift*. For information on captains in the Bristol slave trade see Stephen D. Behrendt, 'The Captains in the British Slave Trade from 1785 to 1807', *Transactions of the Historic Society of Lancashire and Cheshire*, 140 (1990), app., tables E, F, 130–40.

[23] Isaac Hobhouse, Noblet Ruddock and William Baker to Capt. William Barry, 7 Oct. 1725, in Elizabeth Donnan, ed., *Documents Illustrative of the History of the Slave Trade to America*, 4 vols. (Washington, DC, 1930–5), II, p. 327; BRO, Richard Meyler & Co. to Capt. John Fowler, 4 Jan. 1751, 20 Aug. 1752, Account book of the snow *Molly*, Bright Papers; Bristol Industrial Museum, Owners to Capt. Thomas Baker, 1 Aug. 1776, Account book of the snow *Africa*; UMA, Richard Meyler, Henry Bright & Co. to Capt. John Brown, 1747, box 36, Bright Family Papers; Lloyd's of London, Owners to Capt. William Llewellin, 30 Oct. 1771, Account book of the *Hector*.

[24] See the evidence cited in Richardson, ed., *Bristol, Africa and the Eighteenth-Century Slave Trade to America, Vols. 1–3*. Even where destinations are given, they are not always clear: this is true, for instance, of ships listed as trading with 'the Bight'.

Buying slaves involved competition with foreign traders, government ships, and the governors of African forts and castles, all of whom were concerned in the same business. The governors had access to a better supply and assortment of exports and were able to offer higher prices for slaves. They could monopolise the trade for their own purposes and dictate trading patterns with the interior. The state of relations between governors and natives, the existence of wars between different tribal groups, and geographical conditions such as excessive rainfall also affected the supply and price of slaves in Africa.[25] Slave purchases were sometimes facilitated by connections with employees of the forts. Some 406 Negroes were supplied in this way to Bristol vessels in West Africa by Richard Miles between 1771 and 1779.[26] But buying slaves was not always so straightforward. A vessel could remain anchored on a particular part of the African coast for over a month before opening trade if slaves were sickly and dear, and could stay there for several months while slaves were bought, transhipped and relanded. By the early 1790s, for example, Bristol slavers spent an average of 109 days on the African coast while purchasing slaves.[27] Ship captains could find difficulty in bartering goods for slaves by the ounce, bar, copper, piece and various other local units of account. They knew the number of slaves they were expected to purchase but were not always successful in filling up with black cargoes.[28] Thus in 1764 four Bristol ships anchored at James Fort, near the River Gambia, acquired only 289 of the 440 slaves they intended to buy.[29] The purchase of slaves could therefore be impeded by various drawbacks. Once slaving

[25] Depositions of William Muff and George Home, 26 July 1738, 15 Jan. 1738/9, in Donnan, ed., *Documents Illustrative of the History of the Slave Trade*, II, pp. 464, 467; SMV, Deposition of John Sinclair, 1738, African Trade (bundle D); PRO, CO 388/45, pt. 3, fos. 89–91: Deposition of William Brown, 16 June 1753, and fos. 112–19: Memorial of the merchants of Bristol and Liverpool with respect to the complaints exhibited by the said merchants against the officers and servants of the Committee of the Company of Merchants trading to Africa, 26 June 1753; PRO, BT 6/3, Memorial of the Merchants and others of the City of Bristol . . . , 17 Apr. 1777; PRO, C 107/12: John Smith to James Rogers, 27 Feb., 10 Mar. 1791, and John Smith to James Rogers & Co., 17 Apr., 24 Sept. 1791, James Rogers Papers; Thomas Mills to William Wansey & Co., 4 Oct. 1752, in D. W. Thoms, 'West India Merchants and Planters in the Mid-Eighteenth Century with special reference to St. Kitts', 2 vols. (University of Kent M.A. thesis, 1967), II, no. 54.

[26] PRO, T 70/1541: 'An Account of Richard Miles's slave barters with the British shipping during his command as chief of a Fort in the service of the African Committee from the year 1771 to 1780.'

[27] Details taken from 53 voyages for 1791–5 listed in House of Lords Record Office, Main Papers, 28 July 1800 (House of Lords 'A' list).

[28] PRO, T 70/1525, List of Shipping, Gambia, 7 Apr.–11 June 1756; Gloucestershire RO, Joseph [?Dolman] to Capt. Richard Prankard, 9 Dec. 1738, and Capt. Charles Gwynn to Capt. Richard Prankard & Co., 15 Dec. 1754, Miscellaneous Correspondence of Richard Prankard, Parish records of Chard (P74 MI 1/1).

[29] Staffordshire RO, 'List of the Vessels arrived at and sailed from James Fort in the River Gambia in 1764', Dartmouth Papers, D(W)1778/V/251.

had ended on the coast, captains aimed to leave this disease-ridden environment post haste, for 'dispatch' was 'the life of a Guinea voyage'.[30] There were occasions, however, where the length of stay of Bristol vessels on the African coast exceeded the duration of the Atlantic crossing.[31]

During the 'middle passage' Bristol slave captains were beset by further problems. Beef, herrings, bread, rice, yams and beans were usually purchased as provisions in Africa, but many slaves and crew died on the Atlantic crossing from diseases such as smallpox, dysentery and the flux.[32] Sometimes ships were wrecked by stormy weather in the Atlantic.[33] There was the additional problem of controlling Negroes during the voyage. Slaves were often restrained by placing chains around their necks. They were sometimes shackled beneath deck and barricadoes and netting erected to prevent them from insurrection or from leaping overboard. These devices might be accompanied by severe punishment with a cat o' nine tails.[34] Even with these restraints, violence and mutinies sometimes occurred on slaving voyages. There were also instances of slaves jumping overboard as a release from their suffering.[35]

Towards the end of the 'middle passage', complex commercial decisions were necessary. This was the time when Bristol slave captains

30   Bristol Industrial Museum, Owners to Capt. Thomas Baker, 1 Aug. 1776, Account book of the *Africa*. The same remark appears in PRO, C 107/13: Thomas Walker to James Rogers & Co., 25 Sept. 1786, James Rogers Papers.
31   J. E. Inikori, 'The Sources of Supply for the Atlantic Slave Exports from the Bight of Benin and the Bight of Bonny (Biafra)' in Serge Daget, ed., *De la Traite à l'esclavage*, 2 vols. (Société Française d'Histoire d'Outre Mer, Nantes, 1988), II, pp. 31–2.
32   BRO, Richard Meyler & Co. to Capt. John Fowler, 4 Jan. 1751, Account book of the snow *Molly*, Bright Papers; BRO, Henry Bright *et al.* to Capt. James McTaggart, 5 Mar. 1759, Voyage Accounts: the *Swift* (1759); Bodleian Library, James Jones & Co. to Capt. David Williams, 7 Apr. 1792, MS. Eng. misc. b.44; UMA, Francis Bright to Henry Bright, 14, 25 Oct. 1747, 14 July 1748, boxes 7, 85, Bright Family Papers; Jonathan Press, *The Merchant Seamen of Bristol, 1747–1789* (Bristol Branch of the Historical Association, pamphlet no. 38, Bristol, 1976), pp. 11–15. A detailed account of slaves dying on board a Bristol slaving vessel is included in National Maritime Museum, Daybook of the *Castle* (1727).
33   For a vivid description of one Bristol slave ship that was wrecked see J. D. Spinney, 'Misadventures of a Slaver', *Blackwood's Magazine*, no. 1629 (1951), 27–33.
34   John Atkins, *A Voyage to Guinea, Brasil, and the West Indies . . .* (London, 1735), p. 173; Report of Negroes rising on Bristol slave vessels in *The Boston Weekly Newsletter*, 2–9 Sept. 1731; evidence of James Arnold, 1789, in Lambert, ed., *House of Commons Sessional Papers*, LXIX, pp. 127, 133–4; UMA, Richard Meyler, Henry Bright & Co. to Capt. John Brown, 1747, the snow *Bristol Merchant's* Book, box 36, Bright Family Papers; *An Account of the Life and Dealings of God with Silas Told . . .* (London, 1786), pp. 22–4. Some Bristol slave captains dealt with their black cargoes in a more humane way: see *The Genuine Life of Robert Barker . . .* (London, 1809), p. 82.
35   E.g. Richardson, ed., *Bristol, Africa and the Eighteenth-Century Slave Trade to America*, *Vol. 1*, p. 98, *Vol. 2*, p. 75, *Vol. 3*, pp. 62, 111, 134, 149, 179.

settled on the best potential markets for slave sales. Though issued with instructions specifying a range of market options, factors to contact, and expected average sale prices for slaves, considerable discretion in these matters was left to masters.[36] Invariably they opted to sell slaves in Jamaica, the leading slave market in the British Empire, but they could choose among numerous plantation colonies and islands for the sale of their human cargoes. Captains nevertheless found it difficult to gauge the current demand for slaves in different parts of the New World, or the prospect of full return cargoes of seasonal tropical produce.[37] They were also hampered when black cargoes would not sell above the price limits specified by shipowners.[38] An added difficulty lay in securing remittances from areas where plantation debts were endemic.[39] Thus the potential bonanza of the slave trade was offset by heavy mortality rates, expensive transport costs, and difficulties of seasonal timing. Small wonder that British slave merchants achieved on average only a 10 per cent (or thereabouts) annual rate of return on investment.[40] For these reasons, too, Bristol slaving ventures were always a considerable risk and one should expect to find that they fluctuated in profit levels over time.[41] 'It is a precarious trade', the Bristol slave merchant James Jones informed

---

[36] For an example of flexible instructions given by owners of a Bristol slave vessel see above, pp. 74–5.

[37] See BRO, Richard Meyler & Co. to Capt. John Fowler, 4 Jan., 10 Apr. 1751, Account book of the snow *Molly*, Bright Papers; Lloyd's of London, Owners to Capt. William Llewellin, Sept. 1770, 30 Oct. 1771, 3 Aug. 1772, to Alexander, James & Evan Baillie, 28 Feb. 1771, to Miles Brewton & Co., 28 Feb. 1771, and to Richard Hanson, 1 Feb. 1772; PRO, C 107/9: Samuel Chollett & Co. to James Rogers, 25 Feb. 1789, and Lyttock & Maxwell to James Rogers, 25 Feb. 1789, James Rogers Papers. See also above, pp. 74–5. Detailed breakdowns of slaves sold from Bristol ships can be found in Virginia HS, Account sales of slaves on the *Charfield*, 23 July 1717, Tayloe MSS; BRO, Sales of slaves from the snow *Molly*, Mar. 1752, Bright Papers; and Sales of slaves from the *Prince of Wales*, 1772, in Julian P. Boyd, ed., *The Papers of Thomas Jefferson, Vol. 15: 27 March 1789 to 30 November 1789* (Princeton, NJ, 1958), pp. 654–5.

[38] E.g. Robert Colhoun & Thomas Mills to Thomas Harris & Co., 22 Aug. 1752, in Thoms, 'West India Merchants and Planters,' II, no. 50.

[39] This problem is analysed below on pp. 146–9, 163–4.

[40] Roger Anstey, *The Atlantic Slave Trade and British Abolition 1760–1810* (London, 1975), pp. 38–57; David Richardson, 'Profits in the Liverpool Slave Trade: The Accounts of William Davenport, 1757–1784' in Anstey and Hair, eds., *Liverpool, the African Slave Trade, and Abolition*, pp. 60–90; 'The Costs of Survival: The Transport of Slaves in the Middle Passage and the Profitability of the 18th-Century British Slave Trade', *Explorations in Economic History*, 24 (1987), 178–96; 'Profitability in the Bristol–Liverpool Slave Trade', in *The Atlantic Slave Trade: New Approaches*, Société Française d'Histoire d'Outre Mer (1976), pp. 301–6.

[41] Some examples from individual Bristol slaving voyages are given in Richardson, *Bristol Slave Traders*, pp. 7–8.

a parliamentary committee, and one in which profits were 'sometimes . . .
good – sometimes not so'.[42]

Further explanations can be supplied for the changing performance of
Bristol in the slave trade. In the decade after 1698 Bristol merchants
campaigned vigorously with petitions to prevent the revival of the Royal
African Company's monopoly.[43] Bristol's slaving ventures then rose
significantly in the period up to the mid-1730s. Several reasons can be
suggested for this success. The overall ratio of slave deliveries to vessels'
stated complements of slaves reached around 75 per cent in the mid-1720s
and there was a noticeable improvement in the average number of slaves
delivered per voyage in Bristol ships at that time. Down to about 1730
Bristol merchants expanded trade with previously under-exploited
sources of slave supply such as Bonny and Calabar in the Bight of Biafra;
they improved their marketing skills in America; and they took a major
share of several rapidly growing markets for slaves (notably Virginia,
Barbados and Jamaica). All these factors indicate that good profits were
generally made in the early Bristol slave trade.[44]

The buoyancy of the early Bristol slave trade was bolstered by flexible
business arrangements and the sale of slaves to lucrative markets in
Spanish America. Bristol slave merchants maintained regular correspondence with American agents, who furnished them with up-to-date
information on the best slave markets at any given time.[45] Thus Isaac
Hobhouse was informed by his factors that Gold Coast slaves were much
in demand in Jamaica and that it would be advisable not to overdo the
trade with the Bight of Biafra.[46] In organising voyages, Bristol slave
merchants gave several options to masters. Isaac Hobhouse instructed
the captain of the *Dispatch* to pick up orders for the disposal of his slaves
at either Antigua or Nevis, but gave him leave to sell his cargo at
Charleston, South Carolina, if demand for Negroes was low at the two

---

[42] Evidence of James Jones, 1788, cited in Lambert, ed., *House of Commons Sessional
Papers*, LXVIII, p. 44. The fluctuating financial fortunes of some Bristol slave vessels can
be traced in BRO, James Day Account Book, with loose papers enclosed, Acc. 40044(2)
and (3).

[43] Donnan, ed., *Documents Illustrative of the History of the Slave Trade*, II, pp. 131–8;
McGrath, *Merchant Venturers of Bristol*, pp. 131–8; Minchinton, ed., *Politics and the
Port of Bristol*, pp. 2–4, 7–8.

[44] Richardson, ed., *Bristol, Africa and the Eighteenth-Century Slave Trade to America, Vol.
1*, pp. xviii–xxviii.

[45] E.g. ACRL, Richard Assheton to Isaac Hobhouse,?10 Mar. 1726, 18 Feb. 1730,
Jefferies Collection, XIII, which respectively comment on the great demand for slaves at
Jamaica and St Kitts.

[46] ACRL, Tyndall & Assheton to Isaac Hobhouse, 3 Nov. 1729, Jefferies Collection, XIII.
For a brief discussion of Hobhouse as a Bristol slave trader see Rawley, *The Transatlantic
Slave Trade*, pp. 184–6.

West Indian islands.[47] Richard Laugher & Co. ordered their factors in Barbados to sell a cargo of slaves carried by the *America* if the ship arrived before 10 February; if it arrived later, the captain was to leave forty of his Gold Coast slaves there and proceed to Charleston with the rest.[48] Remittances were also handled flexibly. The Barbados agents of the *America* were requested to pay for slaves by sending back ⅝ of the net proceeds on the return voyage (⅖ in good bills of exchange, ⅛ in ginger and ⅜ in Barbados sugar); the remainder could wait until the following year.[49] Other evidence from the 1720s suggests that it was common for ⅝ of the net proceeds to be returned with the ship to Bristol.[50] This material, though fragmentary, hints that remittances for slave cargoes were not hampered by the extensions of credit that later became the norm in the trade.[51]

Bristol's early success in the slave trade was also stimulated by her role in the illegal shipment of slaves. Between 1702 and 1775 some 137,114 of the 497,736 slaves brought to Jamaica (in other words, 28 per cent) were re-exported, usually to Spanish America.[52] The scope of this illegal traffic is also apparent from the annual purchase by the South Sea Company of 4–5,000 slaves from Jamaica for re-export to ports such as Havana, Cartagena, Porto Bello, Buenos Aires, Vera Cruz, Panama, and Santiago de Cuba in the late 1720s.[53] Bristol's role in this trade grew after the reopening of the Asiento when Britain and Spain declared peace, on 9 November 1729. Gold Coast and Angolan slaves were most in demand in the Spanish Empire, where buyers expressed a preference for them rather than for slaves from Calabar.[54] Bristol merchants certainly benefited from the trade: a letter of 1733 revealed that a standstill for Bristolians selling slaves at Jamaica occurred because of trade being stopped at Havana and other places on the Spanish Main by the governors

---

[47] Isaac Hobhouse *et al.* to Capt. William Barry, 7 Oct. 1725, in Donnan, ed., *Documents Illustrative of the History of the Slave Trade*, II, p. 328.

[48] PRO, HCA 15/34: Richard Laugher *et al.* to Crump & Hasell, 10 Oct. 1722.

[49] *Ibid.*

[50] ACRL, Tyndall & Assheton to Isaac Hobhouse, 20 July 1729, Jefferies Collection, XIII; Tyndall & Assheton to Hobhouse & Tyndall, 16 Mar. 1730, in Donnan, ed., *Documents Illustrative of the History of the Slave Trade*, II, p. 388.

[51] See below, pp. 145–9.

[52] Frank Wesley Pitman, *The Development of the British West Indies, 1700–1763* (New Haven, CT, 1917), app. II, pp. 391–2.

[53] ACRL, Tyndall & Assheton to Isaac Hobhouse, 17 Feb. 1729, Jefferies Collection, XIII; Colin A. Palmer, *Human Cargoes: The British Slave Trade to Spanish America, 1700–1739* (Urbana, IL, 1981).

[54] ACRL, Tyndall & Assheton to Isaac Hobhouse, 8 June 1729, Jefferies Collection, vol. XIII; BRO, Tyndall & Assheton to Isaac Hobhouse, 15 Nov. 1729, Acc. 8029[16]f; Tyndall & Assheton to Isaac Hobhouse & Co., 13 Nov. 1729, in Donnan, ed., *Documents Illustrative of the History of the Slave Trade*, II, p. 382.

of those territories.[55] Altogether, about one-third of all slaves taken in Bristol ships to the Americas in the early 1730s were re-exported to Spanish American markets.[56]

Given this success in the first three decades of the eighteenth century, why did Bristol's slave trade decline from the 1740s onwards? One explanation is that her merchants failed to take full advantage of shifts in the centre of gravity of the trade. Bristol's market share of slave deliveries to Virginia fell from 66 per cent in 1718–27 to 46 per cent in 1759–66. More significantly, her portion of slave deliveries dropped from 69 to 25 per cent for Jamaica between 1728–30 and 1761–9 and from 49 to 24 per cent for South Carolina between 1730–9 and 1757–66.[57] The demand for imported slaves increased much more in Jamaica and South Carolina than in Virginia in the years from 1730–1770,[58] so Bristol merchants were obviously failing to compete with slave traders from Liverpool and London in expanding markets. Nor did they respond quickly to the accession of new markets in the Ceded Islands (especially Grenada, Dominica and St Vincent) which were acquired as British settlements at the Treaty of Paris in 1763.[59] By the 1750s and 1760s, the only slave markets where Bristolians competed effectively with Londoners and Liverpudlians were smaller West Indian islands such as St Kitts and Antigua.[60]

Bristol's declining role in expanding slave markets was partly caused by trading difficulties in wartime. Her slaving ventures were significantly cut back in 1744–6, 1755–8 and during the American War of Independence (see table 5.1). Already in 1740 the Bristol merchant Graffin Prankard noted that the Guinea trade had declined to a great extent at Bristol and was unlikely to revive.[61] The situation worsened over the next few years. 'Ye Difference between the Trade of this Town to Africa, before & since ye Warr with France, are very great', Walter Laugher commented in 1744, adding that 'ye Number for many years before were Sixty Sayl of Ships, and upwards, upon an Avarage yearly, and I think since only 5

[55] *South Carolina Gazette*, 17 Feb. 1734.
[56] Richardson, ed., *Bristol, Africa and the Eighteenth-Century Slave Trade to America, Vol. 2*, p. xxi.
[57] *Ibid.*, *Vol. 3*, p. xxviii.
[58] Based on figures of slave imports to these colonies given in *ibid.*, p. 140; Susan Westbury, 'Slaves of Colonial Virginia: Where they came from', *WMQ*, 3rd Series, 42 (1985), 236; and Converse D. Clowse, *Measuring Charleston's Overseas Commerce, 1717–1767* (Washington, DC, 1981), table A-21, p. 31.
[59] Richardson, 'Bristol Slave Trade', pp. 150–2.
[60] Richardson, ed., *Bristol, Africa and the Eighteenth-Century Slave Trade to America, Vol. 3*, p. xxx.
[61] Somerset RO, Graffin Prankard to D. & R. Mackey, 14 Jan. 1740, and to Francis Jennings, 16 July 1740, Graffin Prankard Letterbooks (1738–56), Dickinson Papers, DD/DN 428, 429.

small vessels have been sent'.[62] Bristol slave traders cut back on African voyages at this time because of the threat posed by enemy privateers in the English Channel. They also lobbied parliament to request naval protection for their slave ships on the African coast.[63] Liverpool merchants, by contrast, increased their slaving ventures during the 1740s: they avoided marauders by sending ships around the north of Ireland and into the Atlantic.[64]

Later, during the Seven Years War, Bristol traders were afraid to send ships to Africa and not concerned 'to venture their Fortunes abroad at this Juncture'.[65] The uncertainty of sea lanes during wartime, caused by the activities of enemy privateers, undoubtedly influenced this decision. So, too, did higher insurance premiums.[66] The refusal of the Board of Ordnance to grant licences for exportation of gunpowder at this time also affected the African trade.[67] In response to these wartime disruptions, a good many Bristol slave traders converted their ships into privateers.[68] They also hired out slave vessels for government transport service during the American War of Independence.[69] These were logical changes, for both privateering and slave trading were speculative ventures that had the lure of substantial returns. But attention to privateering at Bristol harmed the port's position in the slave trade *vis-à-vis* Liverpool, and this lost ground was never recovered.[70]

Several other factors affected the downturn in the Bristol slave trade by the 1740s. Investment in slaving voyages was usually spread among several ad hoc partners who joined together for individual ventures and took shares in the ship's outset, cargo and proceeds. Between 1730 and 1760 most Bristol slaving voyages had from two to five shareholders, though some had six, eight or even ten.[71] The voyage of the snow *Bristol*

---

[62] ACRL, Walter Laugher to Edward Southwell, 7 Mar. 1744, Southwell Papers, IX.

[63] Petition of the SMV to the House of Commons, 2 Apr. 1744, and Walter Laugher to MPs, 27 Feb. 1745, in Minchinton, ed., *Politics and the Port of Bristol*, pp. 57, 60–1.

[64] See above, p. 20.

[65] Somerset RO, Isaac Baugh to Henry Strachey, 6 Feb. 1762, folder 7, Strachie MSS.

[66] Petition of the SMV to the Lords Commissioners for executing the office of the Lord High Admiral of Great Britain, 25 Mar. 1762, in Minchinton, ed., *Politics and the Port of Bristol*, p. 95.

[67] SMV, Sargent, Aufrère & Co. to the Master of the SMV, 19 Aug. 1756, bundle 2, Correspondence (1754–1800).

[68] This is well documented in J. W. Damer Powell, *Bristol Privateers and Ships of War* (Bristol, 1930) and Richardson, ed., *Bristol, Africa and the Eighteenth-Century Slave Trade to America, Vol. 3*. The commercial arrangements of Bristol slavers fitted out with letters-of-marque are well illustrated in New York HS, Misc. MSS. Ships: Ship *Cornwall*, Articles of Agreement, 20 Sept. 1759, and BRO, Articles of Agreement for the *Gascoyne* (1781), Acc. 248/2.

[69] PRO T 70/1534: John Cockburn to [? Richard Miles], 30 Nov. 1776.

[70] See above, pp.19–22.

[71] Richardson, 'Bristol Slave Trade', p. 48.

Merchant to Africa and Jamaica in 1747 provides a good example of the spread of ownership. The investors in this venture were Richard Meyler, Henry Bright & Co. and Thomas Power (each with ⅙ shares); William Gordon, John Collett and Samuel Sedgley (each with ⅛ shares); and William Wansey and John Trevaskes (each with 1/16 shares).[72] But such a division of ownership was not necessarily perceived as advantageous: at least one American merchant considered that the Bristol slave trade was 'casual & uncertain' because, with various investors in one venture, it was often impossible to ensure the arrival of a vessel with slaves at a particular market.[73] The spread of ownership may even have contributed to the lack of productivity gains by Bristol slavers in mid-century.[74] Yet equally significant, it seems, was the erosion of Bristol's slaving activity by French competition on parts of the African coast. In the mid-1730s nearly half of Bristol's slave ships apparently purchased their whole complements of slaves on the Windward and Gold Coasts. But the great increase in French slaving on the Gold Coast, especially at Annamaboe, reduced Bristol's trade there to an appreciable degree in the period 1737–44 without the Bristolians increasing their trade to other parts of the African coast.[75] By 1750, Bristol merchants also complained about stagnant trade with the Spaniards: they considered that slave trading with Jamaica would not be worthwhile until the Spanish American market recovered.[76] In the event, the re-export of slaves from Jamaica to Spanish America remained depressed throughout the third quarter of the eighteenth century.[77]

Besides these problems, David Richardson found that Bristol failed to produce lasting dynasties in the slave trade by the 1740s. Five of the leading 26 Bristol slave agents in the 1720s and 1730s died as bachelors and a further ten died without leaving a direct male heir.[78] The leading

---

[72] UMA, Richard Meyler, Henry Bright & Co. to Capt. John Brown, (?) 1747, the snow *Bristol Merchant*'s book, box 36, Bright Family Papers. Other sources that cite the division of shares on Bristol slave vessels include BRO, Account Book of James Day (1729–53), with loose papers enclosed; BRO, Account Book of the *Swift* (1759); Bristol Industrial Museum, Account Book of the snow *Africa*. See also W. E. Minchinton, 'The Voyage of the Snow *Africa*', *The Mariner's Mirror*, 37 (1951), 187–96. For a general discussion of shipownership in Bristol's Atlantic trade see above, pp. 34–8.

[73] Duke UL, Richard Hill to John Guerard, 16 Sept. 1743, Richard Hill Letterbook (1743).

[74] For evidence on this point see above, pp. 48–53.

[75] PRO, CO 388/43: Charles Hayes to the Secretary of the Lords Commissioners for Trade and Plantations, 31 Dec. 1744.

[76] UMA, Henry Bright to Richard Meyler, 25 July, 22 Aug. 1750, box 8, Bright Family Papers.

[77] Richardson, ed., *Bristol, Africa and the Eighteenth-Century Slave Trade to America, Vol. 3*, p. xxiv.

[78] Richardson, *Bristol Slave Traders*, pp. 9–10. See also David Richardson, 'The Slave Merchants of the Outports' (Unpublished paper presented to the Organization of American Historians' Conference, Chicago, 1973).

agents of Bristol slaving voyages (listed in table 5.2) were always an elite group, in the sense that a relatively small number of men managed a high proportion of voyages. Thus by 1789–91 James Jones and Thomas Jones alone accounted for almost 40 per cent of the tonnage of African vessels clearing from Bristol.[79] The leading agents were also specialised: there was little overlap between them and the major tobacco and sugar merchants at Bristol.[80] Given such specialisation plus the complexity of the triangular trade, the need to build up capital and expertise over time, and the well-documented family connections among early Bristol slave traders, this demographic failure, though fortuitous, was yet another nail in the coffin of Bristol as a slave trading port. By contrast, it is not coincidental that many instances of family continuity can be found in the city's most lucrative and successful branch of commerce, the sugar trade.[81]

Problems caused by wartime disruptions, the spread of investment in slave vessels, competition on the African coast and lack of family continuity all made the 1740s a watershed for the Bristol slave trade. From that decade onwards Bristol's Guinea merchants were also outpaced by the business acumen of their Liverpool counterparts. Contemporaries drew attention to the cheaper prices that Liverpudlians sold slaves for in the Americas – while still making profits – and the lower fees they paid their ship captains and factors.[82] Liverpool merchants seem to have had access to as many ships as they required for the trade, and to have kept the business confined to fewer hands than was the case at Bristol. In some instances they clearly speculated, sending out ships for which they did not have security but for which they insisted on no bad debts and on payment for the account of the owners of cargoes.[83] They had the added advantage of being allowed two years' credit for goods by Manchester tradesmen rather than the nine months common in the Bristol slave trade.[84] Appar-

---

[79] J. E. Inikori, 'Market Structure and the Profits of the British African Trade in the Late Eighteenth Century', *JEcH*, 41 (1981), 752.

[80] Cf. the names in table 5.2 with those in tables 6.5 and 7.5 below, pp. 161, 194–5. The extent of concentration among Liverpool slave merchants is debated by Inikori, 'Market Structure', pp. 745–76, and B. L. Anderson and David Richardson, 'Market Structure and the Profits of the British African Trade in the Late Eighteenth Century: A Comment', *JEcH*, 43 (1983), 713–21. Inikori, Anderson and Richardson continued the debate in *JEcH*, 45 (1985), 705–11.

[81] See below, p. 189.

[82] See the contemporary comments quoted in C. Northcote Parkinson, *The Rise of the Port of Liverpool* (Liverpool, 1952), pp. 93–5.

[83] UMA, Richard Meyler to Henry Bright, 23 Oct. 1750, box 7, and Lowbridge Bright to Bright, Milward & Duncomb, 5 Nov. 1773, Lowbridge Bright Letterbook (1765–73), Bright Family Papers; PRO, C 107/14: William Webb to James Rogers, 21 July 1785, James Rogers Papers.

[84] BRO, Henry Bright to Richard Bright, 28 Jan. 1772, Letters of the Brights of Colwall, 1772, Bright Papers; Robert Norris, *A Short Account of the African Slave Trade* (Liverpool, 1788), p. 10.

Table 5.2. *Leading agents of Bristol slaving voyages, 1698–1807*

Agents	Voyages managed	Period of management
James Laroche	132	1728–69
John Fowler	77	1758–77
James Jones	68	1783–95
John Anderson	66	1764–97
John Powell	58	1755–76
James Day	56	1711–42
James Rogers	51	1783–92
Isaac Hobhouse	44	1722–47
Henry Tonge	42	1730–53
Thomas Deane	40	1747–64
Samuel Jacob	40	1716–47
William Hare	38	1729–52
Richard Farr	37	1726–45
Henry Dampier	34	1727–44
William Jefferies	34	1713–47
Thomas Jones	34	1767–94
Walter Lougher	34	1732–60
Edmund Saunders	32	1723–39
Richard Henvill	30	1709–44
Noblet Ruddock	30	1712–25

Source: David Richardson, *The Bristol Slave Traders: A Collective Portrait* (Bristol Branch of the Historical Association, pamphlet no. 60, 1985), pp. 29–30.

ently, they also assorted export cargoes more effectively than Bristolians and sold their wares in Africa for 25 per cent less than their West-Country rivals.[85] By the 1750s and 1760s Liverpool slave merchants showed more enterprise in directing their trade to West African coastal areas such as Sierra Leone, the Cameroons and Gabon whereas Bristolians, adopting a more conservative approach, continued to trade with Angola and the Gold Coast instead.[86]

Liverpool slave traders, in addition, had significant advantages over Bristol in the supply of exports to Africa. Coarse woollen goods were common among exports in the slave trade during Queen Anne's reign, but by 1740 most textiles in the trade were East India commodities.[87] During wartime Bristol Guinea traders sometimes experienced difficulty in obtaining foreign-produced goods, which comprised 50–60 per cent of

[85] PRO, C 107/14: Thomas Walker to James Rogers, 20 June 1789, James Rogers Papers.
[86] Richardson, ed., *Bristol, Africa and the Eighteenth-Century Slave Trade to America, Vol. 3*, pp. xx–xxi.
[87] ACRL, John Pearce to Edward Southwell, 16 July 1740, Southwell Papers.

their exports to Africa.[88] 'Bristol's evident reliance upon foreign supplies of essential trade goods for Africa', it has been claimed, 'was perhaps its Achilles heel as a slaving port in the long term.'[89] By 1765 foreign manufactured goods had increased greatly in price, some by as much as 100 per cent in twenty years. Liverpool slave traders procured these goods cheaply in Holland, where beads and other export items were more widely available, less expensive, and better assorted than in England. They acquired cheap brass battery, arms, gunpowder and spirits from Holland in the Isle of Man, to the great detriment of the Bristol slave trade. No less than 4–6,000 barrels of gunpowder, for instance, were lodged at the Isle of Man between November 1764 and mid-January 1765, all intended for Liverpool ships bound to Africa.[90]

Despite problems experienced in the 1740s and growing competition from Liverpool, Bristol was still the second slaving port in England during the 1750s and the third from the 1760s onwards. The general rate of profit by investors in Bristol slaving ventures at mid-century (as measured by slave complements and deliveries) remained comparable to that achieved elsewhere.[91] Yet Bristol did not recapture the leading role she had played in the trade in the 1720s and early 1730s. Besides the factors already discussed, another commercial problem inhibited such a revival: the difficulty of securing remittances for sales of slaves. This is best illustrated by the experience of the Brights and Meylers, two substantial Bristol merchant families linked by marriage and business. Henry Bright, first an apprentice and later a son-in-law to Richard Meyler, Sr, lived in Bristol, Jamaica and St Kitts for various spells in the 1740s. He settled permanently in Bristol from 1749 onwards. Richard Meyler, Sr, his commercial partner, was always resident in Bristol. In the 1750s their business was assisted by Francis Bright (the brother of Henry) and by Jeremiah Meyler (the nephew of Richard, Sr), both of whom lived in Jamaica where they formed partnerships with merchants at Kingston and Savanna-la-Mar. The business was later taken over by a nephew of Henry Bright called Lowbridge Bright, who lived in Jamaica from 1765 until 1768 before returning to Bristol. Henry Bright, while in Bristol, managed twenty-one slaving voyages between 1749 and 1766. Richard Meyler, Sr

[88] Richardson, 'West African Consumption Patterns', pp. 303–30.
[89] Richardson, ed., *Bristol, Africa and the Eighteenth-Century Slave Trade to America, Vol. 1*, p. xx.
[90] SMV, Isaac Baugh to Robert Nugent, 22 Jan. 1760, and Isaac Elton to Robert Nugent, 15 Jan. 1765, SMV Letterbook (1753–80); PRO, CO 388/95 I (4): Representation of John Murray to the Earl of Halifax, 10 Apr. 1765.
[91] Richardson, ed., *Bristol, Africa, and the Eighteenth-Century Slave Trade to America, Vol. 3*, pp. xv–xviii.

also invested in many of these ventures.[92] Most of the voyages involved trade with Jamaica, the biggest slave market for Bristol and an island where an increase in the supply of slaves in the generation before the American Revolution stimulated productivity on the plantations to meet growing British demand for sugar consumption.[93]

Unfortunately, the Brights and the Meylers found it difficult to extract payment for slaves sold in Jamaica. When no bills of exchange or cash were available there – a frequent occurrence – proceeds for slave cargoes had to be remitted in produce. Henry Bright considered that this led to 'most miserable Returns and the Ruine of a Voyadge'.[94] Evidence on the lack of full return cargoes taken by Bristol slaving vessels supports this contention.[95] Loading sugar and other produce was not a favoured method of remittance in the slave trade because merchants could not be certain of the prices they would receive for goods taken on their own account; so much depended on the state of the Bristol market as well as prevailing prices in Jamaica.[96]

It was always difficult to extract money tied up in mortgage or plantation debts in the West Indies – something which casts doubt on the extent to which the wealth of the Caribbean was repatriated to Britain in the eighteenth century.[97] Richard Pares outlined the contributory factors to 'that malignant organism, a West-India debt' when he showed how planters fell into arrears through a combination of personal extravagance, poor plantation management, exorbitant annuities on existing estates, the purchase of slaves and new plantations, the need to cope with

[92] Information taken from various parts of the Bright Family Papers at the BRO and the UMA. I intend to publish a separate, full account of the West India connections of these Bristol families.

[93] Richardson, ed., *Bristol, Africa and the Eighteenth-Century Slave Trade to America, Vol. 3*, pp. xxi–xxii; David Richardson, 'The Slave Trade, Sugar, and British Economic Growth, 1748–1776,' *Journal of Interdisciplinary History*, 17 (1987), 739–69.

[94] UMA, Henry Bright to Richard Meyler, Sr, 25 July 1749, and Jeremiah Meyler to Henry Bright, 15 Feb. 1752, boxes 8 and 85, Bright Family Papers.

[95] Richard B. Sheridan has argued that after 1750 many slave vessels returned home from the Caribbean in ballast while W. E. Minchinton has suggested, on the contrary, that slave ships sailed home partly laden with staple produce (Sheridan, 'The Commercial and Financial Organisation of the British Slave Trade, 1750–1807', *EcHR*, 2nd Series, II (1958–9), 252–3; Minchinton, 'The Triangular Trade Revisited' in Gemery and Hogendorn, eds., *The Uncommon Market*, pp. 331–52). Evidence for 1762–5 inclusive shows that direct vessels in the Bristol–Jamaica trade took home about twice as much sugar as slave ships from Bristol trading with Jamaica (Morgan, 'Bristol Merchants and the Colonial Trades,' pp. 271–4).

[96] UMA, Lowbridge Bright to Bright, Milward & Duncomb, 24 Sept. 1773, Lowbridge Bright Letterbook (1765–73), Bright Family Papers.

[97] This is discussed in Kenneth Morgan, 'Atlantic Trade and British Economic Growth in the Eighteenth Century' in Peter Mathias and John A. Davis, eds., *International Trade and British Economic Growth from the Eighteenth Century to the Present* (Oxford, 1994).

debts inherited from previous generations, and falling incomes coupled with rising costs.[98] The Brights and the Meylers encountered these problems. In particular they experienced great delays, and hence the risk of bad debts, in selling Gold Coast Negroes in Jamaica in the late 1740s and early 1750s. Such slaves were expensive, selling at around £50 in Jamaican currency. Slaves from Angola, Calabar, Bonny or the Bight of Benin sold more cheaply, for about £30 in Jamaican currency, and remittances were easier to collect for them.[99]

Extension of considerable credit was necessary to sell slaves at good prices. But this could cause problems of payment.[100] The usual method of remittance for slave sales was for factors in the New World to return part of the proceeds at once – in produce, specie or bills of exchange – and the rest at a specified future date (which could be up to eighteen months' time).[101] Yet this procedure left the timing of payment for slaves uncertain given the debt situation in the plantation economies. An added problem was that British merchants sometimes delayed payment on bills drawn on them for slave sales in advance of receiving their own proceeds from seasonal plantation crops.[102] The Brights and the Meylers therefore adopted a system that became widespread in the English slave trade by the mid-eighteenth century: they only accepted remittances in bills of exchange paid at specified times and guaranteed by a merchant house of known trust. Preferably some of the returns were made 'in the bottom' of the ship that delivered the slave cargo. This method of remittance led to slavers leaving the Americas with some of the receipts for slave sales plus the balance still owed – the greater part of the proceeds – in a factor's bills of exchange on his guarantor in England. Under this system, bills were usually payable at not less than nine, twelve and fifteen months' sight after presentation to the drawee in England for acceptance.[103] On one set

[98] Pares, *West-India Fortune*, pp. 239–92.

[99] UMA, Francis Bright to Richard Meyler, Sr, 29 May 1751, Francis Bright Letterbook (1752–3); Francis Bright to Henry Bright, 28 May 1747; Jeremiah Meyler to Richard Meyler, Sr, 22 Apr. 1752, boxes 7, 8, 25, Bright Family Papers.

[100] On the role of credit in the slave trade see Joseph E. Inikori, 'The Credit Needs of the African Trade and the Development of the Credit Economy in England', *Explorations in Economic History*, 27 (1990), 197–231, and Jacob M. Price, 'Credit in the Slave Trade and Plantation Economies' in Barbara L. Solow, ed., *Slavery and the Rise of the Atlantic System* (Cambridge, 1991), pp. 298–323.

[101] See, for example, ACRL, Tyndall & Assheton to Isaac Hobhouse, 13 Mar. 1729, Jefferies Collection, XIII, no. 96; Bristol Industrial Museum, Benjamin King & Robert Arbuthnot to Isaac Hobhouse & Stephen Baugh, 24 Nov. 1740; and above, p. 139.

[102] For examples in the Bristol slave trade see Augustine Moore to Isaac Hobhouse & Co., 8 Mar. 1722, 6 May 1723, in W. E. Minchinton, ed., 'The Virginia Letters of Isaac Hobhouse, Merchant of Bristol', *VMHB*, 66 (1958), 288–9, 294.

[103] The system is well explained in PRO, T 79/30: Printed memorial of J. T. Warre on the debt of Wayles and Randolph, 22 June 1798; BRO, Henry Bright *et al.* to Capt. James McTaggart, 5 Mar. 1759, Bright Papers; Price, 'Credit in the Slave Trade', pp. 311–15;

of voyages that followed this procedure the Brights and the Meylers nominated Bush & Elton, a Bristol merchant firm with whom they were involved in shipowning, as 'security' for the returns.[104] At the Bristol end of the business great emphasis was laid on the Jamaican agents being careful in dealing with bills remitted on Guinea ships. If any bills were protested, Richard Meyler, Sr and Henry Bright would be obliged to pay them because of the bond they had given.[105] As Meyler put it to Francis Bright, when noting that he had to give his partners security for remittances, 'if you fail therein 'twill be of very bad Consequence to me & y[ou]r Bro[ther]'.[106]

Remittances were essential for Bristol slave traders to profit from their ventures, especially since prices for slaves were rising on the African coast in the quarter century before the American Revolution.[107] Yet the problems were not overcome even by such well-positioned merchants as the Brights and the Meylers. 'Loss by Remittances is the Rock more Guinea Houses have splitt upon than any other', Lowbridge Bright advised his Jamaican agents in 1773, 'and you cannot be too provident in guarding against it.'[108] Henry Bright noted in the late 1760s that several Bristol slave ships had recently made bad voyages, and that the last seven of these vessels bound to the West Indies would lose £10,000. One week later he added that 'all our African ships makes Bad Voyages'.[109] He himself had clearly experienced difficulty in securing prompt and full payment. He had 'a very great sum' tied up in Jamaica over many years, a 'good part of which arose from Guinea men sold there'.[110] Other Bristol merchants insisted on long-dated bills of exchange as remittance for slave cargoes delivered to transatlantic markets but found payments difficult to

and David Richardson, 'The British Slave Trade to Colonial South Carolina', *Slavery and Abolition*, 12 (1991), 151–60. For a detailed case study see B. L. Anderson, 'The Lancashire Bill System and its Liverpool Practitioners: The Case of a Slave Merchant' in W. H. Chaloner and Barrie M. Ratcliffe, eds., *Trade and Transport: Essays in Economic History in Honour of T. S. Willan* (Manchester, 1977), pp. 59–97.

[104] UMA, Lowbridge to Bright, Milward & Duncomb, 26 July, 21 Sept. 1773, 26 Jan. 1774, Lowbridge Bright Letterbook (1765–73), Bright Family Papers.

[105] *Ibid.*

[106] UMA, Richard Meyler, Sr to Francis Bright, 3 Dec. 1748, box 7, *ibid.*

[107] See the comments in UMA, Lowbridge Bright to Bright, Milward & Duncomb, 3 Dec. 1773, Lowbridge Bright Letterbook (1765–73), *ibid.*, and PRO, CO 388/45 pt. 3, fos. 89–91: Deposition of William Brown, 16 June 1753.

[108] UMA, Lowbridge Bright to Bright, Milward & Duncomb, 24 Sept. 1773, Lowbridge Bright Letterbook (1765–73), Bright Family Papers.

[109] BRO, Henry Bright to Richard Bright, 16, 23 Dec. 1769, Letters of the Brights of Colwall, 1746–71, Bright Papers.

[110] UMA, Lowbridge Bright to Bright & Milward, 21 Mar. 1771, Lowbridge Bright Letterbook (1765–73), Bright Family Papers.

secure.[111] One firm of guarantees, Lyde & Cooper, were forced to pay when a slave-selling factor in Maryland defaulted.[112] A leading Bristol West India merchant, William Miles, also suffered from lack of payment for slave cargoes for which he had served as guarantor.[113] Another Bristol mercantile house did not settle their debts under the guarantee system until 1811.[114]

After the American Revolution, the Meylers found that two or three years' credit was expected for the sale of slaves in Jamaica. They therefore declined a consignment of Negroes because the bad debts amounted to more than the commissions.[115] The Bristol slave trade in general was an emasculated version of its former self by the 1780s. This was partly because the commercial incentives for re-entry into the trade, in any substantial way, no longer existed. One major Bristol slave merchant, James Rogers, found that slaves were now more expensive than ever to buy in Africa and that remittances due from the Caribbean were still precarious and long-winded.[116] James Jones, another leading Bristol slave trader, felt that restrictions placed on the carriage of slaves by Dolben's Act (1788) would force him to reduce the number of slaves carried on his ships by almost a quarter.[117] He estimated that this would lead to a loss of between £1,400 and £1,500 on ships in the trade larger than 200 tons. 'It is a very uncertain and precarious trade', he added, 'and

---

[111] UMA, Smith & Baillies to Henry Bright, 21 June 1763, *ibid.*; Lloyd's of London, Owners to Capt. William Llewellin, Sept. 1770, and to Richard Hanson, 28 Feb. 1771, Account Book of the *Hector*; Farell & Jones to Wayles & Randolph, 6 Apr. 1772, and to Richard Randolph, 10 Dec. 1773, in Boyd, ed., *The Papers of Thomas Jefferson, Vol. 15*, pp. 652, 665. Later examples of remittance in bills of exchange at 12, 15, 18, 21 and 24 months' sight for slaves delivered by Bristol ships include PRO, C 107/6: John Kennedy to James Rogers & Co., 3 May 1792; C 107/8: Campbell, Baillie & Co. to James Rogers, 26 Mar. 1786, and Francis Grant to James Rogers & Co., 15 Mar. 1791, James Rogers Papers; Sale of 306 slaves from the *Emilia* on the account of Evan Baillie & Co., 5–6 Feb. 1784, cited in Lambert, ed., *House of Commons Sessional Papers*, LXXII, pp. 349–51.

[112] Price, 'Credit in the Slave Trade', p. 321 note 70.

[113] Kenneth Morgan, ed., 'The Letters of William Miles, a Bristol West India Merchant, to John Tharp, a Jamaican Sugar Planter, 1770–1789' in Patrick McGrath, ed., *A Bristol Miscellany* (Bristol Record Society's *Publications*, 37, 1985), pp. 105, 110.

[114] Price, 'Credit in the Slave Trade', pp. 320–1.

[115] UMA, Jeremiah Meyler to Richard Bright, 5 Nov. 1783, Bright Family Papers.

[116] PRO, C 107/5: William Roper to James Rogers, 12 Dec. 1789, and Capt. John Goodrich to James Rogers, 4 Feb. 1790; C 107/6: William Stewart to James Rogers, 8 June 1792; C 107/9: Capt. Thomas Walker to James Rogers, 2 July 1787; C 107/12: John Smith to James Rogers, 30 Apr. 1791; C 107/13: William Woodville, Jr to James Rogers & Co., 16 May 1791, and Samuel Forsyth to James Rogers, 11 June 1792; C 107/14: William Roper to James Rogers, 17 June 1791, James Rogers Papers. I intend to analyse the Rogers Papers in detail in a future publication. A brief appraisal of Rogers as a slave trader appears in Rawley, *The Transatlantic Slave Trade*, pp. 186–9.

[117] Minchinton, ed., *Trade of Bristol in the Eighteenth Century*, p. 173.

if there is not a probable Prospect of considerable Profit, no Man of Property who hath any Knowledge of it would embark or continue in it.'[118] By the mid-1790s the African business had virtually stopped at Bristol and gunmakers, once prominent suppliers to slaving vessels, directed their interests to the country trade instead.[119] Even the prospect of large commissions in the Guinea business was insufficient to tempt Bristol firms back into the trade.[120] Apart from considerations already mentioned, Bristolians may have been deterred from re-entering the trade by the substantial rise in slave prices on the African coast during the eighteenth century.[121]

By the 1780s Bristolians were, to some degree, morally opposed to the slave trade, perhaps because of the strength of Dissenting groups in the city. Harry Gandy, a conveyancer who had sailed on Bristol slaving voyages, now supported the Quaker view of the inhumanity of the traffic.[122] Joseph Harford, an Anglican convert from Quakerism who had been High Sheriff and Mayor of Bristol, told William Wilberforce 'that the slave trade is growing disgraceful'.[123] John Wesley preached a famous sermon at the New Room, Bristol on the immorality of slavery, an occasion when violent shaking – almost a sign of divine wrath – stopped the service for six minutes.[124] These criticisms were effective, for Bristol became the first English provincial town to set up a committee to agitate against the slave trade.[125] Local attacks on the Guinea business continued into the 1790s. One of the prominent anti-slave trade spokesmen at that time was the poet Samuel Taylor Coleridge, who lectured on the topic at the Assembly coffee house on the Quay in 1795.[126]

A Bristol directory for 1794 claimed that 'the ardour for the Trade to Africa for men and women, our fellow creatures and equals, is much

[118] BL, Add. MS 38,416: James Jones to Lord Hawkesbury, 26 July 1788.

[119] Somerset RO, George Dyer to Henry Strachey, 27 Nov. 1795, 22 Apr. 1796, box 27, Strachie MSS, DD/SH c/1165. The provision of gunpowder for the Bristol slave trade is discussed in B. J. Buchanan and M. T. Tucker, 'The Manufacture of Gunpowder: A Study of the Documentary and Physical Evidence Relating to the Woolley Powder Works near Bath', *Industrial Archaeological Review*, 5 (1981), 185–202.

[120] Bristol UL, Tobin & Pinney to Ulysses Lynch, 21 Dec. 1789, Tobin & Pinney Letter-book (1789–92), Pinney Papers.

[121] David Richardson, 'Prices of Slaves in West and West-Central Africa: Toward an Annual Series, 1698–1807', *Bulletin of Economic Research*, 43 (1991), 21–56.

[122] Anthony Benezet, *Some Historical Account of Guinea* . . . (2nd edn., London, 1788), pp. 125–31.

[123] See Wilberforce's diary entry for 5 July 1791, quoted in Peter Marshall, 'The Anti-Slave Trade Movement in Bristol' in McGrath, ed., *Bristol in the Eighteenth Century*, p. 211.

[124] Nehemiah Curnock, ed., *The Journal of John Wesley*, 8 vols. (London, 1909–16), VII, 6 Mar. 1788, pp. 359–60.

[125] Latimer, *History of the Society of Merchant Venturers of the City of Bristol*, p. 185.

[126] Peter Fryer, *Staying Power: The History of Black People in Britain* (London, 1984), p. 212.

abated among the humane and benevolent merchants of Bristol. In 1787 there were but 30 ships employed in this melancholy traffic; while the people of Liverpool, in their indiscriminate rage for commerce and for getting money at all events, have nearly engrossed this Trade.'[127] But this comment conveniently distracts attention away from the importance of West India commerce to Bristol. As Thomas Clarkson found in 1787, when he investigated the slave trade, there was firm Bristol opposition to the Parliamentary movement to abolish the trade even though influential merchants in the city had no desire to increase their slaving ventures.[128] In 1791 the rejection by the Commons of Wilberforce's motion for a bill to abolish the slave trade was greeted in Bristol by a peal of church bells, the firing of cannon on Brandon Hill, a bonfire and fireworks display, and the grant of a half-day holiday to workmen and sailors.[129] The battle in Bristol between the pro-slave trade and abolitionist lobbies is further documented in Clarkson's account, in petitions presented to Parliament, and in the columns of local newspapers.[130] But if Bristol's slave trade had waned by the late eighteenth century so had her participation in the tobacco trade: the next chapter analyses the different reasons for another aspect of entrepreneurial decline in Bristol's colonial trades.

[127] W. Matthews, *The New History, Survey and Description of the City and Suburbs of Bristol, or Complete Guide and Bristol Directory for the Year 1793–4* (Bristol, 1794), pp. 38–9.

[128] Marshall, 'Anti-Slave Trade Movement', pp. 185–215; UMA, Lowbridge Bright to David Duncombe, 6 Apr. 1791, box 16, Bright Family Papers. For Clarkson's report to Parliament on the Bristol slave trade see Lambert, ed., *House of Commons Sessional Papers*, LXIX, pp. 144–56.

[129] Fryer, *Staying Power*, p. 64.

[130] Thomas Clarkson, *The History of the Rise, Progress and Accomplishment of the Abolition of the African Slave Trade by the British Parliament*, 2 vols. (London, 1808), I, pp. 294–367; SMV, Meetings at Merchants' Hall to oppose the abolition of the slave trade, 13, 15 Apr. 1789, and Lowbridge Bright to Jeremiah Osborn, 25 Apr. 1789, in Papers on the African Slave Trade, bundle G; House of Lords Record Office, Main Papers: James Jones, Petition of the Merchants of Bristol against the slave trade, 19 June 1788; Petition of the West India Planters and Merchants of Bristol, 5 July 1788; Petition of the Master, wardens and commonalty of the Merchant Venturers of Bristol, 24 May 1792; Petition of the Merchants, traders and shipowners concerned in the trade to Africa from the Port of Bristol, 31 May 1792; Richards, 'Connection of Bristol', pp. 23–87.

6   The tobacco trade

Tobacco was the most valuable commodity imported into Bristol and other British ports from mainland North America in the seventeenth and eighteenth centuries. On the eve of the American Revolution, tobacco imports into Britain were worth just under £1 million at official prices and almost the same at market prices. This made tobacco at least twice as valuable as coffee and rice, the next most important commodities imported from mainland America.[1] British tobacco imports increased from 38 million lbs. in 1700 to 100 million lbs. in 1771–5. By 1775, Scotland received almost as much tobacco as England (46 million lbs. as opposed to 56 million) and more than four-fifths of the leaf was re-exported, mainly to the European continent.[2] Such growth triggered significant changes in both business operations and the scale of enterprise in the Chesapeake and throughout the Atlantic trading world. The most significant change was the rise of the re-export trade. Demand for tobacco within Britain, by contrast, was relatively inelastic and soon reached a plateau. This was partly because tobacco consumption remained the preserve of adult males, and partly because pipe smoking was associated with the alehouse, which fell into decline in the later eighteenth century.[3] The demand for snuff – an important component of British tobacco consumption – was presumably insufficient to alter these trends. As we shall see, Bristol's tobacco trade, with its emphasis on the domestic market, failed to advance during the eighteenth century as rival British ports gained the upper hand in marketing the crop via the re-export business.

Bristol's declining role in this branch of Atlantic commerce can be traced in the four phases that characterised the tobacco trade before

---

[1] Jacob M. Price, 'Colonial Trade and British Economic Development, 1660–1775' in *La Révolution américaine et l'Europe: colloques internationaux du Centre nationale de la Recherche Scientifique*, no. 577 (Paris, 1979), p. 226.

[2] US Department of Commerce, Bureau of the Census, *Historical Statistics of the United States*, 2 vols. (Washington, DC, 1975), II, Series Z 449–56, p. 1190.

[3] Carole Shammas, *The Pre-Industrial Consumer in England and America* (Oxford, 1990), pp. 78–81.

1800.[4] First came a period from the late 1630s to the 1670s during which the rapid increase of settlement in the Chesapeake was accompanied by expanding tobacco production and a gradual reduction in the costs of producing, transporting and marketing the crop. Bristol merchants, following in the wake of London, entered this initial boom and imported over four million lbs. of tobacco per annum by the early 1670s.[5] Between the 1680s and the 1720s, however, rapid trade fluctuations caused by a slump in tobacco production, poor prices, and long European wars led the London and Bristol markets to approach stagnation. By the 1690s Bristol was second only to London among English tobacco ports, accounting for 10–15 per cent of the total trade, but it did not increase its level of imports between that decade and the 1720s.[6]

Despite a continuing cyclical pattern of prosperity and depression, the tobacco trade recovered its fortunes from the late 1720s onwards. Renewed growth in production, price recovery in the Chesapeake, and ever-increasing European demand for consumption were stimulated by the spread of the nicotine habit, the rise of English and Scottish outport firms in the trade, and the expansion of tobacco growing in a more diversified Chesapeake economy.[7] During this period the west coast outports took a more important role in the trade, with tobacco imports generally moving away from south-western ports such as Bristol, Barnstaple and Bideford to three north-western ports – Liverpool, Whitehaven and Glasgow. The latter forged ahead of their rivals partly through more efficient methods of collecting and shipping tobacco and partly through the natural advantage of relatively sheltered positions away from naval engagements and privateering raids in wartime. British merchants also increased their re-export business to northern Europe. Londoners were particularly active in supplying tobacco to the Dutch market, while Glaswegians concentrated on selling the leaf to the French tobacco

---

[4] This section is based on a reading of Jacob M. Price, *France and the Chesapeake: A History of the French Tobacco Monopoly, 1674–1791, and of its Relationship to the British and American Tobacco Trades*, 2 vols. (Ann Arbor, MI, 1973); John M. Hemphill, 'Virginia and the English Commercial System, 1689–1733: Studies in the Development and Fluctuations of a Colonial Economy under Imperial Control' (Princeton University Ph.D. dissertation, 1964), chs. 1–4; Paul G. E. Clemens, *The Atlantic Economy and Colonial Maryland's Eastern Shore: From Tobacco to Grain* (Ithaca, NY, 1980), pp. 30–9, 111–19; Russell R. Menard, 'The Tobacco Industry in the Chesapeake Colonies, 1617–1730: An Interpretation', *Research in Economic History*, 5 (1980), 109–77; and Allan Kulikoff, *Tobacco and Slaves: The Development of Southern Cultures in the Chesapeake, 1680–1800* (Chapel Hill, NC, 1986), chs. 3 and 4.

[5] Jacob M. Price and Paul G. E. Clemens, 'A Revolution of Scale in Overseas Trade: British Firms in the Chesapeake Trade, 1675–1775', *JEcH*, 47 (1987), 25.

[6] Price, *France and the Chesapeake*, I, p. 180.

[7] Menard, 'Tobacco Industry', pp. 127, 154.

monopoly.[8] The tobacco trade from the American mainland collapsed during the War of Independence: less tobacco reached Britain and Europe in the period 1776–82 than during any single year before the war. Tobacco imports recovered in a fourth phase after 1783 but never regained their pre-war levels. London merchants dominated the British tobacco trade with the new United States, mainly at the expense of the Glasgow tobacco lords.[9]

Table 6.1 charts the changing position of the five major British ports engaged in the tobacco trade. London was always the leading port except during the decade before the American Revolution, when Glasgow overtook the metropolis as the main centre for tobacco importation.[10] This was the culmination of a rapid rise which established the tobacco trade as 'the first big business in Scotland' and gave Glasgow 'a leading position among the commercial cities of Europe'.[11] Whitehaven's involvement in tobacco importation declined after reaching a peak during wartime in the 1740s, and Liverpool's tobacco trade reached its height by 1750.[12] Bristol lagged behind these ports, being passed in the level of tobacco imports by Glasgow in the 1720s, by Liverpool in 1738, and by Whitehaven in 1739. In fact, the Bristol tobacco trade remained stationary: aggregate imports in the 1770s had not advanced beyond the four million lbs. of the 1720s.

Bristol was the only significant port in the trade where more than 50 per cent of the imported leaf was consumed in the home market – as table 6.2 reveals for the early eighteenth century. By contrast, more than 90 per cent of the tobacco entering Glasgow and over 70 per cent arriving at

----

[8] Price, *France and the Chesapeake*, II, appendix, tables 2a-c, pp. 845–9; Jacob M. Price, 'The Rise of Glasgow in the Chesapeake Tobacco Trade, 1707–1775', *WMQ*, 3rd Series, II (1954), 179–99; Richard F. Dell, 'The Operational Record of the Clyde Tobacco Fleet, 1747–1775', *Scottish Economic and Social History*, 2 (1982), 1–16; Paul G. E. Clemens, 'The Rise of Liverpool, 1665–1750', *EcHR*, 2nd Series, 29 (1976), 211–25; T. M. Devine, *The Tobacco Lords: A Study of the Tobacco Merchants of Glasgow and their Trading Activities, c. 1740–1790* (Edinburgh, 1975), pp. 65–6; and David Ormrod, 'English Re-Exports and the Dutch Staple Market in the Eighteenth Century', in D. C. Coleman and Peter Mathias, eds., *Enterprise and History: Essays in Honour of Charles Wilson* (Cambridge, 1984), table 6.1, p. 97.

[9] Price, *France and the Chesapeake*, II, pp. 731–3; US Bureau of the Census, Department of Commerce, *Historical Statistics of the United States*, II, Series Z 449–56, p. 1190; Kulikoff, *Tobacco and Slaves*, p. 157.

[10] On the role of Glasgow in the tobacco trade see the studies in note 8 plus Clemens, *Atlantic Economy*, pp. 112–14, and Stuart M. Butler, 'The Glasgow Tobacco Merchants and the American Revolution, 1770–1800' (University of St Andrews Ph.D. thesis, 1978).

[11] W. R. Brock, *Scotus Americanus: A Survey of Sources for Links between Scotland and America in the Eighteenth Century* (Edinburgh, 1982), pp. 2, 53.

[12] Clemens, *Atlantic Economy*, p. 113; J. V. Beckett, *Coal and Tobacco: The Lowthers and the Economic Development of West Cumberland, 1660–1760* (Cambridge, 1981), pp. 104–8, 204–5; Annie Eaglesham, 'The Growth and Influence of the West Cumberland Shipping Industry, 1660–1800' (University of Lancaster Ph.D. thesis, 1977), pt. 1, ch. 2.

Table 6.1. *British tobacco imports at the five principal centres, 1722–1800 (in thousands of lbs.)*

	London	Bristol	Liverpool	Whitehaven	Port Glasgow and Greenock
1722	19,457	4,109	1,728	1,119	6,533[a]
1723	20,581	4,900	1,569	859	4,166[a]
1724	18,400	3,076	2,008	1,410	5,311[a]
1725	14,272	3,182	1,203	756	4,162[a]
1726	20,114	3,809	2,250	1,955	3,616[a]
1727	27,671	6,870	2,962	1,877	6,537[a]
1728	28,563	4,851	4,051	1,442	6,696[a]
1729	27,296	3,945	3,276	1,896	6,383[a]
1730	23,981	3,410	2,491	2,011	4,495[a]
1731	28,860	4,508	2,431	1,472	3,266[a]
1738	24,889	3,816	4,351	3,168	3,745
1739	30,516	3,799	4,310	3,942	4,713
1740	17,437	4,748	5,358	4,457	4,255
1741	40,025	2,927	5,468	5,413	6,434
1742	23,360	4,311	5,312	6,970	8,569
1743	36,254	3,840	6,129	9,443	9,148
1744	22,805	3,791	4,248	9,359	8,832
1745	24,373	3,243	5,770	7,073	11,173
1746	18,407	3,979	7,195	9,145	8,194
1747	28,189	3,256	9,380	9,266	10,021
1748	27,782	2,861	8,161	10,622	13,537
1749	21,438	4,690	6,004	10,556	17,783
1750	25,668	4,806	5,563	9,013	14,361
1751	26,000	4,506	5,412	n.a.	15,999
1752	33,000	6,963	6,206	n.a.	16,071
1753	37,000	6,544	6,828	n.a.	17,705
1754	33,000	n.a.	6,746	n.a.	13,370
1763	42,000	4,649	4,850	n.a.	30,560
1764	37,000	4,824	3,150	n.a.	23,912
1765	29,000	5,570	3,177	n.a.	32,450
1766	27,000	n.a.	3,298	n.a.	28,731
1771	43,542	4,433	7,020	2,940	48,148
1772	38,789	4,713	6,537	3,576	43,427
1773	34,913	4,668	7,593	7,212	44,471
1784	32,672	2,213	5,825	127	4,205
1785	26,231	1,975	4,613	1,505	9,306
1786	26,554	1,607	4,552	1,882	8,071
1790	33,333	2,461	10,415	118	10,573
1791	29,072	2,341	5,325	1,332	14,407
1792	28,960	1,927	7,481	579	3,467
1799	23,326	1,586	6,504	165	3,706
1800	23,078	2,416	7,683	359	4,147

[a] Indicates year ending at Michaelmas; otherwise at Christmas.
Source: Jacob M. Price and Paul G. E. Clemens, 'A Revolution of Scale in Overseas Trade: British Firms in the Chesapeake Trade, 1675–1775', *Journal of Economic History*, 47 (1987), appendix A, tables 13 and 14, 39–40.

Table 6.2. *Tobacco imports and re-exports at selected English ports, 1722–1731*

	London			Bristol			Liverpool			Whitehaven		
	Imports (lbs.)	Exports (lbs.)	% exported	Imports (lbs.)	Exports (lbs.)	% exported	Imports (lbs.)	Exports (lbs.)	% exported	Imports (lbs.)	Exports (lbs.)	% exported
1722	19,456,793	16,501,310	(85)	4,109,182	1,159,833	(28)	1,727,749	1,153,504	(67)	1,119,194	925,584	(83)
1723	20,581,204	16,367,567	(80)	3,900,372	1,626,824	(42)	1,569,374	1,239,846	(79)	859,015	1,916,844	(223)
1724	18,400,201	12,808,981	(70)	3,076,377	1,491,818	(48)	2,008,204	1,168,706	(58)	1,410,139	625,219	(44)
1725	14,272,169	10,031,632	(70)	3,182,390	1,384,145	(43)	1,203,639	1,009,861	(84)	755,982	1,275,844	(169)
1726	20,113,536	22,134,929	(110)	3,808,804	1,749,643	(46)	2,249,863	1,305,681	(58)	1,955,183	1,187,663	(61)
1727	27,671,005	18,127,596	(66)	6,869,862	2,940,538	(43)	2,962,046	1,900,247	(64)	1,877,015	1,539,530	(82)
1728	28,562,703	18,030,782	(63)	4,851,709	2,012,637	(41)	4,051,207	2,480,027	(61)	1,442,373	2,174,624	(151)
1729	27,295,641	22,716,718	(83)	3,945,031	1,401,337	(36)	3,275,774	2,723,160	(83)	1,895,740	1,591,361	(84)
1730	23,980,765	19,088,124	(80)	3,409,523	1,646,327	(48)	2,491,228	1,585,433	(64)	2,010,907	1,437,701	(71)
1731	28,860,300	19,478,429	(67)	4,508,206	1,585,195	(35)	2,439,582	3,014,839	(124)	1,472,069	2,468,587	(168)
Totals	229,194,317	175,286,068	(77)	41,661,456	16,998,297	(41)	23,969,666	17,581,304	(74)	14,797,617	15,142,957	(114)

Source: Public Record Office, London, T 1/278, fos. 100–2. Identical information is given in T 64/276 B.

London was usually re-exported.[13] Since smuggling was extensive and linked to domestic consumption, the figures in table 6.1 underestimate the amount of tobacco entering Bristol. The degree of understatement is impossible to determine because of the clandestine nature of illegal importation.[14] The most obvious form of smuggling – the running of uncustomed leaf into secluded coves – was not the main problem, for it declined after the government banned the shipping of unprized or bulk tobacco in 1699.[15] Indirect methods of smuggling had a greater impact. Evidence of Bristol merchants relanding tobacco after claiming the drawback to which they were entitled on re-exportation surfaces in a report of 1718, which noted that goods were run from time to time on the stretch of coast between Woodspring and Possets Point in Somerset and Shirehampton and Berkeley in Gloucestershire.[16] A later report of 1764 still referred to tobacco and other commodities being run at Bristol.[17] Probably more significant, in terms of indirect smuggling, were various cases of fraud concerning merchants and customs officials handling tobacco at Bristol in the 1680s, the early 1690s, and in 1703, 1718, and the 1720s, after which increased customs efficiency made examples of cheating rarer.[18]

Despite the significance of smuggling, the Bristol tobacco trade generally lacked buoyancy in the eighteenth century. Table 6.3 shows that the

---

[13] Price, *France and the Chesapeake*, I, p. 591; W. E. Minchinton, ed., *Trade of Bristol in the Eighteenth Century*, p. 15. Annual figures for Bristol's tobacco re-exports for the period 1786–1806 are given in *British Parliamentary Papers* (1806), XIII, Accounts and Papers, IV, pp. 817–19.

[14] The best detailed study of all different aspects of tobacco smuggling is Jacob M. Price, 'The Tobacco Trade and the Treasury, 1685–1733: British Mercantilism in its Fiscal Aspects' (Harvard University Ph.D. dissertation, 1954), chs. 4–8. See also Robert C. Nash, 'The English and Scottish Tobacco Trades in the Seventeenth and Eighteenth Centuries: Legal and Illegal Trade', *EcHR*, 2nd Series, 35 (1982), 354–72, and T. C. Barker, 'Smuggling in the Eighteenth Century: The Evidence of the Scottish Tobacco Trade', *VMHB*, 71 (1954), 387–99.

[15] Price, 'Tobacco Trade and the Treasury,' p. 269.

[16] PRO, T 64/142, fo. 1b.

[17] BL, Add. MS 9,293, fo. 46: 'Report of the State of the Trade of the Several Outports of England and Wales, 1764.' For an incident of snuff smuggling by Bristol merchants see below, p. 179.

[18] Patrick McGrath, ed., *Merchants and Merchandise in Seventeenth-Century Bristol* (Bristol Record Society's *Publications*, 19, 1955), pp. 222–4; Price, 'Tobacco Trade and the Treasury', pp. 573–84, 628–30, 655, 661–2; PRO, T 64/142; PRO, T 64/143: Revenue frauds, London and Western Ports, 1723–32. For an example of a customs fraud at Bristol after 1750 see BL, Add. MS 34,736, fos. 55–79: '9 Jan. 1755, Mr H. Simon: A Copy of his Report to the Commissioners of His Majesties Customs on his Inspection into the Frauds of the Customs in the Port of Bristol.' Robert C. Nash suggests that tobacco hogsheads at Bristol were underweighed by 3 per cent in 1700 and by 15 per cent by 1730 ('The English and Scottish Tobacco Trades in the Seventeenth and Eighteenth Centuries: Legal and Illegal Trade', pp. 358–9, and tables 6 and 7, pp. 366–7).

Table 6.3. *Activity of Bristol tobacco importers, 1702–1799 (annual averages)*

	Hogsheads imported	Number of firms	Imports per firm
1702	6,274.6	202	31.1
1723	4,900.5	188	26.1
1728–32	5,012	89.4	56.1
1733–7	4,870.2	62.4	78.0
1738–42	4,686.2	51.8	90.5
1743–7	4,195.2	35.8	117.2
1748–9	3,631	28	129.7
1754–7	6,905.3	27.3	252.9
1758–62	5,803	21.4	271.2
1763–7	4,610.6	19.6	235.2
1768	3,325	14	237.5
1773–6	3,225	7.8	413.5
1785	2,009	26	77.3
1788–9	2,809.5	12.5	224.8
1791–2	2,071	8	258.9
1793–7	1,537.8	2.6	591.5
1798–9	1,638.5	6	273.1

Sources: i) 1702, 1723: Jacob M. Price and Paul G. E. Clemens, 'A Revolution of Scale in Overseas Trade: British Firms in the Chesapeake Trade, 1675–1775', *Journal of Economic History*, 47 (1987), table 6A, p. 25, where the tobacco imports are given in lbs. I have converted the figures at 794 lbs. per hogshead by using data for 1731, the nearest year where tobacco imports are available in both sets of measures.
ii) 1728–32 to 1789: Society of Merchant Venturers, Bristol, Wharfage Books.
iii) 1791, 1793–6, 1798–9: Avon County Reference Library, Bristol, *Bristol Presentments*, Imports.

number of firms involved in the trade decreased quite dramatically over time. At the beginning of the century, there were more than 200 tobacco importers at Bristol; by the 1770s, less than ten. With the exception of 1785, the number of Bristol tobacco importers remained in single figures after the American Revolution. This decline occurred consistently throughout periods of war and peace. Table 6.4 presents material for sample years to demonstrate more clearly the high concentration ratios in the trade. It reveals that most tobacco importers were medium-size firms (with annual imports between 50 and 499 hogsheads) and that marginal firms (those importing less than 50 hogsheads) were increasingly squeezed out of the trade. It also points to the growing domination of the Bristol tobacco trade by a small, concentrated group of merchants who eliminated their commercial rivals at the same port. A similar pattern emerged at London and Glasgow, where annual tobacco imports were

Table 6.4. *Size of Bristol tobacco importers, 1728–1788*

	1728			1748			1768			1788		
	Number	Weight (hhds.)	% hhds.	Number	Weight (hhds.)	% hhds.	Number	Weight (hhds.)	% hhds.	Number	Weight (hhds.)	% hhds.
Over 1,000 hhds.	1	1,097	16.9	0	0	0.0	0	0	0.0	1	1,109	63.8
500–999 hhds.	1	516	7.9	1	777	26.1	1	971	29.2	0	0	0.0
50–499 hhds.	20	3,869	59.5	12	2,077	69.8	10	2,268	68.2	4	583	33.5
0–49 hhds.	108	1,022	15.7	11	122	4.1	3	86	2.6	3	47	2.7
Totals	130	6,504	100.0	24	2,976	100.0	14	3,325	100.0	8	1,739	100.0

Note: In preparing the table, firms were counted separately where personnel overlapped in any year.
Source: Society of Merchant Venturers, Bristol, Wharfage Books. Cf. Jacob M. Price and Paul G. E. Clemens, 'A Revolution of Scale in Overseas Trade: British Firms in the Chesapeake Trade, 1675–1775', *Journal of Economic History*, 47 (1987), table 7, p. 27.

much higher than at Bristol.[19] This movement from a large to a small number of firms was, in fact, a general phenomenon at all British ports engaged in the tobacco, slave and sugar trades from *circa* 1675 to 1775. It has been characterised as 'a revolution of scale' that stemmed mainly from the advantages brought to larger firms by the increased availability of credit.[20]

Table 6.5 shows the rank order of the major tobacco importers at Bristol. The leading firm, Farell & Jones, was active over a period of eighteen years in the 1760s and 1770s. Most other merchants listed, however, remained in the trade for relatively few years, and their surnames suggest that there was little family continuity from one generation to the next (the major exceptions being the Harfords and the Farells).[21] This was one of several significant differences between the sugar and tobacco trades at Bristol, for sugar importers belonged to a closer-knit group of families.[22] Another difference was that tobacco, sugar and slave merchants were discrete groups. Between 1748 and 1776 only Thomas Knox, John Perks, and Morgan Thomas and various partners appear – and then only occasionally – in these three trades.[23] This division between management of the tobacco and sugar trades was evident at Bristol and London (though not at Liverpool) by the 1720s and at Glasgow by 1770.[24] A third contrast was that Bristol tobacco merchants apparently acquired very little land or property in the Chesapeake, whereas a good many sugar merchants owned West Indian plantations, either in whole or in part.[25] In the 1730s a group of Bristol merchants controlled the management of an ironworks on the Rappahannock River in Virginia and in the 1750s at least four Bristolians had large estates in the same province, but

---

[19] Price, *France and the Chesapeake*, I, p. 568.

[20] Price and Clemens, 'Revolution of Scale', pp. 1–43. The dominance of a few British firms over the tobacco export of one of Virginia's naval districts is brought out in Robert Polk Thomson, 'The Tobacco Export of the Upper James River Naval District, 1773–1775', *WMQ*, 3rd Series, 18 (1961), 394, 401.

[21] The role of the Harfords in the Bristol tobacco trade is discussed in Jacob M. Price, *Capital and Credit in British Overseas Trade: The View from the Chesapeake, 1700–1776* (Cambridge, MA, 1980), pp. 31–3.

[22] See below, pp. 189, 194–5.

[23] Based on an examination of SMV, Wharfage Books and David Richardson, *The Bristol Slave Traders: A Collective Portrait* (Bristol Branch of the Historical Association, pamphlet no. 60, Bristol, 1985), appendix, pp. 29–30. For a comprehensive list of tobacco and sugar importers at Bristol, 1748–80, see Morgan, 'Bristol Merchants and the Colonial Trades', apps. B and C, pp. 325–66. The only occasion when the specialisation of sugar and tobacco merchants was seriously upset was during the American War of Independence: see above, pp. 26–7.

[24] Clemens, 'Rise of Liverpool', p. 219; T. M. Devine, 'Glasgow Merchants in Colonial Trade, 1770–1815' (University of Strathclyde Ph.D. thesis, 1971), pp. 99–103.

[25] See below, p. 186.

Table 6.5. *Leading tobacco importers at Bristol, 1728–1800*

Merchants	Hogsheads imported	Years active in the tobacco trade
Farell & Jones	16,723	1760–8, 1773–6, 1778
Thomas Knox	14,640	1748–9, 1754–61
William Holder	12,509	1785, 1788, 1791–9
Thomas Chamberlayne	11,202	1728–45, 1748, 1755
Joseph Farell	11,117	1728–49, 1755, 1757–60
Lyde & Cooper	10,955	1735–47
Lyonel Lyde	7,308	1728–36, 1741–2, 1745
Edward Harford, Sr	7,133	1728–45, 1749, 1755–6, 1758–68
John King	5,081	1728–49, 1754
John Perks	4,959	1754–8
Sedgley & Hilhouse	4,001	1757–63, 1766
George Whitehead	3,839	1728–46, 1748–9
Edward Harford, Jr	3,768	1754–60, 1763–7, 1774–5
Lidderdale, Harmer & Co.	2,452	1754–7
Sedgley, Hilhouse & Co.	2,254	1754, 1756, 1764, 1766–7
Lidderdale, Harmer & Farell	2,152	1754–6
Morgan Thomas	2,139	1749, 1754–8
Sedgley, Hilhouse & Berry	1,976	1754–6
George Braikenridge	1,371	1791–2, 1794
Stevenson, Randolph & Cheston	1,219	1773–4

Note: The table only includes years where a complete record of tobacco imports is available.
Source: Society of Merchant Venturers, Bristol, Wharfage Books.

these seem to have represented the sum total of direct investment for Bristol in the Chesapeake.[26]

Bristol merchants had ready access to the capital and credit resources that were vital for participation in the tobacco trade. Only one surviving source lists the initial capital put into a Bristol tobacco firm; the amount was £9,000 for the partnership of Stevenson, Randolph & Cheston.[27] This

[26] G. MacLaren Brydon, 'The Bristol Iron Works in King George County', *VMHB*, 13 (1934), 97–102; Price, *Capital and Credit*, p. 46; PRO, Chatham Papers, 30/8/95, fos. 149–50: Thomas Knox to James Abercromby, 4 Jan. 1757. John Harmer and Samuel Gist were probably two of the four Bristolians who owned land in Virginia in the 1750s. Harmer emigrated from Bristol to Virginia in 1733 and acquired 7,080 acres of land in Amherst County, including a tobacco plantation. Gist left Bristol for Virginia in 1739 and made a fortune there, buying several thousand acres in Hanover County before returning to London to set up as a tobacco merchant in 1765 (PRO, AO 13/30/75–212, 570–80, and Peter Wilson Coldham, ed., *American Loyalist Claims* (Washington, DC, 1980), I, pp. 182–4, 218).

[27] Maryland HS, William Stevenson to James Cheston, 5 Aug. 1768, James Cheston Incoming Letters, 1767–April 1771, box 9, Cheston-Galloway Papers. BRO, Articles of Partnership between Edward Cooper and Lyonel Lyde, 24 Sept. 1745, Acc. 17124(2), the only other partnership agreement extant for a Bristol tobacco firm, does not mention the amount of initial capital.

figure falls within the £5–10,000 range, which was the usual amount invested in British firms beginning to trade with Virginia and Maryland before the American Revolution.[28] Such modest capital resources made the mobilisation of long-term credit an essential part of business survival. Borrowing on bond was one way of assembling the wherewithal for trade. One Bristol tobacco merchant, John King, was using this means of raising credit by the early 1730s.[29] A small amount of credit was also available from local banks. Several prominent Bristol tobacco merchants were members of the five banks that opened in the city in the second half of the eighteenth century. Thus Thomas Knox and Edward Harford were founder members of the Bristol Old Bank and the Harford Bank in 1750 and 1769 respectively.[30]

Most of the credit needed in the tobacco trade came neither from bonds nor from banks but from commercial credit supplied by warehousemen in the ports. These intermediaries were often wholesale linendrapers and ironmongers, and some of them possessed considerable capitals. For instance, the Bristol wholesale linendrapers Fisher, Baker & Griffin had a capital of £18,000 in 1739, £30,000 in 1747, and £36,000 in 1754. Paul Fisher, the leading partner, was active in supplying credit in British–Chesapeake trade, for he signed the customs bonds of the John King mentioned above.[31] In addition, several Bristol merchants offered favourable financial terms to Virginia planter-consigners. The Crown allowed a discount of 7 per cent per annum for tobacco duties paid before the due date. American consigners were entitled to this amount if they kept money in their British correspondents' hands, as a few did. But some Bristol merchants attracted business by using their own money to obtain discounts. They then gave half the sum saved to their American correspondents, something that could be done relatively cheaply by borrowing

---

[28] Price, *Capital and Credit*, p. 38. By contrast, the Glasgow tobacco lords, with their large interlocking partnerships, had a capital stock of between £10,000 and £20,000 (*ibid.*, p. 25). On the role of capital in the Glasgow tobacco trade see also Devine, *Tobacco Lords*, ch. 6.

[29] Price, *Capital and Credit*, pp. 46–50.

[30] *Ibid.*, ch. 5; C. H. Cave, *A History of Banking in Bristol from 1750 to 1899* (Bristol, 1899), pp. 9–12. Knox owed some £12,000 to his banking partners when he was declared bankrupt in 1761, while Sedgley, Hilhouse & Randolph, who collapsed seven years later, still owed the Bristol Old Bank over £4,000 in 1775 (ACRL, Extracts from the Diaries of William Dyer, 2 vols., I, fo. 119; Maryland HS, William Stevenson to James Cheston, 5 Aug. 1768, James Cheston Incoming Letters, 1767–April 1771, box 9, Cheston-Galloway Papers; Price, *Capital and Credit*, p. 92). Comparison of information in SMV, Wharfage Books with the names of bankrupt Bristol merchants, 1711–93, given in Minchinton, ed., *Trade of Bristol in the Eighteenth Century*, pp. 184–91, suggests that only two other Bristol tobacco merchants were declared bankrupt in that period: John Perks in 1773 and William Stevenson in 1777.

[31] Price, *Capital and Credit*, p. 116.

money at a peacetime rate of around 4 per cent.[32] One firm, Lippincott & Brown, rather than split the savings earned by their own money, preferred to lend the money at 4 per cent per annum to their correspondents, who could then use it to obtain the discount.[33] This procedure was not understood by the planter, so it was abandoned a few years later.[34] Such a competitive device plus access to commercial credit suggests, however, that at least some leading Bristol tobacco merchants were able to muster sizeable amounts of capital in the mid-eighteenth century.[35]

Participation in the tobacco trade required substantial working capital. In the credit and debt arrangements of the eighteenth-century Chesapeake, British merchants bought goods on credit from tradesmen and sent them to Virginia and Maryland where they were bought, and also resold, on credit. British merchants extended credit first to establish and then to maintain relations with Chesapeake clients, from whom they expected supplies of tobacco. Poor prices for tobacco and other commodities and a restricted supply of money often meant, however, that remittances were not as forthcoming as the merchants hoped. As Jacob M. Price has shown, credit helped to create wealth for Chesapeake planters in the three decades before 1776, and this wealth in turn encouraged an even larger flow of credit because the investment seemed safe. But at a time of slow remittances accumulated credit also led to indebtedness to British merchants. This situation became critical in the decade before 1776, for then the debt of the Chesapeake colonies appears to have doubled while the debt of the colonies as a whole seems to have been fairly static. By 1776 around £2 million was owed by the tobacco colonies of Virginia, Maryland and North Carolina to British merchants.[36] The

---

[32] See the following: Virginia HS, Sales account of Griffiths & Thomas, 20 Nov. 1765, section 16, Adams Family Papers; SHC, Sales accounts of Morgan Thomas & Co., 7 Aug. 1754 and 25 July 1755, of Thomas, Griffiths & Thomas, 30 May 1758, and of Farell & Jones, 20 Aug. 1765, folders 3, 4 and 8, C. W. Dabney Papers; Huntington Library, Sale account of Christopher Lilly, (?) Aug. 1747, BR box 16, Tinsley MSS; LC, Sales accounts of Farell & Jones, 20 July 1764 and (?) 1765, Jones Family Papers, fos. 2513, 2670.

[33] Virginia SL, Sale account of Lippincott & Brown, 24 June 1772, box 6, Allason Papers.

[34] Virginia SL, Circular letter of Henry Lippincott & Co., 7 Feb. 1775, box 7, *ibid.*

[35] Price, *Capital and Credit*, pp. 101, 189 n. 17.

[36] These remarks rely heavily on *ibid.*, ch. 2. The origins of mercantile debt in the Chesapeake are explored in Jacob M. Price, 'Sheffeild v. Starke: Institutional Experimentation in the London–Maryland Trade c. 1696–1706', *Business History*, 28 (1986), 19–39. Two articles by Emory G. Evans also throw much light on debt in the Chesapeake: 'Planter Indebtedness and the Coming of the Revolution in Virginia', *WMQ*, 3rd Series, 19 (1962), 511–33, and 'Private Indebtedness and the Revolution in Virginia, 1776 to 1796', *WMQ*, 3rd Series, 28 (1971), 349–74.

extent of the indebtedness of Bristol firms trading with the Chesapeake is known in only a handful of cases. In an unofficial record of 1790, debts of £80,000 in Virginia were still owed to William Jones (the surviving partner of Farell & Jones) and a sum of £14,000 in Maryland was due to Stevenson, Randolph & Cheston.[37]

Debts arising from over-extended credit were a great concern to Bristol tobacco merchants. This can be seen in two memorials forwarded to Whitehall in 1758 in which they expressed fears that security in the tobacco trade was threatened by two acts passed in Virginia: a measure of 1748 that allowed insolvent debtors to settle outstanding accounts in current money, and an act of 1757 that permitted Virginians to pay off debts with paper bills drawn up as legal tender in the colony. Bristol tobacco merchants felt that both acts put secure debts on an uncertain footing. They joined together with London merchants to put pressure on the British authorities to persuade the Virginia Council and House of Burgesses to amend the legislation. This was eventually achieved with two main results. First, all debts contracted before the passing of the two acts were now to be discharged only in sterling. Second, all subsequent defaults could be paid in bills of credit, but only if the creditor agreed to the arrangement.[38] The worries of Bristol tobacco merchants are further demonstrated by several petitions and requests they dispatched to the government between 1751 and 1763 before the Currency Act of 1764 prohibited the use of paper money as legal tender.[39] The fears of Bristol merchants were exacerbated by spiralling exchange rates in Virginia during the Seven Years War, but these stemmed more from difficulties in the flow of credit and a decline in tobacco prices than (as the Bristolians thought) from the introduction of paper currency.[40]

[37] PRO, Chatham Papers, 30/8/343, fos. 168–9. According to this list, only three Glasgow firms had larger debts owing from Virginia than Farell & Jones. Much information about the debts owed to this particular Bristol firm appears in PRO, T 79/30 and in Julian P. Boyd, ed., *The Papers of Thomas Jefferson, vol. 15: 27 March 1789 to 30 November 1789* (Princeton, NJ, 1958), pp. 642–77. The efforts made by Bristol merchants to recover unpaid Chesapeake debts are discussed in Kenneth Morgan, 'The Organization of the Convict Trade to Maryland: Stevenson, Randolph & Cheston, 1768–1775', *WMQ*, 3rd Series, 42 (1985), 223–5.

[38] PRO, CO 5/1367, fos. 332–41: 'Representation to His Majesty upon two memorials from the merchants of London and Bristol trading to Virginia', 12 July 1758.

[39] PRO, CO 5/1328, fo. 63: Petition of Bristol Merchants, n.d. but probably 1751; PRO, CO 5/1330, fos. 204–5: Farell & Jones to [?], 19 June 1763; Minchinton, ed., *Politics and the Port of Bristol*, p. 79; 'The Political Activities of Bristol Merchants with respect to the Southern Colonies before the Revolution', *VMHB*, 79 (1971), 171–3.

[40] Joseph Ernst, '"Ideology" and an Economic Interpretation of the Revolution' in Alfred F. Young, ed., *The American Revolution: Explorations in the History of American Radicalism* (De Kalb, IL, 1976), pp. 174–5. John J. McCusker shows that there was a higher average rate of growth in the Virginia exchange on London between 1755 and 1763 than at any comparable seven-year period in Virginia between 1691 and 1775 (*Money and Exchange in Europe and America, 1600–1775: A Handbook* (Chapel Hill, NC, 1978), pp. 205, 210–12).

Long-term credit was an essential component of the two basic business methods used in the eighteenth-century tobacco trade: the consignment system and the direct purchase system. The former largely gave way to the latter during the course of the century. This change was closely related to the expansion of tobacco cultivation away from exhausted tidewater land, beyond the fall lines of the major rivers, and into the piedmont interior. The chief differences in the two modes of conducting business lay in the use of employees and in the ownership of tobacco. In the consignment system ship captains – occasionally supercargoes – were authorised by their British principals to solicit tobacco for shipment from planters, who retained ownership of the leaf until it arrived in Britain and was sold on commission by tobacco merchants there. But in the direct purchase system British merchants bought and immediately assumed ownership of tobacco in the Chesapeake. This was achieved by merchants employing either indigenous merchants or resident salaried factors to do their buying on the spot.

The consignment system was most suited to a stage when tobacco production was concentrated in the tidewater area, for the extensive navigable river network of the Chesapeake Bay enabled ship captains to sail their vessels and deal with planters near the tobacco plantations. At first, captains could take ships' boats or other rented small craft right up to many planters' wharves. But the introduction of tobacco inspection acts in Virginia in 1730 and Maryland in 1747 made this illegal by stipulating that tobacco should be stored in central warehouses until ready for shipment. This was just one of several important business changes in the trade during the eighteenth century. The extension of tobacco production into the interior beyond the reach of ocean-going ships, the proliferation of small suppliers that formed part of this expansion, and the strain caused by captains no longer having easy geographical access to planters to assess their credit-standing were three important factors which led to the direct purchase method gaining ascendancy over consignment trading by the third quarter of the century.[41] By that time, direct purchase

---

[41] Among many studies that analyse the organisation of the consignment and store systems are: Samuel M. Rosenblatt, 'The Significance of Credit in the Tobacco Consignment Trade: A Study of John Norton & Sons, 1768–1775', *WMQ*, 3rd Series, 29 (1962), 383–99; James H. Soltow, 'Scottish Traders in Virginia, 1750–1775', *EcHR*, 2nd Series, 12 (1959–60), 83–98; Robert Polk Thomson, 'The Merchant in Virginia, 1700–1775' (University of Wisconsin Ph.D. dissertation, 1955), chs. 2 and 3; Jacob M. Price, 'Economic Function and the Growth of American Port Towns in the Eighteenth Century', *Perspectives in American History*, 8 (1974), 163–72; *France and the Chesapeake*, I, pp. 659–66; Devine, *Tobacco Lords*, ch. 4; John W. Tyler, 'Foster Cunliffe and Sons: Liverpool Merchants in the Maryland Tobacco Trade, 1738–1765', *Maryland Historical Magazine*, 73 (1978), 246–77.

probably accounted for over three-fifths of the total amount of tobacco arriving in Britain.[42] Scottish firms employing resident agents pioneered the move to direct purchase. They supplied most of the 2,000 or so resident factors, storekeepers and assistants who, according to a contemporary estimate, were resident in Virginia by 1776.[43] Their success is summed up in the comment of a Virginian to his London merchant principals in 1769: 'The spirit of consigning is broke, and the Scotch are become the Engrossers.'[44]

The commercial organisation of the tobacco trade around 1770 has been summarised by Jacob M. Price as follows: 'The trade between Britain and the Chesapeake was divided institutionally into two distinct sectors: northern and southern, each of which accounted for about half the trade. The northern sector, centred on Glasgow, Liverpool and (to a declining degree) Whitehaven, was conducted primarily by firms which operated chains of stores in Virginia, Maryland and (to a limited extent) North Carolina where they sold European, West Indian and Asian goods and bought tobacco. The southern sector, centred on London and Bristol, was still primarily a commission business with planters and traders in the Chesapeake consigning tobacco for sale to "factors" or commission merchants in those ports and ordering goods in return.'[45] While this statement is generally correct, significant business changes had occurred by 1770. The success of direct purchase methods employed by the Scots forced many English and Virginian merchants to adopt more aggressive methods to ensure survival in the trade. There were, for instance, various business practices used by British merchants trading with the Upper James River, Virginia by the 1770s. These included trading with planters under the traditional consignment system, employing factors to buy tobacco with cash or bills, and British merchants taking tobacco partly on their own account and partly from Virginian firms acting on commission.[46] On the eve of the American Revolution, there were also Scottish firms operating either retail stores in the piedmont interior or wholesale businesses largely through independent merchant houses in the Chesapeake.[47]

---

[42] Price, *Capital and Credit*, p. 6.

[43] Brock, *Scotus Americanus*, p. 49.

[44] Roger Atkinson to Lyonel and Samuel Lyde, 5 July 1769, in A. J. Morrison, ed., 'Letters of Roger Atkinson, 1769–1776', *VMHB*, 15 (1908), 346.

[45] Jacob M. Price, ed., *Joshua Johnson's Letterbook, 1771–1774: Letters from a Merchant in London to his Partners in Maryland* (London Record Society, 15, 1979), p. xi.

[46] Thomson, 'Tobacco Export', pp. 397–8.

[47] For a case study of a wholesale Scottish firm trading with the Chesapeake see Jacob M. Price, 'Buchanan & Simson, 1759–1763: A Different Kind of Glasgow Firm Trading to the Chesapeake', *WMQ*, 3rd Series, 40 (1983), 3–41.

Between the 1740s and the 1770s, changes in business practice and marketing arrangements affected Bristol's tobacco trade far more than has been hitherto appreciated. Nearly all surviving evidence relating to Bristol tobacco firms in the late seventeenth and early eighteenth centuries, it is true, refers solely to consignment methods.[48] This system was still followed in the mid-eighteenth century by merchants such as John Blagden, Leighton Wood, Lippincott & Brown, and Lidderdale & Harmer.[49] But by then at least one major Bristol tobacco firm – Farell & Jones – had followed London commission merchants into the 'cargo' trade. This was a bifurcation of the consignment system in which British merchants dispatched manufactured goods purchased on twelve to fifteen months credit to indigenous Chesapeake merchants, with the latter guaranteeing payment before the credit period expired.[50] The 'cargo' trade became a dynamic feature of the Chesapeake economy in the period 1763–74.[51] A circular letter sent out in 1770 indicates that Farell & Jones had adopted this method of trade under pressure from London and Liverpool consignment firms and from Virginian correspondents.[52] It is difficult to determine how many other Bristol firms followed this positive way of attracting tobacco shipments, but Stevenson, Randolph & Cheston partly operated such a trade with Maryland from 1768 to 1775.[53]

---

[48] See the correspondence between Bristol tobacco merchants and Virginia planters in Richard Beale Davis, ed., *William Fitzhugh and his Chesapeake World, 1676–1701* (Chapel Hill, NC, 1963), pp. 86, 301, 316–18, 328, 332, 360–5; Louis B. Wright, ed., *Letters of Robert Carter: The Commercial Interests of a Virginia Gentleman* (San Marino, CA, 1940); W. E. Minchinton, ed., 'The Virginia Letters of Isaac Hobhouse, merchant of Bristol', *VMHB*, 66 (1958), 288–9, 296; Virginia HS, Account Book of Stephen Loyde (1708–11) and Account Book and Letterbook (1714–78) of John Tayloe (1687–1747) and John Tayloe (1721–79), Tayloe Papers; Alderman Library, UVA, Robert 'King' Carter Letterbooks (1728–32), Carter Family Papers. See also New York HS, John Custis Accounts (1732–4) with Lyonel Lyde and Lyde & Cooper.

[49] Gloucestershire RO, John Blagden Wastebook (1755/6), 20 Oct. 1755; SHC, John Snelson to Edward Harford, Jr, 1 Feb. 1760, Snelson Letterbook (1757–75); Virginia SL, Lippincott & Brown to William Allason, 22 June 1771, and Sales of Tobacco by Lippincott & Brown, 25 Aug. 1774, boxes 6 and 7, Allason Papers; BL, Add. MS 36,217, fos. 199–205; William R. Perkins Library, Duke University, Entries for 1754 in George Yuille Account Book (1754–7).

[50] On the 'cargo' trade see four studies by Price: *Capital and Credit*, p. 127; *Joshua Johnson's Letterbook*, p. xi; 'One Family's Empire: the Russell-Lee-Clerk Connection in Maryland, Britain, and India', *Maryland Historical Magazine*, 72 (1977), 176–7; and 'The Last Phase of the Virginia–London Consignment Trade: James Buchanan & Co., 1758–1768', *WMQ*, 3rd Series, 43 (1986), 64–98.

[51] Price, *Capital and Credit*, p.128.

[52] The original letter, dated 10 Aug. 1770, is in PRO, T 79/30. It has been reprinted in full in Minchinton, ed., *Trade of Bristol in the Eighteenth Century*, pp. 170–1, and in Price, *Capital and Credit*, app. C, pp. 156–7.

[53] Morgan, 'Organization of the Convict Trade', pp. 208, 224–5.

Possibly other tobacco merchants were too cautious to trade with these altered arrangements. Lippincott & Brown certainly fell into this category, for in 1771 they informed a planter that 'it is not customary with us to take tobacco in payment for goods, but the usual way is to consign tobacco for sales and the neat proceeds to go in payment'.[54]

Several Bristol merchants adapted to changing marketing arrangements in the quarter century before the American Revolution by following the direct purchase method of buying tobacco usually associated with the Scots. In selecting the mode of purchase, some Bristolians probably drew on commercial expertise gained from living in Virginia during their early careers.[55] Sometimes direct purchase was carried out by factors specially dispatched to the Chesapeake to operate retail stores – as, for instance, when James Cheston was sent by his partners, Stevenson & Randolph, to set up a store in a tobacco neighbourhood in Maryland in 1768.[56] On other occasions, the responsibility was entrusted to professional tobacco buyers resident in the Chesapeake (or occasionally to the factors of other firms) acting on commission.[57] Weare & Co. and John Perks employed such factors in Virginia to buy tobacco.[58] Thomas Knox and Morgan Thomas were probably also involved in direct purchase because they operated stores in the Old Dominion.[59] Even consignment firms sometimes used cash buyers speculatively to purchase good quality tobacco expeditiously. Farell & Jones, Edward Harford, Jr, and Morgan Thomas all followed this policy.[60] The factors employed by Bristol firms were usually independent or semi-independent traders. They were there-

[54] Virginia SL, Lippincott & Brown to William Allason, 22 June 1771, box 6, Allason Papers.
[55] G. E. Weare notes that Messrs. Chamberlayne, Farell, Innys, Lidderdale and Harmer were among the 'principal importers of tobacco' at Bristol who had lived in Virginia (*Edmund Burke's Connection with Bristol from 1774 till 1780: with a Prefatory Memoir of Burke* (Bristol, 1894), p. 7). Weare cites no source for this statement but it is taken verbatim from a copy of the *Bristol Gazette* for March 1787.
[56] Maryland HS, William Stevenson to James Cheston, 20 Feb. 1768, James Cheston Incoming Letters, 1767–April 1771, box 9, Cheston-Galloway Papers.
[57] Thomson, 'Merchant in Virginia', pp. 197–8, 207.
[58] *Virginia Gazette*, 10 Sept. 1772; LC, William Reynolds to John Perks, 19 Aug. 1771, William Reynolds Letterbook (1771–9); Alderman Library, UVA, Roger Atkinson to John Perks, 13 Nov. 1769, Roger Atkinson Letterbook (1769–76); SHC, John Snelson to Edward Harford, Jr, 16 May 1770, Snelson Letterbook; William Reynolds to John Norton, 19 Aug. 1771, in Frances Norton Mason, ed., *John Norton & Sons: Merchants of London and Virginia* (Richmond, VA, 1937), p. 177. See also, for a later date, Smithsonian Institution, Benjamin Pollard & Co. to Samuel Span, 23 January 1788, Benjamin Pollard & Co. Letterbook (1787–92).
[59] SHC, John Snelson to Edward Harford, Jr, 26 June 1758, Snelson Letterbook.
[60] Virginia SL, John Syme to Farell & Jones, 2 Feb., 15 Nov. 1764, US Circuit Court, Virginia District, Ended Cases, Record Book 5, E (1796), fos. 467, 480; SHC, John Snelson to Edward Harford, Jr, 20 May 1761, 7 July 1765, Snelson Letterbook; Swem Library, Francis Jerdone to Morgan Thomas, 15 May 1756, 25 Feb., 15 Apr. 1757, 3 Feb. 1758, Francis Jerdone Letterbook (1756–63), Jerdone Family Papers. Thomas paid his factor a 5 per cent commission for executing the task.

fore different from Scottish factors in the Chesapeake, who were salaried employees.

Individual British ports concentrated their tobacco trade on the different rivers of the Chesapeake Bay (shown in map 6). Bristol merchants were particularly active in areas that produced the mild sweetscented tobacco in demand in the home market.[61] The chief areas for the production of such tobacco in the Chesapeake were the banks of the James, York, Rappahannock and Potomac rivers in Virginia. Sweetscented tobacco was delicate in flavour and considered the best quality in the world in the eighteenth century. It was often known as stemmed tobacco because much of it was stripped from the leaf before shipment. London, Liverpool and Glasgow shippers, on the other hand, directed their business more to suppliers of oronoco leaf. This was darker, seldom stripped, generally poorer in quality, and suitable for consumption in continental Europe. It was grown throughout the Chesapeake, but particularly in Maryland and backcountry areas of Virginia.[62]

About four-fifths of the tobacco sent to Bristol in the mid-eighteenth century came from Virginia; the rest came from Maryland.[63] The Bristol interest in Virginia (shown in table 6.6) was especially strong on the York River, a district that had reached its peak by the late 1730s and was not growing thereafter.[64] Bristolians also traded regularly with the Upper James River, but increasingly whittled down their connections with other Virginia naval districts.[65] Even minor Bristol tobacco importers maintained commercial operations on the York and James rivers provided that they could supply shipping, for planters preferred to be certain of freight and wished to avoid damage to tobacco through transportation to another river for shipment.[66] But on rivers where Bristolians rarely ventured, such as the Potomac, planters were unwilling to ship tobacco to Bristol because they had no assurance that the goods they requested would arrive

---

[61] The demand for good quality, sweetscented tobacco in the Bristol market is emphasised in Somerset RO, Graffin Prankard to Cozen Hare, 11 Oct. 1717, Graffin Prankard Letterbook (1712–18), Dickinson Papers, DD/DN 423; Hampshire RO, Henry Wyndham to John Darracott, 20 Feb. 1728/9, 26 Sept. 1730, Henry Wyndham Account Book (1725–53), Acc. 8M49/F12; and Virginia SL, Lippincott & Brown to William Allason, 22 June 1771, box 6, Allason Papers.

[62] For detailed commentary on these points see Carville Earle and Ronald Hoffman, 'Urban Development in the Eighteenth-Century South', *Perspectives in American History*, 10 (1976), 21; Clemens, *Atlantic Economy*, pp. 218–19; and Arthur Pierce Middleton, *Tobacco Coast: A Maritime History of the Chesapeake Bay in the Colonial Era* (Newport News, VA, 1953), pp. 97–8.

[63] Based on PRO, CO 5/1444–1449, and Maryland HS, Annapolis Clearances (1756–75) for 1758, 1761 and 1762. These are the only years in the generation before the American Revolution for which full data are available for all the Chesapeake naval districts.

[64] Price, *France and the Chesapeake*, I, p. 670.

[65] LC, Farell & Jones to Thomas Jones, 10 Aug. 1763, Jones Family Papers, XII, fo. 2330.

[66] George Braxton to Lidderdale & Co., 28 July 1757, in Frederick Horner, *A History of the Blair, Banister, and Braxton Families* (Philadelphia, 1898), p. 144; SHC, John Snelson to Edward Harford, Jr, 29 Oct. 1757, Snelson Letterbook.

in that particular river.[67] Bristol firms rarely traded with ports on the Eastern Shore of Maryland; their trade with that province concentrated on Annapolis and Baltimore on the Western Shore.[68]

Two available sources throw much light on the degree of success achieved by Bristol tobacco merchants employing factors in the best Virginia tobacco country and on merchant-planter operation of the consignment and direct purchase systems. The correspondence of two Scottish factors, William Johnston and Francis Jerdone, reveals that Bristol merchants – unfortunately not specified by name – were using stores and employing factors near the Pamunkey River, a major tributary of the York River, by the late 1730s and early 1740s.[69] These stores were increasing rapidly at that time. They were clustered in the small back-country area of the York River, from which good quality sweetscented tobacco, often from Hanover County, could be purchased.[70] 'There is at this time above 25 stores within 18 miles around me', Jerdone reported in 1743, 'which is more than were at Mr. Johnston's death, & 4 or 5 more expected in this next year from some of the outports.'[71] Some of these stores were run by Bristol firms competing with Scottish factors who were flooding into Virginia and buying tobacco for their principals in Glasgow.

Bristol stores had two chief advantages over rivals in certain parts of the York River basin. One was their commitment to quick bidding for tobacco with cash, for Bristol factors usually began the market by offering higher prices than their competitors in order to acquire the best tobacco.[72] Bristol factors who offered high prices were not doing so simply to buy good grades of tobacco, but also to earn themselves larger commissions.[73] They maintained close links with local tobacco warehouses and were not discouraged from cash purchases at high prices when war broke out with Spain in 1739.[74] The second advantage was keeping an appropriate range of exported goods in their stores at low prices. This helped in sustaining contacts with sellers of tobacco. Nails, kerseys, and woollens were apparently all cheaper from Bristol than from London.[75]

---

[67] HSP, Charles Willing & Son to John Perks, 3 Aug. 1754, Willing Letterbook (1754–61).
[68] Based on Maryland Hall of Records, Port Records for Annapolis (1748–59), Oxford (1742–6) and Patuxent (1745–7).
[69] The business activities of Johnston and Jerdone in Virginia are briefly discussed in Price, 'Buchanan & Simson', pp. 10–11.
[70] Thomson, 'Merchant in Virginia', p. 160.
[71] Swem Library, To Neill Buchanan, 4 Aug. 1743, Letterbook of William Johnston and Francis Jerdone (1738–45). From this source we can infer that Johnston died in 1741 or 1742.
[72] Swem Library, To Freeman Partridge, 12 Sept. 1739, *ibid*.
[73] *Ibid*.
[74] Swem Library, To Neill Buchanan, 4 Feb. 1744 and to Mr Rae, 8 Sept. 1740, *ibid*.
[75] Swem Library, To Neill Buchanan, 5 June, 13 July 1741, *ibid*.

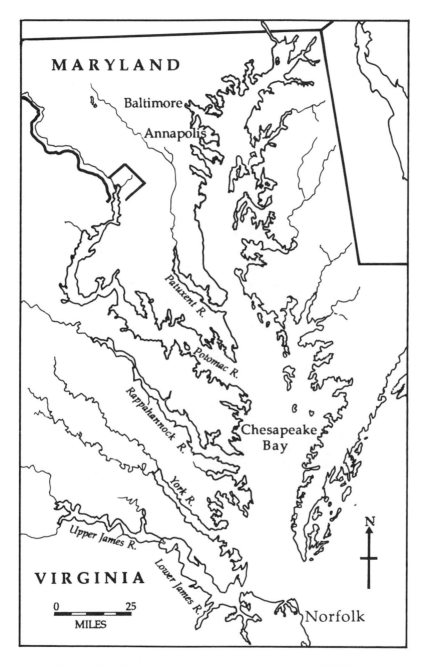

Map 6   Trading regions in the Chesapeake around 1760

Table 6.6. *Virginia tobacco exports to Bristol by district, 1737–1762 (selected years)*

	South Potomac		Upper James		Lower James		York River		Rappahannock	
	N	Hhds.	N	Hhds.	N	Hhds.	N	Hhds.	N	Hhds.
1737	1	100	3	664	1	100	15	3,709	3	744
1738	0	0	3	802	1	100	10	3,113	1	263
1739	0	0	3	944	0	0	10	3,311	2	564
1740	0	0	2	862	0	0	14	4,188	1	307
1741	0	0	3	899	2	72	9	2,956	1	319
1742	0	0	2	839	1	0	10	2,599	1	386
1743	0	0	4	621	1	99	13	3,204	1	321
1744	0	0	6	1,712	0	0	7	2,616	1	321
1745	0	0	1	381	2	160	10	2,848	0	0
1758	1	406	6	2,227	1	84	10	2,641	3	680
1761	1	267	6	2,455	0	0	8	2,518	1	266
1762	0	0	4	1,473	0	0	5	1,573	1	313

Note: The figures include a few ships clearing from Virginia to Bristol without tobacco on board. No tobacco was sent to Bristol from the fifth Virginia naval district, Accomac, so it has been omitted here.
Source: Public Record Office, London, CO 5/1444–1449.

Salt, rum and sugar were also mentioned as articles where Bristol-controlled stores had the upper hand. 'Tis a very great loss to you in not supplying your stores with these three articles', a London merchant was informed, for 'the best of the trade is carried on with them & little can be done without them. I can form no other scheme that will affect the Bristol traders so much, as always having a plenty of these three articles.'[76] Johnston complained in 1740 that the Bristol factors stocked their stores well ahead of their competitors and reminded his principal 'to send in the cargo early in the Spring that the Bristol men may not have the Whip hand of me'.[77]

The success of Bristol factors in running stores on the Pamunkey River in the late 1730s and early 1740s was summed up in the following exasperated comment: 'I wish some way could be fallen upon to prevent the Bristol purchasers from proceeding in the method they do in buying tobacco. This country is so crowded with stores from that place that I am afraid twill be a very difficult matter to make a purchase of 100 hogsheads in 2 or 3 years after this.'[78] The solution was for rivals from other ports to put more capital into stores in the area. One factor advised his London principal that a store with goods to the value of £4,000 in the York River region would crush the competition from Bristol stores, none of which stocked goods worth more than a total of £1,000.[79] Unfortunately, the Johnston–Jerdone correspondence ends just at the point when other ports were beginning to set up stores in the York River area.

Further light is thrown on merchant–planter relations in the Bristol tobacco trade by letters written between 1757 and 1775 by John Snelson, an experienced tobacco grower and buyer living in Hanover County, Virginia, to Edward Harford, Jr, a member of a prominent Bristol Quaker merchant and banking family connected with the trade since the late seventeenth century.[80] Snelson supplied tobacco to Harford partly on consignment from his neighbours and partly via the varied business

[76] Swem Library, To Neill Buchanan, 5 Aug. 1741, *ibid.*
[77] Swem Library, To Neill Buchanan, 8 July, 3 Nov. 1740, *ibid.*
[78] Swem Library, To Buchanan, 20 May 1741, *ibid.*
[79] Swem Library, To Neill Buchanan, 20 Oct. 1741, *ibid.*
[80] PRO, T 52/16, fos. 90–3, refers to several Harfords in the Bristol tobacco trade in 1691. Correspondence from Harford to Snelson has apparently not survived. That some mercantile records of Harford were available earlier in the present century is apparent from the letterbook cited in Alice Harford, *Annals of the Harford Family* (London, 1909), and 'List of Virginians appearing in an Account Book of Edward Harford (1691–1779) and Edward Harford (1720–1806)', deposited at Virginia HS in 1910. Regrettably, the only details given in this list are the names of various Virginians. Both sources seem to be no longer available. They are not to be found, for instance, in the Harford deposit at the BRO.

practices described above. Some tobacco exported by Snelson personally was grown by him, some bought on joint account from neighbouring planters, some purchased on the sole account of Harford.[81] In the latter case, Snelson received a small commission for carrying out the transaction.[82] Harford sent firm written instructions about the quantity, quality and price of tobacco to buy.[83] The difference in quality between tobacco grown in different parts of Virginia was an important consideration. This is why, on one occasion, Snelson informed Harford that he was 'determined not to buy any but sweetscented, as you complain so much of long thin Rappahannocks'.[84] Snelson usually supplied tobacco from his own York River, and only resorted to buying on the James and Rappahannock rivers if prices were substantially lower there.[85]

During the marketing season from November until the end of August, the price of tobacco rose and fell according to the quality of the leaf and the practices of buyers. High prices usually prevailed when the crop was short. In such circumstances, planters were frequently unwilling to consign tobacco because they could sell it more profitably on the spot.[86] Buyers responded by purchasing partly with cash, for planters were often short of ready money.[87] Snelson bought tobacco with both bills of exchange and cash in a setting where strong competition prevailed among buyers for the finer blends of sweetscented tobacco.[88] In June 1759, for instance, when York River tobacco was selling for around 40 shillings per cwt. Snelson hoped it would fall by at least five shillings. 'I wish it had ever been higher', he commented, 'but the Scotch & Bristol purchasers have been the means of getting it up.'[89] Nevertheless, cash transactions brought several advantages. By offering money for 'tip top' crops – the good quality tobacco in demand at Bristol – ship masters avoided waiting

[81] SHC, John Snelson to Edward Harford, Jr, 26 June 1758, 11 June 1759, Snelson Letterbook.
[82] SHC, John Snelson to Edward Harford, Jr, 23 May 1759, ibid.
[83] SHC, John Snelson to Edward Harford, Jr, 8 June 1761, 17 Sept. 1762, ibid.
[84] SHC, John Snelson to Edward Harford, Jr, 22 Apr. 1774, ibid.
[85] SHC, John Snelson to Edward Harford, Jr, 11 July 1769, 16 May 1770, 31 May 1772, 31 May 1773, ibid.
[86] SHC, John Snelson to Edward Harford, Jr, 12 June 1766, ibid.; George Braxton to Lidderdale & Harmer, (?) 1756, in Horner, History of the Blair, Banister, and Braxton Families, p. 142. High tobacco prices in Virginia also resulted from expectations of good sales based on news of favourable prices at British ports (Francis Jerdone to Speirs & Brown, 10 Dec. 1756, WMQ, 1st Series, 16 (1907), 130–1).
[87] Middleton, Tobacco Coast, p. 183.
[88] SHC, John Snelson to Edward Harford, Jr, 11 May 1766 and 25 July 1771, Snelson Letterbook.
[89] SHC, John Snelson to Edward Harford, Jr, 20 June 1759, ibid. In 1759, tobacco prices reached their highest level between 1725 and 1776 (Price, France and the Chesapeake, I, pp. 671–7, II, p. 852).

for hogsheads to arrive from warehouses and buyers eliminated the uncertainty of purchasing tobacco with goods.[90]

Harford could assist Snelson to expedite the purchase of tobacco in several ways. He could ensure that orders reached Virginia before his ships arrived to carry off the crop: late orders caused problems in assembling a tobacco cargo.[91] It was also important to maintain good relations with Virginia correspondents. This could be achieved in two ways in particular. The first was to check that export wares were shipped in good condition and conformed closely to those ordered. This was necessary because exports were mainly supplied to those from whom Snelson expected to receive tobacco, and the receipt of goods in proper order was an inducement for such people to entrust their crop to Snelson.[92] The second way was for Harford to accept bills drawn on him so that they would not be returned protested.[93] Snelson, for his part, paid close attention to the timing of voyages to and from Virginia. Faced with an urgent request for goods, he suggested that Harford should charter space in a ship if one of his own was not available to leave Bristol.[94] Snelson also attempted to load ships quickly, but was sometimes held up by planters promising tobacco and then failing to supply it; by planters not submitting tobacco notes until ships were half loaded; and by delays in gathering tobacco from single hogshead suppliers.[95] But these problems should not be exaggerated. Ships from other British ports were more prone to delays on the York River, 'for its a thing next to impossible to prevail on the planters to part with their tobacco even for ready cash, before the Bristol ships come in'.[96]

Despite supplying good quality tobacco, several Virginia planters found the Bristol tobacco market comparatively small, easily overstocked, subject to uncertain price fluctuations, and restricted by inelastic demand for tobacco in the domestic market.[97] These commercial problems undoubtedly affected the lack of growth in the Bristol tobacco

---

[90] Francis Jerdone to William Buchanan, 26 May 1750, *WMQ*, 1st Series, II (1903), 157.

[91] SHC, John Snelson to Edward Harford, Jr, 5 June, 14 July, 14 Oct. 1758, Snelson Letterbook.

[92] SHC, John Snelson to Edward Harford, Jr, 31 July 1768, 25 July 1771, 27 July 1772, *ibid.*

[93] SHC, John Snelson to Edward Harford, Jr, 25 July 1764, *ibid.*

[94] SHC, John Snelson to Edward Harford, Jr, 5 Aug. 1757, *ibid.* For an example of a complaint made by a Virginia firm to a Bristol merchant who was slow to provide vessels see Smithsonian Institution, Benjamin Pollard & Co. to Samuel Span, 25 Mar. 1789, Benjamin Pollard & Co. Letterbook.

[95] SHC, John Snelson to Edward Harford, Jr, 19 June, 8 Aug. 1765, 31 May 1772, *ibid.*

[96] Francis Jerdone to Speirs & Brown, 15 May 1756, *WMQ*, 1st Series, 16 (1907), 128–9.

[97] Swem Library, Francis Jerdone to Thomas, Griffiths & Thomas, 10 Sept. 1762, Jerdone Letterbook; Nash, 'English and Scottish Tobacco Trades', p. 371.

trade. By the late 1730s and early 1740s, complaints were made about poor tobacco sales at Bristol compared with better returns from London.[98] Almost two decades later these criticisms were reiterated by Snelson, who thought that mean sales at Bristol would discourage planters from shipping their crop there in future.[99] Other Virginians were critical of the Bristol tobacco market, too.[100]

Poor sales sometimes stemmed from outside commercial pressures. In 1761, for instance, Bristol merchants experienced difficulty in selling tobacco to domestic consumers because the north-western ports were disposing of their own tobacco at Bristol at reduced prices.[101] In these circumstances, Harford compromised on the sale price so that large amounts of unsold tobacco did not pile up in warehouses on the quayside.[102] Another reason for low prices was poor appraisal of the current market situation. Thus Snelson frequently suggested that Harford tended to sell too quickly in years when tobacco was in short supply, and therefore failed to command the best prices.[103] To defend the commercial judgement of Bristol merchants, however, it should be mentioned that hasty selling occasionally occurred when American correspondents failed to provide timely advice about the amount of tobacco expected from the Chesapeake.[104]

Most tobacco sold at Bristol was bought in small lots by manufacturers and retailers such as snuffmakers, pigtail spinners, rag cutters and tobacconists, who purchased usually on short credit (60 days) or occasionally for cash at a small discount.[105] Buyers paid particular attention to the

---

[98] LC, John Custis to Mr Lloyd, 1736 and n.d. (but *c.* 1740), John Custis Letterbook (1717–42), Custis Family Papers.

[99] SHC, John Snelson to Edward Harford, Jr, 14 July 1758, Snelson Letterbook.

[100] George Washington to Richard Washington, 7 May 1759, and to Farell & Jones, 30 July 1760, in W. W. Abbot, ed., *The Papers of George Washington: Colonial Series 6: September 1758–December 1760* (Charlottesville, VA, 1988), pp. 319, 442; Virginia HS, John Baylor to Joseph Farrel & Co., 6 July 1762, John Baylor Letterbooks (1757–65); and Theodorick Bland to Farell & Jones, 1 Dec. 1774, in Charles Campbell, ed., *The Bland Papers*, 2 vols. (Petersburg, VA, 1840–3), I, p. 33.

[101] LC, Farell & Jones to Thomas Walker, 10 Aug. 1761, box 162, W. C. Rives Papers: Thomas and Francis Walker Papers. For a similar situation at Bristol in the years from *c.* 1718 to 1722 see PRO, T 1/238 no. 108, James Hilhouse to Daniel Campbell, 18 Dec. 1721, and Jacob M. Price, 'Glasgow, the Tobacco Trade, and the Scottish Customs, 1707–1730', *Scottish Historical Review*, 63 (1984), 14–20.

[102] SHC, John Snelson to Edward Harford, Jr, 20 May 1761, Snelson Letterbook.

[103] SHC, John Snelson to Edward Harford, Jr, 14 July 1758, 8 Sept., 3 Dec. 1767, 16 Sept. 1768, *ibid.*

[104] LC, Farell & Jones to Thomas Walker, 10 Aug. 1761, box 162, W. C. Rives Papers: Thomas and Francis Walker Papers.

[105] Maryland HS, Sedgley, Hilhouse & Berry to Charles Carroll, 10 Sept. 1754, box 7, Carroll-MacCubbin Papers.

scent, colour and substance of the leaf.[106] The sweetscented tobacco preferred in the Bristol market was often kept on hand for several months before being sold. Cheaper tobacco for re-export was normally vended quickly, presumably because it was bought in bulk without much attention to quality differences among the hogsheads on offer.[107] Little information is available on shifts in tobacco prices at Bristol: there is insufficient material to construct price indices. By the 1780s, however, Virginia tobacco from the Rappahannock River sold at Bristol for 1d or 2d per lb. less than that from the James and York rivers.[108]

The manufacturing and retail trade in tobacco had flourished in Bristol since the seventeenth century.[109] In 1722, fifty pipemakers and fifty-seven tobacconists were trading at Bristol.[110] By 1775 there were around twenty tobacconists and similar concerns in the city, operating either from business premises near warehouses on the docks or from snuff mills in the hills around Bristol at places such as Coombe Dingle, Frenchay and Clifton (on the site of the observatory).[111] Despite the sharp fall in tobacco importation during the American War of Independence, there were still nineteen tobacconists and snuffmakers in Bristol in 1783.[112] The three main products made from tobacco – cut tobacco, roll tobacco, and snuff – were all manufactured at Bristol and distributed throughout the city and its hinterland.[113] An anonymous pamphlet of 1751 suggested that tobacco merchants and manufacturers at London differed in personnel but that

---

[106] Virginia SL, Sales accounts of Lippincott & Brown and Henry Lippincott & Co., 24 June 1772, 7 Feb. 1775, boxes 6 and 7, Allason Papers. The second of these accounts specifies the occupations of tobacco buyers. The first does not, but the occupations of several buyers can be identified from Sketchley's *Bristol Directory* (1775). B. W. E. Alford has noted that 'the distinction between tobacconists – who were primarily retailers – and tobacco manufacturers was blurred because . . . tobacconists performed operations which were strictly part of the manufacturing process' (*W. D. & H. O. Wills and the Development of the U.K. Tobacco Industry, 1786–1965* (London, 1973), pp. 7–10).

[107] Price, *Capital and Credit*, pp. 61–2.

[108] HSP, Thomas Clifford, Jr to John Clifford, 17 Sept. 1784, Clifford Correspondence, VII (1783–5), Pemberton Papers. Jacob Price has suggested to me that York River tobacco usually sold for ½d. per lb. more than the French buyers' price cited in *France and the Chesapeake*, I, pp. 671–7.

[109] N. C. P. Tyack, 'The Trade Relations of Bristol with Virginia during the Seventeenth Century' (University of Bristol M.A. thesis, 1930), pp. 55–64.

[110] Bryan Little, *The City and County of Bristol: A Study in Atlantic Civilization* (London, 1954), p. 172.

[111] Sketchley's *Bristol Directory* (1775), pp. 1–110; *Tobacco, Its Culture and Manufacture* (2nd edn., Bristol, 1936), p. 51. A picture of a snuff mill near Bristol is included as a frontispiece to Hugh McCausland, *Snuff and Snuff-Boxes* (London, 1951).

[112] Bailey's *Western and Midland Directory . . . 1783*.

[113] The production techniques of these tobacco products are discussed in Alford, *W. D. & H. O. Wills*, pp. 7–10.

the situation was different at Bristol and Liverpool 'because [there] they are both importers and manufacturers'.[114] The second part of this statement is either incorrect or things had altered by 1775, for Sketchley's *Bristol Directory* of that year reveals that tobacco merchants were clearly distinct from tobacco retailers.

Of all the products made from tobacco, snuff had the most significant local impact in Bristol. Around 1750, when apparently one pound of snuff was consumed weekly on average in a gentleman's family, many corn mills in the Bristol suburbs were converted into snuff mills. The impact of this change was revealed in 1756 when a quarter sessions meeting in the city criticised altering grist mills to snuff mills for anything other than grinding corn.[115] Snuff was more highly manufactured than pipe tobacco and contained a relatively low nicotine content. After first gaining popularity during Queen Anne's reign, it became the most important form of tobacco consumption by the mid-eighteenth century.[116] Success in marketing snuff depended on offering a variety of flavours from the different brands available.[117] But it did not require large capital resources. In the 1740s it was estimated that retail snuff men needed only £50–£100 to set up in business; and in 1775 a Bristol tobacconist, advertising for a partner to manufacture tobacco and snuff, commented that 'no large capital will be required'.[118]

For Bristol merchants supplying the domestic market, the duty on tobacco was a major expenditure and thus of critical importance. Customs charges on tobacco moved upwards cautiously after the sharp increase at the time of the impost of 1685. The nominal duties on imported tobacco were 6⅓d per lb. in the early eighteenth century; they were raised to 7⅓d in 1747/8 and by a further penny in 1759. The total duties were then 8⅓d per lb., a sum which was from three to seven times the price of tobacco in the colonies.[119] The duties increased to 1s 3d per lb. by 1787 and to almost 1s 8d per lb. by the end of the century.[120]

---

[114] *The Present State of the Tobacco Trade, as the Late Act Affects the London Manufacturers, Considered: In a Letter to a Friend* (London, 1751), pp. 7–8.

[115] Latimer, *Annals of Bristol*, pp. 302–3.

[116] Price, 'Tobacco Trade and the Treasury', pp. 698, 712.

[117] Jerome E. Brooks, *The Mighty Leaf: Tobacco through the Centuries* (Boston, 1952), p. 136; 'Committee of the Whole House on the Bill for repealing the Duties on Tobacco and Snuff, and for granting new duties in lieu thereof' in Sheila Lambert, ed., *House of Commons Sessional Papers*, LXXV: *George III: Corn and Tobacco Trades 1789 and 1790*, p. 103.

[118] Price, *Capital and Credit*, p. 98; *Bonner and Middleton's Bristol Journal*, 2 Dec. 1775.

[119] Price, 'Tobacco Trade and the Treasury', p. 2; Middleton, *Tobacco Coast*, pp. 110–11. The different components that made up the tobacco duties are explained in E. E. Hoon, *Organization of the English Customs*, pp. 249–50.

[120] *British Parliamentary Papers* (1844), XII (Cd. 565), p. 500. From 1789 onwards about two-thirds of the duty consisted of an excise on tobacco (*British Parliamentary Papers* (1829), XV (Cd. 340), p. 370).

The burden of the duties was unevenly spread: it fell far more on merchants serving the home market than on those concerned chiefly with re-export. Various drawbacks were available for re-exported tobacco, amounting after 1723 to a full refund of the duties.[121] For domestically consumed tobacco, however, the duties had to be paid in full (though, as already noted, the government allowed a discount for early payment).[122] By the 1780s,when the tobacco duties amounted to five times the value of the commodity, American merchants complained that the charges on tobacco sold at Bristol 'preclude all chance of a profit' and that tobacco was therefore 'not proper for the owners of vessels to ship for the sake of Fr[eigh]t but only on Speculation as Remittances, the Duty being so enormous.'[123] Bristol tobacco merchants, too, must have felt the pinch from high duties (taken out of the gross proceeds of sales) and from lower commission earnings. Bristol manufacturers of tobacco and snuff also found that high duties adversely affected their sales in Devon and Cornwall by the late 1780s.[124] The resort of some 'principal people' in Bristol to smuggling snuff from Guernsey manufacturers around this time no doubt stemmed partly from a perception of excessive taxation by the government.[125]

Bristol tobacco merchants always expressed concern at proposals to raise tobacco duties, for they realised that such measures would particularly affect the profits of tobacco sold in the home market.[126] They unanimously opposed Walpole's excise scheme of 1733, when the prospect of new taxes on tobacco and wine seemed imminent.[127] They also

---

[121] The system of drawbacks in the tobacco trade is outlined in Hoon, *Organization of the English Customs System*, pp. 256–64.

[122] Price, *Capital and Credit*, pp. 61–2.

[123] Hoon, *Organization of the English Customs System*, p. 36, Smithsonian Institution, Benjamin Pollard & Co. to Samuel Span, 26 June 1787, Pollard Letterbook; HSP, Thomas Clifford, Jr to John Clifford, 26 May 1783, 17 July and 17 Sept. 1784 (from which the quotation is taken), Clifford Correspondence, VII (1783–5), Pemberton Papers.

[124] 'Committee of the Whole House on the Bill for repealing the duties on tobacco and snuff ... ', 25 June 1789, in Lambert, ed., *House of Commons Sessional Papers*, LXXV, p. 101.

[125] William L. Clements Library, Thomas Gee to Lord Shelburne, 3 Feb. 1783, Shelburne Papers, CLII, no. 68.

[126] E.g. ACRL, Thomas Chamberlayne & Co. and other Bristol tobacco firms to Foster Cunliffe and other tobacco merchants in Liverpool, 4 Feb. 1748, Southwell Papers; SMV, 'The Memorial of the Merchants of the City of Bristol trading to the Colonies of Virginia and Maryland, 1760'; Petition of the tobacco merchants of Bristol, London and Glasgow to the House of Commons, 10 June 1785, as cited in Jerome E. Brooks, *Tobacco: Its History Illustrated by the Books, Manuscripts and Engravings in the Library of George Arents, Jr.*, 4 vols. (New York, 1937–1943), IV, no. 959, p. 38.

[127] Nicholas Rogers, *Whigs and Cities: Popular Politics in the Age of Walpole and Pitt* (Oxford, 1989), pp. 278–9; *Pennsylvania Gazette*, 7–14 June, 19–26 July 1733; Paul Langford, *The Excise Crisis: Society and Politics in the Age of Walpole* (Oxford, 1975), pp. 56, 113–14.

expressed indignation in 1789 over the government decision to apply the licensing and excise systems to the tobacco trade.[128] But the most notable example of lobbying occurred in 1759 when three leading Bristol tobacco merchants – Joseph Farell, John Perks, and Thomas Knox – contested a decision to lay an additional duty on tobacco domestically consumed. The episode began when Richard Nugent, a Whig MP for Bristol, contacted Knox about plans to alter the tobacco laws in the Parliamentary session of 1759. Knox quickly notified Farell and his partner William Jones, 'as the affair concerned him and me more than any other person in Bristol'.[129] After meeting in Bristol on 17 February 1759 to discuss the issue at the Society of Merchant Venturers, Knox, Farell and Perks were asked by the merchants and manufacturers of Bristol to campaign in London against the proposed excise. Their brief was to argue that an excise would harm the trade and that a small additional duty (upon exports rather than domestically consumed tobacco) would bring more revenue to the government. Between 18 and 21 February the Bristol representatives met Nugent plus senior members of the government, including the prime minister, but were unsuccessful in pleading their case. On being told that the proposed excise was necessary to raise extra taxes for the Seven Years War, Knox informed William Pitt that he hoped the extra money 'could be raised without additional duties, as it might lessen the consumption, as it might promote smuggling, and hurt fair traders'.[130]

The Bristolians failed in their venture partly through lack of support from tobacco merchants at other outports: colleagues at Liverpool, for instance, were notably absent from the capital while proposals for the excise were being aired. The Bristol merchants were also fobbed off in London, being shunted from one official to another. Farell, Knox and Perks feared that an additional duty would lessen home consumption, as had happened – according to their argument – after the subsidy of 1747/8.[131] These reservations were based on self-interest, for the home

---

[128] Petition to the House of Commons, 14 April 1790, in Minchinton, ed., *Politics and the Port of Bristol*, pp. 168–9, and Peter T. Underdown, 'The Parliamentary History of the City of Bristol, 1750–1790' (University of Bristol M.A. thesis, 1948), pp. 358–66.

[129] *A Letter from Mr Thomas Knox of Bristol to the Honourable William Nelson Esq. of Virginia* (Bristol, 1759), pp. 4–11. The following account of this affair is based on this pamphlet, a copy of which is available in the library of the Boston Athenaeum. See also SMV, Robert Nugent to the Master of the Society of Merchant Venturers of Bristol, 16 Feb. 1759, Correspondence, bundle 4. For more extended analyses of this episode see Price, 'Tobacco Trade and the Treasury', pp. 61–71, and Morgan, 'Bristol Merchants and the Colonial Trades', pp. 219–22.

[130] *A Letter from Mr Thomas Knox*, pp. 5, 8–10.

[131] *Ibid.*, p. 6.

Table 6.7. *Tobacco re-exports from Bristol, 1773–1776 (in hogsheads)*

	Africa	Ireland	West Indies	American Mainland Colonies	Europe	Coastwise
1773	46	317	13	15	1,280	4
1774	13	225	50	61	1,504	269
1775	16	174	3	27	784	0
1776	3	1	23	38	198	0

Note: This table does not include exports of clay tobacco pipes or the various sorts of manufactured tobacco. It also does not include the small amounts of tobacco exported in containers such as mats, casks and boxes. Where two destinations for ships were stated in the *Presentments*, I assumed that the tobacco was destined for the second-named place. The table understates the level of tobacco re-exports from Bristol for 1773–6 because 14 of the 181 export *Presentments* for those years are missing.
Source: Avon County Reference Library, Bristol, *Bristol Presentments*, Exports, 1773–6.

market emphasis of Bristol made it sensible for tobacco merchants there to suggest that any additional charges should be placed on re-exported tobacco. Merchants at Glasgow, Whitehaven and Liverpool, with their greater involvement in the re-export business, obviously felt differently, and, as Jacob M. Price suggests, 'the ministry had a sounder view of the whole tobacco trade than did the tobacco merchants of Bristol whose situation in the trade was rather atypical'.[132]

Though Bristol merchants were mainly concerned with the home market for tobacco, they did not completely neglect the re-export trade. By the 1770s, Europe was by far the most important market for re-exported tobacco from Bristol, with Ireland a long way second (see table 6.7). Tobacco was, in fact, the most important commodity re-export from Bristol to Northern Europe in the 1770s.[133] Most tobacco sent to that region was dispatched to Dunkirk and Havre de Grace[134] in France, to Rotterdam and Amsterdam in Holland, and to Bremen and Hamburg in Germany.[135] Tobacco re-exports to France, Holland and Germany for 1773–6 (shown in table 6.8) were dominated by five firms: Stevenson, Randolph & Cheston, who supplied Maryland tobacco to Holland and Germany; James Daltera, who dealt with the French tobacco monopoly; Joseph Glover, who sent tobacco to France and Germany; Richard Champion, who supplied tobacco to all three countries; and Farell &

[132] Price, 'Tobacco Trade and the Treasury', I, pp. 65–6.
[133] Colin Merrett, 'The Trades between Bristol and Northern Europe, 1770–1780' (University of Exeter MA thesis, 1974), pp. 42–3.
[134] I.e. Le Havre.
[135] Based on data in ACRL, *Bristol Presentments*, Exports, 1773–6.

Table 6.8. *Tobacco re-exports from Bristol to Northern Europe, 1773–
1776 (in hogsheads)*

	France	Holland	Germany
1773	655	320	213
1774	258	0	976
1775	150	146	462
1776	0	183	0

Note: The totals understate the amount of tobacco re-exported to Northern Europe be-
tween 1773 and 1776 because 14 of the 181 export *Presentments* are missing for those years.
The total for France for 1773 includes 365 hogsheads shipped by James Daltera on a vessel to
Dieppe and Petersburgh. I have assumed that this cargo was unloaded at Dieppe, since
Daltera is known to have supplied tobacco to France (see below, p. 183).
Source: Avon County Reference Library, *Bristol Presentments*, Exports, 1773–6.

Jones, who re-exported some tobacco to Germany and some to
Ireland.[136]

Much of the tobacco re-exported from Bristol seems to have come from
Maryland. The grades of tobacco grown in that province included cheap,
brown, mild tobacco from the Eastern Shore suitable for the French
market and strong, bright leaf from the Western Shore which was in
demand in Holland and Germany.[137] In general, tobacco from the Western Shore of Maryland was better in quality than that from the Eastern
Shore and was therefore preferred for re-export.[138] William Stevenson,
writing to his step-brother James Cheston in Maryland, considered that
buyers in Bristol were often unaware that tobacco from the Eastern Shore
was cheaper than that from the Western Shore. He added that when
Maryland tobacco was easily available at Bristol 'we shall get but a low
price for it, therefore ye cheapest is most profitable & when it is scarce &
dear they are not so nice as to quality & one will fetch as much as ye other,
so that upon ye whole whenever Tob[acc]o can be purchased lowest, will
be most eligible'.[139]

The re-export markets in Holland and Germany, as noted above,
usually took tobacco of higher quality than the French market. Thus
when a ship arrived too late at Bristol to send tobacco to the Dutch and
German markets, Stevenson noted that he would now have to take

[136] *Ibid.*
[137] Price, ed., *Joshua Johnson's Letterbook*, p. xxv.
[138] Maryland HS, James Cheston to Stevenson, Randolph & Cheston, 8 Oct. 1774, James
Cheston Letterbook, 1772–6, and Stevenson & Randolph to James Cheston, 24 Jan.
1775, James Cheston Incoming Letters, 1775–82, boxes 8 and 15, Cheston-Galloway
Papers.
[139] Maryland HS, William Stevenson to James Cheston, 9 Apr. 1768, James Cheston
Incoming Letters, 1767–Apr. 1771, box 9, *ibid.*

whatever price the French were willing to offer.[140] In fact, poor quality tobacco was often dumped on the French market. 'Was it not for the French', Stevenson & Randolph advised Cheston, 'we should never get rid of it & even they often object to it'.[141] Lippincott & Brown noted, in a year of poor quality tobacco imports, that most of the hogsheads 'were only fit for the French market'.[142] Very little is known about French buying at Bristol except that from the 1730s to the 1760s there were regular annual sales of two or three shiploads carried out for the French tobacco monopoly by Huguenots such as the Dalteras and the Peloquins, who had branches of their families living in Bristol.[143] The small-scale nature of the trade between Bristol and the French tobacco monopoly was an inevitable consequence of the home market orientation of the Bristol tobacco market, which served as a consumption centre for the finer blends of leaf. As the final chapter shows, this emphasis on the domestic market also dominated Bristol's most lucrative branch of transatlantic trade, the commerce in West Indian sugar.

[140] Maryland HS, William Stevenson to James Cheston, 23 Nov. 1773, James Cheston Incoming Letters, Nov. 1773–June 1774, box 13, *ibid.*

[141] Maryland HS, Stevenson & Randolph to James Cheston, 24 Jan. 1775, James Cheston Incoming Letters, 1775–82, box 15, *ibid.*

[142] Virginia SL, Lippincott & Brown to William Allason, 25 Aug. 1774, box 7, Allason Papers.

[143] Price, *France and the Chesapeake*, I, pp. 593–4.

7   The sugar trade

Though historians dispute whether the West Indian islands were, on balance, an economic drain on the wealth of the mother country during the eighteenth century,[1] there is no doubt that cane sugar from the Caribbean was the most valuable British import in the century and a half down to 1820.[2] English sugar imports increased sevenfold from 430,000 cwt. in 1700 to over 3,000,000 cwt. in 1800. Scottish sugar imports more than trebled from an annual average of 19,889 cwt. in 1739–42 to 72,662 cwt. per year in 1773–5.[3] On the eve of the American Revolution, the value of sugar imports into England and Wales was £2,634,000.[4] As these figures suggest, people in Georgian Britain began to acquire a sweet tooth. This important change in diet was also stimulated by the growing importation of tea, coffee and chocolate and by the availability of these groceries to the mass of the population. In the Bristol area, even the poor could afford sugar except at times of economic depression.[5] In England as a whole, *per capita* sugar consumption rose from 1 lb. to 25 lbs. between 1670 and 1770.[6] By 1787–96, English labouring families spent around 10

---

[1] For the debate see Richard B. Sheridan, *Sugar and Slavery: An Economic History of the British West Indies, 1623–1775* (Baltimore and Barbados, 1974), pp. 295–6, 475–86; 'The Wealth of Jamaica in the Eighteenth Century', *EcHR*, 2nd Series, 18 (1965), 292–311; 'The Wealth of Jamaica in the Eighteenth Century: A Rejoinder', *EcHR*, 2nd Series, 21 (1968), 46–61; R. P. Thomas, 'The Sugar Colonies of the Old Empire: Profit or Loss for Great Britain?' *EcHR*, 2nd Series, 21 (1968), 30–45.

[2] Ralph Davis, *The Industrial Revolution and British Overseas Trade* (Leicester, 1979), p. 43.

[3] *Ibid.*; John J. McCusker, 'The Rum Trade and the Balance of Payments of the Thirteen Continental Colonies, 1650–1775' (University of Pittsburgh Ph.D. dissertation, 1970), tables D-1 and D-2, pp. 891–5.

[4] Ralph Davis, 'English Foreign Trade, 1700–1774', *EcHR*, 2nd Series, 15 (1962), 300.

[5] UMA, Richard Meyler to Henry Bright, 5 May 1741, box 5, Bright Family Papers.

[6] McCusker, 'Rum Trade', p. 33. For suggestive remarks on the relationship between demand for sugar and changing consumption patterns see Jacob M. Price, 'The Transatlantic Economy' in Jack P. Greene and J. R. Pole, eds., *Colonial British America: Essays in the New History of the Early Modern Era* (Baltimore, MD, 1984), pp. 30–3, and Sidney W. Mintz, *Sweetness and Power: The Place of Sugar in Modern History* (New York, 1985), pp. 113–19.

per cent of their annual food expenditure on treacle, sugar and tea.[7] Soaring demand at home meant that sugar re-exports were significant only when war disrupted the supply of French-grown sugar to Europe.[8] The two main by-products of sugar, rum and syrupy molasses, also found growing outlets: molasses became the mainstay of New England distilleries while rum, often served as grog or punch, became a popular beverage in Britain and Ireland.[9] These various data reveal that domestic consumption of sugar and rum clearly outstripped the demand for tobacco in eighteenth-century Britain.[10]

'Rum, slaves, tobacco and sugar', W. E. Minchinton has observed, 'were the main ingredients of Bristol's prosperity in the eighteenth century, with sugar the most important'.[11] The significance of sugar and the West India connection to Bristol can be substantiated in various ways. Bristol had twenty sugar refineries in operation by 1750 – a larger number than at any other British outport.[12] By the late 1780s, the annual value of the ships and outward cargoes in her West India trade was £400–500,000 and the estimated value of produce imported from the Caribbean to Bristol was £774,038.[13] Many Bristol sugar importers had lived for spells in the Caribbean, gaining an apprenticeship in trade conditions there that proved invaluable when they later set up as merchants at home. Michael Atkins, John Curtis, William Gordon, Mark Davis, Henry Bright, William Miles and Robert Claxton all followed such careers.[14] Bristol

[7] Carole Shammas, *The Pre-Industrial Consumer in England and America* (Oxford, 1990), pp. 136–7.

[8] Robert Stein, 'The French Sugar Business in the Eighteenth Century: A Quantitative Study', *Business History*, 22 (1980), 7–8; Davis, *Industrial Revolution*, p. 31.

[9] McCusker, 'Rum Trade', pp. 132–3, tables IV-21B and IV-21C, pp. 233–4; Richard B. Sheridan, 'The Molasses Act and the Market Strategy of the British Sugar Planters', *JEcH*, 17 (1957), 62–83.

[10] Shammas, *Pre-Industrial Consumer*, pp. 81–3.

[11] W. E. Minchinton, *The Port of Bristol in the Eighteenth Century*, Bristol Branch of the Historical Association, pamphlet no. 5 (Bristol, 1962), p. 2.

[12] Sheridan, *Sugar and Slavery*, p. 30. I. V. Hall, in a series of articles, has studied the operation of Bristol's sugar refineries: see especially 'Whitson Court Sugar House, Bristol, 1665–1824', *TBGAS*, 65 (1944), 1–97, and 'The Daubenys: Part 1,' *TBGAS*, 84 (1965), app. II, 137–40.

[13] BRO, [Richard Bright], 'Draft of Particulars of the Trade of Bristol, 1788', Bright MSS, Acc. 11168/2c, and 'Particulars of Value of Produce imported from the West Indies into Bristol, 1787–1788', *ibid.*, Acc. 11168/3b. Details from the latter appear to have been incorporated in a *Report of the Lords of the Committee of Council* (London, 1789), pt. IV, n.p.

[14] G. E. Weare, *Edmund Burke's Connection with Bristol, from 1774 till 1780: with a Prefatory Memoir of Burke* (Bristol, 1894), p. 8; Derbyshire RO, Davis, Protheroe &

West India merchants also acquired sugar estates. For instance, Henry and Francis Bright, Robert Gordon, William Gordon, Thomas Harris, James Pedder and the Smyth family all owned plantations in Jamaica; David Hamilton and Devonsheir & Reeve invested in sugar estates in Grenada; Samuel Span owned a plantation in St Vincent; and Reeve, Son & Hill bought land in St Kitts.[15] Many of these men became wealthy. Thus William Miles, after settling in Bristol, 'became immensely rich' as a sugar merchant, so much so that he apparently handed over a cheque for £100,000 when one of his sons married in 1795.[16] Other Bristolians engaged in West India trade also amassed substantial fortunes. Michael Atkins left about £70,000, Henry Bright £50,000, John Curtis £35,000, and William Gordon, Richard Meyler and Walter Lougher £30,000 each.[17] It is hard, on the basis of this evidence, to accept the claim that Bristol's West India interests in the closing decades of the eighteenth century 'were less important than they had been fifty years earlier'.[18]

The wealth and commercial standing of Bristol West India merchants was complemented by their prominent role in local social, business and political life. Several Bristol sugar merchants played major roles in local banking partnerships after 1750. Samuel Munckley and Henry Bright were members of the Harford Bank, while John Curtis was a partner in the firm of Peach, Fowler & Co.[19] Some of these merchants reached the prestigious position of Master of the Society of Merchant Venturers.

Claxton to W. P. Perrin, 24 Nov. 1783, Fitzherbert MSS: West Indian Papers, 239M/E20110; BRO, Camplin & Smith: Accounts with William & John Miles in Jamaica (1759–61), Acc. 11109/15; G. W. Blunt White Library, Mystic Seaport, Connecticut, Israel Pemberton to Richard Willing, 31 July 1731, Israel Pemberton Letterbook (1727–35). For a detailed appraisal of the business careers of Bristol sugar merchants see Kenneth Morgan, 'Bristol West India Merchants in the Eighteenth Century', *TRHS*, 6th Series, 3 (1993).

[15] D. K. Jones, 'The Elbridge, Woolnough and Smyth Families of Bristol, in the Eighteenth Century, with Special Reference to the Spring Plantation, Jamaica' (University of Bristol M.Litt. thesis, 1971); Vere Langford Oliver, ed., *Caribbeana: Miscellaneous Papers Relating to the History, Genealogy, Topography and Antiquities of the British West Indies*, 6 vols. (London, 1909–1919), II, p. 139; PRO, CO 142/31; PCC 419 Stevens, PROB/11/992/136–7; PCC 88 Norfolk, PROB/11/1138/308–312; PCC 511 Crickitt, PROB/11/1527/338 ff; C 54/6143/9ff; C 54/6329/9-15.

[16] ACRL, Extracts from the Diaries of William Dyer, 2 vols., I, fo. 20; H. R. Fox Bourne, *English Merchants*, 2 vols. (London, 1866), II, p. 17.

[17] *FFBJ*, 8 Jan. 1785. The complete list is reprinted in Latimer, *Annals of Bristol*, p. 463.

[18] S. G. Checkland, 'Finance for the West Indies, 1780–1815', *EcHR*, 2nd Series, 10 (1957–8), 465.

[19] C. H. Cave, *A History of Banking in Bristol from 1750 to 1899* (Bristol, 1899), pp. 200–1.

They included Samuel Munckley in 1768 and Samuel Span in 1777.[20] Two West India societies flourished in Bristol from the American War of Independence onwards, and, by the early nineteenth century, one of the two MPs for the city was invariably a direct representative of the West India interest.[21] The links between Bristol and the Caribbean have attracted some descriptive commentary plus a fine business history of the Pinney family and their sugar estates on Nevis.[22] The present discussion, however, is the first detailed analysis of the Bristol sugar trade during its period of greatest prosperity.

Before the American Revolution, the growth of Bristol's sugar imports closely fitted national trends in sugar importation. Recovery in the production and shipping of sugar after the end of the War of the Spanish Succession slowed down by the 1730s. This decade marked the nadir of sugar production in the British Caribbean. Wartime difficulties during the 1740s hindered a quick renascence.[23] Bristol's sugar imports (given in table 7.3) were affected by those problems but generally remained steady down to the end of the War of the Austrian Succession. The situation then changed dramatically. Rising demand for rum and sugar stimulated an increase in production throughout the Caribbean and a doubling of sugar imports into England in general and Bristol in particular between 1748 and 1775.[24] During that period – the 'silver age' of the planters – sugar imports at Bristol rose to exceed 20,000 hogsheads per year by the mid-1770s.[25] Bristol may then have reached the maximum limit of her sugar consumption; certainly a well-informed contemporary merchant thought so.[26] This peak was followed by a slight deterioration in imports during the latter part of the American War of Independence, a conflict during which English sugar arrivals fell by one quarter.[27] Once peace was

---

[20] John Latimer, *The History of the Society of Merchant Venturers of the City of Bristol* (Bristol, 1903), p. 330.

[21] McGrath, *Merchant Venturers of Bristol*, pp. 237–8; MacInnes, *Bristol: A Gateway of Empire*, p. 363.

[22] MacInnes, *Bristol: A Gateway of Empire*, ch. 11; I. V. Hall, 'A History of the Sugar Trade in England with special attention to the Sugar Trade of Bristol' (University of Bristol MA thesis, 1925); Pares, *West-India Fortune*.

[23] McCusker, 'Rum Trade', pp. 229–30; Richard Pares, *War and Trade in the West Indies, 1739–1763* (Oxford, 1936).

[24] McCusker, 'Rum Trade', pp. 229–30; David Richardson, 'The Slave Trade, Sugar, and British Economic Growth, 1748–1776' in Barbara L. Solow and Stanley L. Engerman, eds., *British Capitalism and Caribbean Slavery: The Legacy of Eric Williams* (Cambridge, 1987), pp. 103–33; and table 7.3 below, p. 191.

[25] For the phrase quoted see Richard Pares, *Merchants and Planters, EcHR*, Supplement no. 4 (Cambridge, 1960), p. 40; for the level of Bristol's sugar imports see below, table 7.3, p. 191.

[26] UMA, Lowbridge Bright to Bright, Milward & Duncomb, 26 Jan. 1774, Lowbridge Bright Letterbook (1765–73), Bright Family Papers.

[27] Stein, 'French Sugar Business in the Eighteenth Century', pp. 7–8.

restored, Bristol began to diverge from the national trend of sugar importation. The English sugar trade did not decline after 1783, as was once thought.[28] On the contrary, it boomed towards the end of the century and West India commerce as a whole accounted for a higher proportion of total British trade after the 1770s than before.[29] Yet Bristol's sugar imports declined slightly and only recovered the level of the mid-1770s by 1799 and 1800.[30]

London always remained the most important British port in the sugar trade, accounting for around three-quarters of English sugar imports before 1776.[31] The outports participated in the trade in a smaller way. Sugar importation at Whitehaven was negligible: no more than three vessels per year entered the port from the Caribbean during the eighteenth century.[32] Glasgow's West India commerce only developed rapidly after the American Revolution; before then it was a pale shadow of the Clyde tobacco trade.[33] This left Bristol and Liverpool to vie for the position of leading outport in the sugar trade. Bristol was the second sugar market in England in the 1720s, for the number of ships entering the city from the West Indies was more than double the number arriving at Liverpool from the same region.[34] Thereafter Liverpool began to challenge Bristol for second place, even though Liverpudlians concentrated more on the slave trade than on the direct trade in sugar.[35] Yet Bristol maintained her position. By 1742, her sugar imports still exceeded those

---

[28] For the old and new interpretations see Lowell Joseph Ragatz, *The Fall of the Planter Class in the British Caribbean, 1763–1833: A Study in Social and Economic History* (New York and London, 1928) and John J. McCusker, 'Growth, Stagnation, or Decline? The Economy of the British West Indies, 1763–1790' in Ronald Hoffman, John J. McCusker, Russell R. Menard and Peter J. Albert, eds., *The Economy of Early America: The Revolutionary Period, 1763–1790* (Charlottesville, VA, 1988), pp. 275–302.

[29] Seymour Drescher, *Econocide: British Slavery in the Era of Abolition* (Pittsburgh, 1977), p. 19.

[30] See below, table 7.3, p. 191. By the turn of the century, Bristolians also consumed a substantial quantity of rum, amounting to an annual average of 2,299 puncheons and 94 hogsheads for the period 1798–1801 (BRO, 'Account of Goods imported into Bristol in the years 1798–1801', Bright MSS, Acc. 11168/2(ii)).

[31] McCusker, 'Rum Trade', table D-1, pp. 891–3. For an overview of London's eighteenth-century sugar trade see Christopher J. French, 'The Trade and Shipping of the Port of London, 1700–1776' (University of Exeter Ph.D. thesis, 1980), ch. 4.

[32] J. V. Beckett, *Coal and Tobacco: The Lowthers and the Economic Development of West Cumberland, 1660–1760* (Cambridge, 1981), pp. 103–4; Annie Eaglesham, 'The Growth and Influence of the West Cumberland Shipping Industry, 1660–1800' (University of Lancaster Ph.D. thesis, 1977), pp. 88–92.

[33] T. M. Devine, 'An Eighteenth-Century Business Elite: Glasgow–West India Merchants, c. 1750–1815', *Scottish Historical Review*, 57 (1978), 40.

[34] See above, table 1.3, p. 17.

[35] Paul G. E. Clemens, 'The Rise of Liverpool, 1665–1750', *EcHR*, 2nd Series, 29 (1976), 221.

of Liverpool.[36] By 1773 she was still ahead of Liverpool (see table 7.1). The situation was probably the same in 1775.[37] Indeed, it was not until the late 1790s that Liverpool overtook Bristol's level of sugar imports (see table 7.2).

Concentration and specialisation were two characteristic features of Bristol sugar merchants.[38] The number of firms involved in the trade decreased over time as the importation of sugar rose. This was a consistent trend during periods of war and peace. Thus, as table 7.3 shows, the total number of importers handling sugar at Bristol dropped from over 500 in the late 1720s to 117 in the mid-1770s and to 85 by the end of the century. Table 7.4 presents data for selected years to show the high concentration ratios in the trade. It points to the increasing dominance over time of large sugar merchants (with annual imports greater than 1,000 hogsheads) and to a corresponding decline in the number of marginal importers (those with less than 50 hogsheads). Over the course of the century, the small fry were clearly being squeezed out of a trade dominated by a fairly small, concentrated group of leading merchants. This 'revolution of scale', as noted in the previous chapter, also occurred in the tobacco and slave trades from c. 1675 to 1775: larger firms had the capital and credit resources to dominate entire sectors of transatlantic trade by the era of the American Revolution.[39]

Table 7.5 presents the rank order of the major Bristol sugar merchants. Michael Atkins, William Miles and Robert Gordon – the three leading importers – were all active in the trade for over a quarter of a century. The duplication of surnames such as Bright, Meyler, Gordon, Baillie, Becher and Davis suggests that there was greater family continuity among sugar merchants than was common among tobacco importers. Such continuity helped merchants to accumulate commercial expertise over several generations. There were other differences, too. Some Bristol West India merchants acquired shares in Caribbean sugar estates, whereas very few Bristol tobacco traders owned property or land in the Chesapeake. Bristol's sugar and tobacco trades also operated in a discrete manner: there was very little overlap in personnel. The only exception were a few merchants who imported both staple commodities, especially during the American War of Independence when clandestine tobacco supplies in the Caribbean were eagerly snapped up by Bristol sugar merchants with

---

[36] *Ibid.*, p. 221 note 1.

[37] In 1775, sugar exports from Jamaica to Bristol and Liverpool were 16,268 and 8,077 hogsheads respectively (William L. Clements Library, Shelburne Papers, LXXVII, fo. 84).

[38] For a comprehensive list of sugar importers at Bristol, 1748–80, see Morgan, 'Bristol Merchants and the Colonial Trades', app. C, pp. 336–66.

[39] Cf. the points made in this and the next paragraph with information on pp. 143–4, 158–62.

Table 7.1. *Sugar exports from the British West Indies to London,*
Bristol, Liverpool, and Glasgow, 1773 (in hogsheads)

	London	Bristol	Liverpool	Glasgow	Totals
Jamaica	49,556	13,615	10,468	3,285	76,924
Nevis	4,465	750	0	150	5,365
St Vincent	8,043	0	886	372	9,301
Montserrat	2,784	0	181	0	2,965
Tortola	1,072	183	2,528	0	3,783
Dominica	4,383*a*	152	147	0	4,682
Tobago	1,289	0	0	0	1,289
Grenada	24,185	855	241	580	25,861
Barbados	8,414	4,663	1,384	0	14,461
Antigua	11,647	0	206	95	11,948
St Kitts	7,953	678	1	436	9,068
Totals	123,791	20,896	16,042	4,918	165,647

Note: *a* 256,270 lbs of foreign sugar excluded.
b To convert the various weights and measures given in this source into hogsheads, I have
followed John J. McCusker, 'The Rum Trade and the Balance of Payments of the Thirteen
Continental Colonies, 1650–1775' (University of Pittsburgh Ph.D. dissertation, 1970),
appendix C, pp. 778–81. The following ratios have been used: 3 hogsheads = 4 tierces; 1
hogshead = 4 barrels *or* 600 lbs.; 1 cwt. = 100 lbs. (using the short hundredweight common
in the West Indies at that time).
Source: Public Record Office, London, BT 6/83, fos. 42–53. Similar material for 1774 is
given in *ibid.*, fos. 56–67.

Table 7.2. *British sugar imports at the five principal centres, 1790–1800*
(in cwt.)

	London	Bristol	Liverpool	Whitehaven	Port Glasgow and Greenock
1790	1,238,749	248,801	231,336	4,743	132,690
1791	1,188,328	229,802	218,329	2,872	131,693
1792	1,338,549	244,358	231,594	2,812	139,627
1799	2,145,491	314,039	419,828	8,714	141,369
1800	1,851,857	269,362	499,937	11,115	187,510

Source: British Parliamentary Papers, Commons, 1802–3, VIII, pp. 1099–427 (no. 138).
I have omitted imports of prize sugar.

established business connections there. Greater overlap existed between
Bristol slave traders and sugar merchants. Firms followed by '& Co.' in
table 7.5 were nearly all *ad hoc* slaving groups in which several individuals
had combined in order to cope with the peculiarly high risks and potential
profits of the traffic in black cargoes.

Table 7.3. *Activity of Bristol sugar importers, 1728–1800 (annual averages)*

	Hogsheads imported	Number of firms	Imports per firm
1728–32	13,604	512.6	26.5
1733–7	10,818	366.2	29.5
1738–42	12,096	374.4	32.3
1743–7	10,816	318.2	34
1748–9	12,062	310.5	38.8
1754–7	13,259	274.8	48.2
1758–62	13,930	171.4	81.3
1763–7	13,729	163.2	84.1
1768	15,803	155	102
1773–7	21,815	117.4	185.8
1778–80	18,252	82.7	220.7
1785	22,811	103	221.5
1788	20,903	76	275.0
1789–90	20,906	n.a.	n.a.
1791–2	18,098	62	291.9
1793–7	16,515	69	239.3
1798–1800	21,094	85	248.2

Sources: 1728–88, 1792, 1797: Society of Merchant Venturers, Bristol, Wharfage Books. 1789–90: Bristol Record Office, 'Account of Goods Imported into Bristol in the Years 1789–92', Bright MSS, Acc. 11168/2d (i).
1791, 1793–6, 1798–1800: Avon County Reference Library, Bristol, *Bristol Presentments.*

Tables 7.6 and 7.7 demonstrate the specialisation of Bristol interests in the Caribbean. They reveal that Jamaica usually supplied half of the sugar arriving at Bristol.[40] A breakdown of sugar imports for twenty leading West India merchants in the city in the 1770s (see table 7.7) shows that five firms – Lowbridge & Richard Bright, Mark Davis & Co., Samuel Delpratt, Meyler & Maxse, and John Fowler & Co. – traded exclusively with Jamaica. A further five firms – Mark Davis, Robert Gordon, Davis & Protheroe, Robert Lovell, William Miles, and John Fisher Weare – also imported most of their sugar from Jamaica. Several more leading sugar firms traded mainly with one Caribbean island. David Parris (later styled Parris, Smith & Daniel) imported sugar almost entirely from Barbados. Samuel Span dealt mainly with St Kitts. Only three firms out of twenty divided their attention between two or more islands. Samuel Munckley traded chiefly with Jamaica and Barbados; David Hamilton concentrated on Tobago and Grenada; and Bright, Baillie & Bright took sugar from various islands in the Lesser Antilles. But though many of

---

[40] This is also substantiated by statistics in SMV, Wharfage Books, 1764–8, and BL, Add. MS 12,413: Edward Long's Collections for the History of Jamaica, fo. 8r.

Table 7.4. Size of Bristol sugar importers, 1728–1788

	1728			1748			1768			1788		
	Number	Weight (hhds.)	% hhds.	Number	Weight (hhds.)	% hhds.	Number	Weight (hhds.)	% hhds.	Number	Weight (hhds.)	% hhds.
Over 1,000 hhds.	0	0	0.0	1	1,893	15.5	3	6,203	39.3	8	15,754	75.4
500–999 hhds.	4	2,586	18.7	2	1,084	8.9	4	2,881	18.2	4	2,240	10.7
50–499 hhds.	63	7,558	54.4	47	7,355	60.3	34	5,706	36.1	14	2,467	11.8
0–49 hhds.	492	3,738	26.9	225	1,871	15.3	114	1,013	6.4	50	442	2.1
Totals	559	13,882	100.0	275	12,203	100.0	155	15,803	100.0	76	20,903	100.0

Note: In preparing the table, firms were counted separately where personnel overlapped in any year.
Source: Society of Merchant Venturers, Bristol, Wharfage Books. Cf. Jacob M. Price and Paul G. E. Clemens, 'A Revolution of Scale in Overseas Trade: British Firms in the Chesapeake Trade, 1675–1775', *Journal of Economic History*, 42 (1987), table 11, p. 35.

these merchants specialised in trade with a few Caribbean islands, they did not confine their commercial activities just to the sugar trade. This is presumably why, in a contemporary trade directory, only Lowbridge & Richard Bright and William Miles are referred to as 'Jamaica merchants' and only Davis & Protheroe and Meyler & Maxse are listed as 'West India merchants'.[41] This lends support to the suggestion that only a few specialised dealers gained a foothold before 1776 in the English outports and Scotland.[42]

To understand the commercial organisation of the Bristol sugar trade it is essential to see how far Bristolians adhered to the commission system. Sugar was originally bought on the spot in the West Indies either by independent merchants or by supercargoes. From the late seventeenth century onwards, however, the emergence of large estates and sugar monoculture in the Caribbean, the rise of a substantial class of planters, and the concentration of the economic interests of the West Indies upon England all helped to develop the growth of a commission trade in sugar. Under this system planters shipped their sugar to English merchants, who were usually paid $2\frac{1}{2}$ per cent on the sales for selling the sugar and carrying out miscellaneous services. These tasks included purchasing supplies and provisions, acting as quasi-bankers by extending credit and accepting bills of exchange, supplying ships for the sugar harvest, paying customs duties and freight charges on sugar vessels, arranging for warehousing of the cargo, communicating market information to planters' attorneys, and making insurance on ships and cargoes (for an extra $\frac{1}{2}$ per cent commission). Sugar commission agents in British ports were therefore important intermediaries between producers and consumers – though, of course, the chief financial burdens remained with the planters until the sugar was sold.[43]

Extensive commitment to the sugar commission system emerged gradually during the first half of the eighteenth century. Unlike the tobacco trade, there are unfortunately no studies that trace the detailed chronology of this development. But it is clear that the lead was taken by the metropolis. In the 1690s London sugar merchants were divided

---

[41] Bailey's *Western and Midland Directory* (1783), pp. 178, 181, 187.
[42] Sheridan, *Sugar and Slavery*, p. 322.
[43] On the commission system see K. G. Davies, 'The Origins of the Commission System in the West India Trade', *TRHS*, 5th Series, 2 (1952), 89–107; Richard B. Sheridan, 'Planters and Merchants: The Oliver Family of Antigua and London, 1716–1784', *Business History*, 13 (1971), 104–13; *Sugar and Slavery*, pp. 282, 284, 290–4, 319–22, 328–32; and D. W. Thoms, 'The Mills Family: London Sugar Merchants of the Eighteenth Century', *Business History*, 11 (1969), 3–10.

Table 7.5. *Leading sugar importers at Bristol, 1728–1800*[a]

Merchants	Hhds. imported	Years active in the sugar trade
Michael Atkins	40,289	1730–49, 1754–63
William Miles	36,543	1764–8, 1773–80, 1785, 1788, 1791–5
Robert Gordon	35,070	1747, 1749, 1754–68, 1773–9
Protheroe & Claxton	31,897	1785, 1788, 1791–1800
Thomas Daniel & Sons	20,993	1785, 1788, 1791–1800
Evan Baillie	20,271	1785, 1788, 1791–9
John Maxse	17,126	1785, 1788, 1791–1800
John Curtis	16,342	1748–9, 1754–68
James Laroche	15,226	1728–49, 1754–68, 1773–8
Meyler & Maxse	14,445	1773–80, 1785
Mark Davis	12,043	1729–33, 1735, 1737, 1740–9, 1754–68, 1773–80
Isaac Hobhouse	11,966	1728–49, 1754–8
Lowbridge & Richard Bright	11,939	1775–80, 1785, 1788, 1791–1800
John Fisher Weare	11,733	1773–80, 1785, 1788, 1791–1800
Samuel Munckley	11,501	1743–4, 1746–8, 1754–68, 1773–80, 1785, 1788, 1799
John Gordon, Sr	11,133	1774–80, 1785, 1788, 1791–1800
Samuel Delpratt	10,501	1764–8, 1773–9
Munckley, Gibbs & Co.	10,427	1773–8, 1791–1800
Samuel Span	10,158	1762–3, 1766, 1768, 1773–80, 1785, 1788, 1791, 1793
Thomas Harris	6,914	1748–9, 1754–68, 1773–80, 1785, 1788, 1791–3, 1796–7
David Dehany	6,896	1738–47
Devonsheir & Co.	6,064	1755, 1757, 1759–66
Evan Baillie & Sons	5,867	1799–1800
William Hare & Co.	5,723	1728–30, 1732–45, 1749, 1754
W. & J. Gordon	5,513	1785, 1788, 1791
Walter Jacks	5,450	1774, 1778–80, 1785, 1788, 1791–1800
Robert Lovell	4,872	1768, 1774–80
James Laroche & Co.	4,842	1728–32, 1734, 1736, 1738, 1740–9, 1754–7, 1761–3, 1765–6
David Parris	4,778	1764–8, 1773–4
Richard Meyler, Sr	4,757	1728–49, 1754–64, 1767–8
Thomas Penington	4,726	1728–32, 1734–48, 1754, 1756–65, 1767–8, 1774
Jeremiah Innys	4,564	1736–49, 1754–9
Henry Swymmer	4,507	1749, 1754–68, 1773
William Hare	4,462	1731–49, 1754
Michael Becher	4,319	1728–49, 1754–7
Tobin & Pinney	4,318	1785, 1788, 1791–5, 1798
Henry Bright	4,246	1746–8, 1754–68, 1773–7

Table 7.5. *contd.*

Merchants	Hhds. imported	Years active in the sugar trade
John Gordon, Jr	4,062	1791–4
Samuel & John Span	3,835	1791–6
David Hamilton	3,740	1766–8, 1773–9
Samuel & John Span & Co.	3,554	1796–1800
John Becher	3,539	1728–43
Thomas Deane	3,528	1737, 1741, 1743–9, 1754–68, 1773–8
Tudway & Smith	3,522	1754–63
James Bonbonous	3,514	1745–9, 1754–67, 1774–6, 1778–80, 1785, 1788, 1792, 1794, 1797–9
Richard Farr	3,511	1728–40, 1754–60
William Gordon	3,436	1728, 1731–49, 1754–7
Mark Davis & Co.	3,352	1742–4, 1746–8, 1755, 1759, 1761, 1763, 1773–6
Devonsheir, Reeve & Co.	3,154	1746–8, 1755–61
Tobin, Pinney & Tobin	2,991	1796–7, 1799–1800

Sources: Society of Merchant Venturers, Bristol, Wharfage Books; Avon County Reference Library, Bristol, *Bristol Presentments.*
Note: [a] only includes years where a complete record of sugar imports is available.

between those already trading as commission agents and those operating on their own account. By *circa* 1750, they virtually all traded on commission.[44] Sugar commission houses existed outside of London by the 1730s, but most outport agents appear to have been merchants trading on their own account.[45] There are no studies of the situation at Liverpool. At Glasgow various trading methods were used, but most sugar merchants operated the commission.system by the late eighteenth century.[46] Most Bristol sugar merchants transacted business on commission by 1750. This was particularly true in the Jamaica trade, in which Robert Lovell, William Miles, Michael Miller, John Curtis, Samuel Munckley, Mark Davis, Protheroe & Claxton, and Davis & Protheroe were agents serving

[44] D. W. Jones, 'London Overseas-Merchant Groups at the End of the Seventeenth Century and the Moves against the East India Company' (Oxford University D.Phil. thesis, 1970), p. 205.
[45] Richard B. Sheridan, 'The Sugar Trade of the British West Indies from 1660 to 1756 with Special Reference to the Island of Antigua' (University of London Ph.D. thesis, 1951), pp. 248–9.
[46] T. M. Devine, 'Glasgow Merchants in Colonial Trade, 1770–1815' (University of Strathclyde Ph.D. thesis, 1971), ch. 4.

Table 7.6. *Distribution of Bristol sugar imports by island of origin, 1702–1742 (selected years, in cwt.)*

	1702	1711	1721	1731	1742
Antigua	9,300	5,400	5,100	9,300	8,000
Barbados	4,500	12,800	6,800	23,000	21,200
Jamaica	18,900	48,800	68,600	92,300	96,200
Montserrat	4,700	4,400	5,700	1,900	800
Nevis	14,900	6,000	4,200	4,000	0
St Kitts	0	0	7,200	13,900	6,400
Other	0	100	1,300	0	0
Totals	52,300	77,500	98,900	144,400	132,600

Source: Public Record Office, London, Bristol Port Books, E 190. Based on data compiled by Paul G. E. Clemens, Roberta Clemens and Lex Renda.

the needs of various plantations.[47] Commission houses were also active in trade with the Leeward Islands. Isaac Elton sold sugar from Montserrat in this way.[48] The Pinney plantations in Nevis consigned some sugar on commission to Peter Eaton, James Laroche, and William Reeve, Son & Hill and, after 1783, the Pinneys themselves set up as sugar commission merchants in Bristol.[49] The Tudways also used this method of trade to dispatch sugar from their Antigua estate to Bristol.[50]

Though the commission system dominated the Bristol sugar trade by 1750, a number of merchants chose to operate on their own account and risk. They employed either factors or ship captains to purchase sugar. Snippets of evidence show that some Bristolians followed this practice in

---

[47] Somerset RO, Robert Lovell to Ezekiel Dickinson, 19 Jan. 1782, William Dickinson Letters, 1780–3, Dickinson Papers, DD/DN 271; Cambridge RO, Business Letters of William Miles to John Tharp, 1771–7, Tharp Papers; BRO, Account Sales of Sugar in series, Ashton Court MSS: The Woolnough Papers, AC/WO 16(50); Huntington Library, John Curtis to Roger Hope Elletson, 18 Apr. 1768, and Samuel Munckley to Roger Hope Elletson, 23 July 1770, STB box 25, Brydges Family Papers, Stowe Collection; Derbyshire RO, Correspondence and Accounts of Bristol Merchants, Fitzherbert MSS: West Indian Papers, 239M/E19935-20239; National Library of Scotland, Sales of sugar from the *Clarendon*, 31 Jan. 1794, Nisbet Papers: Chisholme Papers (MS 5,464), fo. 166. For earlier examples of sugar commission trading at Bristol see Somerset RO, Sales Accounts of Abraham Birkin for 1700 and 1713, Helyar Muniments, DD/WHh/1089 pts. 2 and 6.

[48] BRO, Isaac Elton Ledger (1746–51), fos. 48, 50–2.

[49] Bristol UL, John Pinney to James Laroche, 17 Sept. 1764, 30 June 1765, 26 May 1766, to William Reeve, Son & Hill, 19 June 1769, 12 June 1770, and to Peter Eaton, 29 Oct. 1773, Letterbook of J. F. Pinney I and John Pinney (1761–75), Pinney Papers; Pares, *West-India Fortune*, chs. 8–13.

[50] Somerset RO, Account Sales of Sugar at Bristol, box 12, Tudway of Wells MSS, DD/TD.

Table 7.7. Sources of sugar imported by leading Bristol West India merchants, 1770–1780 (in hogsheads)

	Jamaica	Barbados and St Kitts	Barbados	St Kitts	Antigua and St Kitts	Antigua	Nevis	Tobago	Grenada	St Vincent	Dominica	Tortola	St Lucia
Bright, Lowbridge & Richard	3,322*	0	0	0	0	0	0	0	0	0	0	0	3
Bright, Baillie & Bright	0	179	0	1,257	18	0	1,053	11	951	333	0	0	0
Champion, Richard	0	0	0	0	0	0	0	0	0	0	118	917*	0
Davis, Mark	1,262*	0	0	88	0	0	12	0	0	0	0	0	0
Davis, Mark & Co.	920*	0	0	29	0	0	0	0	0	0	0	0	0
Davis & Protheroe	6,543*	30	0	361	39	0	56	0	0	0	0	0	0
Delpratt, Samuel	2,989*	0	0	0	0	0	0	0	0	0	0	0	0
Fowler, John & Co.	989*	0	0	0	0	0	0	0	0	0	0	0	0
Gordon, Robert	10,183*	0	0	0	0	0	30	17	0	0	0	0	0
Hamilton, David	0	0	13	0	0	0	0	468	669*	0	0	0	0
Lovell, Robert	2,754*	0	0	60	0	0	0	0	0	0	0	0	0
Meyler & Maxse	9,239*	0	0	0	0	0	0	5	0	0	0	0	0
Miles, William	12,533	0	25	12	0	0	0	130	0	0	0	0	0
Munckley, Samuel	1,803*	186	1,263	5	0	126	0	164	0	0	0	0	0
Parris, David	0	0	892*	0	0	65	0	0	0	0	0	0	0
Parris, Smith & Daniel	0	38	2,955*	42	10	45	47	80	8	0	0	0	0
Daniel, Thomas	0	0	979*	0	0	10	25	4	0	0	0	0	0
Reeve, William Son & Hill	0	0	193	1,005*	0	0	765	0	189	245	0	0	0
Span, Samuel	59	50	0	1,501*	198	177	46	310	52	0	443	0	0
Weare, John Fisher	1,279*	0	14	0	0	122	0	914	116	0	0	0	73

* = island from which merchants imported most of their sugar.

Source: Avon County Reference Library, Bristol, Bristol Presentments, Imports, 1770, 1775, 1778–1780. The figures in the table understate the level of sugar imports at Bristol for 1770 and 1775, during which years the Presentments are missing for five and fourteen issues respectively.

trade with Jamaica and St Kitts from the late 1720s to the mid-1750s.[51] In the 1750s, Corsley Rogers, Jr and Edward Pye Chamberlayne employed the services of a factor to buy muscovado and clayed sugar in Barbados. This was a trade on joint account in which Rogers and Chamberlayne sent exports to the factor, who kept one-third of the proceeds and remitted the other two-thirds in sugar as early in the crop as possible.[52] During the Seven Years War, Thomas Harris allowed a firm in Guadeloupe to buy 1,000 lbs. of best muscovado sugar for a sum not exceeding £2,000. He also instructed the captain of the *Ruby* to purchase sugar on the spot at either Jamaica, St Kitts, Nevis or Guadeloupe.[53] Various members of the Bright and Meyler families also purchased sugar directly in Jamaica in the three decades before American Independence.[54] In the 1760s and 1770s, Samuel Munckley acquired sugar on his own account. Bills of lading for his ships indicate that he received sugar in this way from a large number of agents in Barbados.[55]

Arrangements for the direct purchase of sugar are well illustrated in letters written by Samuel Munckley & Co. to captains of the *Fanny*. This ship, in which Munckley himself owned a half share, sailed directly between Bristol and Barbados on eleven consecutive yearly crossings between 1777 and 1788.[56] On the second voyage Captain Thomas Richards, who held a one-eighth share in the vessel, was instructed to send good bills of exchange as part remittance for an export cargo delivered to Barbados. For the other part, the owners hoped that Richards could buy fifty hogsheads of clayed or muscovado sugar.[57] On later voyages of the *Fanny*, the owners sometimes gave the master even more opportunity to use his initiative. On the fifth voyage the owners hoped that, if a full cargo of sugar was difficult to pick up, the captain would purchase some Dutch or French prize sugar in Barbados. They were willing to lay out the net proceeds of the export cargo for this

51 BRO, Tyndall & Asheton to Isaac Hobhouse, 15 Nov. 1729, Isaac Hobhouse Papers, Acc. 8029(16)f; UMA, Richard Meyler to William Wells, 3 Dec. 1732, Richard Meyler Ledger and Letterbook (1725–35), and Henry Bright to Jeremiah Ames, 24 Mar. 1740, and to Richard Meyler, 16 May 1742, Henry Bright Letterbook (1739–48), boxes 37 and 25, Bright Family Papers; PRO, HCA 30/259: invoices of sugar shipped to Bristol by John & Edward Foord of Jamaica, 30 Sept. 1756, 4 Oct. 1756, (?) Oct. 1756.
52 ACRL, Corsley Rogers, Jr & Edward Pye Chamberlayne to Bartholomew Smith, 27 Jan. 1755, Letterbook of Corsley Rogers, Jr & Edward Pye Chamberlayne (1755–6).
53 BRO, Thomas Harris to Pedder, Shaw & Margarett, 10 Oct. 1761, and to Capt. Daniel Henderson, 20 Dec. 1760, 10 Oct. 1761, Voyage Accounts: the *Ruby* (1758–63), Acc. 39654 [1].
54 This is fully documented in the Bright Family Papers at the BRO and the UMA.
55 BRO, Bills of Lading, Samuel Munckley Papers, AC/MU/2.
56 BRO, Account Book of the *Fanny*, Acc. 12162.
57 BRO, Samuel Munckley & Co. to Capt. Thomas Richards, Second Voyage of the *Fanny*, *ibid*.

purpose. They instructed the captain to draw on them for an extra £1,000 and gave him discretion to offer prices higher than the limits specified, if need be.[58]

By the mid-eighteenth century, the shipping of sugar from the Caribbean to Bristol was largely carried out by vessels trading on fixed direct routes on a regular basis.[59] These ships were mainly owned at Bristol. They dominated the trade to such an extent that some Bristol merchants, even influential ones, were refused sugar cargoes by factors in the West Indies tied to dealing with the constant traders.[60] Regular trading patterns were supplemented by shipping arrangements that brought sugar to market by the beginning of the sales season in late summer. Various strategies were available to expedite such sailings. Planters sometimes ordered their sugar to be divided among several ships, so that at least some of the crop stood a chance of arriving at an early market in Bristol.[61] Alternatively they arranged for the crop to be dispatched, in varying proportions, to several ports to maximise commercial connections in Bristol, Liverpool and London.[62] These strategies helped to avoid poor sales arising from late ships arriving at a glutted sugar market in Bristol – a situation that could lead to meagre profits, a possible loss of business reputation, and difficulties in securing full loads of produce the next year.[63]

The shipping of sugar across the Atlantic, however, was subject to several commercial problems – delays in the Caribbean, poor loading of cargoes, and disruptions caused by war. Delays were sometimes caused by sugar being unavailable at certain harbours.[64] But they also resulted from the time needed to gather hogsheads, tierces and barrels from various plantations in order to provide full shipments at the harbour or open road where vessels lay anchored. Samuel Munckley's bills of lading indicate that a fairly large number of shippers supplied small consign-

---

[58] BRO, Samuel Munckley & Co. to Capt. Thomas Richards, Fifth Voyage of the *Fanny*, *ibid*.

[59] See above, pp. 84–5, 87.

[60] See above, pp. 81–2; PRO, C 107/13: James R. Maud to James Rogers, 28 July 1785, James Rogers Papers; Pares, *West-India Fortune*, pp. 210–12.

[61] National Library of Jamaica, Samuel Cleland to Thomas Hall, 5 Mar. 1764, Letters of Samuel Cleland to Thomas Hall (1760–71); Cambridge RO, William Miles to John Tharp, 4 July, 18 Aug. 1781, 22 Oct. 1782, 10 Jan. 1783, Tharp Papers; Somerset RO, Sugar shipped from the Tudway plantations in Antigua to England, 1749–81, Tudway of Wells MSS, DD/TD.

[62] National Library of Scotland, James Chisholme to James Craggs, 2 Mar. 1794, 24 Dec. 1797, 15 Dec. 1799, James Chisholme Letterbook (1793–1812), fos. 18, 55, 70, Nisbet Papers: Chisholme Papers (MS 5,476).

[63] See below, p. 212, and PRO, C 107/14: Walter Atkin to James Rogers, 14 Apr. 1790, James Rogers Papers.

[64] See above, pp. 81–2.

ments to make up a full sugar cargo for a particular vessel – a process that frequently took longer than a month.[65] This long-drawn-out assembly procedure could be exacerbated by planters and ship captains haggling over freight charges. A good instance occurred in 1773 when Foord & Delpratt, agents in Jamaica, informed their Bristol correspondents that a delay in loading the ship *Byron* was owing to 'a grand dispute' between planters and captains about whether the freight for sugar should be 3/9 or 4/- per cwt.[66]

Planters could be recalcitrant in such situations. In one case they resolved collectively not to ship their sugars to Bristol unless captains attached to that port would take the same freight as the Londoners.[67] This decision reflected the close ties between island agencies in Jamaica and major London commission houses – another cause of delay for Bristol vessels in loading sugar cargoes. Sometimes Bristol ships did not receive any sugar until every London vessel was served, even though the Londoners arrived later at the island: 'the Planters never ship for Bristol', one Jamaican factor noted, 'if they can have their Goods taken in for London'.[68] This preference probably stemmed from close commercial ties with some London firms and expectations of high selling prices for sugar in the large metropolitan market. But though Bristol ships were sometimes at a competitive disadvantage against London vessels, planters and merchants in the Caribbean still gave them the preference for sugars on freight over ships arriving from the North American mainland.[69]

The shipping of sugar was also beset by frequent bad loading of cargoes. Often sugars did not arrive in Bristol in the same condition in which they were put on board ship in the Caribbean. The main problems were pilferage and inadequate stowage plus damage caused by salt water leaking into poorly made casks.[70] The change in the quantity of sugar during a voyage was inevitable, however, for sugar lost weight in shipment. On average around 10 per cent of the sugar loaded in the Carib-

[65] BRO, Bills of Lading, Samuel Munckley Papers, AC/MU/2.

[66] BRO, Foord & Delpratt to Samuel Munckley & George Champion, 9 June 1773, *ibid.*, AC/MU/1 (13).

[67] BRO, Lord Westport to Samuel Munckley, 11 Nov. 1773, *ibid.*, AC/MU/1(33).

[68] Derbyshire RO, Mark Davis & Co. to W. P. Perrin, 14 June 1774, Fitzherbert MSS: West Indian Papers, 239M/E19953. Cf. UMA, Francis Bright to Henry Bright, 27 July 1748, box 85, Bright Family Papers.

[69] New Hampshire HS, Thomas Williams to Capt. John Langdon, 1 Oct. 1764, box 1, folder 22, Langdon Papers (1716–1841).

[70] Derbyshire RO, Davis & Protheroe to W. P. Perrin, 6 Apr. 1780, Fitzherbert MSS: West Indian Papers, 239M/E20045; BRO, Letter of 31 Aug. 1730 and [? Henry Woolnough] to Mary Elbridge, 23 Oct. 1743, Ashton Court MSS: The Woolnough Papers, AC/WO 16/8m and 26; McCusker, 'Rum Trade', pp. 774–5.

bean and 25 per cent of that shipped from Jamaica was lost in this way.[71] Muscovado sugar lost more weight in shipment than higher quality clayed sugar.[72] Merchants who tried to calculate the loss of weight in sugar cargoes on the Atlantic crossing faced difficulties, for there were significant differences between insurance weights and King's Beam weights and between the short hundredweight of 100 lbs. – the standard unit in the sugar trade in the British Caribbean – and the long hundredweight of 112 lbs., which was used when the sugar was sold in Britain.[73]

The five major international wars in the eighteenth century sometimes seriously upset the seasonal rhythms of the sugar trade, even though there was usually adequate convoy protection for fleets in the Jamaica trade.[74] War led to high freight and insurance rates.[75] Commission merchants were also obliged to employ a larger capital in the sugar trade in wartime, for freight and other charges had to be met before the sugar was sold.[76] The commercial problems experienced by Bristol West India shippers are well documented for the American War of Independence. These merchants and shipowners were keen to procure sugar for Bristol rather than for a rival port, so they informed their captains that 'we would prefer half a loading to this place to a full loading for London or any other port'.[77] The intention here was to avoid the loss of profits incurred by short-freighted ships: to send vessels with light loads was to cross the ocean for no purpose.

Sugar merchants also knew that insurance premiums fluctuated markedly at the approach of war and during hostilities; that ships in the

[71] McCusker, 'Rum Trade', pp. 139–42, 798.
[72] BRO, Samuel Munckley & Co. to Capt. Thomas Richards, Fifth Voyage of the *Fanny*, Account Book of the *Fanny*. Most sugar produced in the Caribbean was muscovado, which is why more clayed sugar was not shipped.
[73] Derbyshire RO, Davis & Protheroe to W. P. Perrin, 16 Oct. 1777, Fitzherbert MSS: West Indian Papers, 239M/E19999; John J. McCusker, 'Weights and Measures in the Colonial Sugar Trade: The Gallon and the Pound and their International Equivalents', *WMQ*, 3rd Series, 30 (1973), 606–7.
[74] Further discussion of Jamaican fleets and convoy provision is given above on pp. 21, 63. For a useful case study of the effects of war on shipping see T. M. Devine, 'Transport Problems of Glasgow–West India Merchants during the American War of Independence, 1775–1783', *Transport History*, 4 (1971), 266–304.
[75] Freight and insurance charges for London–Jamaica ships operating between 1748 and 1783 are given in J. R. Ward, 'The Profitability of Sugar Planting in the British West Indies, 1650–1834', *EcHR*, 2nd Series, 31 (1978), tables 1 and 2, 199–200.
[76] Pares, *War and Trade in the West Indies*, pp. 515–16.
[77] William L. Clements Library, Bush & Elton to Capt. William Mattocks, 23 Mar. 1775, and Lowbridge & Richard Bright to Capt. William Mattocks, 23 Dec. 1775, 8th and 9th voyages of the *Kingston Packet*, Bristol Shipping Account Books, III. For similar instructions at earlier dates see University of the West Indies Library, Mona, Henry Bright *et al.* to Capt. John Tillidge, 28 Feb. 1753, and to Capt. John Lorain, 28 Feb. 1756, Account Book of the *Sarah* (1753–8), and Richard Meyler & Co. to Capt. John Lorain, 8 Sept. 1761, in Minchinton, ed., *Trade of Bristol in the Eighteenth Century*, p. 164.

Jamaica trade paid higher insurance rates than vessels trading with other West Indian islands; and that the hurricane season increased the risks of shipping in the Caribbean and hence insurance rates, too.[78] Thus in 1775 the owners of the *Kingston Packet* hoped that their ship captain would procure a cargo in Jamaica for Bristol before the double insurance took place at the beginning of the hurricane season in early August.[79] On another voyage of the same vessel, in 1776, the owners instructed the captain to buy sugar and rum at Anatto Bay, on the north-east side of Jamaica, and to be ready to sail for Bristol in January when lower insurance premiums were available.[80] They also noted that, in addition to marine insurance, other shipping costs such as seamen's wages and provisions were now 'so exorbitantly high' with the coming of war that 'every ship must loose a great sum of money by the voyage unless there is a proportionable Advance on the homeward freight and which we are very certain must soon take place; if it does not many People will not send out their ships. The Advance on the Outward Freights will not pay the extra outward Insurance on all the ships that go to the West Indies.'[81]

The risk of attack by enemy privateers during wartime led many Bristol shipowners to instruct captains to sail in convoy on both legs of direct voyages. Outward convoys were usually picked up at Cork,[82] whereas return convoys sailed from a specified rendezvous point in Jamaica. In 1782, the owners of the *Industry* emphasised the importance of joining the return convoy when they ordered their captain to sail from Jamaica to Bristol with an early convoy even if this meant leaving with a few casks short of his loading.[83] Many Bristol shipowners also wanted their captains to join convoys where possible and stay with them as far as they were appointed to go. They outlined the correct procedure to follow.[84] If no convoy was available, captains should agree on signals, sail and keep

[78] Devine, 'Transport Problems of Glasgow West-India Merchants', pp. 285–7; Ward, 'Profitability of Sugar Planting', table 2, p. 200.

[79] William L. Clements Library, Bush & Elton and Lowbridge & Richard Bright to Bright, Milward & Duncomb, 23 Mar. 1775, 8th voyage of the *Kingston Packet*, Bristol Shipping Account Books, III.

[80] William L. Clements Library, Bush, Elton & Bush and Lowbridge & Richard Bright to Capt. William Mattocks, 31 Aug. 1776, 10th voyage of the *Kingston Packet, ibid.*

[81] William L. Clements Library, Bush, Elton & Bush and Lowbridge & Richard Bright to Capt. William Mattocks, 5 Sept. 1776, 10th voyage of the *Kingston Packet, ibid.*

[82] William L. Clements Library, Bush, Elton & Bush and Lowbridge & Richard Bright to Capt. John Honeywell, 20 Dec. 1782, 3rd voyage of the *Industry, ibid.*

[83] William L. Clements Library, Bush, Elton & Bush and Lowbridge & Richard Bright to Capt. James Henderson, 15 Jan. 1782, 2nd voyage of the *Industry, ibid.*

[84] *Ibid.*; William L. Clements Library, Bush, Elton & Bush and Lowbridge & Richard Bright to Capt. William Ball, 11 Dec. 1780, 1st voyage of the *Industry, ibid.*

company with any ship or ships that were homeward bound.[85] Collective pressure by Bristol West India merchants was exerted on captains who tried to leave convoys to sail alone. In October 1776, a general meeting of these merchants resolved that captains should be discouraged from disobeying the orders of convoy commanders and from leaving convoys altogether.[86] But this ruling was not all that effective. In March 1777 there were reports that 'many Captains have already unwarrantably left the Convoy they sailed in Company with, by which means they have run an additional and unnecessary risque & many have lost their ships thereby'.[87] Masters knew that attempts to reach port ahead of the fleet could result in shipwreck, but, if successful, they avoided one important snag of convoys – large numbers of ships arriving home at the same time and depressing the sugar market.

The correspondence of William Miles, a leading Bristol merchant in the Jamaica trade, further illustrates the shipping problems prevalent during the American War of Independence. These letters provide a good instance of a merchant gambling by sending out ships in wartime without convoy protection or insurance. In 1781 Miles dispatched the *Lord North* as a runner in an attempt to provide provisions on time in Jamaica. He considered that the ship was well enough armed to be safe sailing without convoy.[88] Unfortunately, the *Lord North* was captured by an enemy privateer just after Miles had lost two other vessels. Miles grasped his dilemma: 'If I send out a ship to run it – as for instance the Lord North, that don't answer, because it does not meet with the approbation of the Planters to risque their propertys in running Ships. If it goes with convoy, then it is not in my power to hasten the arrivals of the ships, under such convoy, and in that case [they] are always too late.'[89] Other Bristolians also consigned West Indiamen without convoy protection. They were critical of the timing of sending outward convoys from Cork to the Caribbean. They considered that convoys should leave in early January rather than late February-to-early-March, so that ships could be loaded in

---

[85] William L. Clements Library, Bush, Elton & Bush and Lowbridge & Richard Bright to Capt. William Mattocks, 31 Aug. 1776, 10th voyage of the *Kingston Packet*, *ibid*.

[86] *Bonner and Middleton's Bristol Journal*, 26 Oct. 1776.

[87] William L. Clements Library, Bush & Elton and Lowbridge & Richard Bright to Capt. James Henderson, 5 Mar. 1777, 1st voyage of the *Severn*, Bristol Shipping Account Books, III.

[88] Cambridge RO, William Miles to John Tharp, 10 Mar. 1781, Tharp Papers. Extracts from this manuscript material are presented in Kenneth Morgan, ed., 'Calendar of Correspondence from William Miles, a West Indian Merchant in Bristol, to John Tharp, a Planter in Jamaica, 1770–1789' in Patrick McGrath, ed., *A Bristol Miscellany* (Bristol Record Society's *Publications*, 37, 1985), pp. 79–121. Citations to this material in this chapter are to the original manuscripts rather than to the calendar.

[89] Cambridge RO, William Miles to John Tharp, 15 June 1782, Tharp Papers.

the West Indies to come home with the first return convoys. They also thought that the Admiralty did not intend to act upon their complaints. Thus in 1782 several Bristol merchants armed about twelve of their best ships and sent them out without convoy to reach the West Indies in time to be quickly loaded for the first convoy home.[90]

Towards the end of the war, Miles found that West India shipping faced additional problems. In 1781 he noted that there were short crops in Jamaica and that inexperienced ship masters had to be employed in the trade.[91] 'The War now operates so severe upon the Trade of this Kingdom that its going to ruin', he remarked at the end of that year. 'The best of the Gentlemen in Trade connected with the islands hardly know what to do Our ships in general little more than half full, Wages never so high at any period before.'[92] The regularity of hurricanes added to these difficulties. Between 1780 and 1786 no less than six hurricanes spread ruin and destruction throughout the Caribbean each summer, whereas they normally occurred only once every seven or eight years.[93] Once peace occurred, however, the Bristol sugar trade began to recover its fortunes.

The Bristol sugar market was particularly active in the late summer, when the first fleets arrived from the Caribbean, but sales continued throughout most of the year. Apart from damaged sugar, which was usually sold at public auction, most sugar sales at Bristol were arranged by commission merchants and carried out by brokers. Sugar was sold to small merchants, grocers and bakers, and occasionally to distillers, apothecaries and coopers, who were the chief occupational groups involved in operating Bristol sugar refineries. From time to time, brewers and speculators also bought sugar.[94] Payment was usually made in bills of exchange, either on the spot or within three months.[95] Before the American Revolution, Bristol sugar merchants benefited from relatively modest sugar duties (which, by 1776, amounted to 6s. 3%₁₀d. per cwt.).

---

90 SMV, William Miles *et al.* to Philip Stephens, 26 Oct. 1782, Bristol West India Society: Book of Proceedings (1782–1804).
91 Cambridge RO, William Miles to John Tharp, 4 July 1781, Tharp Papers.
92 Cambridge RO, William Miles to John Tharp, 5 Dec. 1781, *ibid.*
93 Richard B. Sheridan, 'The Crisis of Slave Subsistence in the British West Indies during and after the American Revolution', *WMQ*, 3rd Series, 33 (1976), 625–6.
94 Hall, 'The Daubenys: Part 1', app. II, pp. 137–40. For an analysis of the Bristol sugar market after 1783 see Pares, *West-India Fortune*, pp. 186–206.
95 Derbyshire RO, Davis & Protheroe to W. P. Perrin, 18 Mar. 1779, Fitzherbert MSS: West Indian Papers, 239M/E20027; Bristol UL, Pinney & Tobin to William Colhoun, 25 July 1785, and to James French, 9 Aug. 1793, Tobin & Pinney Letterbooks (1784–9 and 1792–6), Pinney Papers; UMA, Richard Meyler to Thomas Young, 30 Sept. 1734, and to John Green, 15 Nov. 1734, Richard Meyler Ledger and Letterbook (1725–35), box 37, Bright Family Papers. When sugar was selling slowly the credit period was sometimes stretched to four months (UMA, Lowbridge Bright to John McMillan, 29 Sept. 1770, Lowbridge Bright Letterbook (1765–73), *ibid.*).

Though they complained, to no avail, when the duties were raised in 1781 from 6s. 7$\frac{13}{20}$d. per cwt. (set in 1779) to 11s. 8$\frac{7}{10}$d. per cwt., they still made good profits from commissions on the sale of sugar lots.[96] By the 1770s, leading West India merchants at Bristol could earn around £1,600 per year from sugar sales.[97] Even though the duties on each hundredweight of sugar were later raised to 12s 3$\frac{2}{5}$d. in 1782, to 12s 4d. in 1787, and to 15s. in 1791, they usually only comprised one-sixth (at most) of the sale price.[98]

Various types of sugar were sold in Bristol. The market there was suited to well cured sugar that was light in colour for, according to one merchant, 'a white cast and strong body are the signs of perfection; what is deemed straw colour or yellow is not so good'.[99] Sugars of particular textures and colours attracted different types of retailers. Sometimes the sugar available was more suitable for sugar bakers than grocers and vice-versa.[100] Large hard-grained sugar commanded high prices from bakers, who preferred strength in their sugar. Low soft-grained sugar was cheaper and more to the liking of grocers, who liked colour rather than strength in their sugar.[101] As far as possible, grocers and bakers both avoided buying brown, moist, syrupy sugar: this was so poor in quality that it was not worth paying freight and duties to ship it home.[102]

Jamaica and the Leeward Islands produced muscovado sugar, a coarse brown substance which was the result of the initial boiling and processing

[96] For details of the sugar duties and Bristolians' complaints about them see Lowell Joseph Ragatz, *Statistics for the Study of British Caribbean Economic History, 1763–1833* (London, 1927), table VI, p. 10, and SMV, West India Society Minutes (1782–1804), 12 Mar. 1783, and two petitions for Mar. 1783 (one dated 13 Mar.), bundle 25A, Miscellaneous Correspondence.

[97] Calculated from the commission earnings and sugar imports of Mark Davis & Co. and Davis & Protheroe, 1774–82, given in Derbyshire RO, Fitzherbert MSS: West Indian Papers, 239M/E19952–20074, and SMV, Wharfage Books. The commission earnings of another Bristol firm – the Pinneys in the 1830s and 1840s – are discussed in Pares, *West-India Fortune*, pp. 204–6.

[98] Based on a comparison of the sugar duties given in Ragatz, *Statistics*, table VI, p. 10, with the following sugar sales accounts at Bristol: BRO, Account sales of sugar, The Woolnough Papers, AC/WO 16(50), Ashton Court MSS; Derbyshire RO, Fitzherbert MSS: West Indian Papers, 239M/E 19952–20096; Guildhall Library, Daybook of Sales of West Indian Produce begun by Samuel Munckley in 1775, Anthony Gibbs & Sons Papers, MS 11,069A.

[99] Bristol UL, Pinney & Tobin to William Ferrier, 20 Sept. 1786, Pinney & Tobin Letterbook (1784–89), Pinney Papers; Cambridge RO, William Miles to John Tharp, 7 Feb. 1788, Tharp Papers (from which the quotation is taken).

[100] Bristol UL, Pinney & Tobin to William Colhoun, 23 June 1791, Pinney & Tobin Letterbook (1789–92), Pinney Papers.

[101] UMA, Richard Meyler to Henry Bright, 6 Mar., 21 Nov. 1741, boxes 5 and 6, Bright Family Papers; Pares, *West-India Fortune*, p. 190.

[102] BRO, Henry Bright *et al.* to Pedder, Shaw & Margarett, 10 Oct. 1761, Voyage Accounts: the *Ruby* (1758–63); Derbyshire RO, Protheroe & Claxton to W. P. Perrin, 12 July, 22 Oct. 1784, Fitzherbert MSS: West Indian Papers, 239M/E20129.

carried out in the Caribbean. Most of the other islands – in this case, Monte Christi, Grenada and Barbados – produced both muscovado and crude white or clayed sugar.[103] Of all the British Caribbean islands, Barbados was the only one where a large proportion of the sugar was clayed. Around 1770 probably about 75 per cent of the sugar produced in Barbados was clayed, though by then virtually none of this reached Britain.[104] Table 7.8 indicates the range of sugars that could be bought in the Bristol market and the prices they fetched.[105] It shows that white sugar was graded by numbers according to quality. Thus in August 1764 Devonsheir & Reeve sold muscovado sugar at prices between 28 and 42 shillings per cwt. The highest price was expected for sugar from St Kitts, which produced the best muscovado of any island in the British Caribbean.[106] The several grades of white clayed sugars were offered at rather higher prices – between 38 and 53½ shillings per cwt. This is not surprising since Barbados white sugar was superior in quality to any muscovado

Table 7.8. *Sugar sale prices offered by Devonsheir & Reeve of Bristol, 22 August 1764 (in shillings per cwt.)*

Sugar Jamaica muscovado	28–39
St Kitts	32–42
Antigua	26–36
Montserrat	30–40
Nevis	29–40
Barbados	28–38
1st clayed	52
2nd clayed	45–48
3rd clayed	38–42
Monte Christi muscovado	27–37
Monte Christi whites	40–53/6
Grenada muscovado	28–38
Grenada whites	38–49

Source: New England Historic Genealogical Society, Price current of Devonsheir & Reeve, 22 August 1764, box 26, folder 3, Hancock Papers. Cf. Baker Library, Harvard Business School, Price current of William Reeve, Son & Hill, 2 April 1772, box 14, file 22: Prices current, Bristol, 1765–72, Samuel Abbot Papers.

[103] For detailed commentary on the sugar production of these islands see McCusker, 'Rum Trade', ch. 4.
[104] *Ibid.*, p. 203 and table D-15, p. 919.
[105] Cf. Boston Public Library, Price current of Devonsheir & Reeve, 25 Oct. 1765, The Chamberlain Collection of Autographs: The Hancock Papers, II (1763–1816). For useful comments on the various grades of unrefined sugar see McCusker, 'Rum Trade', pp. 987–8 note 17.
[106] McCusker, 'Rum Trade', p. 175.

produced in the Leeward Islands and Jamaica.[107] Bristol sugar grocers therefore preferred to buy Barbados clayed sugar rather than 'weak Jamaicas'.[108] They presumably found that the difference between clayed and muscovado sugars was more important in determining price than variations in the sugars supplied by individual islands or plantations.[109] The list of individual grades of sugar suggests that Devonsheir & Reeve intended to sell each grade in separate lots. Nevertheless some commission merchants considered that if sugars supplied from a particular island were highly varied in quality, then it was best to sell them together at an average price.[110]

Apart from the difference in prices for various grades of sugar at any time, there were also seasonal and monthly variations in prices. The seasonal rhythm was influenced most of all by crop time and the shipping season. Prices tended to 'break' around the end of May when the first West Indiamen reached Bristol. They continued to fluctuate over the summer months until the end of September when the last major sugar crop of the year was brought home by the 'first of August' fleet. From the autumn to the spring there were few seasonal fluctuations in prices because very little new sugar arrived in British ports over the winter months to disturb the market seriously. But by late May the yearly round of seasonal price fluctuations began again.[111] Within each month prices also fluctuated. The sugar 'marketts in England you must be convinced from experience are very fluctuating', Henry Cruger, Jr informed Aaron Lopez in 1765, for 'in the course of a Month, they often rise or fall 20 per cent'.[112]

Table 7.9 presents information on sugar sale prices at Bristol for the period 1763–83. These data reveal the fluctuations within an overall upward trend in prices from around 38–40 shillings per cwt. in the 1760s to 65–70 shillings per cwt. in the early 1780s. Rising sugar prices from 1763 to 1776, at a time of increased consumption, are indicative of strong demand for sugar in a protected market in peacetime. But the table also

---

[107] Ibid., p. 165.
[108] UMA, Lowbridge Bright to Nathaniel Milward, 15 July 1771, Bright Letterbook (1765–73), Bright Family Papers.
[109] Cf. Richard Pares, 'The London Sugar Market, 1740–69', EcHR, 2nd Series, 9 (1956–7), 258–60.
[110] BRO, Thomas French to J. H. Smyth, 19 June 1762, Ashton Court MSS: The Woolnough Papers, AC/WO 16(46d); Pares, West-India Fortune, pp. 188–9.
[111] Pares, West-India Fortune, p. 194.
[112] Henry Cruger, Jr to Aaron Lopez, 11 Oct. 1765, in Worthington C. Ford, ed., The Commerce of Rhode Island, 2 vols. (MHS Collections, 7th Series, 9, Boston, 1914), I, p. 128. The fluctuations of sugar prices within each month are well documented in Guildhall Library, Daybook of sales of West India Produce begun by Samuel Munckley in 1775, MS 11,069A.

shows that the War of Independence had a significant impact on sugar prices. Price increases came swiftly during this war – a time of reduced sugar imports into Britain. Price levels in Series A reached 51 shillings per cwt. in August 1778, 60 shillings in December 1779, and a peak of 67 shillings in January 1782. In Series B, prices rose from 30–40 shillings per

Table 7.9. *Sale prices of Jamaican sugar at Bristol, 1763–1783 (in pounds and shillings per hundredweight)*

			Series A			
July	1763	38/–		December	1771	42/6
August	1763	43/–		October	1772	43/6
March	1764	38/–		October	1773	44/–
July	1764	36/6		February	1774	38/–
November	1764	37/6		January	1776	39/–
October	1765	42/–		August	1778	51/–
April	1766	39/–		December	1778	56/–
September	1766	36/–		December	1779	60/–
September	1768	38/6		September	1780	57/–
November	1768	40/–		January	1782	67/–
April	1770	39/6		October	1783	44/–
November	1770	36/–				

			Series B			
March	1774	38/–		October	1777	53/–
		40/–		June	1778	46/–
March	1775	35/–		November	1778	55/–
November	1775	34/6		March	1779	49/–*
		31/–		April	1779	55/–
January	1776	32/–		September	1779	54/–
		27/–		December	1779	59/–
		32/6		May	1780	63/–
		28/6		June	1780	62/–
August	1776	38/–		July	1780	62/–
September	1776	33/–		August	1780	55/–
		36/–		November	1780	58/6
		31/6		January	1781	54/–
December	1776	35/–*		March	1781	60/6
		46/–		January	1782	68/6
April	1777	46/–				66/–
						70/–

* = damaged sugar.
Sources: Series A: Bristol Record Office, Account Sales of Sugar in Series, Ashton Court MSS: The Woolnough Papers, AC/WO 16(50). Series B: Derbyshire Record Office, Fitzherbert MSS: West Indian Papers, 239 M/E 19952–20074.
Note: I have averaged the prices for each month.

cwt. at the start of the war to 63 shillings in May 1780 and to a top price of 70 shillings in January 1782. The range of sale prices widened during the war. In Series A, for instance, sugar prices oscillated between 36 and 44 shillings per cwt. between 1763 and 1776 but fluctuated from 39 to 67 shillings per cwt. between 1776 and 1783. Finally, there was a substantial fall in sugar prices towards the end of the war. Thus in Series A prices fell by one-third from 67 shillings per cwt. in January 1782 to 44 shillings in October 1783. Table 7.10 provides further evidence of fluctuations in sugar prices at Bristol. It confirms some of the trends in table 7.9, especially the price increase for sugar between the beginning and the end of the American Revolution. It also underscores the strong dietary demand for sugar since, by the renewal of war in the 1790s, prices were consistently greater than 60 shillings per cwt.

The state of the sugar market and level of prices at different ports helped to trigger many of these fluctuations, for sugar prices became increasingly integrated throughout Britain towards the end of the eighteenth century. In some years, Bristol grocers and sugar bakers were heavily influenced by price trends at Liverpool. By offering lower prices, Liverpudlians could engross the inland trade among consumers normally served from Bristol and thus bring the sugar market at the latter place to a standstill. Sugar did not recover its price at Bristol in such circumstances until the Liverpool market was drained or prices fell in other markets.[113] The Bristol market was even more sensitive to changes in sugar prices at London. This is not surprising since these were the two leading British ports for West India trade, and absentee plantation owners often divided their sugar cargoes between London and Bristol.[114] Nevertheless, the response of Bristol merchants to sugar imports at London, and to whether the sugar market there was generally buoyant or depressed, has largely passed unrecognised in the secondary literature.

Sugar prices at Bristol 'broke' only after the opening of the London sugar market. Bristol merchants were always anxious about how prices would compare, since a fall in the London market often led to dull sugar

[113] Bristol UL, Tobin & Pinney to George Webbe, 6 Aug. 1799, to John Taylor, 15 Aug. 1799, and to J. C. Miles, 29 Oct. 1799, Tobin & Pinney Letterbook (1796–1800), Pinney Papers; Derbyshire RO, Davis & Protheroe to W. P. Perrin, 11 May 1778, and Protheroes & Claxton to W. P. Perrin, 10 Aug. 1799, Fitzherbert MSS: West Indian Papers, 239M/E20007 and 20235.

[114] E.g. Somerset RO, 'A List of Sugar shipped from Parham plantation from Feb. last to 23 July 1767', box 11, bundle 4, Tudway of Wells MSS, DD/TD; Bristol UL, John Pinney to James Laroche, 30 June 1765, and to William Reeve, 28 May 1768, Letterbook of J. F. Pinney and John Pinney (1761–75), Pinney Papers.

Table 7.10. *Sugar sale prices at Bristol, 1775–1800 (in shillings per cwt.)*

	January	February	March	April	May	June	July	August	September	October	November	December
1775	—	—	—	—	—	—	36.4	40.8	38.3	33.5	35.5	42.1
1776	32.0	41.1	—	31.0	30.0	38.1	45.4	34.7	46.3	50.1	40.9	43.1
1777	42.4	42.2	43.0	50.0	46.3	44.3	42.9	45.6	50.5	58.1	65.0	56.5
1778	51.0	59.7	49.0	51.0	—	—	44.5	54.8	48.1	60.1	46.0	50.3
1779	—	—	52.7	—	—	53.5	43.0	57.3	58.4	60.4	58.4	64.1
1780	57.9	—	52.0	50.0	—	—	—	56.9	59.7	64.6	58.3	54.7
1781	59.4	—	56.0	52.2	63.6	63.0	—	—	—	72.3	64.4	65.0
1782	68.4	—	—	—	—	71.5	66.0	65.9	66.1	62.8	56.3	47.0
1783	44.5	—	—	—	46.0	41.0	48.0	48.5	48.7	46.8	66.0	41.6
1784	46.5	—	—	—	—	42.5	43.9	43.7	45.0	44.0	54.4	47.9
1785	58.7	43.8	—	47.3	45.6	49.4	48.1	51.1	47.9	53.5	56.2	62.1
1786	50.0	45.5	—	45.5	—	—	50.0	56.8	54.3	55.8	57.0	57.8
1787	61.5	55.5	52.3	46.5	48.8	48.0	47.4	53.1	49.7	55.9	50.7	52.8
1788	46.0	—	—	—	—	—	46.9	52.2	45.2	56.3	44.1	—
1789	44.4	—	46.0	—	—	—	51.2	56.4	50.0	53.0	54.7	56.0
1790	53.0	55.2	51.5	—	—	—	60.0	62.5	66.4	65.2	59.5	56.0
1791	65.5	—	—	—	67.2	66.3	69.4	72.8	75.3	—	73.6	78.5
1792	—	79.7	80.5	—	69.7	68.2	69.8	—	73.0	72.8	76.2	75.5
1793	74.0	—	—	—	73.0	59.0	71.0	70.7	65.8	68.5	76.3	80.6
1794	86.8	—	84.5	—	—	—	48.3	52.0	—	62.0	56.2	57.7
1795	57.0	60.9	—	—	—	73.0	72.5	72.0	82.6	84.8	87.2	80.0
1796	—	98.0	—	83.5	82.0	—	—	82.0	81.7	79.5	86.1	78.5
1797	79.0	78.3	83.5	84.5	—	—	82.5	79.0	82.4	80.4	79.1	—
1798	82.3	83.5	79.6	—	88.5	89.0	83.9	83.8	85.5	84.5	90.3	—
1799	84.5	87.4	84.0	85.0	85.0	—	85.4	81.5	93.7	69.5	—	—
1800	65.4	65.8	—	—	—	59.0	64.1	63.3	69.4	78.0	84.0	86.0

Source: Guildhall Library, London, Daybook of Sales of West India Produce begun in 1775 by Samuel Munckley, Anthony Gibbs & Son Papers, MS 11,069A.

Note: I have averaged the prices for each month.

sales at Bristol.[115] 'Our prices are not yet broke', Davis & Protheroe informed a plantation owner in 1782, 'and the Refiners tell us they must be low, i.e. from 50 to 60/-. We wait the opening of the London market and as we have more than our proportion to Bristol in the late Fleet, fear ours will be under it this year.'[116] This comment gains further point when one notes that sugar prices at the outports were usually slightly higher than in London, mainly because outport markets were smaller and subject to less certain payment.[117]

Bristol commission merchants attempted to mitigate fears about price fluctuations by enquiries about the state of the London market.[118] By comparison of prices Mark Davis 'found fine sugars to sell full as high if not higher with you [i.e. London] than in our market, but low and midling several shillings higher with us than with you'.[119] This suggests that prices varied according to the different qualities of sugar in both markets, though whether these particular distinctions were true in most years is hard to say. But the larger metropolitan market was certainly more susceptible than Bristol to rapid price increases.[120] Bristol merchants, unlike their London counterparts, were unable to command a sale on any day of the week, for their sugars sometimes came to market only once a week or fortnight.[121]

Perhaps the most significant influence of the London sugar market on that of Bristol was the way in which falling prices in the former affected the latter, especially at times of high imports. At such times Bristol sugar bakers tended to buy sparingly and reluctantly; they preferred to wait for falling London prices to induce lower prices at Bristol before purchasing large amounts of sugar.[122] William Miles expressed this succinctly in 1774 when he noted that 'the London market has been falling, which has

---

[115] Bristol UL, Tobin, Pinney & Tobin to George Webbe, 15 Dec. 1796, Tobin, Pinney & Tobin Letterbook (1796–1800), Pinney Papers; Derbyshire RO, Protheroe & Claxton to W. P. Perrin, 23 June 1794, Fitzherbert MSS: West Indian Papers, 239M/E20164; HSP, Thomas Penington & Son to Thomas Clifford, 15 Oct. 1759, Clifford Correspondence, II (1757–60), Pemberton Papers.

[116] Derbyshire RO, Davis & Protheroe to W. P. Perrin, 12 Aug. 1782, Fitzherbert MSS: West Indian Papers, 239M/E20082.

[117] Ward ,'Profitability of Sugar Planting', p. 199.

[118] E.g. Derbyshire RO, Mark Davis & Co. to W. P. Perrin, 20 Jan. 1775, Fitzherbert MSS: West Indian Papers, 239/E19958.

[119] Derbyshire RO, Mark Davis & Co. to W. P. Perrin, 22 Mar. 1774, *ibid.*, 239M/E19949.

[120] Derbyshire RO, Davis & Protheroe to W. P. Perrin, 23 June 1779, *ibid.*, 239M/E20031. For a detailed examination of price fluctuations in the London market see Pares, 'London Sugar Market, 1740–69', pp. 263–70.

[121] Derbyshire RO, Davis & Protheroe to W. P. Perrin, 19 Sept. 1776, and Protheroe & Claxton to W. P. Perrin, 4 Dec. 1793, Fitzherbert MSS: West Indian Papers, 239M/E19980 and 20158.

[122] Derbyshire RO, Davis & Protheroe to W. P. Perrin, 6 Nov. 1777, 11 Mar. 1778, *ibid.*, 239M/E20000 and 20004.

affected this . . . full 2/- p[er] hundredweight and I greatly fear will fall 2 to 3/- p[er] hundredweight more – for the import into England must be great – and that all the buyers know'.[123] There was one further adverse way in which commercial factors in London affected the state of the Bristol sugar market. If only a small amount of sugar was available at Bristol at a time of high sugar imports into London, it was usually possible for regular Bristol buyers to pay cheaper prices in the metropolis. Thus on one occasion James Laroche explained to John Pretor Pinney that 'our Sugar Bakers, finding that they could buy from 5 to 6/- p[er] hundredweight cheaper at London than here ... went last week & bought about 2,000 h[ogs]h[ea]ds, which has put a damp to our markett.'[124] The bakers must have considered that this would be profitable even though the charge of bringing sugars from London to Bristol was about 3 shillings per cwt.[125] A good many other Bristolians also followed this practice.[126] Knowledge of these price differentials spread to the Caribbean and some planters sent sugar cargoes to specific ports on the basis of this information.[127]

Fluctuating prices in the Bristol sugar market were also caused by various other factors. Sugar prices at Bristol tended to be dull during the fair and at times when great crops were reported in the West Indies.[128] On the other hand, additional duties plus dabbling by speculators could cause price rises.[129] A glut of sugar after the arrival of the West India fleet at Bristol usually led to poor sale prices, while the arrival of ships with half-full sugar cargoes at an understocked market often led to good sale prices.[130] But the likelihood of high sugar prices at Bristol when demand

[123] Cambridge RO, William Miles to John Tharp, 15 July 1774, Tharp Papers.
[124] Bristol UL, James Laroche to John Pretor Pinney, 13 Sept. 1763, Domestic Papers (1656–1800), Pinney Papers.
[125] *Ibid.*
[126] Bristol UL, Tobin & Pinney to Monsieur Dessall, 18 Nov. 1794, Tobin & Pinney Letterbook (1792–6), *ibid.*; BRO, Henry Bright *et al.* to MacNeal & Sadler, 20 Dec. 1760, Voyage Accounts: the *Ruby* (1758–63); Derbyshire RO, Protheroe & Claxton to W. P. Perrin, 22 Oct. 1784, Fitzherbert MSS: West Indian Papers, 239M/E20129; UMA, Price current of Richard Meyler, 3 Nov. 1766, and Lowbridge Bright to Parker & Collins, 2 Nov. 1770, to John McMillan, 7 Dec. 1770, and to William Thompson & Co., 18 Dec. 1773, Lowbridge Bright Letterbook (1765–73), Bright Family Papers.
[127] UMA, David Duncombe to Lowbridge Bright, 22 Dec. 1789, box 9, Bright Family Papers.
[128] Bristol UL, Pinney & Tobin to J. M. Shaw, 6 June 1785, to James Tyson, 2 Apr. 1787, and to Boddington & Bettesworth, 7 Sept. 1791, Pinney & Tobin Letterbooks (1784–9 and 1789–92), Pinney Papers.
[129] Bristol UL, Pinney & Tobin to Ulysses Lynch, 1 Nov. 1790, and to Edward Braxier, 7 Mar. 1791, Pinney & Tobin Letterbook (1789–92), *ibid.*
[130] Cambridge RO, William Miles to John Tharp, 3 Dec. 1771, 20 Sept. 1774, Tharp Papers; Somerset RO, John Maxse to Robert Tudway, 6 Sept. 1793, 12 Aug. 1794, boxes 11 and 13, Tudway of Wells MSS, DD/TD; Bristol UL, Tobin & Pinney to J. M. Shaw, 23 June 1784, and to George Webbe, 2 Oct. 1793, Tobin & Pinney Letterbooks (1784–9 and 1792–6), Pinney Papers.

exceeded supply was sometimes upset by other considerations. In 1781, for instance, an important by-election absorbed the attention of Bristolians and distracted them from sugar sales.[131] At other times poor commercial information about the probable size of sugar imports had an adverse effect on sales.[132] Of crucial importance in determining the buoyancy of the sugar market was the size and quality of the Jamaica crop (which provided the bulk of the import) rather than the nature of the crop elsewhere in the Caribbean.[133] But prices also varied as a result of unforeseen causes: a fall in Bristol sugar prices in October 1799 was attributed to a larger influx of sugar than usual, decreased consumption due to recent high prices, an excess of foreign sugar imported into Hamburg, the alarming failure of several sugar firms in the same city, the continuance of the continental war, and expectations of a large supply of sugar from Surinam.[134]

The greatest uncertainty about sugar prices was caused by war. This is best illustrated by reference to the Bristol sugar market during the American War of Independence. Short supplies of raw sugar in these years led to British sugar imports falling by one quarter. This diminished import led to swift price increases plus a wider gulf between top and bottom prices than in peacetime.[135] High sugar prices at Bristol quickly led to a fall in consumption and to cutbacks in the activity of local sugar refineries.[136] 'The fact is', as William Miles put it, 'we used to have 18 to 22 Sugar Houses fully at work, now there is not as much refined as eight of those houses could do if fully worked. This occasions a slow and heavy sale and the advance nothing comparatively speaking.'[137] By the early 1780s, speculators were putting their money into government securities rather than into buying sugar.[138] In addition, a large amount of foreign sugar from Tortola and St Thomas was being sold at lucrative rates that undercut the prices obtained for sugar from British-owned plantations.[139] By the end of 1782, with rumours that peace was near, sugar sales at

[131] Somerset RO, Ezekiel Dickinson to William Dickinson, 8 Mar. 1781, William Dickinson Letters (1780–3), Dickinson Papers, DD/DN 271.

[132] Derbyshire RO, Mark Davis & Co. to W. P. Perrin, 22 Mar. 1774, Fitzherbert MSS: West Indian Papers, 239M/E19949.

[133] Bristol UL, Pinney & Tobin to J. R. Herbert, 1 Aug. 1785, Pinney & Tobin Letterbook (1784–9), Pinney Papers.

[134] Bristol UL, Tobin, Pinney & Tobin to Edward Huggins, 29 Oct. 1799, Tobin, Pinney & Tobin Letterbook (1796–1800), ibid.

[135] See above, pp. 207–9.

[136] Cambridge RO, William Miles to John Tharp, 16 July 1782, Tharp Papers; Somerset RO, James Sutton to Ezekiel Dickinson, 20 May 1781, William Dickinson Letters (1780–3), Dickinson Papers, DD/DN 271.

[137] Cambridge RO, William Miles to John Tharp, 10 Mar. 1781, Tharp Papers.

[138] Ibid.

Bristol became dull and then stopped altogether.[140] William Miles estimated that he would lose £20,000 by the fall in sugar consumption and prices when peace was declared but that thereafter 'things will go on better and with more certainty'.[141]

The continual round of fluctuating sugar prices meant that a high degree of judgement was necessary in order to decide exactly when sugar should be sold. Commission merchants often received advice on this matter from their planter principals. In 1777, for instance, John Pinney complained to his Bristol factor that low prices resulted from sugar lots 'being sold before the rise of the market', and requested in future that 'if a good price for my sugars cannot be obtained upon their arrival, you will keep them until Dec[embe]r or Janu[ar]y ab[ou]t which time I observe the markets generally rise'.[142] Yet too much caution on the part of principals was just as detrimental as rash decisions to sell quickly after the arrival of the fleet. Davis & Protheroe realised that it was sometimes best to sell sugar without taking the advice of their principal for, as they noted to him, 'we know that some former years you suffered considerably by being over-scrupulous on this head'.[143] This implies that it was expensive to keep holding back sugar from sale.

Selling sugar cargoes soon after their arrival in Bristol was particularly difficult when buyers felt that prices were too high. In February 1774 Mark Davis placed samples of his principal's sugar in a broker's office with the intention of selling the sugar for thirty-eight shillings per cwt. Sugar bakers bid thirty-seven shillings and sixpence for them but Davis refused the offer.[144] Haggling over sixpence per cwt. was not a petty matter: agents needed to keep within the bounds of prices offered for specific grades of sugar by other commission merchants. Quick sales at prices below those charged by rivals were precarious because they usually brought down the overall average prices in the market, and the costs of freight and sugar duties were also generally prohibitive.[145]

[139] Cambridge RO, William Miles to John Tharp, 22 Oct. 1782, 10 Jan. 1783, *ibid*.

[140] Cambridge RO, William Miles to John Tharp, 30 Nov. 1782, Tharp Papers; Derbyshire RO, Davis & Protheroe to W. P. Perrin, 23 July 1782, Fitzherbert MSS: West Indian Papers, 239M/E20079.

[141] Cambridge RO, William Miles to John Tharp, 6 May 1783, Tharp Papers. For further evidence on the uncertainty of sugar prices when war was expected see Cambridge RO, William Miles to Edward Brazier, 28 Sept. 1787, and to William Colhoun, 17 Nov. 1787, *ibid*.

[142] Bristol UL, John Pinney to Peter Eaton, 18 Apr. 1777, John Pinney Letterbook (1775–8), Pinney Papers.

[143] Derbyshire RO, Davis & Protheroe to W. P. Perrin, 19 Sept. 1776, Fitzherbert MSS: West Indian Papers, 239M/E19980.

[144] Derbyshire RO, Mark Davis & Co. to W. P. Perrin, 7 Feb. 1774, *ibid*., 239M/E19947.

[145] Cambridge RO, William Miles to John Tharp, 10 Jan. 1783, Tharp Papers.

Added to the problem of whether to sell sugar quickly or to keep stocks in the hope of better prices was the ever-present rivalry between importers and shopkeepers that had prevailed in Bristol since the Tudor and Stuart periods. In the case of sugar, this took the form of competition between the commission agents and their chief buyers.[146] The tension between these two groups was reflected in one Bristol merchant's reference to 'the cunning grocers'.[147] Occasionally this rivalry resulted in formal protests, as in 1753 when English sugar refiners and grocers (mainly from London and Bristol) petitioned the House of Commons about the high prices which factors charged for sugar.[148] This resort to petitioning brought no satisfaction to grocers and refiners, but they had less formal and more effective ways of competing with commission agents at sugar sales. The tactics of sugar bakers and refiners suggest that there was fierce competition between them and commission merchants over the sale price of sugar.[149] Buyers often knew as much as sellers about when large crops were expected in the West Indies, and were therefore partly able to anticipate low prices.[150] In addition, sugar bakers sometimes negotiated favourable credit arrangements with commission agents, thereby effectively getting lower prices by forcing merchants to sell later consignments at reduced rates. Davis & Protheroe perceived this problem, and suggested how it might be solved,when in 1776 they commented that 'our Bakers have for two years past found means to extend the Credit and hitherto we have been obliged to comply or relax in price but we hope soon by uniting together to overcome these difficulties'.[151]

Nevertheless, the available evidence suggests that sugar bakers were able to combine more effectively than sugar commission merchants for business purposes. The bakers kept a vigilant eye on sugar prices in Bristol and London and often stayed out of the market altogether when their warehouses were full of refined sugar, when demand was slack, and when a considerable fall in prices was expected with the arrival of the

---

[146] David Harris Sacks, *The Widening Gate: Bristol and the Atlantic Economy, 1450–1700* (Berkeley and Los Angeles, 1991), pp. 80–3. For a similar situation in the metropolis see Walter M. Stern, 'The London Sugar Refiners around 1800', *The Guildhall Miscellany*, 3 (1954), pp. 31–2.

[147] Somerset RO, Abraham Birkin to William Helyar, 8 Oct. 1701, Helyar Muniments, DD/WHL/1089–90.

[148] Sheridan, *Sugar and Slavery*, p. 72.

[149] Cf. Pares, *West-India Fortune*, ch. 9.

[150] E.g. Cambridge RO, William Miles to John Tharp, 18 May 1774, Tharp Papers.

[151] Derbyshire RO, Davis & Protheroe to W. P. Perrin, 18 Mar. 1776, Fitzherbert MSS: West Indian Papers, 239M/E19975.

Jamaica fleet.[152] Sometimes they refrained from buying until they were ready to put sugar into the pan.[153] By taking this action, sugar bakers hoped to gain the whip-hand over commission agents. 'Our Bakers are at present so much out of humour with the prices asked that they keep out of the market and we have had no sale for some time', Davis & Protheroe wrote in February 1777, 'and until the Bakers are obliged to come to market we must stand still or relax in our prices.'[154] This waiting game between sugar bakers and commission agents was common.[155] More-over, the bakers could be firm in their stance. In 1781 they collectively decided not to buy any imported sugar unless the casks were tared.[156] By that time they had been trying for twelve years to ensure that all casks were tared, but their action on this occasion was probably influenced not just by trading difficulties in wartime but also by the large increase in sugar duties in that year. The sugar bakers persevered in their action and eventually succeeded. William Miles stood out against this action until he 'was deserted and left alone', by which time he was obliged to comply or keep all his sugar.[157]

Sugar bakers operated refineries in Bristol on the banks of the rivers Frome and Avon. They competed with one another for riverside accommodation because water was needed for almost every process of sugar refining. In particular, hard lime water from wells was widely used. As far as possible, sugar works were built near to main roads and the centre of Bristol business at the Exchange. They had quite extensive premises to accommodate large furnaces, open pans and utensils, as well as draught horses and carts. They absorbed a fair amount of local capital, perhaps as much as £200,000 in the sixty years after 1720, and became a very

---

[152] See above, p. 214; Derbyshire RO, Mark Davis & Co. to W. P. Perrin, 7 Feb. 1774, and Protheroe & Claxton to W. P. Perrin, 16 Aug. 1793, Fitzherbert MSS: West Indian Papers, 239M/E19947 and 20151; Bristol UL, Pinney & Tobin to J. S. Budgen, 22 June 1786, and to B. & T. Boddington, 17 Sept. 1787, Pinney & Tobin Letterbook (1784–9), Pinney Papers.

[153] UMA, Richard Meyler to Henry & Francis Bright, 8 Feb. 1749, box 85, Bright Family Papers.

[154] Derbyshire RO, Davis & Protheroe to W. P. Perrin, 15 Feb. 1777, Fitzherbert MSS: West Indian Papers, 239M/E19988.

[155] E.g. Derbyshire RO, Davis & Protheroe to W. P. Perrin, 15 Feb. 1783, *ibid.*, 239M/E20095; Bristol UL, Pinney & Tobin to William Colhoun, 8 Nov. 1786, and to Edward Brazier, 7 Feb. 1792, Pinney & Tobin Letterbooks (1784–9 and 1789–92), Pinney Papers; UMA, Richard Meyler to Davies & Wilson, 12 Dec. 1734, and to Henry Bright, 10 July 1741, Loose Correspondence, and Richard Meyler Ledger and Letter-book (1725–35), boxes 6 and 37, Bright Family Papers.

[156] The tare was the difference between the gross weight and net weight of a cask.

[157] Cambridge RO, William Miles to John Tharp, 10 Mar. 1781, Tharp Papers. For the level of duties see above, pp. 204–5.

noticeable feature of industrial development in Georgian Bristol.[158] Today all signs of this once-flourishing industry have disappeared from central Bristol and a leap of the imagination is necessary to visualise the time when such refineries were a dominant part of the city's urban development.

After being refined, most sugar was consumed in the home market. Bristol supplied refined sugar to its own population and to consumers in Gloucestershire, Herefordshire, Worcestershire, Shropshire, Warwickshire, Wiltshire, Somerset, Devon, Dorset and South Wales.[159] The rest of the sugar was re-exported. Small quantities of muscovado and refined sugar were sent by Bristol merchants to Europe, West Africa, North America and the Caribbean. The most important re-export market for sugar after 1733 was Ireland. Sugar was often sent there at times of a dull market in Bristol.[160] Sugar re-exports from Bristol to Ireland were divided between commission merchants (who sent muscovado sugar) and sugar bakers and refiners (who sent refined sugar). Several Irish ports received small amounts of sugar from Bristol but Dublin was easily the largest market.[161]

During the eighteenth century, Bristol's transatlantic commerce was increasingly dominated by trade with the Caribbean. For the year beginning 1 April 1787 the value of total West Indian imports at Bristol was £774,000, of which sugar accounted for £643,000.[162] The wealth accruing to Bristolians from their Caribbean trading connections led, however, to a rather conservative approach to business affairs: many merchants rested contentedly on their laurels and became unwilling to diversify. Thus John Pinney felt that those merchants who had attempted to gain moderate profits from moderate risks had 'succeeded much better than such as have engaged in wild and unlimited schemes and speculations in hopes of *larger profits*'.[163] Warning his partner James Tobin to be cautious in taking on new correspondents, he also commented that 'you had better have a snug little business and safe than an extensive one which

[158] Details in this paragraph are taken from BRO, I. V. Hall's research notes on Bristol sugar refineries, boxes 7 and 12.

[159] BRO, [Richard Bright], 'Particulars of the Trade of Bristol, 1788', Bright MSS; Maureen Weinstock, *More Dorset Studies* (Dorchester, 1960), pp. 86–7.

[160] Sheridan, 'The Molasses Act and the Market Strategy of the British Sugar Planters', pp. 75–6; Derbyshire RO, Davis & Protheroe to W. P. Perrin, 7 Jan. 1777, Fitzherbert MSS: West Indian Papers, 239M/E19985.

[161] Based on ACRL, *Bristol Presentments*, Exports, 1773–6.

[162] BRO, [Richard Bright], 'Particulars of Value of Produce imported from the West Indies to Bristol, 1787–8', Bright MSS, Acc. 11168/3b.

[163] Bristol UL, Tobin & Pinney to Ulysses Lynch, 31 Aug. 1789, Tobin & Pinney Letterbook (1789–92), Pinney Papers.

may produce a contrary effect'.[164] Other contemporaries echoed these sentiments. A visitor to Bristol in 1790 found that the leading traders were 'principally rich respectable West India Merch[an]ts who do not go out of their usual line of business & averse to speculation.'[165] An earlier observation, made by the Jamaican agents of a Bristol firm, stated, in a similar vein, that 'Bristol . . . is rich enough but don't care to launch out much'.[166]

[164] Quoted in Pares, *West-India Fortune*, p. 176.
[165] HSP, Robert Phillips to Phillips, Cramond & Co., 7 Apr. 1790, Cramond, Phillips & Co. Correspondence.
[166] UMA, Bright & Milward to Henry Bright, 15 June 1773, box 16, Bright Family Papers.

Conclusion

During the Tudor and Stuart periods, Bristol was transformed from a medieval trading city to a centre of early modern capitalism. The quest for imports from the New World, the formation of business ties with overseas agents, and extensive use of credit all helped to open her economic gates and provide a platform for future commercial development. By 1700 she was already an Atlantic entrepôt whose international trade touched nearly every foreign market.[1] Throughout the eighteenth century Bristol's Atlantic commerce grew significantly in absolute terms, her merchants responded to new commercial pressures and opportunities, and a great deal of local capital was poured into international trade and the industries connected with it. This created wealth in the Bristol merchant community and supported a wide range of artisan activities linked to the production and consumption of goods. Bristol, it should be remembered, was a leading centre of growth industries between 1660 and 1800: sugar refining, soap making, glass and pottery manufacture, and the metal industries all flourished in the city during that period.[2] Moreover, Bristol's role as 'metropolis of the west' helped her to dominate the internal and external trade of the entire south-west region.[3] With significant population growth as well as economic development, Bristol remained one of the five largest English cities between the late seventeenth and early nineteenth centuries, and the only one outside the metropolis to maintain this position. The other leading provincial capitals of the late Stuart era – York, Norwich, Exeter – failed to maintain similar demographic and economic growth by the Regency period.[4] The pros-

---

[1] David Harris Sacks, *The Widening Gate: Bristol and the Atlantic Economy, 1450–1700* (Berkeley and Los Angeles, 1991), pp. xvi, 12, 60, 331, 350.

[2] Jonathan Barry, 'The Cultural Life of Bristol, 1640–1775' (Oxford University D.Phil. thesis, 1985), pp. 249–50.

[3] W. E. Minchinton, 'Bristol – Metropolis of the West in the Eighteenth Century', *TRHS*, 5th Series, 4 (1954), 69–85.

[4] Elizabeth Baigent, 'Bristol Society in the Later Eighteenth Century with Specific Reference to the Handling by Computer of Fragmentary Historical Resources' (Oxford University D.Phil. thesis, 1985), pp. 31, 37–8.

perity of Georgian Bristol was reflected in the increased number of published maps, plans and directories that listed prominent traders in the city.[5]

Yet despite this success, Bristol still experienced relative commercial decline. Failure to provide sufficient port improvements led to congestion in the city docks for the increased number and size of West Indiamen and other large vessels by the late eighteenth century. This vital constraint on the volume of trade was only relieved partially by the construction of the Floating Harbour between 1804 and 1809. By contrast Liverpool and, to a lesser extent, Glasgow benefited from better improvements to port facilities to cope with expanding overseas trade. By the 1780s Liverpool also outpaced Bristol in the export trade to the Americas. This was owing to the different commodity composition of her exports, more reliable internal communications with the industrial Midlands, and closer links with a rapidly industrialising hinterland. Industry gradually became part of the commercial orbit of Liverpool, whereas at Bristol it did not. Instead of following the example of Liverpudlians, who invested heavily in their own hinterland, Bristolians put more money into South Wales and places farther afield.[6] At the turn of the nineteenth century there was no industry of national significance in Bristol or new developments in her industrial base or hinterland to stimulate increased channels of distribution for overseas trade. These commercial difficulties within Bristol and its surrounding area suggest some modification to Alan F. Williams' verdict that 'the partial eclipse of the port' in the later eighteenth century 'may be accounted for more by new developments outside Bristol and its hinterland than by untoward circumstances within the area'.[7] They also indicate that W. E. Minchinton was only partly correct in concluding that 'the shift in the economic centre of gravity of Great Britain was the main cause of the relative decline of Bristol as a port'.[8]

The material analysed in this book shows, in addition, that the impact of war and the commercial decisions made by Bristol merchants in the slave, sugar and tobacco trades contributed greatly to the relative decline of Bristol as a maritime centre. During wartime, Bristol shipowners were quick to shift their activities away from purely commercial trading ventures towards privateering. They pursued this activity with a notable

[5] J. H. Bettey, *Bristol Observed: Visitors' Impressions of the City from Domesday to the Blitz* (Bristol, 1986), pp. 80–1.

[6] M. J. Daunton, 'Towns and Economic Growth in Eighteenth-Century England' in Philip Abrams and E. A. Wrigley, eds., *Towns in Societies: Essays in Economic History and Historical Sociology* (Cambridge, 1978), pp. 266–9.

[7] Alan F. Williams, 'Bristol Port Plans', p. 180.

[8] W. E. Minchinton, 'The Port of Bristol in the Eighteenth Century' in McGrath, ed., *Bristol in the Eighteenth Century*, p. 158.

degree of success, but sometimes found it difficult, once peace was restored, to recover their share of commodity trade from the encroachments made by other ports. The Bristol slave and tobacco trades, in particular, were altered dramatically by these trading problems. During the War of the Austrian Succession and the Seven Years War, Liverpool and Glasgow benefited from safer shipping lanes distant from enemy privateers. In the same war years Liverpudlians put many ships into commercial trading as letter-of-marque vessels. Bristolians, on the other hand, preferred to convert slaving vessels into privateers which, though they often took lucrative prizes, were non-trading ventures.[9] These developments enabled Glasgow and Liverpool to increase their shares in the tobacco and slave trades respectively at the expense of Bristol at a time when the Atlantic economy was expanding and when rapid changes were occurring in marketing arrangements.

There is also evidence of entrepreneurial failure by Bristol merchants in these trades. In the slave trade, early generations of Bristol merchants failed to provide continuity in business. Later, Bristolians were slow to shift the purchase of Negroes to areas of better opportunity on the West African coast. They also did not tap expanding markets for slaves as rapidly as Liverpudlians, who sold their slaves more cheaply and effectively. Bristol's slave trade had greatly diminished by 1793, almost fifteen years before Parliament abolished the traffic. Bristol revived her African commerce in the nineteenth century, but this was primarily a trade in palm oil that was unconnected with the former slaving activity.[10] In the tobacco trade, the inability or unwillingness of Bristolians to diversify fully into the re-export business, despite long-standing trading connections with Europe, enabled Glasgow and Liverpool firms to capture a greater share of the trade. Bristol's concentration on the domestic market for tobacco and the better grades of leaf limited her overall market penetration in the tobacco trade. Possibly some of these problems could have been reduced by significant productivity advances in the shipping deployed in the slave and tobacco trades, but such gains did not materialise.

The sugar trade was the greatest success story in Bristol's eighteenth-century Atlantic trade. It was always in a more favourable position than the tobacco trade in terms of the level of imports, duties, commercial organisation and marketing arrangements. The concentration of Bristol

---

[9] David J. Starkey, *British Privateering Enterprise in the Eighteenth Century* (Exeter, 1990), p. 271.

[10] Martin Lynn, 'Bristol, West Africa and the Nineteenth-Century Palm Oil Trade', *Historical Research: The Bulletin of the Institute of Historical Research*, 64 (1991), 359–74.

merchants in this trade made much commercial sense because possible avenues of diversification, such as the tobacco and slave trades, were areas where Bristol had been overhauled already; the sugar trade was the most remunerative overseas trade of all; and it was crucial in enabling Bristol to maintain second place among the outports in 1800 in the customs revenue collected from imports. But business problems existed even in this branch of commerce. Leading Bristol merchants, according to several emphatic contemporary comments, were rigidly fixed in this particular trade by the late eighteenth century.[11] Richard Pares once suggested that Bristol West India merchants were a self-satisfied, inward-looking, complacent clique by that time, for whom competitive business enterprise had become diluted by intermarriage within the group and comfortable settled commercial arrangements. 'It would not have been very genteel', he commented in an eloquent phrase, 'for fellow-members of a small dining-club, connected together by the marriages of their children, to wage war to the knife on each other by cutting freight rates or instructing their captains to snatch consignments from each others' ships'.[12] Though this evaluation has not convinced all historians,[13] no less a figure than John Wesley once remarked in a sermon that 'the chief besetting sins' of Bristol, a city he knew very well, were love of money and love of ease, a sentiment that matches Pares' portrayal.[14] Inability to adapt to changing economic circumstances seems therefore to have been present in late eighteenth-century Bristol: it resulted from concentration, specialisation and an emphasis on the domestic market. The situation did not change rapidly thereafter: lack of adaptability imbued the whole commercial ethos of the city by the 1830s.[15]

Specialisation, concentration, and the pursuit of specific lines of trade are the keys to the contrasting performance of Bristol and other outports in the eighteenth century. In 1700 a large number of merchant firms and shopkeepers at various British ports were involved in transatlantic trade. By 1800, there was a dramatic reduction in the number of ports and

[11] See above, pp. 217–18.
[12] Pares, *West-India Fortune*, p. 212.
[13] E.g. McGrath, *Merchant Venturers of Bristol*, p. 94.
[14] Entry for 15 Sept. 1786 in Nehemiah Curnock, ed., *Journal of John Wesley*, 8 vols. (London, 1909–16), VII, p. 209.
[15] B. W. E. Alford, 'The Economic Development of Bristol in the Nineteenth Century: An Enigma?' in Patrick McGrath and John Cannon, eds., *Essays in Bristol and Gloucestershire History* (Bristol, 1976), pp. 261–3, 266. For a contrasting view that plays down business conservatism as a main factor in Bristol's relative decline see B. J. Atkinson, 'An Early Example of the Decline of the Industrial Spirit? Bristol Enterprise in the First Half of the Nineteenth Century', *Southern History*, 9 (1987), 71–89.

merchants engaged to a significant degree in the same trades.[16] What gradually emerged between the beginning and end of the century was that each of the west-coast outports became ever more committed to one major type of Atlantic commerce: Liverpool to the slave trade, Glasgow to the tobacco trade, Bristol to the sugar trade.[17] Bristol merchants concentrated more and more of their resources on the sugar trade because of the increasing complexity and uncertainty of commercial relations in a large trading bowl. This was reinforced by time and communication lags, seasonal variations in imperfect markets, wartime disruptions, and the need to consolidate connections with specific agents in particular places to secure business relations. By the mid-eighteenth century these trading problems made it difficult for a port to recover lost ground in a branch of commerce, or for merchants to shift from one major Atlantic trade to another. Bristol's increasing specialisation in the sugar trade was therefore a logical development, but it provided a narrow base for the diversification of enterprise by 1800. Small wonder that C. M. MacInnes considered that Bristol's trade had become dangerously specialised by that time.[18]

Bristol's foreign trade continued along traditional lines down to the mid-nineteenth century.[19] The West Indies continued to be a major source of prosperity until the repeal of the sugar duties in 1846, sometimes being worth twice as much as the rest of Bristol's overseas trade. In 1833 one leading merchant declared that Bristol would be a fishing port without the West India trade.[20] This concentration of economic activity, however, was not entirely a boon: perhaps too much Bristol capital was poured into the Caribbean and not enough into local enterprises.[21] It is true, of course, that port industries such as shipbuilding, sugar refining, and cocoa, chocolate and tobacco manufacture flourished in the city after 1800.[22] But it is revealing that the three last-named of those industries

---

[16] Jacob M. Price, 'Who Cared about the Colonies? The Impact of the Thirteen Colonies on British Society and Politics, circa 1714–1775' in Bernard Bailyn and Philip D. Morgan, eds., *Strangers within the Realm: Cultural Margins of the First British Empire* (Chapel Hill, NC, 1991), pp. 420–1.

[17] Cf. Jacob M. Price, 'The Rise of Glasgow in the Chesapeake Tobacco Trade, 1707–1775', *WMQ*, 3rd Series, 11 (1954), 190.

[18] MacInnes, *Bristol: A Gateway of Empire*, p. 358.

[19] David Large, ed., *The Port of Bristol, 1848–1884* (Bristol Record Society's *Publications*, 36, 1984), p. ix.

[20] MacInnes, *Bristol: A Gateway of Empire*, p. 370.

[21] A. J. Pugsley, 'Some Contributions towards the Study of the Economic History of Bristol in the Eighteenth and Nineteenth Centuries' (University of Bristol MA thesis, 1921), ch. 5, p. 7.

[22] Charles Harvey and Jon Press, 'Industrial Change and the Economic Life of Bristol since 1800' in Charles Harvey and Jon Press, eds., *Studies in the Business History of Bristol* (Bristol, 1988), pp. 4–6.

were import-linked, reflecting the city's strength in trading with the Americas, rather than connected to export industries that would probably have given a greater boost to industrial and demographic growth in Bristol and her hinterland. Bristol's Achilles heel in overseas trade may well have been a failure to diversify away from concentration on the domestic market and a tendency to keep all the eggs in one basket. Yet in the economic world of the early industrial revolution it was vital for ports to expand their areas of trade, to take advantage of the spiralling process inherent in Atlantic commerce, and to expand avenues of commerce so that foreign and domestic demand could be linked effectively – and that, of course, is what Liverpool signally achieved after 1783 and Bristol did not.

Appendix

The sources for reconstructing voyage patterns are listed in the notes to table 3.1. Since certain of these records may be unfamiliar to readers, the usefulness of each source is outlined here.[1]

1. *Manuscript records at the Society of Merchant Venturers, Bristol*

The Annual List of Shipping (1747–87) and the Ships' Muster Rolls (1748–94) came into being with the establishment of the Merchant Seamen's Fund for disabled seamen in 1747. This was a pioneer contributory pension scheme financed by employed seamen, who had sixpence per month deducted from their wages in order to make up the fund.[2] The money was collected by ship captains at the end of each voyage and was recorded on a muster roll so that the Controller of Customs could check the figures. Seamen became eligible for relief if they were temporarily out of work through illness or injury. The Society of Merchant Venturers administered the fund for Bristol.[3]

The Annual List of Shipping, compiled from late September to late September, according to the civic year in Bristol, records the following information in columns:

1. Time when Paid the 6d. p mo.
2. Ship or Vessels Name.
3. Of What Place.

[1] For a reconstruction of thirty round-trip transatlantic voyages from Bristol, all beginning in 1764, see Morgan, 'Bristol Merchants and the Colonial Trades', app. A, pp. 313–24.

[2] 20 Geo. II c. 38. Seamen's sixpences had been collected from London and the outports for the maintenance of Greenwich Hospital, London, since 1696. For commentary on these records see Ralph Davis, 'Seamen's Sixpences: An Index of Commercial Activity, 1697–1828', *Economica*, New Series, 23 (1956), 328–43, plus N. A. M. Rodger, 'Some Practical Problems Arising from the Study of the Receiver of Sixpences Ledgers', *The Mariner's Mirror*, 62 (1976), 223–4, 270.

[3] McGrath, *Merchant Venturers of Bristol*, pp. 197–8; Jon Press, 'The Collapse of a Contributory Pension Scheme: The Merchant Seamen's Fund, 1747–1851', *Journal of Transport History*, New Series, 5 (1979), 91–104.

4. Of What Burthen: Tons.
5. Number of Men usually Sail'd with.
6. Master's Name.
7. Whence Arriv'd, or of what Trade.
8. To What Time last PAID. Day. Month. Year.
9. Time of the First Man's Entry. Day. Month. Year.
10. Time of the last Man's *Discharge*, or end of the Voyage. Day. Month. Year.
11. No. of Months &c. for a Man.
12. Money Receiv'd. £. s. d.

Every column except 1, 8, 11, and 12 furnishes pertinent information for working out shipping routes.

The Muster Rolls record the following information, again mainly in columns:

1. Name of Ship and Master.
2. From Whence.
3. Mens Names.
4. Usual Places of Abode.
5. When enter'd into Pay, and where.
6. When discharg'd, deserted or what became of them.
7. In what Ship or Vessel the last Voyage.
8. Time Serv'd. Months, Days.

The data given under 1, 2, 5, and 6 were all useful in working out shipping patterns. Sometimes the headings of Muster Rolls provide a clear indication of a ship's entire voyage pattern. In all such cases, checks with other sources revealed that these details were correct.[4]

From the early seventeenth century, the Society of Merchant Venturers leased the right to collect wharfage dues – an important source of its income – from the Corporation of Bristol.[5] From 1607 these dues were imposed on goods brought from overseas belonging to both freemen and non-freemen of the city; and from 1667 the dues also had to be paid on exports sent from Bristol by non-members of the Society.[6] The annual Wharfage Books – running from September to September – form an almost unbroken series for the mid-eighteenth century.[7] Quarterly lists of ships entering the port of Bristol are given in these records, along with the

[4] For reasons that are not clear, these Bristol Muster Rolls are much more informative about ports of call and colonial destinations than the eighteenth-century Liverpool Muster Rolls in PRO, BT 98/47.
[5] The society also collected other port dues such as anchorage, keyage and plankage.
[6] McGrath, *Merchant Venturers of Bristol*, pp. 46, 71, 73, 150.
[7] The only years in the period 1749–75 for which volumes are missing or incomplete are 1750–3 and 1769–72.

dates when vessels paid their dues, the places of ownership and tonnage of individual ships, and the ports or regions from which ships had arrived. The Wharfage Books are especially important because no inward Port Books survive for Bristol after 1741.[8]

2.   Manuscript records in the Public Record Office, London

The Port Books were established by the Exchequer in 1564 and discontinued in 1799. There are several sets of these records for individual ports, each kept by different customs officials. On outward-bound voyages the Customer 'allowed' certain goods duty free to masters and mariners, and so, where possible, it is important to take data from books kept by the Searcher, who checked the cargoes loaded and was not concerned with the collection of duty. The surviving Bristol Port Books are not easy to use, partly because entries relating to a single vessel are scattered over several folios and partly because they are 'so badly damaged by damp and mildew as to be almost illegible'.[9] Nevertheless, the books yield essential information for the study of shipping routes, including the names of vessels and their masters, the ports to which ships were bound, and the dates when merchants loaded items of cargo aboard ship.[10]

Colonial Naval Officers' Returns are the best-known source for entrance and clearance of ships in colonial waters.[11] They were, in effect, colonial port records prepared at customs districts in British America by an administrative official known as the naval officer.[12] The returns, which were compiled for each quarter of the year, provide the following information in columns:

[8] W. E. Minchinton's selection of documents in *Trade of Bristol in the Eighteenth Century* fails to include any items from the three major sources discussed in this section of the appendix.

[9] C. M. Andrews, *Guide to the Materials for American History to 1783, in the Public Record Office of Great Britain. II: Departmental and Miscellaneous Papers* (London, 1914), p. 128. For the period 1749–75, outward Port Books for Bristol are available for 1752–66 and for 1771–5.

[10] Full particulars on the Port Books and their reliability are given in G. N. Clark, *Guide to English Commercial Statistics, 1696–1782* (London, 1938), pp. 52–6; Sven-Erik Aström, 'The Reliability of the English Port Books', *Scandinavian Economic History Review*, 16 (1968), 125–36; and Donald Woodward, 'Sources for Maritime History (III): The Port Books of England and Wales', *Maritime History*, 3 (1973), 147–65. The format of the entries in the Bristol Port Books is illustrated in Minchinton, ed., *Trade of Bristol in the Eighteenth Century*, pp. 22–3.

[11] See above, pp. 36–7, 40, 48–52, 56–7, 60. Some of these returns are now located in repositories other than the PRO. This is true of the shipping records listed as (d), (e) and (f) under table 3.1 (pp. 60–1).

[12] The duties of this officer are summarised in Thomas C. Barrow, *Trade and Empire: The British Customs Service in Colonial America, 1660–1775* (Cambridge, MA, 1967), p. 78.

1. Time of Entry.
2. Ships & Vessells names.
3. Masters Names.
4. Kind of Built.
5. Number of Tons, Guns, Men.
6. Where & When Built.
7. Where & When Registered.
8. Owners Names.
9. Quality & Quantity of Each Vessells Cargoe.
10. From Whence/Where bound.
11. Where & When Bond Given.

For working out voyage patterns, the material given in columns 1, 2, 3, 5, 9 and 10 is of direct importance. The main problem in using these returns is their incomplete coverage. Some include only entrance or clearance data; quarters are often missing; and some colonies have no extant copies for the mid-eighteenth century.[13] Changing jurisdictions for different colonial customs districts means that a great deal of territory is not covered by these records. In addition, many ships were not formally entered or cleared at ports when trading between nearby colonies such as Pennsylvania and New Jersey.[14] And for at least one colony (Virginia) there are duplicate returns that record slightly different details for some ships.[15] These deficiencies do not detract from the value of this source, but they clearly indicate that one cannot rely on the returns alone for reconstructing shipping routes.

Mediterranean Passes were documents issued to defend British ships against interference by Barbary pirates off the North African coast. The practice of granting such passes was formalized in treaties of 1662 with

[13] Pennsylvania and Newfoundland fall into the latter category (John J. McCusker, 'An Introduction to the Naval Officer Shipping Lists' (unpublished manuscript, 1976), pp. 7, 27, 29–32). McCusker's study, the most comprehensive guide to these records, is more illuminating than W. E. Minchinton, *The Naval Office Shipping Lists for Jamaica, 1683–1818* (E. P. Microform Ltd., Wakefield, 1977) and W. E. Minchinton and Peter Waite, *The Naval Office Shipping Lists for the West Indies, 1678–1825 (excluding Jamaica)* (E. P. Microform Ltd., Wakefield, 1981). Excerpts from the Naval Officers' Returns, illustrating Bristol-based voyages, are printed in Minchinton, ed., *Trade of Bristol in the Eighteenth Century*, pp. 16–19, 36–41. Readers of this volume are warned, however, that there are many mistakes in the transcription of statistics from manuscript sources. For example, material transcribed from the South Carolina Naval Officers' Returns (pp. 16–17) contains at least one hundred errors of omission or commission.

[14] McCusker, 'An Introduction to the Naval Officer Shipping Lists' (unpublished manuscript, 1976), pp. 7, 24, 29–32. For an excellent map of the British Customs Districts ('Ports') in North America plus commentary on their geographical extent *c.* 1770 see Lester J. Cappon *et al.*, eds., *Atlas of Early American History: The Revolutionary Era, 1760–1790* (Princeton, NJ, 1976), pp. 40, 119–20.

[15] Peter V. Bergstrom notes that one ship in four appears more than once in the returns for Virginia ('Markets and Merchants: Economic Diversification in Colonial Virginia, 1700–1775' (University of New Hampshire Ph.D. dissertation, 1980), pp. 7–8).

Tripoli and 1682 with Algiers. The ledgers of the passes list shipping information in columns:

1. No. of Pass.
2. Date of Certificate.
3. Nature of the Ship.
4. Ships Names.
5. Of what Place.
6. Burthen.
7. Guns.
8. At what Place.
9. Masters Names.
10. Men: British Foreign.
11. Built: British, Irish &c. Foreign.
12. Whither bd directly from the Place the Pass is recd at.
13. Whither bound from thence.
14. Names of ye Custom House Officers at the Out ports who sign Certificates for Passes.
15. Securities for the Return of the Pass: Names Places of Abode Occupation.
16. Date of Pass.
17. By whom signed.
18. To whom Del[ivere]d or Sent.
19. When Returned.

Columns 2, 3, 4, 5, 8, 9, 12, and 13 are particularly useful for determining shipping patterns. There are some limitations to these records, however. They include only about two-thirds of vessels leaving British ports on transatlantic voyages; they exclude ships that were not British-owned; and the destinations they give are sometimes a signal of a ship's intentions – the passes were issued a month or more before vessels sailed – rather than a specification of the route actually followed.[16] These problems mean, once again, that the passes need to be used with other material in order to reconstruct shipping tracks.

3. *Other Manuscript Sources*

The Richard Neale Daybook – kept by a customs officer at Pill, a creek near Bristol – records the names and tonnage of ships, their dates of

---

[16] For discussions of the purpose and effectiveness of Mediterranean Passes see M. S. Anderson, 'Great Britain and the Barbary States in the Eighteenth Century', *Bulletin of the Institute of Historical Research*, 29 (1956), 99–101; Rupert C. Jarvis, 'Sources for the History of Ships and Shipping', *Journal of Transport History*, 3 (1958), 227; Elaine G. Cooper, 'Aspects of British Shipping and Maritime Trade in the Atlantic, 1775–1783'

entrance and clearance, and the ports to which they were bound or from which they had arrived. It provides a comprehensive record of vessels trading at Bristol between 3 August 1761 and 14 February 1764.[17]

The Customs House Tonnage Books for Philadelphia came into existence as a result of a law passed by the Pennsylvania Assembly in 1764 that levied a duty of sixpence per measured ton on all vessels entering and leaving the port of Philadelphia. This source provides a full listing of ships entering and clearing that port between 1 November 1765 and 27 August 1776. It records the date when the duty was paid, the names of vessels and their masters, from whence, to whom belonging or consigned, and the tonnage.[18]

4.   Newspapers

Shipping lists in Bristol and colonial newspapers are a valuable source for tracing the movements of vessels in colonial waters, especially when other records do not exist. The format of these lists and the information they contain vary, but most state the names of ships and masters and their destinations in British America, and sometimes the date of arrival or departure. Since few West Indian newspapers survive for the eighteenth century, Bristol newspapers are particularly helpful in tracking down the Caribbean destinations of vessels.

5.   Other Printed Sources

Lloyd's List appeared regularly from 1740 onwards. It is organised by port and then by date, and records the vessels that arrived at and sailed from those ports. Each entry gives the name of the vessel, the surname of its master, and the names of the ports whence arrived or whither bound.[19]

(University of Exeter M.A. thesis, 1975), Appendix; and David Richardson, *The Mediterranean Passes* (E. P. Microform Ltd., Wakefield, 1983). H. E. S. Fisher has demonstrated that falsely obtained passes were sometimes used by foreign vessels to secure immunity from the Barbary corsairs ('Lisbon, its English Merchant Community and the Mediterranean in the Eighteenth Century' in P. L. Cottrell and D. H. Aldcroft, eds., *Shipping, Trade and Commerce: Essays in Honour of Ralph Davis* (Leicester, 1981), pp. 30–2).

17 Extracts from this daybook for the period 26 May–21 June 1762 are printed in Minchinton, ed., *Trade of Bristol in the Eighteenth Century*, pp. 42–5, where the year is incorrectly given as 1763.

18 The Tonnage Duty Books are described in Thomas M. Doerflinger, *A Vigorous Spirit of Enterprise: Merchants and Economic Development in Revolutionary Philadelphia* (Chapel Hill, NC, 1986), pp. 388–9.

19 John J. McCusker, 'European Bills of Entry and Marine Lists: Early Commercial Publications and the Origins of the Business Press: Part II: British Marine Lists and Continental Counterparts', *Harvard Library Bulletin*, 21 (1983), 316–28.

However, this source was of limited use for my purposes since the coverage of Bristol vessels is very patchy.

The Bristol Presentments are available in a broken series mainly from 1770. These printed bills of entry and clearance of vessels using the port of Bristol include details of the names of ships and their masters, whence arrived or whither sailed, the dates of entrance and clearance, and a full breakdown of cargoes and the merchants lading them.[20] The Presentments are most valuable for years where no Port Books or Wharfage Books survive.

Finally, ships' tonnages can present tricky problems before 1786, when ship registry became compulsory under 26 Geo. III c. 60. Three main types of ship's tonnage were in use before then, each calculated on a different basis, but this does not pose a problem for the present study because all the tonnages given in the records used (except for the Philadelphia Tonnage Duty Book) are registered tons rather than cargo or measured tons.[21]

---

[20] John J. McCusker, 'European Bills of Entry and Marine Lists: Early Commercial Publications and the Origins of the Business Press: Part I: Introduction and British Bills of Entry', *ibid.*, pp. 246–9. Table 6 of this article (p. 247) summarises all known extant copies of the Bristol Bills of Entry, 1748–90. For extracts from these records see Minchinton, ed., *Trade of Bristol in the Eighteenth Century*, pp. 48–50 (with errors of omission) and pp. 55–71. Three stray copies of the *Bristol Presentments* for 1748 are included in the National Library of Wales, Aberystwyth, Hopton Court Deeds and Documents, nos. 1934–6. A copy of the *Bristol Presentment* for 24 Nov. 1760 is available at Lloyd's Insurance Library. These are the earliest surviving copies of these documents.

[21] The matter of tonnage is discussed in Christopher J. French, 'Eighteenth-Century Shipping Tonnage Measurements', *JEcH*, 33 (1973), 434–43, and in McCusker, 'Tonnage of Ships Engaged in British Colonial Trade during the Eighteenth Century', *Research in Economic History*, 6 (1981), 73–105. My research finds close agreement among various sources on the tonnage of individual ships (Morgan, 'Bristol Merchants and the Colonial Trades', app. A, pp. 310–12).

Bibliography

A   MANUSCRIPT SOURCES

COLLECTIONS IN THE BRITISH ISLES

Aberystwyth
National Library of Wales:
   Hopton Court Deeds and Documents, nos. 1934–6

Birmingham

Birmingham Central Library:
   Samuel Galton Senior Letterbooks, 1741–55

Bristol
Avon County Reference Library:
   Extracts from the Diaries of William Dyer (2 vols.)
   Letters of Corsley Rogers Jr and Edward Pye Chamberlayne, 1755–6 (19717)
   Papers relating to the Ship *Milford* (21257)
   Journal of the *Black Prince*, 1762–4 (4764)
   Jefferies MSS, vols. VIII and XIII (B 7952)
   Southwell papers, vols. VIII–X (B 11159–61)
   Braikenridge Collection, vol. VI
Bristol Industrial Museum:
   Account Book of the Snow *Africa*, 1774–6
   Letter from Benjamin King & Robert Arbuthnot to Isaac Hobhouse & Stephen
      Baugh, 24 Nov. 1740
Bristol Record Office:
   Account Book of the *Fanny*, 1777–88 (12162)
   Articles of Partnership between Edward Cooper and Lyonel Lyde, 1745
      (17124(2))
   Ashton Court MSS:
      The Woolnough Papers (AC/WO/16)
      Business Papers and Bills of Lading of Samuel Munckley (AC/MU)
   Logbook of the *Lloyd*, 1771–2 (38082)
   Articles of Agreement for the *Gascoyne*, 1781 (248/2)
   I. V. Hall Research Notes on Bristol Sugar Refineries (boxes 7 and 12)
   Miscellaneous Letters and other Documents Relating to Bristol, 1679–1742

Richard Neale Daybook, 1761–4 (04399)

James Day Account Book, 1729–53 (40044(2))

Isaac Hobhouse Letters, 1723–36 (8029(163))

Isaac Elton Ledger, 1746–51 (24390)

Camplin & Smith: Accounts with William & John Miles in Jamaica, 1759–61
    (11109/15)

Bright MSS:

  Draft of Particulars of the Trade of Bristol, 1788 (11168/2c)

  Account of Goods Imported into Bristol in the Years 1798–1801
     (11168/2d(ii))

  Particulars of Value of Produce Imported from the West Indies into Bristol,
     1787–8 (11168/3b)

  General View of the Question Respecting the Improvement of the Harbour
     of Bristol, n.d., but *c.* early 1790s (11168/5f)

*Bright Family Papers:

  Letters of the Brights of Colwall, 1746–71 (M/F F45)

  Letters of the Brights of Colwall, 1772 (M/F F45)

  Letters of the Brights of Colwall, 1773–1837 (M/F F46)

  Account Book of the *Molly*, 1750 and 1752 (M/F F47)

Voyage Accounts: the *Ruby*, 1758–63, the *Swift*, 1759, the *Sally*, 1768, the
    Triton, 1777–90, the *Druid*, 1790–1791 (39654[1–5])

Bristol University Library:

  D.M.15: Estimates of Slave Cargoes for 1769

  Samuel Gale, 'A Tour Through Several Parts of England A.D.1705'

  Pinney Papers:

    Domestic Papers, 1656–1800

    Letterbook of J. F. Pinney I and John Pinney, 1761–75

    John Pinney Letterbook, 1775–8

    Pinney & Tobin Letterbook, 1784–9

    Tobin & Pinney Letterbooks, 1789–96

    Tobin, Pinney & Tobin Letterbook, 1796–1800

Society of Merchant Venturers:

  Annual List of Ships, 1747–87

  Ships' Muster Rolls, 1747–70

  Wharfage Books

  Letters addressed to the Master of the Society, 1754–1800

  Letterbook, 1753–80

  Letters Received by the Society, 1747–8

  Bristol West India Society Book of Proceedings, 1782–1804

  Papers on the African Slave Trade (bundles D and G)

  Papers on the Abolition of the Slave Trade, 1788–91

  Docks: Miscellaneous Papers, 1784–92

  Case and Papers Relative to the Time of Paying or Securing the Customs due on
    the Importation of Goods and Merchandise, 1760

Cambridge

Cambridgeshire Record Office:

  Chippenham Estate Records:

Tharp Family Papers:
   Business Letters of William Miles of Bristol to John Tharp of Trelawney,
      Jamaica, 1771–7 (R55/7/122(0)2)
   Letters mainly from William Miles to John Tharp (R55/7/128(b))
Cambridge University Library:
   Cholmondeley (Houghton) MSS: Section 13

Cork
Cork Archives Department:
   Richard Hare Letterbook, 1771–2 (U259)

Edinburgh
Scottish Record Office:
   Account Book of McNeil, Sadler & Claxton, 1758–81 (CS 96/4370)
   Unextracted Processes (CS 237/T4/1)
National Library of Scotland:
   Nisbet Papers:
      Chisholme Papers (MS 5464)
      James Chisholme Letterbook, 1793–1812 (MS 5476)

Gloucester
Gloucestershire Record Office:
   Parish Records of Chard:
      Miscellaneous Correspondence of Richard Prankard (P74/MI/1/1)
   Waste book of John Blagden, 1755/6

Kidderminster
Kidderminster Public Library:
   Knight Manuscripts:
      Stour Works General Account, 1772–3
      Brindgwood Iron Works Accounts, 1753–4

Liverpool
Liverpool Central Library:
   Holt and Gregson Papers, vols. X and XIX

London
British Library:
   Additional MSS:
      9,293 fos. 45–6: Report of the State of the Trade of the several Outports of
            England and Wales, 1764
      12,413 Edward Long's Collections for the History of Jamaica
      12,436 List of Landholders in Jamaica c.1750
      22,676 Miscellaneous Papers Relating to the Island of Jamaica, 1661–1765
      32,800 Newcastle Papers
      34,736 fos. 55–79: Papers Relating to Frauds in the Customs at Bristol, 1755
      34,181 Abstracts of Wills Relating to Jamaica, 1625–1792
      36,217 fos. 99–205: Case between John Lidderdale and John Harmer of
            Bristol and John Chiswell of Virginia, 1758

    38,416 Liverpool Papers, CCXXVII: Papers Relating to the Slave Trade, 1787–1823

Lansdowne MSS:
  1,219

The Guildhall Library:
  Papers of Anthony Gibbs and Sons:
    MS 11,021 vol. I
    MS 11,069A Daybook of Sales of West India Produce begun by Samuel Munckley in 1775

House of Lords Record Office:
  Main Papers, 1788, 1792, 1799

Lloyd's Insurance Library:
  Account Book of the *Hector*, 1770–3
  Bristol Presentment, 24 Nov. 1760

National Maritime Museum, Greenwich:
  Logbooks of the *Lloyd*, 1767–9
  Logbook of the *African Queen*, 1790 (Log/M/64)
  Daybook of the *Castle*, 1727 (AMS/4)

Public Record Office, Chancery Lane:
  Chancery Records:
    Close Rolls C 54/6143, 6329
  Chancery Masters' Exhibits:
    C 107/1–15 James Rogers Papers
  Records of the Exchequer, Kings Remembrancer:
    E 190 Bristol Port Books
  High Court of Admiralty Papers:
    HCA 15/34 Instance Papers
    HCA 25/56–75 Letters of Marque, 1777–83
    HCA 26/60 Letters of Marque, 1777
    HCA 30/259 Intercepted Mails and Papers, 1756–62
  Prerogative Court of Canterbury:
    PROB 11 Wills

Public Record Office, Kew:
  Admiralty Papers:
    ADM 7/77–116 Mediterranean Passes
  Audit Office Papers:
    AO 13/30, 32 Loyalist Claims
  Board of Trade Papers:
    BT 6/3 Miscellanea
    BT 6/83 America and West Indies: Commercial Intercourse, 1784
    BT 6/186 Jamaica Naval Officers' Returns
    BT 98/47 Liverpool Muster Rolls, 1787
  Chatham Papers:
    30/8/81 Revenue Papers
    30/8/95 North America: Miscellaneous Papers, 1742–57
    30/8/343 Papers Relating to North American States, 1780–98
  Colonial Office Papers:
    CO 5/508–11 South Carolina Naval Officers' Returns

CO 5/709–10 Georgia Naval Officers' Returns
CO 5/750 Maryland Naval Officers' Returns
CO 5/848–51 Massachusetts Naval Officers' Returns
CO 5/967–9 New Hampshire Naval Officers' Returns
CO 5/1036 New Jersey Naval Officers' Returns
CO 5/1222–8 New York Naval Officers' Returns
CO 5/1328, 1330, 1367 Board of Trade Correspondence: Virginia
CO 5/1442–50 Virginia Naval Officers' Returns
CO 27/12–13 Bahamas Naval Officers' Returns
CO 33/15–17 Barbados Naval Officers' Returns
CO 76/4 Dominica Naval Officers' Returns
CO 106/1 Grenada Naval Officers' Returns
CO 142/14–23 Jamaica Naval Officers' Returns
CO 142/131 Jamaica Quit Rent Book, 1754
CO 157/1 Leeward Islands Naval Officers' Returns
CO 187/1 Nevis Naval Officers' Returns
CO 221/30–1 Nova Scotia Naval Officers' Returns
CO 388/43, 45, 95 Board of Trade (Commercial) Papers
Customs Papers:
CUST 3/4-80, 82 Inspector General's Ledgers, Imports and Exports, 1700–80
Home Office Papers:
HO 55/6/8 Petition from the Citizens of Bristol Condemning the Actions of the Present Government, 1769
HO 55/11/9 Condemnation of the American Rebellion by the Mayor and Inhabitants of Bristol, 1775
HO 55/11/64 Condemnation of the American Rebellion by the Merchants, Traders and Other Citizens of Bristol, 1776
Treasury Office Papers:
T 1/238, 523
T 1/484, 488, 498, 506 Virginia Naval Officers' Returns
T 52/16 Treasury Miscellanea – King's Warrants
T 64/48–9 Barbados Naval Officers' Returns
T 64/72 Jamaica Naval Officers' Returns
T 64/142 Report on the Complaints against the officers at Bristol, 1718
T 64/143 Revenue Frauds, London and Western Ports, 1723–32
T 64/276A & B
T 70/1516, 1518, 1525, 1534, 1541, 1549 (1) African Companies: Detached Papers
T 79/30 American Loyalist Claims

Losset, by Campeltown
Family Papers of MacNeal of Tirfergus, Ugadale and Losset (bundle 5)

Matlock
Derbyshire Record Office:
  Fitzherbert Manuscripts:

West Indian Papers: Correspondence and Accounts of Bristol Merchants
with W. P. Perrin (239M/E 19935–20241)

Oxford
Bodleian Library:
  MS Eng. misc. b.44:
    fos. 93–94: James Jones & Co. to Captain David Williams, 7 April 1792

Stafford

Staffordshire Record Office:
  Dartmouth Papers:
    List of Vessels Arrived at and Sailed from James Fort, River Gambia, 1764
      (D(W) 1778/V/251)

Taunton
Somerset Record Office:
  Dickinson Papers:
    Caleb Dickinson Diary, 1740 (DD/DN 230)
    William Dickinson Letters, 1780–3 (DD/DN271)
    Graffin Prankard Letterbook, 1712–18 (DD/DN 423)
    Graffin Prankard Letterbook, 1738–56 (DD/DN 428)
    Graffin Prankard Letterbook, 1740–2 (DD/DN 429)
  Graham-Clarke (Hestercombe) MSS:
    Shipping Articles, 1745–62 (DD/GC/73)
  Helyar Muniments, Coker Court (DD/WHh/1089 and 1090)
  Strachie MSS (DD/SH/c/1165/box 27)
  Stradling MSS:
    Letterbook of R. Anstice, 1769–81 (DD/S/ST23)
  Tudway of Wells MSS:
    West Indian Papers (boxes 11–13) (DD/TD)

Trowbridge
Wiltshire Record Office:
  Thomas Goldney Account Book, 1741–68 (473/295)

Winchester
Hampshire Record Office:
  Henry Wyndham Account Book, 1725–53 (8M49/F12)

COLLECTIONS IN PORTUGAL

Lisbon
Arquivo Nacional da Torre do Tombo:
  Junta do Comercio, Maço 311, ord. 442
    Com Privilegio Real. Navios que entravam neste Rio de Lisboa e salinam

COLLECTIONS IN THE WEST INDIES

Kingston, Jamaica
National Library of Jamaica:
Letters of Samuel Cleland to Thomas Hall, 1760–71 (MS 1069)

Mona, Jamaica
University of the West Indies Library:
Account Book of the *Sarah*, 1753–8

COLLECTIONS IN THE UNITED STATES OF AMERICA

San Marino, California
Henry E. Huntington Library:
Stowe Collection:
Brydges Family Papers (STB box 25)
Tinsley Manuscripts:
Tobacco Sales Account, 1747 (BR box 16)

Mystic Seaport, Connecticut
G. W. Blunt White Library:
Israel Pemberton Letterbook, 1727–35

Washington, District of Columbia
Library of Congress:
Papers of the Jones Family of Northumberland County, Virginia, vols. XII–
XIV: 1762–6
William Reynolds Letterbook, 1771–9
William C. Rives Papers:
Thomas and Francis Walker Papers:
General Correspondence, 1745–1801 (box 162)
Samuel Smith Papers:
Samuel Smith Letterbook, 1772–4 (box 7)
Stephen Collins Papers, vols. X, XIII, XLI
Stephen Collins Letterbook, 1760–73 (vol. LVII)
Nicholas Low Papers (box 3)
Custis Family Papers:
John Custis Letterbook, 1717–42
Archives Centre, National Museum of American History, Smithsonian
Institution:
Benjamin Pollard & Co. Letterbook, 1787–92

Savannah, Georgia
Georgia Historical Society:
Joseph Clay & Co. Letterbook, 1772–4

Chicago, Illinois
The Newberry Library:
  Ayer MSS:
    Logbook of the *Wennie*, 1765–6 (Ayer MS 817)

Annapolis, Maryland
Maryland State Archives, Hall of Records:
  Port of Annapolis: Entrances and Clearances, 1748–59 (Maryland 1372-2;
      1/32/1/9)
  Port Records for Oxford, 1742–6
  Port Records for Patuxent, 1745–7

Baltimore, Maryland
Maryland Historical Society:
  Carroll-MacCubbin Papers: box 7 (MS 219)
  Cheston-Galloway Papers (MS 1994):
    James Cheston Letterbooks, 1768–82 (box 8)
    James Cheston Incoming Letters, 1767–82 (boxes 9, 13, 15)
  Brice-Jennings Papers (MS 1997)
  Smith Letterbooks (MS 1152):
    Letterbook of John Smith & Sons, 1774–86
  Port of Annapolis: Entrances and Clearances, 1756–75 (MS 21)

Boston, Massachusetts
Baker Library, Graduate School of Business Administration, Harvard
      University:
  Papers of Samuel Abbot, 1732–1812
    Foreign Letters and Accounts, 1757–87 (box 5)
    Prices Current, Bristol, 1765–72 (box 14)
  John Rowe Letterbook, 1759–62
  Reynell & Coates Collection
Boston Public Library Rare Books and Manuscripts Division:
  The Chamberlain Collection of Autographs:
    The Hancock Papers: vol. II, 1763–1816
Massachusetts Historical Society:
  Gardiner, Whipple & Allen Papers, vol. II
  S. P. Savage Papers:
    vol. I, 1702–50
  Lee Family Papers:
    Jonathan Jackson Letterbook, 1765–74
    Benjamin Dolbeare Letterbook, 1739–67
New England Historic Genealogical Society:
  Richard Clarke Invoice Book, 1767–75
  John Fayerweather Papers (MS 80)
  Thomas Hubbard Papers (MS 76)
  Hancock Papers:
    John Hancock Letterbook, 1762–82 (JH-6)
    John Hancock Foreign Letters, 1764–91 (box 27)

John Hancock Foreign Invoices, Foreign Bills, Foreign Freight, Foreign
     Sales, Customs, 1764–92 (box 28)
John Hancock Price Currents etc., 1766–93 (box 26)
Thomas Hancock Letterbook, 1750–62 (TH-4)
Thomas Hancock Foreign Letters, 1728–64 (box 7)

Cambridge, Massachusetts
Houghton Library:
  William Palfrey Papers (bMS AM 1704)

Salem, Massachusetts
James Duncan Phillips Library, The Essex Institute:
  Samuel Curwen Papers:
    Samuel Curwen Letterbook, 1771–5

Worcester, Massachusetts
American Antiquarian Society:
  Salisbury Family Papers

Ann Arbor, Michigan
William L. Clements Library, University of Michigan:
  *Bristol Shipping Account Books: vols. II, III and IV: Captaincy Appoint-
     ments and Shipping Records for various vessels in the Jamaica trade
     owned by Bristol merchants, 1776–87
  *Accounts of the *Tryall*, 1757–8 (Bristol Shipping Account Books, vol. I)
  Shelburne Papers, vols. LXXVIII, CLII

Detroit, Michigan
Burton Historical Collection, Detroit Public Library:
  John Moffatt Letterbook, 1762–3

Concord, New Hampshire
New Hampshire Historical Society:
  Boyd Papers, 1773–1821:
    George Boyd Letters, 1773–5
  Langdon Papers, 1716–1841:
    John Langdon Papers (boxes 1 and 2)
  Moffatt-Whipple Papers, 1651–1820:
    John Moffatt Invoice Book, 1737–55

Portsmouth, New Hampshire
MacPhaedris-Warner House:
  MacPhaedris-Warner Papers
Portsmouth Athenaeum:
  Larkin Papers

New York City
Montgomery Collection, Rare Book and Manuscript Library, Columbia Uni-
     versity Library:

John Ludlow Letterbook, 1752–63 (MS 126)
New York Genealogical and Biographical Society:
  Bristol Account with Cruger & Co., 1784–9
New York Historical Society:
  Bancker Papers:
    Evert Bancker Invoice Book, 1764–74
  Henry & John Cruger Wastebook, 1762–8
  Henry & John Cruger Letterbook, 1765–7
  Joshua Delaplaine Papers
  Samuel Coates Papers (box 1, 1738–84)
  Stewart and Jones Letterbook, 1786–95
  Sanders Papers:
    Barent, Robert and John Sanders: Invoice Book of Imported Goods,
        1737–49
    John Sanders Letterbook, 1749–73
  David Clarkson Invoices, 1751–5
  John Custis Accounts, 1732–44
  Miscellaneous MSS: Ships: Articles of Agreement for the *Cornwall*, 1759
  William Bedlow Journal, 1759
New York Public Library Rare Books and Manuscripts Division:
  Philip Cuyler Letterbook, 1755–60
  Stewart & Jones Letterbook, 1784–6
  Stewart & Jones Papers
  Richard Champion Letterbook, 1773–5
  Thomas Moffatt Letterbook, 1714–16

Chapel Hill, North Carolina
Southern Historical Collection, University of North Carolina Library:
  Charles W. Dabney Papers:
    Tobacco Sales Accounts, 1754, 1755, 1758, 1765
  Frederick's Hall Plantation Books:
    John Snelson Letterbook, 1757–75
  Miscellaneous Papers: Indenture Tripartite: An Instrument of Assignment by
        Christopher Rolleston, London, Surviving Partner of the late Edward
        Neufville, Bristol, 1789

Durham, North Carolina
Duke University Library:
  Richard Hill Letterbook, 1743
  Hogg & Clayton: Letterbook and Accounts, 1762–71
  George Yuille Account Book, 1754–7

Carlisle, Pennsylvania
Dickinson College:
  Thomas Fisher Journals, 1762–4

Doylestown, Pennsylvania
Bucks County Historical Society:
  Kuhn & Risberg Letterbooks, 1779–88 (B-205, 206)

Harrisburg, Pennsylvania
Pennsylvania State Archives:
*Baynton-Wharton-Morgan Papers:
    Letters from John Noble of Bristol to Baynton, Wharton and Morgan of
        Philadelphia, 1760–7 (reels 3, 4 and 5 of microfilm edition)
Joshua Gilpin Journals, vol. XXVIII
Record Group 4: Records of the Office of the Comptroller General-Register of
    Vessels:
    Duty on Tonnage, 1775–6

Haverford, Pennsylvania
Haverford College Quaker Collection:
Edward Wanton Smith Collection

Philadelphia, Pennsylvania
American Philosophical Society:
    Israel Pemberton, Jr Letterbook, 1744–7 (APS768)
Historical Society of Pennsylvania:
    Cadwallader Collection:
        Thomas Cadwallader Section:
            Custom House Tonnage Books, 1765–75
    Coates and Reynell Papers, 1702–1843:
        John Reynell Letterbooks, 1729–84
        John Reynell Correspondence, 1729–84
        John Reynell Invoice Book, 1736–58
    Henry Drinker Papers, 1756–1869:
        James and Drinker Letterbooks, 1756–85
        Diary of Henry Drinker, 1759
    Owen Jones Papers:
        Jones & Wister Letterbook, 1759–70
        Jones & Wister Invoice Book, 1759–62
    John Kidd Letterbook, 1749–63
    Pemberton Papers, 1641–1800:
        Clifford Correspondence (vols. V–VII, X, 1766–85, 1790–4)
        Clifford Letterbooks, 1759–89
    John Reynell Papers:
        Correspondence
    Willing & Morris Letterbook, 1754–61
    Jonathan Dickinson Letterbook, 1715–21
    Richard Waln Papers:
        Foreign Correspondence, 1761–90 (box 5)
    Cramond, Philips and Co.: Correspondence, 1789–91

Swarthmore, Pennsylvania
Friends Historical Library, Swarthmore College:
    Samuel Rowland Fisher Journals, 1767–8, 1783–4

Providence, Rhode Island
Rhode Island Historical Society:
  Champlin Papers

Columbia, South Carolina
South Caroliniana Library:
  Ball Family Papers
  Isaac King Letterbook, 1783–98

Charlottesville, Virginia
Alderman Library, University of Virginia:
  Roger Atkinson Letterbook, 1769–76
  Robert 'King' Carter Letterbook, 1728–32

Newport News, Virginia
Mariners' Museum:
  Logbooks of the *Minerva* (1772, 1776)

Richmond, Virginia
Virginia Historical Society:
  Adams Family Papers:
    Section 16: Sales Account of Griffiths & Thomas of Bristol (1765)
      (MSS/AD/98a 219)
  John Baylor Letterbook, 1757–65
  Alice Harford:
    List of Virginians appearing in an Account Book of Edward Harford, Sr and
      Edward Harford, Jr of Bristol, 1910 (MSS5: 3H 2235:1)
  Tayloe Papers:
    Account Book of Stephen Loyde (1708–11) and Account Book and Letter-
      book of John Tayloe (1687–1747) and John Tayloe (1721–79)
      (MSS/T2118b1)
Virginia State Library and Archives:
  David and William Allason Papers:
    William Allason Letterbook, 1770–89
    Letters and Papers, 1759–75 (boxes 2, 6, 7)
  Federal Records Collection:
    US Circuit Court, Virginia District, Ended Cases 1790–1861: Record Book
      5, E, 1796

Williamsburg, Virginia
Earl Gregg Swem Library, College of William and Mary:
  Jerdone Papers:
    Letterbook of William Johnston and Francis Jerdone, 1738–45
    Letterbook of Francis Jerdone, 1756–63

COLLECTIONS IN AUSTRALIA

Parkville, Melbourne
University of Melbourne Archives:
  Bright Family Papers:
    Francis Bright Letterbook, 1752–3
    The Snow *Bristol Merchant*'s Book, 1746–7
    Allen Bright Letterbook, 1751–62
    Henry Bright Letterbook, 1739–48
    Lowbridge Bright Letterbook, 1765–73
    Boxes of Business Correspondence
    Loose Business Correspondence
    Richard Meyler Ledger and Letterbook, 1725–35
*available on microfilm

B   PRINTED SOURCES

(A) BRITISH NEWSPAPERS

Bonner and Middleton's Bristol Journal (Bristol, 1775–6, 1785)
Bristol Gazette (Bristol, 1787)
Bristol Oracle (Bristol, 1742, 1749)
Bristol Weekly Intelligencer (Bristol, 1750–1, 1757)
Farley's Bristol Newspaper (1725–6)
Felix Farley's Bristol Journal (Bristol, 1752–68, 1773, 1785, 1788, 1790, 1825)

(B) WEST INDIAN NEWSPAPERS

Barbados Mercury (Bridgetown, 1766)

(C) AMERICAN NEWSPAPERS

American Weekly Mercury (1722–3, 1727–9, 1732, 1736, 1744)
Boston Evening Post (Boston, 1749–66)
Boston Gazette, or Weekly Journal (Boston, 1749–68)
Boston Weekly Newsletter (Boston, 1731, 1749–68)
Maryland Gazette (Annapolis, 1749–68)
Massachusetts Gazette and Boston Newsletter (Boston, 1764)
New York Gazette (New York City, 1760)
New York Gazette (Weyman) (New York City, 1765–7)
New York Gazette, or Weekly Post Boy (New York City, 1759)
New York Mercury (New York City, 1756/7, 1763–4)
New York Weekly Journal (New York City, 1749–50)
Pennsylvania Gazette (Philadelphia, 1749–68)
Pennsylvania Journal and Weekly Advertiser (Philadelphia, 1763–6)
South Carolina Gazette (Charleston, 1734, 1749–68)
Virginia Gazette (Williamsburg, 1749–66)
Virginia Gazette (Purdie and Dixon) (Williamsburg, 1766–74)

Virginia Gazette (Rind) (Williamsburg, 1766–74)

C   OTHER PRINTED SOURCES

Abbot, W. W., ed., *The Papers of George Washington: Colonial Series 6: September 1758–December 1760* (Charlottesville, VA, 1988).
An Account of the Life, and Dealings of God with Silas Told . . . (London, 1786).
Atkins, John, *A Voyage to Guinea, Brasil, and the West Indies . . .* (London, 1735).
Bailey, *Western and Midland Directory: Or Merchant's and Tradesman's Useful Companion for the Year 1783*.
Barrett, William, *The History and Antiquities of the City of Bristol* (Bristol, 1789; facsimile reprint, Gloucester, 1982).
Benezet, Anthony, *Some Historical Account of Guinea . . .* (2nd edn., London, 1788).
Boyd, Julian P., ed., *The Papers of Thomas Jefferson, Vol. 15: 27 March 1789 to 30 November 1789* (Princeton, NJ, 1958).
Bristol Directory (1791).
Bristol Presentments: Exports: 1773–80; Imports: 1770, 1775, 1778–80.
British Parliamentary Papers, 1802–3, vol. VIII (Cd. 138); 1806, vol. XIII (Accounts and Papers, IV); 1829, vol. XV (Cd. 340); 1844, vol. XII (Cd. 565).
Brooks, Jerome E., ed., *Tobacco: Its History Illustrated by the Books, Manuscripts and Engravings in the Library of George Arents, Jr.*, 4 vols. (New York, 1937–43).
Campbell, Charles, ed., *The Bland Papers*, 2 vols. (Petersburg, VA, 1840–3).
Champion, Richard, *Considerations on the Present Situation of Great Britain and the United States of America . . .* (2nd edn., London, 1784).
Clarkson, Thomas, *The History of the Rise, Progress, and Accomplishment of the Abolition of the African Slave Trade by the British Parliament*, 2 vols. (London, 1808).
Coldham, Peter Wilson, *American Loyalist Claims*, vol. 1 (Washington, DC, 1980).
Bonded Passengers to America, vol. V: Western Circuit, 1664–1775 (Baltimore, 1983).
Curnock, Nehemiah, *The Journal of John Wesley*, 8 vols. (London, 1909–16).
Davis, Richard Beale, ed., *William Fitzhugh and his Chesapeake World, 1676–1701* (Chapel Hill, NC, 1963).
Donnan, Elizabeth, ed., *Documents Illustrative of the History of the Slave Trade to America*, 4 vols. (Washington, DC, 1930–5).
Elsas, Madeleine, ed., *Iron in the Making: Dowlais Iron Company Letters, 1782–1860* (Cardiff, 1960).
Ford, Worthington C., *et al.*, eds., *The Commerce of Rhode Island, 1726–1800*, Massachusetts Historical Society Collections, 7th Series, 9, 2 vols. (Boston, 1914).
The Genuine Life of Robert Barker . . . (London, 1809).
Guttridge, George H., *The American Correspondence of a Bristol Merchant, 1766–1776: Letters of Richard Champion*, University of California Publications in History, no. 22 (Berkeley, CA, 1934).

Hamer, Philip M., Rogers, George C. *et al.*, eds., *The Papers of Henry Laurens* (Columbia, SC, 1968–).

Hawes, Lilla M., ed., 'The Letterbook of Thomas Rasberry, 1758–1761', *Georgia Historical Quarterly*, 41 (1957), 48–70.

Jarvis, Rupert C., ed., *Customs Letter-books of the Port of Liverpool, 1711–1813* (Chetham Society's Publications, 3rd Series, 6, Manchester, 1954).

Jensen, Merrill, ed., *English Historical Documents, IX: American Colonial Documents to 1776* (London, 1955).

Jessopp, Augustus, ed., *The Lives of the Right Hon. F. North . . . Hon. Sir D. North, Vol. I* (London, 1890).

Keith, Alice Barnwell, ed., *The John Gray Blount Papers*, 2 vols. (Raleigh, NC, 1952, 1959).

Lambert, Sheila, ed., *House of Commons Sessional Papers of the Eighteenth Century* (Wilmington, Delaware, 1975), vols. LXVII–IX, LXXII, LXXIII, LXXV.

Lamoine, George, ed., *Bristol Gaol Delivery Fiats 1741–1799* (Bristol Record Society's *Publications*, 40, 1989).

Large, David, ed., *The Port of Bristol 1848–1884* (Bristol Record Society's *Publications*, 36, 1984).

A Letter from Mr. Thomas Knox of Bristol to the Hon. William Nelson Esq. of Virginia (Bristol, 1759).

'Letters of Francis Jerdone', *William and Mary Quarterly*, 1st Series, 11 (1903), 153–60, 236–42 and 16 (1907), 126–32.

McCusker, John J., compiler, 'Ships Registered at the Port of Philadelphia before 1776: A Computerized Listing' (on deposit at the Historical Society of Pennsylvania).

McGrath, Patrick, ed., *Merchants and Merchandise in Seventeenth-century Bristol* (Bristol Record Society's *Publications*, 19, 1955).

Mann, Julia de Lacy, ed., *Documents Illustrating the Wiltshire Textile Trades in the Eighteenth Century* (Wiltshire Record Society, 19, Devizes, 1964).

Martin, Benjamin, *The Natural History of England* (1759).

Mason, Frances Norton, ed., *John Norton & Sons: Merchants of London and Virginia* (Richmond, VA, 1937).

Matthews, W., *The New History, Survey and Description of the City of Bristol, or Complete Guide and Bristol Directory for the Year 1793–4* (Bristol, 1794).

Memoirs of the Life and Travels of the late Charles MacPherson, Esq. in Asia, Africa and America . . . (Edinburgh, 1800).

Minchinton, W. E., ed., *The Trade of Bristol in the Eighteenth Century* (Bristol Record Society's *Publications*, 20, 1957).

'The Virginia Letters of Isaac Hobhouse, Merchant of Bristol', *Virginia Magazine of History and Biography*, 66 (1958), 278–301.

Politics and the Port of Bristol in the Eighteenth Century: The Petitions of the Society of Merchant Venturers 1698–1803 (Bristol Record Society's *Publications*, 23, 1963).

Minchinton, W. E., King, Celia and Waite, Peter, eds., *Virginia Slave-Trade Statistics, 1698–1775* (Richmond, VA, 1984).

Morgan, Kenneth, ed., 'Calendar of Correspondence from William Miles, a West Indian Merchant in Bristol, to John Tharp, a Planter in Jamaica, 1770–1789' in Patrick McGrath, ed., *A Bristol Miscellany* (Bristol Record Society's *Publications*, 37, 1985), pp. 79–121.

An American Quaker in the British Isles: The Travel Journals of Jabez Maud Fisher, 1775–1779 (Oxford, 1992).

Bristol's Transatlantic Commerce in the Eighteenth Century (Bristol Record Society's *Publications*, forthcoming).

Morrison, A. J., ed., 'Letters of Roger Atkinson, 1769–1776', *Virginia Magazine of History and Biography*, 15 (1908) 345–59.

Norris, Robert, *A Short Account of the African Slave Trade* (Liverpool, 1788).

Oliver, Vere Langford, ed., *Caribbeana: Miscellaneous Papers relating to the History, Genealogy, Topography and Antiquities of the British West Indies*, 6 vols. (London, 1909–19).

Porter, Kenneth Wiggins, ed., *The Jacksons and the Lees: Two Generations of Massachusetts Merchants*, 2 vols. (Cambridge, MA, 1937).

The Present State of the Tobacco Trade, as the late act affects the London Manufacturers, Considered: in a letter to a friend (London, 1751).

Price, Jacob M., ed., *Joshua Johnson's Letterbook, 1771–1774: Letters from a Merchant in London to his Partners in Maryland* (London Record Society, 15, 1979).

Report of the Lords of the Committee of Council (London, 1789).

Richardson, David, ed., *Bristol, Africa and the Eighteenth-Century Slave Trade to America, I: The Years of Expansion, 1698–1729* (Bristol Record Society's *Publications*, 38, 1986).

Bristol, Africa and the Eighteenth-Century Slave Trade to America, II: The Years of Ascendancy, 1730–1745 (Bristol Record Society's *Publications*, 39, 1987).

Bristol, Africa and the Eighteenth-Century Slave Trade to America, III: The Years of Decline, 1746–1769 (Bristol Record Society's *Publications*, 42, 1991).

Sketchley, James, *Bristol Directory* (Bristol, 1775, facsimile reprint, Bath, 1971).

Sketchley's and Adams's Tradesman's True Guide: Or an Universal Directory for the Towns of Birmingham, Wolverhampton, Walsall, Dudley . . . (1770).

Stock, Leo Francis, ed., *Proceedings and Debates of the British Parliaments respecting North America*, 5 vols. (Washington, DC, 1924–1941).

The Stranger in Liverpool; or an Historical and Descriptive View of the Town of Liverpool and its Environs (Liverpool, 1820).

Taylor, Robert J., ed., *Papers of John Adams, vol. 2, December 1773–April 1775* (Cambridge, MA, 1977).

Tobacco, its Culture and Manufacture (2nd edn., Bristol, 1936).

The Unfortunate Shipwright: Or Cruel Captain: Being a Faithful Narrative of the Unparalleled Sufferings of Robert Barker, late Carpenter, on board the Thetis Snow, of Bristol, in a Voyage to the Coast of Guinea and Antigua (London, 1760).

U.S. Bureau of the Census, Department of Commerce, *Historical Statistics of the United States, Colonial Times to 1970*, 2 vols. (Washington, DC, 1976).

Watson, Winslow C., *Men and Times of the Revolution; or, Memoirs of Elkanah Watson . . .* (2nd edn., New York, 1856).

White, Philip L. ed., *The Beekman Mercantile Papers, 1746–1799*, 3 vols. (New York, 1956).

Wright, Louis B., ed., *Letters of Robert Carter: The Commercial Interests of a Virginia Gentleman* (San Marino, CA, 1940).

D   SECONDARY SOURCES

Albion, Robert G., 'Sea Routes' in Critchell Rimington, ed., *Merchant Fleets: A Survey of the Merchant Navies of the World* (New York, 1944), pp. 19–39.

Alford, B. W. E., *W. D. & H. O. Wills and the Development of the U.K. Tobacco Industry, 1786–1965* (London, 1973).

'The Economic Development of Bristol in the Nineteenth Century: An Enigma?' in Patrick McGrath and John Cannon, eds., *Essays in Bristol and Gloucestershire History* (Bristol, 1976), pp. 252–83.

Anderson, B. L., 'The Lancashire Bill System and its Liverpool Practitioners: The Case of a Slave Merchant' in W. H. Chaloner and Barrie M. Ratcliffe, eds., *Trade and Transport: Essays in Economic History in Honour of T. S. Willan* (Manchester, 1977), pp. 59–97.

Anderson, B. L. and Richardson, David, 'Market Structure and the Profits of the British African Trade in the Late Eighteenth Century: A Comment', *Journal of Economic History*, 43 (1983), 713–21.

Anderson, M. S., 'Great Britain and the Barbary States in the Eighteenth Century', *Bulletin of the Institute of Historical Research*, 29 (1956), 87–107.

Andrews, C. M., *Guide to the Materials for American History to 1783, in the Public Record Office of Great Britain, II: Departmental and Miscellaneous Papers* (London, 1914).

'Colonial Commerce', *American Historical Review*, 20 (1914–15), 43–63.

Anstey, Roger, *The Atlantic Slave Trade and British Abolition, 1760–1810* (London, 1975).

Ashton, T. S., *Economic Fluctuations in England, 1700–1800* (Oxford, 1959).

Aström, Sven-Erik, 'The Reliability of the English Port Books', *Scandinavian Economic History Review*, 16 (1968), 125–36.

Atkinson, B. J., 'An Early Example of the Decline of the Industrial Spirit? Bristol Enterprise in the First Half of the Nineteenth Century', *Southern History*, 9 (1987), 71–89.

Baigent, Elizabeth, 'Economy and Society in Eighteenth-Century English Towns: Bristol in the 1770s' in Dietrich Denecke and Gareth Shaw, eds., *Urban Historical Geography: Recent Progress in Britain and Germany* (Cambridge, 1988), pp. 109–24.

Bailyn, Bernard, *Voyagers to the West: Emigration from Britain to America on the Eve of the Revolution* (New York, 1986).

Baines, Thomas, *History of the Commerce and Town of Liverpool* (Liverpool, 1852).

Barker, T. C., 'Smuggling in the Eighteenth Century: The Evidence of the Scottish Tobacco Trade', *Virginia Magazine of History and Biography*, 71 (1954), 387–99.

Barrow, Thomas C., *Trade and Empire: The British Customs Service in Colonial America, 1660–1775* (Cambridge, MA, 1967).

Baxter, W. T., *The House of Hancock: Business in Boston, 1724–1775* (Cambridge, MA, 1945).

Beckett, J. V., *Coal and Tobacco: The Lowthers and the Economic Development of West Cumberland, 1660–1760* (Cambridge, 1981).

Behrendt, Stephen D., 'The Captains in the British Slave Trade from 1785 to 1807', *Transactions of the Historic Society of Lancashire and Cheshire*, 140 (1990), 79–140.

Bell, Herbert C., 'The West India Trade before the American Revolution', *American Historical Review*, 22 (1917), 272–87.

Bettey, J. H., *Bristol Observed: Visitors' Impressions of the City from Domesday to the Blitz* (Bristol, 1986).

'The Capture of the *Baltic Merchant*, 1740', *The Mariner's Mirror*, 76 (1990), 36–9.

'Graffin Prankard, an Eighteenth-Century Bristol Merchant', *Southern History*, 12 (1990), 34–47.

Bird, James, *The Major Seaports of the United Kingdom* (London, 1963).

Botsford, Jay Barrett, *English Society in the Eighteenth Century as Influenced from Oversea* (New York, 1924).

Bradley, James E., *Popular Politics and the American Revolution in England: Petitions, the Crown, and Public Opinion* (Macon, GA, 1986).

Breen, T. H., 'An Empire of Goods: The Anglicization of Colonial America, 1690–1776', *Journal of British Studies*, 15 (1986), 467–99.

'"Baubles of Britain": The American and Consumer Revolutions of the Eighteenth Century', *Past and Present*, 119 (1988), 73–104.

Brock, William R., *Scotus Americanus: A Survey of Sources for Links between Scotland and America in the Eighteenth Century* (Edinburgh, 1982).

Brooks, Jerome E., *The Mighty Leaf: Tobacco through the Centuries* (Boston, 1952).

Bruchey, Stuart, 'Success and Failure Factors: American Merchants in Foreign Trade in the Eighteenth and Early Nineteenth Centuries', *Business History Review*, 32 (1958), 272–92.

The Roots of American Economic Growth, 1607–1861 (London, 1965).

Brydon, G. MacLaren, 'The Bristol Iron Works in King George County', *Virginia Magazine of History and Biography*, 13 (1934), 97–102.

Buchanan, B. J., 'Aspects of Capital Formation: Some Insights from North Somerset, 1750–1830', *Southern History*, 8 (1986), 73–93.

Buchanan, B. J. and Tucker, M. T., 'The Manufacture of Gunpowder: A Study of the Documentary and Physical Evidence Relating to the Woolley Powder Works near Bath', *Industrial Archaeology Review*, 5 (1981), 185–202.

Buchanan, R. A., 'The Construction of the Floating Harbour in Bristol, 1804–9', *Transactions of the Bristol and Gloucestershire Archaeological Society*, 88 (1969), 184–204.

Buchanan, R. A. and Cossons, Neil, *The Industrial Archaeology of the Bristol Region* (Newton Abbot, 1969).

Buckley, Francis, 'The Early Glasshouses of Bristol', *Journal of the Society for Glass Technology*, 9 (1925), 36–61.

Cappon, Lester J. *et al.*, *Atlas of Early American History: The Revolutionary Era, 1760–1790* (Princeton, NJ, 1976).

Cave, C. H., *A History of Banking in Bristol from 1750 to 1899* (Bristol, 1899).

Chapman, Stanley D., 'British Marketing Enterprise: The Changing Roles of Merchants, Manufacturers, and Financiers, 1700–1860', *Business History Review*, 53 (1979), 205–34.

Chartres, John A., 'The Marketing of Agricultural Produce in Metropolitan Western England in the Late Seventeenth and Eighteenth Centuries' in M. A. Havinden, ed., *Husbandry and Marketing in the South-West, 1500–1800* (Exeter Papers in Economic History, no. 8, 1973).

Chaudhuri, K. N., *The Trading World of Asia and the English East India Company, 1660–1760* (Cambridge, 1978).

Checkland, S. G., 'Finance for the West Indies, 1780–1815', *Economic History Review*, 2nd Series, 10 (1957–8), 461–9.

Clark, G. N., *Guide to English Commercial Statistics, 1696–1782* (London, 1938).

Claypole, W. A. and Buisseret, D. J., 'Trade Patterns in Early English Jamaica', *Journal of Caribbean History*, 5 (1972), 1–19.

Clemens, Paul G. E., 'The Rise of Liverpool, 1665–1750', *Economic History Review*, 2nd Series, 29 (1976), 211–25.

The Atlantic Economy and Colonial Maryland's Eastern Shore: From Tobacco to Grain (Ithaca, NY, 1980).

Clowse, Converse D., *Measuring Charleston's Overseas Commerce, 1717–1767: Statistics from the Port's Naval Lists* (Washington, DC, 1981).

Cordingly, David, 'Nicholas Pocock's Voyages from Bristol' in *Sea Studies: Essays in Honour of Basil Greenhill on the Occasion of his Retirement* (Greenwich, 1983), pp. 27–32.

Corfield, P. J., *The Impact of English Towns, 1700–1800* (Oxford, 1982).

Crafts, N. F. R., *British Economic Growth during the Industrial Revolution* (Oxford, 1985).

Craig, Robin, 'Printed Guides for Master Mariners as a Source of Productivity Change in Shipping, 1750–1914', *Journal of Transport History*, 3rd Series, 3 (1982), 23–35.

Crouzet, François, 'Toward an Export Economy: British Exports during the Industrial Revolution', *Explorations in Economic History*, 17 (1980), 48–93.

Crowhurst, R. P., 'The Admiralty and the Convoy System in the Seven Years' War', *The Mariner's Mirror*, 57 (1971), 163–73.

The Defence of British Trade, 1689–1815 (Folkestone, 1977).

Curtin, Philip D., *The Atlantic Slave Trade: A Census* (Madison, WI, 1969).

Daunton, M. J., 'Towns and Economic Growth in Eighteenth-Century England' in Philip Abrams and E. A. Wrigley, eds., *Towns in Societies: Essays in Economic History and Historical Sociology* (Cambridge, 1978), pp. 245–77.

Davies, K. G., 'The Origins of the Commission System in the West India Trade', *Transactions of the Royal Historical Society*, 5th Series, 2 (1952), 89–107.

The Royal African Company (London, 1957).

Davis, Ralph, 'Seamen's Sixpences: An Index of Commercial Activity, 1697–1828', *Economica*, New Series, 23 (1956), 328–43.

The Rise of the English Shipping Industry in the Seventeenth and Eighteenth Centuries (London, 1962).

'English Foreign Trade, 1700–1774', *Economic History Review*, 2nd Series, 15 (1962–3), 285–303.

'Untapped Sources and Research Opportunities in the Field of American Maritime History from the Beginning to about 1815' in *Untapped Sources and Research Opportunities in the Field of American Maritime History: A Symposium* . . . (Mystic Seaport, CT, 1966), pp. 11–26.

A Commercial Revolution: English Overseas Trade in the Seventeenth and Eighteenth Centuries (London, 1967).

The Rise of the Atlantic Economies (London, 1973).

'Maritime History: Progress and Problems' in Sheila Marriner, ed., *Business and Businessmen: Studies in Business, Economic and Accounting History* (Liverpool, 1978), pp. 169–97.

The Industrial Revolution and British Overseas Trade (Leicester, 1979).

Davisson, William I., 'The Philadelphia Trade', *Western Economic Journal*, 3 (1965), 310–11.

Davisson William I. and Bradley, Lawrence J., 'New York Maritime Trade: Ship-Voyage Patterns, 1715–1765', *New York Historical Society Quarterly*, 55 (1971), 309–17.

Day, Joan, *Bristol Brass: A History of the Industry* (Newton Abbot, 1973).

Deane, Phyllis and Cole, W. A., *British Economic Growth, 1688–1959* (2nd edn., Cambridge, 1967).

Dell, Richard F., 'The Operational Record of the Clyde Tobacco Fleet, 1747–1775', *Scottish Economic and Social History*, 2 (1982), 1–16.

Devine, T. M., 'Transport Problems of Glasgow–West Indian Merchants during the American War of Independence, 1775–83', *Transport History*, 4 (1971), 266–304.

The Tobacco Lords: A Study of the Tobacco Merchants of Glasgow and their Trading Activities, c. 1740–1790 (Edinburgh, 1975).

'An Eighteenth-Century Business Elite: Glasgow–West India Merchants, c. 1750–1815', *Scottish Historical Review*, 67 (1978), 40–67.

Doerflinger, Thomas M., *A Vigorous Spirit of Enterprise: Merchants and Economic Development in Revolutionary Philadelphia* (Chapel Hill, NC, 1986).

'Farmers and Dry Goods in the Philadelphia Market Area, 1750–1800' in Ronald Hoffman, John J. McCusker, Russell R. Menard and Peter J. Albert, eds., *The Economy of Early America: The Revolutionary Period, 1763–1790* (Charlottesville, VA, 1988), pp. 166–95.

Drake, B. K., 'Continuity and Flexibility in Liverpool's Trade with Africa and the Caribbean', *Business History*, 18 (1976), 85–97.

Drescher, Seymour, *Econocide: British Slavery in the Era of Abolition* (Pittsburgh, 1977).

Earle, Carville and Hoffman, Ronald, 'Urban Development in the Eighteenth-Century South', *Perspectives in American History*, 10 (1976), 7–78.

Eden, F. M., *The State of the Poor*, 3 vols. (London, 1797).

Egnal, Marc, 'The Changing Structure of Philadelphia's Trade with the British West Indies, 1750–1775', *Pennsylvania Magazine of History and Biography*, 99 (1975), 156–79.

'The Economic Development of the Thirteen Continental Colonies, 1720 to 1775', *William and Mary Quarterly*, 3rd Series, 32 (1975), 191–222.

Egnal, Marc and Ernst, Joseph A., 'An Economic Interpretation of the American Revolution', *William and Mary Quarterly*, 3rd Series, 29 (1972), 3–30.

Ekirch, A. Roger, *Bound for America: The Transportation of British Convicts to the Colonies, 1718–1775* (Oxford, 1987).

Enfield, William, *An Essay Towards the History of Liverpool* (London, 1774).

Ernst, Joseph A., '"Ideology" and an Economic Interpretation of the Revolution' in Alfred F. Young, ed., *The American Revolution: Explorations in the History of American Radicalism* (De Kalb, IL, 1976), pp. 159–85.

Evans, Emory G., 'Planter Indebtedness and the Coming of the Revolution in Virginia', *William and Mary Quarterly*, 3rd Series, 19 (1962), 511–33.

'Private Indebtedness and the Revolution in Virginia, 1776 to 1796', *William and Mary Quarterly*, 3rd Series, 28 (1971), 349–74.

Eversley, D. E. C., 'The Home Market and Economic Growth in England, 1750–1780' in E. L. Jones and G. E. Mingay, eds., *Land, Labour and Population in the Industrial Revolution: Essays presented to J. D. Chambers* (London, 1967), pp. 206–59.

Fairchild, Byron, *Messrs. William Pepperrell: Merchants at Piscataqua* (Ithaca, NY, 1954).

Fage, J. D., *A History of West Africa* (Cambridge, 1969).

Farnie, D. A., 'The Commercial Empire of the Atlantic, 1607–1783', *Economic History Review*, 2nd Series, 15 (1962–63), 205–18.

Farr, Grahame, 'Severn Navigation and the Trow', *The Mariner's Mirror*, 32 (1946), 66–95.

'Bristol Channel Pilotage: Historical notes on its administration and craft', *The Mariner's Mirror*, 39 (1953), 27–44.

Shipbuilding in the Port of Bristol (Greenwich, 1977).

Fisher, H. E. S., *The Portugal Trade: A Study of Anglo–Portuguese Commerce 1700–1770* (London, 1971).

'Lisbon, its English Merchant Community and the Mediterranean in the Eighteenth Century' in P. L. Cottrell and D. H. Aldcroft, eds., *Shipping, Trade and Commerce: Essays in Honour of Ralph Davis* (Leicester, 1981), pp. 23–44.

Fox Bourne, H. R., *English Merchants*, 2 vols. (London, 1866).

French, Christopher J., 'Eighteenth-Century Shipping Tonnage Measurements', *Journal of Economic History*, 33 (1973), 434–43.

'Productivity in the Atlantic Shipping Industry: A Quantitative Study', *Journal of Interdisciplinary History*, 17 (1987), 613–38.

'The Longevity of Ships in Colonial Trade: Some Further Evidence', *International Journal of Maritime History*, 3 (1991), 155–63.

'"Crowded with Traders and a Great Commerce": London's Dominion of English Overseas Trade, 1700–1775', *The London Journal*, 17 (1992), 27–35.

Fryer, Peter, *Staying Power: The History of Black People in Britain* (London, 1984).

Galenson, David W., *White Servitude in Colonial America: An Economic Analysis* (Cambridge, 1981).

Gemery, Henry A. and Hogendorn, Jan S., 'Technological Change, Slavery, and the Slave Trade', in Clive Dewey and A. G. Hopkins, eds., *The Imperial*

Impact: Studies in the Economic History of Africa and India (London, 1978), pp. 243–58.

Goldenberg, Joseph A., 'An Analysis of Shipbuilding Sites in *Lloyd's Register* of 1776', *The Mariner's Mirror*, 59 (1973), 419–35.

Shipbuilding in Colonial America (Charlottesville, VA, 1976).

Greenacre, Francis, *Marine Artists of Bristol: Nicholas Pocock (1740–1821), Joseph Walter (1783–1856)* (Bristol, 1982).

Hall, I. V., 'Whitson Court Sugar House, Bristol, 1665–1824', *Transactions of the Bristol and Gloucestershire Archaeological Society*, 65 (1944), 1–97.

'The Daubenys: Part 1' and 'The Daubenys: Part 2', *Transactions of the Bristol and Gloucestershire Archaeological Society*, 84 and 85 (1965 and 1966), 113–40 and 175–201.

Hamilton, Henry, *The English Brass and Copper Industries to 1800* (1926; 2nd edn., London, 1967).

Harford, Alice, *Annals of the Harford Family* (London, 1909).

Harper, Lawrence A., *The English Navigation Laws: A Seventeenth-Century Experiment in Social Engineering* (New York, 1939).

Harrington, Virginia D., *The New York Merchant on the Eve of the Revolution* (New York, 1935).

Harvey, Charles, and Press, Jon, 'Industrial Change and the Economic Life of Bristol since 1800' in Charles Harvey and Jon Press, eds., *Studies in the Business History of Bristol* (Bristol, 1988), pp. 1–32.

Head, C. Grant, *Eighteenth Century Newfoundland: A Geographer's Perspective* (Toronto, 1976).

Hewson, J. B., *A History of the Practice of Navigation* (Glasgow, 1951).

Hoon, E. E., *The Organisation of the English Customs System, 1696–1786* (2nd edn., Newton Abbot, 1968).

Hoppit, Julian, *Risk and Failure in English Business, 1700–1800* (Cambridge, 1987).

Horn, James, 'Servant Emigration to the Chesapeake in the Seventeenth Century' in Thad W. Tate and David L. Ammerman, eds., *The Chesapeake in the Seventeenth Century: Essays on Anglo-American Society* (Chapel Hill, NC, 1979), pp. 51–95.

Horner, Frederick, *A History of the Blair, Banister, and Braxton Families* (Philadelphia, 1898).

Hunt, William, *Bristol* (Bristol, 1895).

Hyde, Charles K., *Technological Change and the British Iron Industry, 1700–1870* (Princeton, NJ, 1977).

Hyde, F. E., *Liverpool and the Mersey: An Economic History of a Port, 1700–1970* (Newton Abbot, 1971).

Inikori, J. E., 'The Import of Firearms into West Africa 1750–1807: A Quantitative Analysis', *Journal of African History*, 18 (1977), 339–68.

'Market Structure and the Profits of the British African Trade in the Late Eighteenth Century', *Journal of Economic History*, 41 (1981), 745–76, and a rejoinder, *ibid.*, 43 (1983), 723–8.

'The Sources of Supply for the Atlantic Slave Exports from the Bight of Benin and the Bight of Bonny (Biafra)' in Serge Daget, ed., *De La Traite à*

L'Esclavage, 2 vols. (Société Française d'Histoire d'Outre Mer, Nantes, 1988), II, pp. 25–43.

'The Credit Needs of the African Trade and the Development of the Credit Economy in England', *Explorations in Economic History*, 27 (1990), 197–231.

Jackson, Gordon, 'The Ports' in Derek H. Aldcroft and Michael J. Freeman, eds., *Transport in the Industrial Revolution* (Manchester, 1983).

The History and Archaeology of Ports (Tadworth, Surrey, 1983).

James, Francis G., 'Irish Colonial Trade in the Eighteenth Century', *William and Mary Quarterly*, 3rd Series, 20 (1963), 574–84.

Jameson, H. B., 'Bonded Servants on the North American Continent in the Eighteenth Century: Some New Evidence from Bristol', *Transactions of the Bristol and Gloucestershire Archaeological Society*, 99 (1981), 127–40.

Jarvis, Rupert C., 'Sources for the History of Ships and Shipping', *Journal of Transport History*, 3 (1958), 212–34.

'Fractional Shareholding in British Merchant Ships with Special Reference to 64ths', *The Mariner's Mirror*, 45 (1959), 301–19.

'Eighteenth-Century London Shipping' in A. E. J. Hollaender and William Kellaway, eds., *Studies in London History Presented to Philip Edmund Jones* (London, 1969), pp. 403–25.

Jenkins, Philip, 'The Tory Tradition in Eighteenth-Century Cardiff', *Welsh History Review*, XII (1984), 180–96.

Jenkins, Rhys, 'The Copper Works at Redbrook and Bristol', *Transactions of the Bristol and Gloucestershire Archaeological Society*, 63 (1942), 145–67.

Jensen, Arthur L., *The Maritime Commerce of Colonial Philadelphia* (Madison, WI, 1963).

John, A. H., 'Iron and Coal on a Glamorgan Estate, 1700–1740', *Economic History Review*, 13 (1943), 93–103.

The Industrial Development of South Wales, 1750–1850 (Cardiff, 1950).

Johnson, Keach, 'The Baltimore Company seeks English Markets: A Study of the Anglo-American Iron Trade, 1731–1755', *William and Mary Quarterly*, 3rd Series, 16 (1959), 37–60.

Jones, Donald, *Captain Woodes Rogers' Voyage Round the World 1708–1711* (Bristol Branch of the Historical Association, pamphlet no. 79, Bristol, 1992).

Kellett, J. R., 'Glasgow' in M. D. Lobel, ed., *Historic Towns of the British Isles*, vol. I (London, 1969).

Klein, Herbert S., 'Slaves and Shipping in Eighteenth-Century Virginia,' *Journal of Interdisciplinary History*, 5 (1975), 383–412.

'Economic Aspects of the Eighteenth-Century Atlantic Slave Trade' in James D. Tracy, ed., *The Rise of Merchant Empires: Long-Distance Trade in the Early Modern World, 1350–1750* (Cambridge, 1990), pp. 287–310.

Koninckx, Christian, *The First and Second Charters of the Swedish East India Company (1731–1766)* (Korkrijk, Belgium, 1980).

Kulikoff, Allan, *Tobacco and Slaves: The Development of Southern Cultures in the Chesapeake, 1680–1800* (Chapel Hill, NC, 1986).

Lamb, D. P., 'Volume and Tonnage of the Liverpool Slave Trade 1772–1807' in Roger Anstey and P. E. H. Hair, eds., *Liverpool, the African Slave Trade,* and Abolition (Historic Society of Lancashire and Cheshire, Occasional Series, vol. 2, 1976), pp. 91–112.

Langford, Paul, *The Excise Crisis: Society and Politics in the Age of Walpole* (Oxford, 1975).

Langton, John, 'Liverpool and its Hinterland in the late Eighteenth Century' in B. L. Anderson and P. J. M. Stoney, eds., *Commerce, Industry and Transport: Studies in Economic Change on Merseyside* (Liverpool, 1983), pp. 1–25.

Latimer, John, *The Annals of Bristol in the Eighteenth Century* (Bristol, 1893).
The History of the Society of Merchant Venturers of the City of Bristol (Bristol, 1903).

Lawson, Murray G., 'The Routes of Boston's Trade, 1752–1765', *Transactions of the Colonial Society of Massachusetts*, 38 (1947–51) (Boston, 1959), 81–120.

Lemire, Beverly, *Fashion's Favourite: The Cotton Trade and the Consumer in Britain, 1660–1800* (Oxford, 1991).

Little, Bryan, *The City and the County of Bristol: A Study in Atlantic Civilization* (London, 1954).

Lloyd, Christopher, *Atlas of Maritime History* (London, 1975).

Lobel, M. D. and Carus-Wilson, E. M., *Bristol: Historic Towns Atlas* (London, 1975).

Lord, John, and Southam, Jem, *The Floating Harbour: A Landscape History of Bristol City Docks* (Bristol, 1983).

Lynn, Martin, 'Bristol, West Africa and the Nineteenth-Century Palm Oil Trade', *Historical Research: The Bulletin of the Institute of Historical Research*, 64 (1991), 359–74.

McCausland, Hugh, *Snuff and Snuff-boxes* (London, 1951).

McCusker, John J., 'The Current Value of English Exports, 1697–1800', *William and Mary Quarterly*, 3rd Series, 28 (1971), 607–28.

'Sources of Investment Capital in the Colonial Philadelphia Shipping Industry', *Journal of Economic History*, 32 (1972), 146–57.

'Weights and Measures in the Colonial Sugar Trade: The Gallon and the Pound and their International Equivalents', *William and Mary Quarterly*, 3rd Series, 30 (1973), 599–624.

'An Introduction to the Naval Officer Shipping Lists' (unpublished manuscript, 1976).

Money and Exchange in Europe and America, 1600–1775: A Handbook (Chapel Hill, NC, 1978).

'The Tonnage of Ships Engaged in British Colonial Trade during the Eighteenth Century', *Research in Economic History*, 6 (1981), 73–105.

'European Bills of Entry and Marine Lists: Early Commercial Publications and the Origins of the Business Press', *Harvard Library Bulletin*, 21 (1983), 209–55 and 316–39.

'The Shipowners of British America before 1775' (unpublished typescript, 1985).

'Growth, Stagnation, or Decline? The Economy of the British West Indies, 1763–1790' in Ronald Hoffman, John J. McCusker, Russell R. Menard and Peter J. Albert, eds., *The Economy of Early America: the Revolutionary Period, 1763–1790* (Charlottesville, VA, 1988), pp. 275–302.

McCusker, John J. and Menard, Russell R., *The Economy of British America, 1607–1789* (Chapel Hill, NC, 1985).

McGowan, Alan, *The Ship: The Century Before Steam: The Development of the Sailing Ship, 1700–1820* (London, 1980).

McGrath, Patrick, 'The Society of Merchant Venturers and the Port of Bristol in the Seventeenth Century', *Transactions of the Bristol and Gloucestershire Archaeological Society*, 72 (1953), 105–28.

    The Merchant Venturers of Bristol: A History of the Society of Merchant Venturers of the City of Bristol from its Origin to the Present Day (Bristol, 1975).

    'Bristol and America, 1480–1631' in K. R. Andrews, N. P. Canny and P. E. H. Hair, eds., *The Westward Enterprise: English Activities in Ireland, the Atlantic, and America, 1480–1650* (Liverpool, 1978), pp. 81–102.

McGrath, Patrick, ed., *Bristol in the Eighteenth Century* (Newton Abbot, 1972).

MacInnes, C. M., *Bristol: A Gateway of Empire* (Bristol, 1939).

    'The Port of Bristol' in H. A. Cronne, T. W. Moody and D. B. Quinn, eds., *Essays in British and Irish History* (London, 1949), pp. 200–17.

    'Bristol and Overseas Expansion' in C. M. MacInnes and W. F. Whittard, eds., *Bristol and its Adjoining Counties* (Bristol, 1955), pp. 219–30.

    'Bristol and the Slave Trade' in Patrick McGrath, ed., *Bristol in the Eighteenth Century* (Newton Abbot, 1972), pp. 161–84.

McIntyre, Sylvia, 'The Mineral Water Trade in the Eighteenth Century', *Journal of Transport History*, New Series, 2 (1973–4), 1–19.

Mackeson, John F., *Bristol Transported* (Bristol, 1987).

Malone, Joseph J., 'England and the Baltic Naval Stores Trade in the Seventeenth and Eighteenth Centuries', *The Mariner's Mirror*, 58 (1972), 375–95.

Mann, Julia de Lacy, *The Cloth Industry in the West of England from 1640 to 1880* (Oxford, 1971).

Mannion, John, 'The Waterford Merchants and the Irish-Newfoundland Provisions Trade, 1770–1820', in Paul Butel and L. M. Cullen, eds., *Trade and Industry in France and Ireland in the Seventeenth and Eighteenth Centuries* (Paris, 1980), pp. 27–43.

Marcy, Peter T., 'Bristol's Roads and Communications on the Eve of the Industrial Revolution, 1740–1780', *Transactions of the Bristol and Gloucestershire Archaeological Society*, 87 (1968), 149–72.

    'Eighteenth Century Views of Bristol and Bristolians' in Patrick McGrath, ed., *Bristol in the Eighteenth Century* (Newton Abbot, 1972), pp. 11–40.

Marshall, Peter, 'The Anti-Slave Trade Movement in Bristol' in Patrick McGrath, ed., *Bristol in the Eighteenth Century* (Newton Abbot, 1972), pp. 185–215.

    'A Refuge from Revolution: the American Loyalists' Residence in Bristol' in Patrick McGrath and John Cannon, eds., *Essays in Bristol and Gloucestershire History* (Bristol, 1976), pp. 200–16.

    Bristol and the American War of Independence (Bristol Branch of the Historical Association, pamphlet no. 41, 1977).

Mathias, Peter, *The Brewing Industry in England, 1700–1830* (Cambridge, 1959).

    The Transformation of England: Essays in the Economic and Social History of England in the Eighteenth Century (London, 1979).

Menard, Russell R., 'The Tobacco Industry in the Chesapeake Colonies, 1617–1730: An Interpretation', *Research in Economic History*, 5 (1980), 109–77.

'Transport Costs and Long-Range Trade, 1300–1800: Was there a European-"Transport Revolution" in the Early Modern Era?' in James D. Tracy, ed., *The Political Economy of Merchant Empires* (Cambridge, 1991), pp. 228–75.

Merritt, J. E., 'The Triangular Trade', *Business History*, 3 (1960), 1–7.

Meyer, W. R., 'English Privateering in the War of the Spanish Succession, 1702–13,' *The Mariner's Mirror*, 69 (1983), 435–46.

Middleton, Arthur Pierce, *Tobacco Coast: A Maritime History of Chesapeake Bay in the Colonial Era* (Newport News, VA, 1953).

Minchinton, W. E., 'The Voyage of the Snow *Africa*', *The Mariner's Mirror*, 37 (1951), 187–96.

'Bristol – Metropolis of the West in the Eighteenth Century', *Transactions of the Royal Historical Society*, 5th Series, 4 (1954), 69–89.

The British Tinplate Industry: A History (Oxford, 1957).

'Shipbuilding in Colonial Rhode Island', *Rhode Island History*, 20 (1961), 119–24.

'Richard Champion, Nicholas Pocock, and the Carolina Trade', *South Carolina Historical Magazine*, 65 (1964), 87–97 with a note, 70 (1969), 97–103.

'The Stamp Act Crisis: Bristol and Virginia', *Virginia Magazine of History and Biography*, 73 (1965), 145–55.

'The Political Activities of Bristol Merchants with Respect to the Southern Colonies before the Revolution', *Virginia Magazine of History and Biography*, 79 (1971), 167–89.

'The Port of Bristol in the Eighteenth Century' in Patrick McGrath, ed., *Bristol in the Eighteenth Century* (Newton Abbot, 1972), pp. 127–60.

'The Slave Trade of Bristol with the British Mainland Colonies in North America, 1699–1770', in Roger Anstey and P. E. H. Hair, eds., *Liverpool, the African Slave Trade and Abolition* (Historic Society of Lancashire and Cheshire, Occasional Series, 2, Liverpool, 1976), pp. 39–59.

The Naval Office Shipping Lists for Jamaica, 1683–1818 (E. P. Microform Ltd., Wakefield, 1977).

'The Merchants of Bristol in the Eighteenth Century' in *Sociétés et groupes sociaux en Aquitaine et an Angleterre*: Fédérations Historiques du Sud-ouest (Bordeaux, 1979), pp. 185–200.

'The Triangular Trade Revisited' in Henry A. Gemery and Jan S. Hogendorn, eds., *The Uncommon Market: Essays on the Atlantic Slave Trade* (New York, 1979), pp. 331–52.

'Gli Scambi Commerciali di Bristol con le Indie Occidentali et l'America meridionale, 1780–1830', *Revista di Storia Economica*, New Series, 4 (1987), 212–33.

'The British Slave Fleet, 1680–1775: The Evidence of the Naval Office Shipping Lists' in Serge Daget, ed., *De la Traite à l'esclavage*, 2 vols. (Nantes, 1988), I, pp. 395–427.

'Characteristics of British Slaving Vessels 1698–1775', *Journal of Interdisciplinary History*, 20 (1989), 53–81.

Minchinton, W. E., ed., *The Growth of English Overseas Trade in the Seventeenth and Eighteenth Centuries* (London, 1969).

Minchinton, W. E., and Waite, Peter, *The Naval Office Shipping Lists for the West Indies, 1678–1825 (excluding Jamaica)* (E. P. Microform Ltd., Wakefield, 1981).

Mintz, Sidney W., *Sweetness and Power: The Place of Sugar in Modern History* (New York, 1985).

Miquelon, Dale, *Dugard of Rouen: French Trade to Canada and the West Indies, 1729–1770* (Montreal and London, 1978).

Morgan, Kenneth, 'The Organization of the Convict Trade to Maryland: Stevenson, Randolph and Cheston, 1768–1775', *William and Mary Quarterly*, 3rd Series, 42 (1985), 201–27.

'Shipping Patterns and the Atlantic Trade of Bristol, 1749–1770', *William and Mary Quarterly*, 3rd Series, 46 (1989), 506–38.

'The Organization of the Colonial American Rice Trade' (Paper presented to the Organization of American Historians' Conference, Washington, DC, 1990).

'Bristol and the Atlantic Trade in the Eighteenth Century', *English Historical Review*, 107 (1992), 626–50.

'Convict Transportation from Devon to America', in H. E. S. Fisher, Basil Greenhill and Joyce Youings, eds., *A New Maritime History of Devon*, vol. I (1993), pp. 121–2.

'Bristol West India Merchants in the Eighteenth Century', *Transactions of the Royal Historical Society*, 6th series, 3 (1993).

'Atlantic Trade and British Economic Growth in the Eighteenth Century' in Peter Mathias and J. A. Davis, eds., *International Trade and British Economic Growth from the Eighteenth Century to the Present Day* (Oxford, 1994).

'The Bright Family Papers', *Archives* (forthcoming).

Mui, Hoh-Cheung and Mui, Lorna H., *Shops and Shopkeeping in Eighteenth-Century England* (London, 1989).

Nash, Gary B., 'The Early Merchants of Philadelphia: The Formation and Disintegration of a Founding Elite' in Richard S. Dunn and Mary Maples Dunn, eds., *The World of William Penn* (Philadelphia, 1986), pp. 337–62.

Nash, Robert C., 'The English and Scottish Tobacco Trades in the Seventeenth and Eighteenth Centuries: Legal and Illegal Trade', *Economic History Review*, 2nd Series, 35 (1982), 354–72.

'Irish Atlantic Trade in the Seventeenth and Eighteenth Centuries', *William and Mary Quarterly*, 3rd Series, 42 (1985), 329–56.

North, Douglass C., 'Sources of Productivity Change in Ocean Shipping, 1600–1850', *Journal of Political Economy*, 76 (1968), 953–70, reprinted in Robert W. Fogel and Stanley L. Engerman, eds., *The Reinterpretation of American Economic History* (New York, 1971), pp. 163–74.

O'Brien, Patrick, 'European Economic Development: The Contribution of the Periphery', *Economic History Review*, 2nd Series, 35 (1982), 1–18.

O'Brien, P. K. and Engerman, S. L., 'Exports and the Growth of the British Economy from the Glorious Revolution to the Peace of Amiens' in Barbara L. Solow, ed., *Slavery and the Rise of the Atlantic System* (Cambridge, 1991), pp. 177–209.

Ormrod, David, 'English Re-Exports and the Dutch Staple Market in the Eighteenth Century' in D. C. Coleman and Peter Mathias, eds., *Enterprise and History: Essays in Honour of Charles Wilson* (Cambridge, 1984), pp. 89–115.

Palmer, Colin A., *Human Cargoes: The British Slave Trade to Spanish America, 1700–1739* (Urbana, IL, 1981).

Pares, Richard, *War and Trade in the West Indies, 1739–1763* (Oxford, 1936).

A West-India Fortune (London, 1950).

'The London Sugar Market, 1740–1769', *Economic History Review*, 2nd Series, 9 (1956–7), 254–70.

Merchants and Planters, Economic History Review, supplement no. 4 (Cambridge, 1960).

Parkinson, C. Northcote, *The Rise of the Port of Liverpool* (Liverpool, 1952).

Parry, J. H., 'Transport and Trade Routes' in E. E. Rich and C. H. Wilson, eds., *The Cambridge Economic History of Europe, IV: The Economy of Expanding Europe in the Sixteenth and Seventeenth Centuries* (Cambridge, 1967), pp. 155–219.

Trade and Dominion: The European Oversea Empires in the Eighteenth Century (London, 1971).

Picton, J. A., *Memorials of Liverpool, Historical and Topographical*, 2 vols. (London, 1875).

Pitman, Frank Wesley, *The Development of the British West Indies, 1700–1763* (New Haven, CT, 1917).

Pountney, W. J., *Old Bristol Potteries* (Bristol, 1920).

Powell, A. C., 'Glassmaking in Bristol', *Transactions of the Bristol and Gloucestershire Archaeological Society*, 47 (1925), 211–57.

Powell, J. W. Damer, *Bristol Privateers and Ships of War* (Bristol, 1930).

Press, Jonathan, *The Merchant Seamen of Bristol, 1747–1789* (Bristol Branch of the Historical Association, pamphlet no. 38, 1976).

'The Collapse of a Contributory Pension Scheme: The Merchant Seamen's Fund, 1747–1851', *Journal of Transport History*, New Series, 5 (1979), 91–104.

Pressnell, L. S., *Country Banking in the Industrial Revolution* (Oxford, 1956).

Price, Jacob M., 'The Rise of Glasgow in the Chesapeake Tobacco Trade, 1707–1775', *William and Mary Quarterly*, 3rd Series, 11 (1954), 179–99.

'The Economic Growth of the Chesapeake and the European Market, 1697–1775', *Journal of Economic History*, 24 (1964), 496–511.

France and the Chesapeake: A History of the French Tobacco Monopoly, 1674–1791, and of its Relationship to the British and American Tobacco Trades, 2 vols. (Ann Arbor, MI, 1973).

'Economic Function and the Growth of American Port Towns in the Eighteenth Century', *Perspectives in American History*, 8 (1974), 123–86.

'A Note on the Value of Colonial Exports of Shipping', *Journal of Economic History*, 36 (1976), 704–24.

'One Family's Empire: The Russell-Lee-Clerk Connection in Maryland, Britain and India, 1707–1857', *Maryland Historical Magazine*, 72 (1977), 165–225.

'Colonial Trade and British Economic Development, 1660–1775' in *La Révolution Américaine et l'Europe*, Colloques internationaux du Centre Nationale de la Recherche Scientifique, no. 577 (Paris, 1979), pp. 221–42.

Capital and Credit in British Overseas Trade: The View from the Chesapeake, 1700–1776 (Cambridge, MA, 1980).

'Buchanan & Simson, 1759–1763: A Different Kind of Glasgow Firm trading to the Chesapeake', *William and Mary Quarterly*, 3rd Series, 40 (1983), 3–41.

'Glasgow, the Tobacco Trade, and the Scottish Customs, 1707–1730', *Scottish Historical Review*, 63 (1984), 1–36.

'The Transatlantic Economy' in Jack P. Greene and J. R. Pole, eds., *Colonial British America: Essays in the New History of the Early Modern Era* (Baltimore, 1984), pp. 18–42.

'The Last Phase of the Virginia–London Consignment Trade: James Buchanan & Co., 1758–1768', *William and Mary Quarterly*, 3rd Series, 43 (1986), 64–98.

'Sheffield v. Starke: Institutional Experimentation in the London–Maryland Trade *c*. 1696–1706', *Business History*, 28 (1986), 19–39.

'What Did Merchants Do? Reflections on British Overseas Trade, 1660–1790', *Journal of Economic History*, 49 (1989), 267–84.

'Who Cared about the Colonies? The Impact of the Thirteen Colonies on British Society and Politics, *circa* 1714–1775' in Bernard Bailyn and Philip D. Morgan, eds., *Strangers within the Realm: Cultural Margins of the First British Empire* (Chapel Hill, NC, 1991), pp. 395–436.

'Credit in the Slave Trade and Plantation Economies' in Barbara L. Solow, ed., *Slavery and the Rise of the Atlantic System* (Cambridge, 1991), pp. 293–339.

'Transaction Costs: A Note on Merchant Credit and the Organization of Private Trade' in James D. Tracy, ed., *The Political Economy of Merchant Empires* (Cambridge, 1991), pp. 276–97.

Price, Jacob M. and Clemens, Paul G. E., 'A Revolution of Scale in Overseas Trade: British Firms in the Chesapeake Trade, 1675–1775', *Journal of Economic History*, 47 (1987), 1–43.

Ragatz, Lowell Joseph, *Statistics for the Study of British Caribbean Economic History, 1763–1833* (London, 1927).

The Fall of the Planter Class in the British Caribbean, 1763–1833: A Study in Social and Economic History (New York and London, 1928).

Raistrick, Arthur, *Quakers in Science and Industry* (London, 1950).

Dynasty of Ironfounders: The Darbys and Coalbrookdale (London, 1953).

Ralph, Elizabeth, *Guide to the Archives of the Society of Merchant Venturers of Bristol* (Bristol, 1988).

Ramsay, G. D., *English Overseas Trade during the Centuries of Emergence: Studies in some Modern Origins of the English-Speaking World* (London, 1957).

Rawley, James A., *The Trans-Atlantic Slave Trade* (New York, 1981).

Rediker, Marcus, *Between the Devil and the Deep Blue Sea: Merchant Seamen, Pirates, and the Anglo-American Maritime World, 1700–1750* (Cambridge, 1987).

Rees, D. Gareth, 'Copper Sheathing: An Example of Technological Diffusion in the English Merchant Fleet', *Journal of Transport History*, New Series, 1 (1971/2), 85–94.

Richardson, David, 'The Slave Merchants of the Outports' (unpublished paper delivered at the Organization of American Historians' Conference, Chicago, 1973).

'Profitability in the Bristol–Liverpool Slave Trade' in *The Atlantic Slave Trade:*

New Approaches, Société Française d'Histoire d'Outre-Mer (1976), pp. 301–6.

'Profits in the Liverpool Slave Trade: the Accounts of William Davenport, 1757–1784' in Roger Anstey and P. E. H. Hair, eds., *Liverpool, the African Slave Trade, and Abolition* (Historic Society of Lancashire and Cheshire Occasional Series, 2, Liverpool, 1976), pp. 60–90.

'West African Consumption Patterns and their Influence on the Eighteenth-Century English Slave Trade' in Henry A. Gemery and Jan S. Hogendorn, eds., *The Uncommon Market: Essays on the Atlantic Slave Trade* (New York, 1979), pp. 303–30.

The Mediterranean Passes (E. P. Microform Ltd., Wakefield, 1983).

The Bristol Slave Traders: A Collective Portrait (Bristol Branch of the Historical Association, pamphlet no. 60, 1985).

'The Slave Trade, Sugar, and British Economic Growth, 1748–1776', *Journal of Interdisciplinary History*, 18 (1987), 739–69, reprinted in Barbara L. Solow and Stanley L. Engerman, eds., *British Capitalism and Caribbean Slavery: The Legacy of Eric Williams* (Cambridge, 1987), pp. 103–33.

'The Costs of Survival: the Transport of Slaves in the Middle Passage and the Profitability of the 18th Century British Slave Trade', *Explorations in Economic History*, 24 (1987), 178–96.

'The Eighteenth-Century British Slave Trade: Estimates of its Volume and Coastal Distribution in Africa', *Research in Economic History*, 12 (1989), 151–95.

'Slave Exports from West and West-Central Africa, 1700–1810: New Estimates of Volume and Distribution', *Journal of African History*, 30 (1989), 1–22.

'Prices of Slaves in West and West-Central Africa: Toward an Annual Series, 1698–1807', *Bulletin of Economic Research*, 43 (1991), 21–56.

'The British Slave Trade to Colonial South Carolina', *Slavery and Abolition*, 12 (1991), 125–72.

Rodger, N. A. M., 'Some Practical Problems Arising from the Study of the Receiver of Sixpences Ledgers', *The Mariner's Mirror*, 62 (1976), 223–4, 270.

Rogers, Nicholas, *Whigs and Cities: Popular Politics in the Age of Walpole and Pitt* (Oxford, 1989).

Rosenberg, Nathan, 'Factors affecting the Diffusion of Technology', *Explorations in Economic History*, 10 (1972), 3–33.

Rosenblatt, Samuel M., 'The Significance of Credit in the Tobacco Consignment Trade: A Study of John Norton & Sons, 1768–1775', *William and Mary Quarterly*, 3rd Series, 29 (1962), 383–99.

Rowlands, Marie B., *Masters and Men in the West Midland Metalware Trades before the Industrial Revolution* (Manchester, 1975).

Sacks, David Harris, *The Widening Gate: Bristol and the Atlantic Economy, 1450–1700* (Berkeley and Los Angeles, 1991).

Schumpeter, Elizabeth B., *English Overseas Trade Statistics, 1697–1808* (Oxford, 1960).

Scott, *Chronicles of Canongate* (1829).

Shammas, Carole, *The Pre-Industrial Consumer in England and America* (Oxford, 1990).

Shepherd, James F. and Walton, Gary M., *Shipping, Maritime Trade, and the Economic Development of Colonial North America* (Cambridge, 1972).

Sheridan, Richard B., 'The Molasses Act and the Market Strategy of the British Sugar Planters', *Journal of Economic History*, 17 (1957), 62–83.

'The Commercial and Financial Organisation of the British Slave Trade, 1750–1807', *Economic History Review*, 2nd Series, 11 (1958–9), 249–63.

'The British Credit Crisis of 1772 and the American Colonies', *Journal of Economic History*, 20 (1960), 161–86.

'The Wealth of Jamaica in the Eighteenth Century', *Economic History Review*, 2nd Series, 18 (1965), 292–311.

'The Wealth of Jamaica in the Eighteenth Century: A Rejoinder', *Economic History Review*, 2nd Series, 21 (1968), 46–61.

'Planters and Merchants: The Oliver Family of Antigua and London, 1716–1784', *Business History*, 13 (1971), 104–13.

Sugar and Slavery: An Economic History of the British West Indies, 1623–1775 (Baltimore and Barbados, 1974).

'The Crisis of Slave Subsistence in the British West Indies during and after the American Revolution', *William and Mary Quarterly*, 3rd Series, 33 (1976), 615–41.

Siebert, Wilbur H., 'The Colony of Massachusetts Loyalists at Bristol, England', *Proceedings of the Massachusetts Historical Society*, 45 (1912), 409–14.

Smith, Abbot Emerson, *Colonists in Bondage: White Servitude and Convict Labor in America, 1607–1776* (Chapel Hill, NC, 1947).

Soltow, James H., 'Scottish Traders in Virginia, 1750–1775', *Economic History Review*, 2nd Series, 12 (1959–60), 83–98.

Souden, David, '"Rogues, whores and vagabonds?" Indentured Servant Emigrants to North America, and the Case of Mid-Seventeenth Century Bristol', *Social History*, 3 (1978), 23–41.

Spinney, J. D., 'Misadventures of a Slaver', *Blackwood's Magazine*, no. 1629 (1951), 26–37.

Spooner, Frank C., *Risks at Sea: Amsterdam Insurance and Maritime Europe, 1766–1780* (Cambridge, 1983).

Starkey, David J., *British Privateering Enterprise in the Eighteenth Century* (Exeter, 1990).

Steele, Ian K., 'Moat Theories and the English Atlantic, 1675 to 1740', *Canadian Historical Association Papers* (1978), pp. 18–33.

The English Atlantic, 1675–1740: An Exploration of Communication and Community (Oxford, 1986).

Steensgaard, Niels, *The Asian Trade Revolution of the Seventeenth Century: The East India Companies and the Decline of the Caravan Trade* (Chicago, 1974).

Stein, Robert, *The French Slave Trade in the Eighteenth Century: An Old Regime Business* (Madison, WI, 1979).

'The French Sugar Business in the Eighteenth Century: A Quantitative Study', *Business History*, 22 (1980), 3–17.

Stern, Walter M., 'The London Sugar Refiners around 1800', *The Guildhall Miscellany*, 3 (1954), 25–36.

Supple, Barry, 'The Nature of Enterprise' in E. E. Rich and C. H. Wilson, eds.,

The Cambridge Economic History of Europe, V: The Economic Organisation of Early Modern Europe (Cambridge, 1977), pp. 393–461.

Taylor, E. G. R., *The Haven-Finding Art: A History of Navigation from Odysseus to Captain Cook* (London, 1956).

Thomas, R. P., 'The Sugar Colonies of the Old Empire: Profit or Loss for Great Britain?', *Economic History Review*, 2nd Series, 21 (1968), 30–45.

Thomas, R. P. and McCloskey, D. N., 'Overseas Trade and Empire, 1700–1860' in D. N. McCloskey and R. C. Floud, eds., *The Economic History of Britain since 1700, Vol. I. 1700–1860* (Cambridge, 1981), 87–102.

Thoms, D. W., 'The Mills Family: London Sugar Merchants of the Eighteenth Century', *Business History*, 11 (1969), 3–10.

Thomson, Robert Polk, 'The Tobacco Export of the Upper James River Naval District, 1773–75', *William and Mary Quarterly*, 3rd Series, 18 (1961), 393–401.

Trinder, Barrie, *The Industrial Revolution in Shropshire* (London and Chichester, 1973).

Truxes, Thomas M., *Irish-American Trade, 1660–1783* (Cambridge, 1988).

Tyler, John W., 'Foster Cunliffe and Sons: Liverpool Merchants in the Maryland Tobacco Trade, 1738–1765', *Maryland Historical Magazine*, 73 (1978), 246–77.

Underdown, P. T., 'Bristol and Burke' in Patrick McGrath, ed., *Bristol in the Eighteenth Century* (Newton Abbot, 1972), pp. 41–62.

Walker, F., 'The Port of Bristol', *Economic Geography*, 15 (1939), 109–24.

Walker, Iain C., *The Bristol Clay Tobacco-Pipe Industry* (Bristol, 1971).
  Clay Tobacco-Pipes, with particular reference to the Bristol Industry, 4 vols. (Ottawa, 1977).

Wallerstein, Immanuel, *The Modern World System, Vol. II: Mercantilism and the Consolidation of the European World-Economy, 1600–1750* (New York, 1980).

Walton, Gary M., 'Sources of Productivity Change in American Colonial Shipping 1675–1775', *Economic History Review*, 2nd Series, 20 (1967), 67–78.
  'A Measure of Productivity Change in American Colonial Shipping', *Economic History Review*, 2nd Series, 11 (1968), 268–82.
  'New Evidence on Colonial Commerce', *Journal of Economic History*, 28 (1968), 363–89.
  'Trade Routes, Ownership Proportions and American Colonial Shipping Characteristics' in *Les Routes de l'Atlantique*, Travaux de Neuvième Colloque International d'Histoire Maritime, Seville, 1967 (Paris, 1969), pp. 471–505.
  'Obstacles to Technical Diffusion in Ocean Shipping 1675–1775', *Explorations in Economic History*, 8 (1970–1), 124–40.

Ward, J. R., *The Finance of Canal Building in Eighteenth-Century England* (Oxford, 1974).
  'Speculative Building at Bristol and Clifton, 1783–1793', *Business History*, 20 (1978), 3–18.
  'The Profitability of Sugar Planting in the British West Indies, 1650–1834', *Economic History Review*, 2nd Series, 31 (1978), 197–213.

Weare, G. E., *Edmund Burke's Connection with Bristol, from 1774 till 1780: With a Prefatory Memoir of Burke* (Bristol, 1894).

Weinstock, Maureen, *More Dorset Studies* (Dorchester, 1960).

Westbury, Susan, 'Slaves of Colonial Virginia: Where they came from', *William and Mary Quarterly*, 3rd Series, 42 (1985), 228–37.

White, Philip L., *The Beekmans of New York in Politics and Commerce, 1647–1870* (New York, 1956).

Wiles, R. M., *Freshest Advices: Early Provincial Newspapers in England* (Columbus, OH, 1965).

Willan, T. S., 'The River Navigation and Trade of the Severn Valley, 1600–1750', *Economic History Review*, 8 (1937–8), 68–79.

   The English Coasting Trade, 1600–1750 (Manchester, 1938).

   An Eighteenth Century Shopkeeper: Abraham Dent of Kirkby Stephen (Manchester, 1970).

Williams, Alan F., 'Bristol Port Plans and Improvement Schemes of the Eighteenth Century', *Transactions of the Bristol and Gloucestershire Archaeological Society*, 81 (1962), 138–88.

   'Bristol and C. M. MacInnes: The Canadian Dean of Gateway of Empire', *British Journal of Canadian Studies*, 1 (1986), 303–17.

Williams, David M., 'The Shipping of the North Atlantic Cotton Trade in the Mid-Nineteenth Century' in David Alexander and Rosemary Ommer, eds., *Volumes not Values: Canadian Sailing Ships and World Trades* (St John's, Newfoundland, 1979), pp. 305–29.

Williams, Eric, *Capitalism and Slavery* (Washington, DC, 1944).

Williams, J. E., 'Whitehaven in the Eighteenth Century', *Economic History Review*, 2nd Series, 7 (1956), 393–404.

Williams, L. J., 'A Carmarthenshire Ironmaster and the Seven Years' War,' *Business History*, 2 (1959), 32–43.

Wilson, R. G., 'The Supremacy of the Yorkshire Cloth Industry in the Eighteenth Century' in N. B. Harte and K. G. Ponting, eds., *Textile History and Economic History: Essays in Honour of Miss Julia de Lacy Mann* (Manchester, 1973), pp. 225–46.

Witt, Cleo, Weeden, Cyril, and Schwind, Arlene Palmer, *Bristol Glass* (Bristol, 1984).

Woodward, Donald, 'Sources for Maritime History (III): The Port Books of England and Wales', *Maritime History*, 3 (1973), 147–65.

E   UNPUBLISHED THESES

Baigent, Elizabeth, 'Bristol Society in the Later Eighteenth Century with Special Reference to the Handling by Computer of Fragmentary Historical Sources' (Oxford University D.Phil. thesis, 1985).

Barry, Jonathan, 'The Cultural Life of Bristol, 1640–1775' (University of Oxford D.Phil. thesis, 1985).

Bergstrom, Peter V., 'Markets and Merchants: Economic Diversification in Colonial Virginia, 1700–1775' (University of New Hampshire Ph.D. dissertation, 1980).

Bigelow, Bruce M., 'The Commerce of Rhode Island with the West Indies before the American Revolution' (Brown University Ph.D. dissertation, 1930).

Bradley, Lawrence, J. 'The London/Bristol Trade Rivalry: Conventional History and the Colonial Office 5 Records for the Port of New York' (Notre Dame University Ph.D. dissertation, 1971).

Butler, Stuart M., 'The Glasgow Tobacco Merchants and the American Revolution, 1770–1800' (University of St Andrews Ph.D. thesis, 1978).

Clemens, Paul G. E., 'From Tobacco to Grain: Economic Development on Maryland's Eastern Shore, 1660–1750' (University of Wisconsin Ph.D. dissertation, 1974).

Cooper, Elaine G., 'Aspects of British Shipping and Maritime Trade in the Atlantic, 1775–1783' (University of Exeter MA thesis, 1975).

Crowhurst, R. P., 'British Oceanic Convoys in the Seven Years' War, 1756–1763' (University of London Ph.D. thesis, 1970).

Davies, G. J., 'England and Newfoundland: Policy and Trade, 1660–1783' (University of Southampton Ph.D. thesis, 1980).

Devine, T. M., 'Glasgow Merchants in Colonial Trade, 1770–1815' (University of Strathclyde Ph.D. thesis, 1971).

Dickson, David, 'An Economic History of the Cork Region in the Eighteenth Century' (University of Dublin Ph.D. thesis, 1977).

Dructor, Robert M., 'The New York Commercial Community: The Revolutionary Experience' (University of Pittsburgh Ph.D. dissertation, 1975).

Eaglesham, Annie, 'The Growth and Influence of the West Cumberland Shipping Industry, 1660–1800' (University of Lancaster Ph.D. thesis, 1977).

French, Christopher J., 'The Role of London in the Atlantic Slave Trade, 1680–1776' (University of Exeter MA thesis, 1970).

'The Trade and Shipping of the Port of London, 1700–1776' (University of Exeter Ph.D. thesis, 1980).

Hall, I. V., 'A History of the Sugar Trade in England with Special Attention to the Sugar Trade of Bristol' (University of Bristol MA thesis, 1925).

Handcock, W. Gordon, 'An Historical Geography of the Origins of English Settlement in Newfoundland: A Study of the Migration Process' (University of Birmingham Ph.D. thesis, 1979).

Hemphill, John M.,* 'Virginia and the English Commercial System, 1689–1733: Studies in the Development and Fluctuations of Colonial Economy under Imperial Control' (Princeton University Ph.D. dissertation, 1964).

Hillier, Susan E., 'The Trade of the Virginia Colony, 1606 to 1660' (University of Liverpool Ph.D. thesis, 1971).

Jones, D. K., 'The Elbridge, Woolnough and Smyth Families of Bristol, in the Eighteenth Century, with special reference to the Spring Plantation, Jamaica' (University of Bristol M.Litt. thesis, 1972).

Jones, D. W., 'London Overseas Merchant Groups at the End of the Seventeenth Century and the Moves against the East India Company' (University of Oxford D.Phil. thesis, 1970).

Klopfer, Helen L., 'Statistics of the Foreign Trade of Philadelphia, 1700–1860' (University of Pennsylvania Ph.D. dissertation, 1936).

Larsen, Grace H., 'Profile of a Colonial Merchant: Thomas Clifford of Pre-

Revolutionary Philadelphia' (Columbia University Ph.D. dissertation, 1955).

McCusker, John J.,* 'The Rum Trade and the Balance of Payments of the Thirteen Continental Colonies, 1650–1775' (University of Pittsburgh Ph.D. dissertation, 1970).

Matthews, Keith, 'A History of the West of England-Newfoundland Fishery' (University of Oxford D.Phil. thesis, 1968).

Merrett, Colin, 'The Trades between Bristol and Northern Europe, 1770–1780' (University of Exeter MA thesis, 1974).

Morgan, Kenneth, 'Bristol Merchants and the Colonial Trades, 1748–1783' (University of Oxford D.Phil. thesis, 1984).

Nash, Robert C., 'English Transatlantic Trade, 1660–1730: A Quantitative Study' (University of Cambridge Ph.D. thesis, 1982).

Pickering, Joanne, 'The Bristol–American Export Trade, 1773–1775' (University of Exeter MA thesis, 1983).

Pope, D. J., 'Shipping and Trade in the Port of Liverpool, 1783–1793' (University of Liverpool Ph.D. thesis, 1970).

Price, Jacob M., 'The Tobacco Trade and the Treasury, 1685–1733: British Mercantilism in its Fiscal Aspects' (Harvard University Ph.D. dissertation, 1954).

Pugsley, Alfred J., 'Some Contributions towards the Study of the Economic Development of Bristol in the Eighteenth and Nineteenth Centuries' (University of Bristol MA thesis, 1921).

Quilici, Ronald H., 'Turmoil in a City and an Empire: Bristol's Factions, 1700–1775' (University of New Hampshire Ph.D. dissertation, 1976).

Rees, D. Gareth, 'The Role of Bristol in the Atlantic Slave Trade, 1710–1769' (University of Exeter MA thesis, 1970).

Richards, A. M., 'The Connection of Bristol with the African Slave Trade, with some account of the currents of public opinion in the city' (University of Bristol MA thesis, 1923).

Richardson, David, 'The Bristol Slave Trade in the Eighteenth Century' (University of Manchester MA thesis, 1969).

Sacks, David H.,* 'Trade, Society and Politics in Bristol Circa 1500–Circa 1640' (Harvard University Ph.D. dissertation, 1977).

Savadge, W. R., 'The West Country and the American Mainland Colonies, 1763–1783, with Special Reference to the Merchants of Bristol' (University of Oxford B.Litt. thesis, 1952).

Sheridan, Richard B., 'The Sugar Trade of the British West Indies from 1660 to 1756 with Special Reference to the Island of Antigua' (University of London Ph.D. thesis, 1951).

Thoms, D. W., 'West India Merchants and Planters in the Mid-Eighteenth Century, with Special Reference to St. Kitts' (University of Kent MA thesis, 1967).

Thomson, Robert Polk, 'The Merchant in Virginia, 1700–1775' (University of Wisconsin Ph.D. dissertation, 1955).

Tyack, N. C. P., 'The Trade Relations of Bristol with Virginia during the Seventeenth Century' (University of Bristol MA thesis, 1930).

Underdown, Peter T., 'The Parliamentary History of the City of Bristol, 1750–1790' (University of Bristol M A thesis, 1948).

* Published as a book by Garland Press.

Index

Abercarn, 102
Acapulco, 15
Adams, John, 10
Admiralty, 21, 206
Admiralty Court, 38
Africa, 12, 127; exports to, 28, 144–5,
  150; forts and castles in, 135; value of
  Bristol's trade with, 131; and shipping
  routes, 69, 72–3, 76–7; size of ships
  trading to, 44; slave ships to, 50–1,
  141–2; and the slave trade, 131–6,
  140–2, 144, 149–50; supply of slaves
  in, 135, 142, 148; tobacco re-exports
  to, 181; see also African coast
African coast, 19, 130, 134–6, 140, 142,
  148, 150, 228
agents, in Barbados, 139, 198; in Britain,
  105–6, 109; in the Chesapeake, 165–6,
  168, 170, 173; colonial, 53, 70–1, 74–5,
  81, 223; in Jamaica, 148, 218; in
  Philadelphia, 78; in the slave trade,
  142–4; in the sugar trade, 195, 198–9,
  215–16
ale, 98
alehouse, 152
Alicante, 71
Allason, William, 82
America, 13, 16–18, 23, 25–6, 28, 34, 38,
  41–2, 56, 59–60, 80, 93, 97–8, 104,
  112, 116, 118, 124, 133, 138, 140, 143,
  147, 152, 154, 181, 217, 220, 224
American colonies, 59, 78, 113
American Revolution, 10–11, 25, 40, 42,
  57, 146, 148, 152, 166, 168, 184, 189;
  and Bristol privateering, 38; and the
  Bristol slave trade, 140–1; and the
  Bristol sugar trade, 187–9, 201–14;
  and the Bristol tobacco trade, 154;
  and Bristol's transatlantic trade, 25–7
Amsterdam, 10, 12, 25, 181
Anatto Bay, Jamaica, 202
anchorages, 29

anchorsmiths, 40
Anderson, John, 144
Anglican, 150
Angola, 9, 130, 144, 147
Anguilla, xvii
Annamaboe, 142
Annapolis, 170–1
Annual List of Shipping, 225–6
Antigua, xvi, 12, 24, 74–5, 120, 138, 140,
  190, 196–7, 206
anvils, 95
Apthorp, Stephen, 75, 110, 112
artisans, 95, 219
Asiento, 139
Atkins, Michael, 81, 185–6, 189, 194
Atlantic, 1–7, 13, 18, 22–3, 33–4, 38, 41,
  67, 74–5, 107, 119, 123–4, 127, 133,
  152, 199, 201, 219, 223–4; community
  of traders in, 9; exports in, 90, 95,
  103–4; shipping routes in, 11, 20, 25,
  55–8, 67, 84, 88, 141; weather in, 67,
  136; see also individual colonies, states
  and islands
Austin & Laurens, 70, 74–5
Australia, 5
Avon Gorge, 29
Avonmouth, 32

Bagg, Stephen, 95
Bahamas, xvii
Baillie, Evan, 194
Baillie & Sons, Evan, 194
Baillie family, 189
baizes, 107
ballast, 70–1, 78, 98
Baltic, 13, 15, 17
Baltimore, 12, 115, 170–1
banking in Bristol, 2, 160, 186
bankruptcies, 21, 29, 113
bankrupts, 70, 97
bar, 135

Barbados, xvi, 10, 12, 24, 95, 123; and Bristol ships, 38; Bristol slave trade, 138–9; and the Bristol sugar trade, 190–1, 197–8, 206, 206–7; indentured servants to, 125; and shipping routes, 59, 63, 71, 75, 77
Barbary pirates, 228
Barcelona, 12, 71, 79
bar iron, 104
Barnards & Harrison, 117
Barnstaple, 34, 103
Bath, 98–9
Baynton, Wharton & Morgan, 79
Bay of Honduras, 24, 117
beads, 133, 145
beans, 120
beaver hats, 89
Becher, John, 195
Becher, Michael, 194
Becher family, 189
beef, 123
Beekman, James, 122
beer, 95, 98, 99
Belle Isle, xvi
Bence & Lock, 95
Benin, 130, 147
Berkeley, Glos., 157
Bermuda, 12
Bewdley, Worcs., 100
Bideford, 34, 153
Bight of Biafra, 138
bills of exchange: in the export trade, 108, 110, 117; in the slave trade, 139, 146–8; in the sugar trade, 193, 204; in the tobacco trade, 166, 174–5
bills of lading, 199
Birmingham, 97, 101, 104–5, 109, 121
Birmingham goods, 101
Black Country, 121
Blagden, John, 167
blankets, 104
Board of Ordnance, 141
Bobbins, 106
Bonbonous, James, 195
bonds, 162
Bonny, 74, 130, 138, 147
Book of Rates, 91
Booth, Champion & Co., 95
borrowing on bond, 162
Boston, 10, 12, 113, 122; exports to, 91, 95–6, 102, 105, 116–17; and non-importation, 93, 122; and shipping routes, 63, 65, 70–1, 78
bottles, 98
boxes, 109
Braikenridge, George, 161

brass, 97, 119, 145
bread, 26
Bremen, 181
breweries, 97
brewers, 204
bricks, 97
Bright, Francis, 71, 145, 148, 186
Bright, Henry, 37, 145–6, 148, 185–6, 194
Bright & Co., Henry, 142
Bright, Lowbridge, 79, 115, 145, 148
Bright, Richard, 121
Bright, Lowbridge & Richard, 37, 191, 193–4, 197
Bright family, 145–8, 189, 198
Bright, Baillie & Bright, 191, 197
Bright, Milward & Duncomb, 37
Brigs, 41, 75
Bristol: banks at, 186; business records at, 5; clergy at, 9; coasting trade, 99; coffee houses at, 7, 67; commerce of before 1700, 1, 219; and competition with Liverpool, 18, 20–2, 26–8, 31–2, 106–7, 132–3, 140–1, 143–5, 151, 153–5, 188, 209, 220–1; and competition with London, 120, 210–12; custom house at, 7; customs records of, 5; customs receipts at, 21, 23, 27–8; economic crisis at, 29; exchange at, 7, 67; fairs at, 100–1; and its hinterland, 4, 99; industries at, 97–9, 219, 223–4; and internal communications, 99–100; and the ironworks, 102–3; major Atlantic markets of, 12; market for commodities at, 117, 175–81, 188, 203–17; merchant community at, 2, 21, 23, 26, 102, 164; 'metropolis of the West', 3, 99; newspapers at, 67; politics at, 23, 25; poor in area of, 184; port development at, 29–33; port installations and trades at, 8; quays at, 7–8, 31, 33; relative decline as a port, 3–4, 11, 140–52, 220, 222; shipping at, 38, 40–5; shipping records at, 225–7, 229–30; shipowning at, 15, 34–8, 75; size of, 3–4, 219; South Wales, 102–3, 220; streets at, 9; Tolzey at, 7; trade with Ireland, 123–4; and tradesmen at, 93, 95–6, 101–2; value of exports from, 91; wealth of, 131–2; and the West Midlands, 104–5; and see also Africa; American Revolution; capital; Chesapeake; convict trade; Credit; Europe; Exports; indentured servant

trade; Ireland; Jamaica; New
England; Newfoundland; New York;
Philadelphia; privateering; St Kitts;
Seven Years War; shipping routes;
slave trade; Society of Merchant
Venturers; sugar refineries; sugar
trade; West Indies.
Bristol, topography of: Blackboy Hill,
128; Brandon Hill, 151; Clifton, 2,
177; Dean's Marsh, 40; Frenchay, 177;
Merchants' Hall, King Street, 7;
Redcliffe Backs, 40; St Augustine's
parish, 40; St James's parish, 22; St
Philip's parish, 106; St Vincent's
Rock, 29; Seven Stars pub, 128;
Wapping, 40
Bristol Brass Wire Company, 97
Bristol Channel, 19, 29, 32, 99
Bristol City Council, 31
Bristol Corporation, 7, 226
Bristol Directory (1791), 100
Bristol Exchange, 7, 67, 82, 216
Bristol Presentments, 91, 93, 97, 231
Bristol West India Associations, 187
British Isles, 34, 127
Britain, 59, 66, 80, 83, 88, 90, 116, 120,
139, 152, 154, 166, 185, 201, 206, 209
British America, xvi, 13, 16–17, 21–2,
25, 66–7, 227, 230
buckles, 109
Buenos Aires, 139
Bullin, James, 101
Burke, Edmund, 25
Bush & Elton, 37, 99, 148
butter, 123
button and 'toy' maker, 105
buttons, 105, 109

Cadiz, 12, 62, 71, 79
Calabar, 130, 138–9, 147
callicoes, 106
callimancoes, 103, 106
camblets, 103
Cameroons, 144
Canada, xvi, 13–14, 35, 39–40, 42–5, 59,
60, 93–4
canals, 4, 107, 121–2
Canary Islands, 12
Cape Fear, North Carolina, 59
Cape Hampton, Virginia, 59
Cape Verde islands, xvii, 9, 12
capital: at Bristol, 219, 223; in Bristol
sugar refineries, 216; in Bristol's
industries, 97; in the export trade,
112, 114–15; in the tobacco trade, 161,
163, 173, 178

capital investment, 31, 102, 131
captains, 225; in the slave trade, 128,
134, 138–9, 143; in the sugar trade,
82–4, 198, 200–3, 206, 222; in the
tobacco trade, 82–4, 174
Cardiff, 102
'cargo' trade, 82, 167
Caribbean, *see* West Indies
Carolinas, 13, 16, 36, 75, 95–6
carpeting, 105
carriers, 120
Cartagena, 62, 139
cash, 109, 112, 115, 146, 166, 170, 174,
176
cash purchases, 111
ceramics, 97
Chamberlayne, Edward Pye, 198
Chamberlayne, Thomas, 161
Champion, Richard, 25, 41, 181, 197
Champion, William, 97
Champion's wet dock, 31
chandlers, 97
Charleston, 12, 25, 59, 62–3, 70–1, 74–5,
138–9
chartered ships, 125
Chesapeake, 1, 5, 36, 171; Bristol
investment in, 159–60, 189; Bristol
shipping engaged with, 13, 25, 42;
exports to, 93, 96; convicts in, 126–7;
debts in, 114, 163–4; and shipping
routes, 59; stores in, 110, 168; and the
tobacco trade, 15, 36, 80, 82–3, 152–3,
162–9, 176; *see also* Maryland;
Virginia
Chesapeake Bay, 82, 169, 171
Cheston, James, 115, 168, 182–3
Child, Samuel, 95
chintz, 106, 134
Chippenham, 104
chocolate, 97, 184, 223
chronometer, 67
cider, 95, 98–9
Clark, John, 99
Clarkson, Thomas, 128, 151
Claxton, Robert, 185
clayed sugar, 208–9
clay tobacco pipes, 97, 181
Clifford & Co., Thomas, 111
clothiers, 103–4
cloths, 118
Clutsam, William, 81
Coalbrookdale, 102–3
coalfields, 85
coarse manufacturers, 91
coasting trade, 99
cocoa, 223

cod, 13, 78
cod trade, 56
coffee, 2, 152, 184
coffee houses, 7, 23, 67
Coghlan, Peach & Co., 99
Coleridge, Samuel Taylor, 150
Collett, John, 142
coloured plains, 108
Colston, Edward, 128
commissions, 18, 106, 108, 123, 150, 165, 174, 179
commission system, 83, 193, 195–6, 214, 216–17
Company of Merchants trading to Africa, 131
compasses, 67
concentration in trade, 158
Connecticut, xvi
consignment system, 82, 165–8, 173
consumer revolution, 90
Controller of Customs, 225
convicts, 11, 124–7
convoys, 20, 62–3, 124, 202–3, 206
Cooper, Elaine G., 57
copper, 97–8, 102–3, 120, 135
copper sheathing, 47
copper smelting, 97
copperware, 40
cordage, 89
Cork, 12, 34, 74, 123–4, 202, 206
corn mills, 178
Cornwall, 99, 179
Corsaires, 20
cotton, 89, 90, 102, 105–8, 123
cotton and linen checks, 107
cotton mills, 107
Coventry, 105–6
Cowles, William, 102
Cowper, Lancelot, 96, 98, 118
cranes, 31
crapes, 106
credit, 26, 108, 219; in the export trade, 80, 109–16, 118; over-extension of, 4, 112–13; in the slave trade, 143, 147, 149; in the sugar trade, 193, 215; in the tobacco trade, 159–60, 162–5, 176
credit crises, 113
crews, 47–9, 84
crown glass, 98
Cruger, Jr, Henry, 70, 75, 78, 113, 120, 209
Cruger & Mallard, 96, 98
Cuba, 12, 24, 83
Curaçao, 9, 117
Currency Act (1764), 164
Curtis, John, 71, 185–6, 194–5

customer, 227
customs, 157, 178, 193
customs districts, 227
Customs House Tonnage Books, Philadelphia, 230–1
customs officers, 7
cutlery, 119
Cuyler, Philip, 111, 119
Cyprus gauze, 106

Daltera, James, 181
Daltera family, 183
Dampier, Henry, 144
Daniel, Thomas, 197
Daniel & Sons, Thomas, 194
Darby, Abraham I, 102
Dartmouth, 34
Davis, Mark, 37, 185, 191, 194–5, 197, 211, 214
Davis & Co., Mark, 191, 195, 197
Davis family, 189
Davis & Protheroe, 191, 193, 195, 197, 211, 214–16
Day, James, 144
Deane, Thomas, 144, 195
debts, 26, 80; in the export trade, 112–16; mortgage and plantation debts, 146; in the slave trade, 143, 147, 179; in the tobacco trade, 163–4
Deerskins, 11, 66
Dehany, David, 194
Delpratt, Samuel, 191, 194, 197
Devizes, 104
Devon, 34, 99, 104, 179, 217
Devonsheir & Co., 194
Devonsheir & Reeve, 74, 111, 114, 117, 186, 203, 208–9
Devonsheir, Reeve & Co., 195
Devonsheir, Reeve & Lloyd, 78, 111, 119
directories, 220
direct purchase system, *see* sugar trade; tobacco trade
discounts, 108–9, 111–12, 162–3, 176
distillers, 207
distilleries, 185
docks, 31–2, 220
Dolben's Act (1788), 149
Dominica, xvii, 12, 23–4, 140, 190, 197
Dorset, 34, 217
double bays, 103
Dowlais, 102
drawbacks, 179
drawboys, 106
druggets, 107
druggists, 93

dry goods, 89, 112
Dublin, 12, 34, 217
Dudley, 104
duffel blankets, 108
duffils, 103
Dunkirk, 181
Dunster, 104
duroys, 103
duties, in the sugar trade, 193, 207, 215, 221; in the tobacco trade, 162, 178–80
dyers, 122
dyestuffs, 2
dyewood, 117

earthenware, 89, 97, 118
East India Company, 45
East Indian textiles, 134, 144
Eaton, Peter, 196
economic crisis (1793), 29
Elton, Isaac, 196
English Channel, 11, 19, 141
Europe, 2, 5, 20, 35; Bristol's trade with, 13, 15, 17–18, 50–1, 55, 78, 221; and shipping routes, 55, 59, 64–6, 68, 72; and the sugar trade, 185, 217; and the tobacco trade, 153–4, 169, 181–2; see also by countries
European demand, 59, 80
European goods, 166
European ports, 58
everlastings, 103
exchange rates, 164
Exchequer, 227
excise, 23, 179–80
Exeter, 99, 104, 219
exports, 4, 23, 26; and Bristol manufactures, 97–9; and Bristol tradesmen, 93, 95, 101, 106; at Bristol fairs, 100; finance of, 108–15; from England, 2, 89–94; from Liverpool, 28, 107; and glut of, 118; price competition of, 119–20; supply of, 96–107, 115–16, 120–3; seasonal rhythm of, 118–19; value of Bristol's exports, 91

Fairs, 100–1, 212
Fall goods, 81, 118
Farell, Joseph, 36, 162, 180
Farell family, 159
Farell & Jones, 81, 91, 96, 159, 162, 164, 167–8, 181–2
Farr, Richard, 37, 123, 144, 195
Farr family, 25
fearnoughts, 103
Felix Farley's Bristol Journal, 66

Fernando Po, 130
fine manufactures, 91
fish, 66, 78
Fisher, Paul, 162
Fisher, Baker & Griffin, 162
fisheries, 1, 26
flannels, 89
fleet, 204, 211–12, 214
flint glass, 98
Floating Harbour, Bristol, 32, 220
Florida, xvi
Florida Channel, 83
foodstuffs, 66, 89
Foord & Delpratt, 200
fore-and-aft sails, 46
forks, 101, 106
Fowler, John, 144
Fowler & Co., John, 191, 197
Fownes, George, 95
France, 28, 90, 107, 181–2
Frank, Thomas, 110, 115
frauds, 157
Freeman, John and Copper Company, 95, 97–8
Freeman, William, 104, 114
Freeman & Oseland, 118
free ports, 23
freight earnings, 85
freight rates, 27, 46, 201, 222
French, Christopher J., 57
French privateers, 20–1
French prizes, 20
French slave trade, 142
Fry, Fripp & Co., 95
furniture, 119
fustians, 103, 122

Gabon, 144
Gandy, Harry, 150
Garlick, Edward, 102
Germany, 107, 181–2
Georgia, xvi
Getley, James, 102
Gibbs, George, 38
Gibraltar, 62
ginger, 11, 139
Glasgow, 12, 16, 34, 91, 132; economic development of, 2, 3; exports from 106; and the tobacco trade, 3, 20, 153–4, 158–9, 166, 169–70, 181, 221, 223; port development at, 32, 220; ships entering, 17; and the sugar trade, 159, 188, 190, 195
glass, 28, 97
glasshouses, 98
glass manufacture, 219

glassware, 89, 98–9, 109, 118
glass warehouses, 93, 98
globes, 66
Gloucester, 99
Gloucestershire, 157, 217
Glover, Joseph, 181
Goldney, Thomas, 103
Goldney family, 103
Gordon, Jr, John, 195
Gordon, Sr, John, 194
Gordon, Robert, 37, 186, 189, 191, 194, 197
Gordon, William, 142, 185–6, 195
Gordon, W. & J., 194
Gordon family, 189
Government securities, 213
Grain, 25
grand larceny, 126
Gravenor, Edward and William, 105
Green Island, 22
Greenock, 17, 155, 190
Grenada, xvii, 12, 24, 74, 95, 140, 186, 190–1, 206, 208
Griffiths, Thomas, 26, 36
grist mills, 178
grog, 185
Guadeloupe, xvii, 75, 198
guarantors, 147–9
Guarda costas, 16
Guinea, 128–9, 132, 134, 136, 134–4, 148, 150
gunmakers, 150
gunpowder, 132, 141, 145
guns, 84, 103, 109, 132–3, 145

Haberdashers, 101
half says, 107
Halifax, Nova Scotia, 12, 106
Hall, J., 95
Halliday, John and William, 75
Hamburg, 181, 213
Hamilton, David, 186, 191, 195, 197
Hancock, John, 78, 113
Hancock, Thomas, 111
handkerchiefs, 107
Hanover County, Virginia, 83, 170, 173
Harbour Grace, Newfoundland, 9
hardware, 11, 28, 89, 101, 105, 109, 121
Hare, Richard, 124
Hare, William, 144, 194
Hare & Co., William, 194
Harford, Jr, Edward, 83, 96, 160, 161, 168, 173–6
Harford, Sr, Edward, 161
Harford, James, 102
Harford, Joseph, 150

Harford family, 60
harrateens, 103
Harris, Thomas, 194, 198
Hauliers, 7
Havana, 139
haven master, 7
Havre de Grace (i.e. Le Havre), 181
Henvill, Richard, 144
Herefordshire, 217
herrings, 123
Hispaniola, 24
Hobhouse, Isaac, 138, 144, 194
Holder, William, 161
Holland, 145, 181–2
hosiery, 101–2
Hotwell water, 95
Hotwells, 40
Huguenots, 183
Hungroad, 29, 30, 125
hurricane season, 83
hurricanes, 206

Iberian peninsula, 1, 74
Imports, 2; see also rice, sugar; tobacco
indentured servants, 11, 124–7
India, 106, 134
India bafts, 134
India dimities, 106
India persians, 106
Indigo, 11
industrial archaeology, 97
inns, 99
Innys, Jeremiah, 194
insurance, 79, 141, 202
insurance rates, 27, 46, 201–2
invoices, 108
Ireland, 20, 141, 185; trade with Bristol, 13, 17; exports from, 28, 123–4; and shipping routes, 53, 64, 68–9, 73, 76–7; and shipownership, 35; and sugar re-exports, 217; and tobacco re-exports, 181–2
Irish Sea, 20
Irving, Thomas, 34, 36
iron, 11, 103
iron manufactures, 104
iron pots, 103
ironmasters, 100
ironmongers, 93, 96, 105, 162
ironmongery, 119, 122
ironware, 89, 96, 103
ironworks, 102–3, 126, 159

Jacks, Walter, 194
Jackson, Jonathan, 111
Jackson & Bromfield, 111–12

Jacob, Samuel, 144
Jamaica, 12, 24; trade with Bristol, 9,
    13–14, 23, 26, 40; Bristol merchants
    in, 9–10, 22, 145, 186; exports to,
    94–6, 98; net worth of settlers in, 90;
    shipping in, 31, 33, 42–3, 124, 201–4,
    206, 216; and shipownership, 37; and
    the slave trade, 73, 75, 137–40, 142,
    145–9; and the sugar trade, 81, 83–4,
    186, 190–1, 193, 195, 197–8, 200–9,
    213, 218; see also productivity trends
    in shipping
James & Drinker, 74
James Fort, River Gambia, 135
James River, 169, 174, 177
japanned ware, 101
Jefferies, William, 144
Jerdone, Francis, 170
Jefferson, Thomas, 91
jewellery, 101
Johnston, William, 170, 173
Jones, James, 137, 143–4, 149
Jones, Thomas, 143–4
Jones, William, 110, 115, 122, 164, 180
Jones & Son, Joseph, 26
Jones & Wister, 118

Kendal, 105
kerseys, 103–4, 170
kettles, 103
Kidderminster goods, 101
King, John, 161, 162
King, William, 95
Kingroad, 29–30, 116, 125
Kingston, 22, 75, 81, 145
Kinsale, 123
Kintyre, 5
knives, 101, 106
Knox, Thomas, 160–1, 168, 180

labour shortages, 121–2
Labrador, xvi, 9, 78
Lancashire, 4, 7, 107
Lancaster, 26–7
Laroche, James, 144, 194, 196, 212
Laroche & Co., James, 194
Laugher & Co., Richard, 139
Laugher, Walter, 140, 144, 186
Laugher & Hancox, 104–5
leather, 97
leatherware, 95
Leeds, 105–6
Leek, 106
Leeward Islands, 21, 59, 71, 75, 123,
    196, 208

Leeward Passage, 83
Leghorn, 71, 79
Leicester, 106
Lesser Antilles, 191
Letter-of-marque ships, 21, 27, 221
Lidderdale, John, 36, 121
Lidderdale & Harmer, 167
Lidderdale, Harmer & Co., 161
Lidderdale, Harmer & Farell, 161
lighterage, 125
lighters, 33
linen, 89, 107, 113, 118
linen checks, 121
linendrapers, 93, 101, 162
links, 109
Lippincott & Co., Henry, 82
Lippincott & Brown, 96, 163, 167–8, 183
liquor, 133
Lisbon, 12, 59, 71, 74
Liverpool, 5, 12, 117, 224; economic
    development of, 2, 28; and the export
    trade, 4, 91, 107, 121, 145; port
    development at, 31–2, 220; rise of, 3,
    28; ships of, 18, 220–1; shipping routes
    at, 20; and the slave trade, 63, 132–3,
    140, 143–5, 151, 221, 223; and the
    sugar trade, 160, 188–90, 195, 199,
    210; and the tobacco trade, 26–7,
    153–6, 160, 166–7, 169, 178, 180–1,
    221; and trade with Jamaica, 22; value
    of commerce at, 13, 21, 27; volume of
    trade with North America, 16–18
livestock, 124
Lloyd's List, 230
Lloyd's Register, 41
loading efficiencies, 50–2, 84
London, 12; bankruptcies at, 113, 116;
    and the slave trade, 129, 132–3, 140;
    and the export trade, 91, 106, 119–20,
    170, 173; as a port, 9, 10, 32; and
    shipping, 45, 57; and shipownership,
    34; and the sugar trade, 18, 159, 188,
    190, 193, 195, 199–201, 210–12, 215;
    and the tobacco trade, 27, 153–9,
    166–7, 169, 173, 176–7, 180; trade of,
    2, 16–17, 22, 28
Longurelach copper works, 102
Lopez, Aaron, 113, 209
Lovell, Robert, 96, 191, 194
Lower James River, 171–2
Lower South, xvi, 13–14, 22, 43, 94
Lucas, Thomas, 99
Lucea, Jamaica, 22
Lundy Island, 19
Lyde, Lyonel, 162
Lyde & Cooper, 149, 161

Macclesfield, 106
MacInnes, C. M., 223
MacNeal, Hector, 80
MacPhaedris, Archibald, 123
Madeira, xvii, 12, 55, 59, 123
mahogany, 117
Malaga, 62, 71
Mallard, John, 25
Manchester, 100, 106–8
Manchester checks, 107
Manchester stripes, 107
Manchester tapes, 106
manufactured wares, 89
manufacturers, 7, 104, 109, 115, 120–1, 123, 176–7, 179
maps, 66
marine atlases, 66
marine insurance, *see* insurance; insurance rates
Martha Brae, Jamaica, 22
Martin, Benjamin, 99
Martinique, xvii, 12, 59
Maryland, xvi, and the convict trade, 126–7; debts in, 26, 114, 149, 164; exports to, 96, 105; imports from, 11; and the slave trade, 149; and the tobacco trade, 15, 159, 163–7, 181–2
Massachusetts, xvi, 111
Massachusetts Loyalists, 10
Masters, *see* captains
Matthews' *Bristol Directory*, 98
Maxse, John, 194
McCusker, John, J., 46
Mediterranean, 11, 79
Mediterranean Passes, 57, 228–9
Melbourne, 5
Melingriffith tinplate works, 102
mercers, 100–1
Merchant Seamen Fund, 225
Meriwether, Capt. David, 83
Merseyside, 32
Merthyr Tydfil, 102
metal industry, 105, 219
metal 'toys', 104, 109
metalware, 11, 95–6, 109
Meyler, Jeremiah, 145
Meyler, Sr Richard, 18, 70, 74, 142, 145, 148, 186, 194
Meyler Family, 145–9, 189, 198
Meyler & Maxse, 96, 191, 193–4, 197
Middle Colonies/States, xvi, 13–14, 22, 25, 36, 43, 66, 78, 93, 94
Middle Passage, 129, 136–7
Midlands, 4, 28, 104, 220
Miles, Richard, 135
Miles, William: wealth of, 186; as

guarantor for slave cargoes, 149; as a shipowner, 37, 84, 203–4, 206; and the sugar trade, 84, 96, 185–6, 189, 191, 193–5, 197, 203–4, 206, 211, 213–14, 216
Miles, William and John, 75
Milford, 74
Miller, Michael, 195
milliners, 100
Minchinton, W. E., 185, 220
mineral water, 98
Minikin bays, 103
mittens, 106
molasses, 185
Monamy, Peter, 33
money supply, 110, 117, 163
Monte Christi, 203, 208
Montego Bay, 122
Montserrat, xvi, 190, 203
Morant Bay, 22
mortgage debts, 146
MPs, 187
Munckley, Samuel, 37–8, 186–7, 191, 194–5, 197–9, 205
Munckley & Co., Samuel, 198
Munckley, Gibbs & Co., 194
muscovado sugar, 123, 208–9, 217
Muster Rolls, 225–6

nailmakers, 122
nails, 89, 104, 108, 120, 122, 170
Naples, 71
Nash, R.C., 46
naval officers, 227
Naval Officers' Returns, 56–7, 227–8
naval stores, 2, 11, 15
navigation, 66–7
Navigation Acts, 11, 55
Neale, Richard, 229
Neufville & Rolleston, 96
Nevis, xvi, 10, 24, 74, 95, 125, 138, 187, 190, 196–8, 203
newspaper advertisements, 126
newspapers, 66, 230
Newburyport, 111
New Calabar, 131
New England, xvi, 36; Bristol shipping and, 13–14, 16, 43; distilleries in, 185; exports to, 94, 112–14; fisheries, 1; imports from, 66, 117; naval stores in, 11
Newfoundland, xvi, 12; Bristol merchants in, 9; and the cod trade, 13, 34, 78–9; export trade, 95–6; and fisheries, 1, 26; provisions, 123; and shipping routes, 55, 59, 62–4, 66

New Hampshire, xvi, 16, 71, 75, 120
New Jersey, xvi, 228
New Providence, 24
New York, xvi, 10–12, 70; Bristol's trade
    with, 16, 117; and the export trade,
    28, 95–6, 100, 106, 119, 121–2; and
    non-importation, 93; and
    shipownership, 36; and shipping
    routes, 57, 71, 74, 78
New York City, 25
Nicaragua wood, 117
Noble, John, 78–9
non-importation, 22–3, 93, 122
Norfolk, 74, 171
North Roger, 95
North America, 1–2, 7, 11, 13, 15–16,
    22, 25–6, 28, 34–5, 39–41, 44, 79,
    89–90, 92–4, 103, 110, 112–13, 116,
    118, 124, 152, 217
North American colonies, xvi, 18, 20,
    35, 40, 45
North Atlantic, 57, 71
North Carolina, xvi, 114, 163, 166
Norwich, 106, 219
Nottingham, 101, 106
Nova Scotia, xvi, 79
Nugent, Richard, 180

octants, 66
oil, 71, 117
Old Calabar, 134
Old Harbour, Jamaica, 22, 81
Oporto, 71, 74, 78
Oseland, John, 114
osnaburghs, 107
ounce, 135
outports, 2–3, 13, 16–18, 211, 222–3
outset, 141

packers, 7, 120
packets, 66
pack horses, 100
palm oil, 221
Pamunkey River, 170, 173
Panama, 139
paper currency, 164
Pares, Richard, 146, 222
Parliament, 7, 132, 151, 180
Parris, David, 37, 191, 194, 197
Parris, Smith & Daniel, 191, 197
Patuxent River, 171
Peach & Henderson, 95
Peach & Pierce, 100, 121–2
Peach, Fowler & Co., 186
Pedder, James, 186
Peloquin family, 183

Penington, Thomas, 118, 194
Penistones, 103
Pennsylvania, xvi, 16, 36, 105, 117, 228,
    230
Perks, John, 36, 160, 161, 168, 180
perpets, 103
Perry, 98
Perry & Hayes, 95, 104, 110
petty larceny, 126
pewter, 108
Philadelphia, 12, 230; Bristol's trade
    with, 25, 36; and the export trade,
    95–6, 102, 106, 114, 118–19, 121, 125;
    and the indentured servant trade, 126;
    merchants of, 5, 9, 10, 117; non-
    importation, 93; and shipping routes,
    62–3, 68, 71, 74, 78–9
piece, 135
pigtail spinners, 176
Pill, 30, 229
pilots, 29
Pimento, 11
Pinney, John Pretor, 212, 214, 217
Pinney & Tobin, 37
Pinney family, 196
pipemakers, 177
pipe smoking, 18, 152
pipe tobacco, 178
Piscataqua, 96
pitch, 11, 15
Pitt the Elder, William, 180
plains, 103
plantation debts, 146
plantation equipment, 96, 120
plantations, 95, 98, 160, 186, 189, 193,
    214
planters, 166, 174, 187, 193, 199–200
plated goods, 101
Plymouth, 34
Pocock, Nicholas, 33
Poole, 34
Pope, Alexander, 33, 98
Pope, Munckley & Co., 95
population, 90
porcelain, 25
pork, 123
Port Antonio, 22
Port Books, 91, 227, 231
port dues, 4, 19, 32, 79
Port Glasgow, 32, 155, 190
porter, 98
porters, 40
Portishead, 29, 32
Porto Bello, 139
Portsmouth, 12, 71, 75, 120
Portugal, 117

Possets Point, 157
posts, 66
pot ash, 117
Potomac River, 169, 171, 172
pots, 95
pottery, 28, 219
Powell, John, 95, 144
Power, Thomas, 142
Prankard, Graffin, 103, 140
Price, Jacob M., 163, 166, 181
prices, 119, 124, 126, 135, 153
Principé, 130
printed guides, 66
privateering, 49, 83, 141, 153, 202, 206;
    from America, 26; from Bristol, 5, 15,
    19–22, 27, 38, 141, 220–1; from
    France, 19–20, 62; from Spain, 19
Privy Council, 32
prize captures, 20, 27, 38, 221
productivity trends in shipping, 45–54,
    84–7
profits, 79, 124, 137–8, 143, 150, 179,
    217
Protheroe & Claxton, 194–5
provisions, 11, 78, 96, 117, 123–4, 202
Puerto Rico, 24
punch, 185

Quakers, 71, 103, 150
quay wardens, 7
quays, 7, 31
Quebec, xvi, 12, 995
Queensware, 109

Rabone, Joseph, 105
Rabone & Co., Joseph, 104
rag cutters, 176
Rappahannock river, 82, 160, 169,
    171–2, 174, 177
raw materials, 89, 100, 116
Reeve, William, 71, 90, 110–111, 122
Reeve, William, Son & Hill, 103, 114,
    116, 186, 196–7
re-exports, see sugar trade; tobacco
    trade
refined sugar, 95, 217
Reform Bill Riots (1831), 5
remittances: and the export trade, 81,
    108, 113–14; and the slave trade, 137,
    145–6, 148–9; and the sugar trade,
    139, 198; and the tobacco trade, 179
Reynolds, Richard, 102–3
Reynolds, Getley & Co., 102
Rhode Island, xvi, 75, 113
ribbons, 105
rice, 2, 11, 13, 66, 74, 129, 131, 152

Richard Neale Daybook, 229–30
Richards, James, 38
Richards, Thomas, 38, 198
Richardson, David, 142
risk, 37, 59, 66
River Avon, 7, 29, 32, 40, 99, 216
River Clyde, 32, 188
River Frome, 7, 216
River Gambia, 135
River Mersey, 32
River Severn, 99–100, 102, 121
River Trent, 99
River Wye, 99
roads, 99–100
Rogers, Jr, Corsley, 198
Rogers, James, 144, 149
Rogers, Robert, 96
Rogers, Woodes, 15
ropemakers, 93
Rosenberg, Nathan, 46
Ross, 34
Rotterdam, 12, 181
Royal African Company, 129, 132, 138
Ruddock, Noblet, 144
rum, 11, 26, 173, 185, 187
rum distilling, 97

saddlery, 95
sagathies, 103
sailcloth, 89
sailmakers, 40
sailors, 7
St Croix, 26
St Domingue, 12, 83
St Eustatius, 12, 25–6, 59
St Kitts, xvi, 24, 145; Bristol investors
    in, 186; and the export trade, 95–6;
    and shipping routes, 59, 63, 74–6; and
    the slave trade, 75, 140; and the sugar
    trade, 190–1, 197–8, 203, 208
St Lucia, 197
St Thomas, 26, 214
St Vincent, xvii, 24, 74, 140, 186, 190,
    197
salt, 173
Santiago de Cuba, 139
Sao Thomé, 130
satins, 106
Saunders, Edmund, 144
Savanna-la-Mar, 12, 22, 120, 145
scarf twist, 106
schooners, 41
Scipio Africanus, 128
scissors, 106
Scotland, 5, 105, 124, 154, 193
Scotch goods, 101

Seamen, 128, 225
Searcher, 227
Sedgley, Samuel, 142
Sedgley & Hilhouse, 162
Sedgley, Hilhouse & Berry, 161
Sedgley, Hilhouse & Co., 161
Sedgley, Hilhouse & Randolph, 127
Senegambia, 130
serges, 103, 107
Severn trows, 33, 99–100
Seven Years War, 221; and Bristol
   privateering, 38; and Bristol shipping,
   47, 53; Bristol's trade in, 21–2; and the
   export trade, 116, 121; and shipping
   routes, 59–60, 62; and the slave trade,
   132; and the sugar trade, 198; and the
   tobacco trade 164, 180
shallows, 103, 107, 122
Shapland, Thomas, 95
Sheffield, 101, 106
Shephard, Joseph, 101
ship decks, 41
ship registry, 231
ship sales, 41
ship size, 42–5, 47
shipbuilding, 38–42, 223
shipping costs, 41, 47
shipping routes, 55–8, 60; direct/shuttle,
   58–9, 60, 62–3, 66, 70, 80–8;
   multilateral, 58–60, 62–3, 66, 70–1,
   75–80; and navigation, 66–7; and
   slaving voyages, 59–60, 63, 74–5;
   sources on, 225–31; see also Barbados,
   Boston, Jamaica, Newfoundland,
   Philadelphia, South Carolina, St Kitts,
   Virginia
shipping shares, 37–8, 142
ship's husband, 34
shipowners, 7, 34–8, 63, 70, 74, 78, 85,
   142, 220
ships, 41, 46–9
Ships: America, 139; Ann, 85; Arundell
   75; Brislington, 74; Bristol Merchant,
   141–2; Bristol Packet, 74; Byron, 200;
   Dispatch, 62, 138; Eagle, 85;
   Manchester, 42; Milford, 85; Pelham,
   71; Planter, 85; Ruby, 198; St James,
   85; St Philip, 20; Santa Theresa, 20;
   Sarah, 123; Swift, 74–5; True Patriot,
   85; Union, 124; Virginia Packett, 85;
   Wennie, 59
shipwrights, 7, 40
Shirehampton, 157
Shirtcliffe, John, 101
shoemakers, 93
shoes, 95

shoopkeeper, 95, 101, 110, 215, 222
short cloths, 103
shot, 103
Shrewsbury, 104
Shropshire, 102–4, 108, 121, 217
Sierra Leone, 130, 144
silk, 89, 102–3
silver goods, 101
single bays, 35
Sketchley, James, 93
Sketchley's Bristol Directory, (1775), 178
slave coast, 130
slave sales, 137, 145, 147
slave trade, 3, 5, 128–30; decline at
   Bristol, 27–8, 140–51; and exports in,
   133–5, 144–5; growth at Bristol,
   138–40; and the 'middle passage', 136;
   number of Bristol voyages in, 129,
   131–3; opposition to, 150–1; and
   payment for slaves, 139; and
   privateering, 20; and purchase of
   slaves, 134–5, 142; shipowning and,
   34, 141–2; shipping and, 48–9;
   shipping routes and, 56, 59–60, 63,
   74–5; and slave merchants, 142–4,
   145–9; and slave sales, 137–9, 147; and
   Spanish America, 139–40, 142; value
   of, 131; and war, 140–1; wealth from,
   132, 137; see also Africa; remittances
slavery, 150
slaves, 23, 127
sloops, 41
Smith, Jr, Joseph, 96
Smith, Son & Russell, 104
smuggling, 157, 179–80
Smyth family, 186
Snelson, John, 173–6
snows, 41
snuff, 18, 152, 178–9
snuffmakers, 93, 97
snuff mills, 177–8
soap, 95, 97
soapmakers, 93, 97
soapmaking, 219
Society of Merchant Venturers, 3, 7, 21,
   31, 63, 132, 180, 186, 225–6
Somerset, 99, 103–4, 106, 157, 217
South America, 24
South Carolina, xvi, 10; debts in, 26;
   exports to, 96, 102; imports from, 11,
   66; and shipping routes, 59, 62–3, 72,
   74; and the slave trade, 138, 140
Southern American Colonies, 35
Southampton, 99
South Sea Company, 139
South Wales, 99, 102–3, 217, 220

Spain, 117, 139, 170
Span, Samuel, 26, 186–7, 191, 194, 197
Span, Samuel & John, 195
Span, Samuel & John & Co., 195
Spanish America, 139, 142
Spanish cloth woollen goods, 89
Spanish privateers, 18–19, 21
specialisation, 143, 189, 191, 193, 222–3
speculators, 213
specie, 147
spirits, 145
'Spring' goods, 81, 118
Staffordshire, 121
Stamp Act, 23, 90, 112, 114, 122
Steen, Marguerite, 128
steering wheel, 46
Stephens, John, 123
Stevenson, William, 182
Stevenson & Randolph & Cheston, 114–15, 127, 159, 161, 164, 167, 181
stockings, 95
stocking maker and hosier, 101
stoves, 166, 170, 173
stuff, 95, 104
Sugar Act, 24
sugar bakers, 97, 207–8, 210–12, 215–16
sugar grocers, 207–8, 210, 215
sugar refineries, 7, 97, 185, 213, 216–17, 219, 223
sugar refiners, 93, 97, 211, 215
sugar trade, 2–3, 6, 11, 12, 66, 80, 96, 131, 159, 173; and the Bristol market, 83, 206, 208–16; and Bristol merchants, 85, 143, 159, 185–6, 189–92, 194–5; and clayed sugar, 198, 208–9; commission system, 83, 193, 195–6, 200; and direct purchase, 196, 198–9; and English sugar imports, 184, 187–8, 191; and muscovado sugar, 198, 208–9; and plantations, 186, 189; and re-exports, 217; and shipping, 50–1, 81–2, 84, 199–206; and the slave trade, 129; and sugar duties, 207; and sugar sales, 203–5, 208–16; see also London; Liverpool; remittances
Summers, Richard, 102
supercargoes, 193
suppliers, 115–16, 119, 121
Surinam, 213
Swansea, 99, 102
Swymmer, Henry, 194

tallow chandlers, 93
tallow candles, 93
tammies, 103
tanners, 97

tar, 11, 15
tares, 216
taxes, 180
Taylor & Sons, Samuel, 99
tea, 184–5
tea tongs, 109
Teignmouth, 34
temper lime, 120
Teredo worms, 47
textiles, 11, 89, 106–7, 133
The Sun is My Undoing, 128
Thomas, Morgan, 111, 159, 161, 168
Thomas, Griffiths & Thomas, 121
thread hose, 106
tides, 29
tiles, 97
timber, 15
tin, 108
tinplate, 100, 102, 104
tobacco trade, 2, 11, 37, 66, 129, 131, 151, 220–3; and the Bristol market, 6, 28, 175; and Bristol merchants, 36, 143, 153, 158–62, 164, 189; and Bristol shipping, 15, 26, 81; capital and credit in, 159, 162–3; captains, 82–4; and the 'cargo' trade, 82, 167–8; and the Chesapeake rivers, 82, 160, 166, 169–75; and clandestine supplies, 26–7; and the consignment system, 82, 165–8, 170, 173; and direct purchase, 82, 165–6, 168, 170, 173; and duties, 178–80; factors in, 168–70, 173; and the growth of Bristol's trade, 152, 155–6, 158; and hogsheads, 50; and oronoco tobacco, 169; and stores, 166, 168, 170, 173; and re-exports, 96, 152, 156–7, 177, 181–3; shipping routes, 80–5; and smuggling, 157, 180; and snuff, 18, 152, 177–9; and sweetscented tobacco, 18, 169, 174, 177; and tobacco inspection acts, 165; and debt, 163–4; and tobacco prices, 177; see also Glasgow; Liverpool; London; Whitehaven
tobacco inspection acts, 165
tobacco notes, 175
tobacco planters, 82
tobacconists, 93, 176–8
Tobago, xvii, 24, 190–1, 197
Tobin, James, 217
Tobin & Pinney, 194
Tobin, Pinney & Tobin, 195
Tonge, Henry, 144
tonnages, 231
tons, registered, 45
Topsham, 34

Tortola, xvii, 12, 24, 96, 190, 197, 214
towboats, 29, 33
Townshend duties (1767), 122
tradesmen, 108, 116, 163
trade winds, 55
transport, 106
transport costs, 121, 137
treacle, 185
Trevaskes, John, 142
Trinity, Newfoundland, 62
Tudway & Smith, 195
Tudway family, 196
Turkey carpets, 91
Turnpike roads, 99–100
Turpentine, 11, 15
Turton, Joseph, 105
Turton & Co., John, 105
Twine, Richard, 38

United States of America, 5, 10, 40, 90,
    121, 154
unsolicited goods, 118
Upper James River, Virginia, 166, 171–2
Upper South, xvi, 12–14, 42–3, 94

vendue, 118
Vera Cruz, 139
Virginia, xvi, 4, 10, 28, 121; and Bristol
    shipping, 33, 36, 42, 172, 175; and the
    Bristol slave trade, 52, 63, 138, 140;
    and the Bristol tobacco trade, 15, 81,
    83, 159–60, 162–6, 168–77; and the
    convict trade, 126; debts in, 26, 114,
    163–4; exports to, 91, 95–6; imports
    from, 11; and the indentured servant
    trade, 125; ironworks in, 159;
    legislation in 164; and Naval Officers'
    Returns, 228; and productivity trends
    in shipping, 45–50, 52–4; and shipping
    routes, 52, 57, 59, 63, 69, 74, 80–6, 88;
    see also tobacco trade

wages, 79, 116
waggons, 99–100
Wakefield, 100
Waldo, Joseph, 105
Wales, 94, 98, 184
Walton, Gary M., 45, 57
Wansey, William, 142
War of Jenkins's Ear, 18
War of the Austrian Succession, 18–20,
    140, 187, 221
War of the Quadruple Alliance, 15
War of the Spanish Succession, 15, 25,
    132, 187
warehousemen, 162

warehouses, 97, 101, 105, 165, 170,
    175–7
Warminster, 104
Warrens, Cannington & Co., 99
water bailiffs, 7
Waterford, 74, 123
Watkins, Benjamin, 95
Wayles, John, 91
wealth, 163
Weare, John Fisher, 191, 194, 197
Weare & Co., 168
weavers, 106, 121
weaving trade, 106
Welch, Wilkinson & Startin, 104, 109
Welsh Marches, 99
Wesley, John, 150, 222
West Africa, 1, 74, 129–30, 133–5, 144,
    217
West Country, 105–7, 144
West India fleet, 26
West India interest, 187
West Indies, xvi, 1–2, 4–5, 11, 20, 23–4,
    26, 37, 45, 66, 80, 124, 151, 184, 186,
    188–91, 193, 197, 200–2, 208, 213, 215,
    217; and the Bristol tobacco trade, 27,
    181; exports to, 89, 92–5, 103; factors
    in, 199; navigation in, 83; population
    of, 90; provisions to, 123; and shipping
    at British ports, 17, 85; and shipping
    from Bristol, 13–16, 18, 34–5, 39–40,
    42–4, 206, 212; and sugar duties, 223;
    value of Bristol ships and exports to,
    28, 91, 185; wealth of, 146; see also
    slave trade; sugar trade; individual
    West Indian islands
West Midlands, 96, 99, 104
Westmoreland parish, Jamaica, 22
Westmoreland, 105
West Riding, 107
wharfage, 226
Wharfage Books, 226–7, 231
wheat, 11, 78
white plains, 120
White Rock Copper company, 102
Whitehall, 164
Whitehaven, 2, 5; hinterland of, 3; and
    the slave trade, 132; and the sugar
    trade, 188, 190; and the tobacco trade,
    153–6, 166, 181; trade of, 16–17, 106
Whitehead, George, 161
Whydah, 130
Wilberforce, William, 150–1
Williams, Alan F., 220
Willing, Thomas, 118
Wilton carpets, 91
Wiltshire, 104, 217

window glass, 89, 98–9
Windward Islands, 21
Windward Passage, 83
wine, 98, 117, 123, 179
Wine islands, xvii, 55, 69, 77
Wiveliscombe, 104
Wood the Elder, John 7
Wood, Leighton, 36, 167
Woodspring, 157
woollen drapers, 101
woollen manufacturers, 100
woollens, 90, 100–1, 103–5, 107, 119–20,
    144, 170
Worcester, 106
Worcestershire, 104, 217

worsted stuffs, 103
worsteds, 103
Wright's *American Negotiator*, 10
wrought iron, 95, 102
wrought leather, 89

York, 219
Yorkshire, 100, 107
Yorkshire goods, 101
York River, Virginia, 36, 81, 169–75,
    177
Youghall, 123

zinc, 97